Relationship Pathways

From Adolescence to Young Adulthood

Brett **Laursen**
Florida Atlantic University

W. Andrew **Collins**
University of Minnesota

Editors

Los Angeles | London | New Delhi
Singapore | Washington DC

Los Angeles | London | New Delhi
Singapore | Washington DC

FOR INFORMATION:

SAGE Publications, Inc.

2455 Teller Road

Thousand Oaks, California 91320

E-mail: order@sagepub.com

SAGE Publications Ltd.

1 Oliver's Yard

55 City Road

London EC1Y 1SP

United Kingdom

SAGE Publications India Pvt. Ltd.

B 1/I 1 Mohan Cooperative Industrial Area

Mathura Road, New Delhi 110 044

India

SAGE Publications Asia-Pacific Pte. Ltd.

33 Pekin Street #02-01

Far East Square

Singapore 048763

Acquisitions Editor: Vicki Knight
Associate Editor: Lauren Habib
Editorial Assistant: Kalie Koscielak
Production Editor: Eric Garner
Copy Editor: Megan Markanich
Typesetter: C&M Digitals (P) Ltd.
Proofreader: Laura Webb
Indexer: Jean Casalegno
Cover Designer: Candice Harman
Marketing Manager: Liz Thornton
Permissions Editor: Adele Hutchinson

Printed in the United States of America

Library of Congress Cataloging-in-Publication Data

Relationship pathways : from adolescence to young adulthood / Brett Laursen, W. Andrew Collins, editors.

p. cm.
Includes bibliographical references and index.

ISBN 978-1-4129-8739-4 (pbk.)

1. Adolescence. 2. Adolescent psychology. 3. Teenagers—Family relationships. 4. Teenagers—Sexual behavior. 5. Interpersonal relations. I. Laursen, Brett Paul. II. Collins, W. Andrew, 1944-

BF724.R393 2012

155.5—dc23   2011031176

This book is printed on acid-free paper.

11 12 13 14 15 10 9 8 7 6 5 4 3 2 1

Brief Contents

Detailed Contents

Preface

A decade ago, we proposed a musical analogy to describe changes in close relationships across the second decade of life. We argued that relationship development during these years resembles a fugue (Collins & Laursen, 2000). A fugue is a musical composition characterized by distinct melodic themes that are elaborated successively and interwoven to create a single, well-defined structure. Close relationships across the years that span the transition into and out of adolescence follow an analogous pattern. Affiliations with friends, romantic partners, siblings, and parents unfold along varied and discrete trajectories for much of this time and then coalesce during the early 20s into integrated interpersonal structures.

Our views are informed by two influential depictions of development. The first is Hartup's (1979) depiction of the emergence of unique social worlds during childhood. In this view, family and peer relationships are two social worlds that develop increasingly independent of one another as children spend more time out of the home and in school and other peer-dominated contexts. The second is Werner's (1957) thesis that development proceeds from a state of globality to a state of increasing differentiation and hierarchic differentiation.

Relationships provide an essential context for human development. Social experiences are organized around relationships (Hartup & Laursen, 1999). We contend that close relationships are global and undifferentiated during the early years of life. Distinctions between family members first emerge as different patterns of interaction are established with mothers, fathers, and siblings that promote the acquisition of a diverse set of skills and abilities. The peer social world emerges from this context.

Most early friendships are formed with playmates under the supervision of family members. Gradually, however, different principles come to govern exchanges with peers and those with family members, and the interactions in these relationships change accordingly (Laursen & Bukowski, 1997). By the end of childhood, families and peers occupy two distinct social worlds.

Differentiation and articulation continue across adolescence. At the transition into adolescence, peer relationships are fairly global and undifferentiated. Children discriminate between friends and nonfriends, but convenience and propinquity have as much to do with these relationships as loyalty and intimacy. Relationship differentiation evolves as a new appreciation of social exchange and shared power alter the form and function of peer relationships (Laursen & Hartup, 2002). Experience and cognitive maturity create new relationship categories and expectations. Nuanced distinctions between peer dyads arise, as close friends are distinguished from other friends and acquaintances. Just as parents provide a base for children's first forays into the peer social world, friends provide a base for contact with potential romantic partners (Laursen, 1996). Eventually males and females establish a new form of peer relationship by altering friendship exchanges to incorporate the unique attributes of romantic interconnections (Laursen & Jensen-Campbell, 1999). Thus, peer groups beget friendships, which in turn beget romantic relationships.

Mid- to late adolescence marks the high water point for relationship differentiation. Then the tide turns. Once these distinct relationship forms have been established, the next developmental task is to organize them into a coherent whole (Collins & Laursen, 2004). The transition from adolescence into young adulthood marks a gradual hierarchic integration in the form and function of close relationship processes. Just as distinct musical themes are integrated in the resolution of a fugue, the social worlds of friends and family merge into a unified social structure that incorporates important features of both relationship systems and that manifests communal properties.

Research on adolescent relationships has rapidly expanded during the past decade. Keeping apace with research advances is a difficult challenge. Harder still is integrating the literature into a coherent whole. This volume is designed to guide the reader through the research on close relationships before, during, and after adolescence. We are fortunate that some of the world's foremost experts on adolescent relationships agreed to summarize what is known in their respective fields of expertise.

The volume begins with a section on family relationships. Separate chapters are devoted to sibling relationships and parent–child relationships during the transition into adolescence and during the transition into young adulthood. The second and third sections concern peer relationships. Two chapters examine friendships during the transition into adolescence and during the transition into young adulthood. There are also chapters on peer networks, heterosexual romantic relationships, and same-sex romantic relationships. The last section focuses on developmental pathways and processes. This section defines relationships processes and describes individual and contextual factors that influence them. For ease of navigation, most of the chapters in the volume share a common outline: Conceptual and/or Theoretical Overview, Recent Empirical Advances and Future Directions.

The volume is designed for scholars who study adolescent and young adult relationships. We use the term *scholars* advisedly. Students will profit from the comprehensive, rigorous, and accessible overview of key content areas. Investigators will want to hear about the latest developments in the field. To accomplish these aims, we've asked the contributors to summarize key findings in the field and to illustrate recent advances on the topic with findings from their own work. The result offers insight into the conceptual themes and empirical precedents that shape contemporary research by scholars who set the pace for the field of adolescent relationships. Our contributors hail from Canada, Germany, Israel, the Netherlands, and the United States. Although geographically diverse, they share a commitment to empirical rigor and communication with others who are interested in youth. Both are apparent in this collection.

A volume of this magnitude requires enormous effort from many parties. It has been a great privilege to collaborate once again with my mentor and friend, Andy Collins. Vicki Knight of Sage showed interest in our project when other publishers did not; she and Kalie Koscielak patiently shepherded the book through to completion. We are gratified by the cooperation we received from our colleagues; most who were invited to participate agreed to do so. Our contributors were a timely and responsive bunch. The field is in good hands. Many friends and collaborators shaped and supported our work over the years—too many to mention by name. We trust you know who you are. Our families merit special acknowledgment. Erika, Kirsten, and Erik, and Carolyn, Caroline, and Drew and Julie: We are thankful for your forbearance, wisdom, love, and support.

We are appreciative of the comments and suggestions provided by the following reviewers:

Lori S. Anderson, University of Wisconsin–Madison

B. Bradford Brown, University of Wisconsin–Madison

Antonius H. N. Cillessen, Radboud University, Nijmegen, The Netherlands

Nancy Darling, PhD, Oberlin College

Anna Beth Doyle, PhD, Concordia University

Judy Garber, Vanderbilt University

Cliff McKinney, Mississippi State University

Rainer K. Silbereisen, Friedrich Schiller University of Jena, Germany

As we set to the task of preparing our chapters, we were deeply saddened to learn of the untimely death of one of the contributing authors. Duane Buhrmester and his wife, Linda, died in a mountain climbing accident in Colorado on July 27, 2010. A tribute to their lives can be found online at http://duaneandlindab.com/Duane_and_Linda_Buhrmester/Home.html. Duane, an expert on adolescent relationships with friends, siblings, and romantic partners, was a doctoral student of Wyndol Furman's at the University of Denver. After a brief stint at UCLA, he served as a professor for 20-plus years at the University of Texas at Dallas. His research was first rate; many of his publications enjoy enviable citation rates. He was particularly well-known for his work on interpersonal competence and need fulfillment in friendships; he also developed several questionnaires that are commonly used by other researchers. Duane was a fixture in the world of peer relationships. Preconferences devoted to the topic at the biennial meetings of the Society for Research on Child Development and the Society for Research on Adolescence invariably featured Duane in roles as chair, presenter, moderator, and commentator. He contributed frequently to discussions and his remarks were often entertainingly provocative. He was witty, smart, and charming. He was also a caring mentor and a dedicated professor, who always put students first. Duane Buhrmester enriched the lives of many, and his absence is keenly felt.

—Brett Laursen
Fort Lauderdale
January 2011

⫸ REFERENCES

Collins, W. A., & Laursen, B. (2000). Adolescent relationships: The art of fugue. In C. Hendrick & S. S. Hendrick (Eds.), *Close relationships: A sourcebook* (pp. 59–69). Thousand Oaks, CA: Sage.

Collins, W. A., & Laursen, B. (2004). Changing relationships, changing youth: Interpersonal contexts of adolescent development. *Journal of Early Adolescence, 24,* 55–62.

Hartup, W. W. (1979). The social worlds of childhood. *American Psychologist, 34,* 944–950.

Hartup, W. W., & Laursen, B. (1999). Relationships as developmental contexts: Retrospective themes and contemporary issues. In W. A. Collins & B. Laursen (Eds.), *The Minnesota Symposia on Child Psychology: Vol. 30. Relationships as developmental contexts* (pp. 13–35). Hillsdale, NJ: Lawrence Erlbaum.

Laursen, B. (1996). Closeness and conflict in adolescent peer relationships: Interdependence with friends and romantic partners. In W. M. Bukowski, A. F. Newcomb, & W. W. Hartup (Eds.), *The company they keep: Friendships in childhood and adolescence* (pp. 186–210). New York: Cambridge University Press.

Laursen, B., & Bukowski, W. M. (1997). A developmental guide to the organisation of close relationships. *International Journal of Behavioral Development, 21,* 747–770.

Laursen, B., & Hartup, W. W. (2002). The origins of reciprocity and social exchange in friendships. In B. Laursen & W. G. Graziano (Eds.), *Social exchange in development: New Directions For Child and Adolescent Development* (No. 95), 27–40.

Laursen, B., & Jensen-Campbell, L. A. (1999). The nature and functions of social exchange in adolescent romantic relationships. In W. Furman, B. B. Brown, & C. Feiring (Eds.), *The development of romantic relationships in adolescence* (pp. 50–74). New York: Cambridge University Press.

Werner, H. (1957). The concept of development from a comparative and organismic point of view. In D. B. Harris (Ed.), *The concept of development: An issue in the study of human behavior* (pp. 125–148). Minneapolis: University of Minnesota Press.

About the Editors

Brett Laursen is professor of psychology and director of Graduate Training at Florida Atlantic University. His research focuses on parent–child and peer relationships during childhood and adolescence and the influence of these relationships on individual social and academic adjustment. Dr. Laursen is a Docent Professor of Social Developmental Psychology at the University of Jyväskylä, Finland. He is currently the Methods and Measures Editor at the *International Journal of Behavioral Development*. Dr. Laursen is a fellow of the American Psychological Association (Division 7, Developmental) and a fellow and charter member of the Association for Psychological Science. In 2008, he received an honorary doctorate from Örebro University, Sweden. Dr. Laursen has edited or coedited several books and monographs, the most recent being the *Handbook of Developmental Research Methods*.

W. Andrew Collins is a Morse-Alumni Distinguished Teaching Professor of Child Development and Psychology at the University of Minnesota. A graduate of Stanford University, Dr. Collins conducts research on parent and peer relationships and influences during adolescence and young adulthood. He is principal investigator of the Minnesota Longitudinal Study of Risk and Adaptation, in which participants have been followed from birth to age 34. Currently editor of the *Monographs of the Society for Research in Child Development*, he is a fellow of both the American Psychological Association and the American Psychological Society. He served as president of the Society for Research on Adolescence from 2000 to 2002. Dr. Collins has edited or coedited several books and monographs and has contributed numerous book and handbook chapters, as well as articles in scholarly journals.

List of Contributors

Ibis Alvarez-Valdivia
School of Psychology
University of Ottawa
Ottawa, Canada

Timothy W. Boyd II
Department of Psychology
University of North Carolina at Greensboro
Greensboro, NC

Susan Branje
Research Centre Adolescent Development
Faculty of Social and Behavioural Sciences
Utrecht University
Utrecht, The Netherlands

Duane Buhrmester
School of Behavioral and Brain Science
The University of Texas at Dallas
Richardson, TX

José M. Causadias
Institute of Child Development
University of Minnesota
Minneapolis, MN

Chong Man Chow
School of Behavioral and Brain Sciences
The University of Texas at Dallas
Richardson, TX

W. Andrew Collins
Institute of Child Development
University of Minnesota
Minneapolis, MN

Kirby Deater-Deickard
Department of Psychology
Virginia Tech
Blacksburg, VA

Dawn DeLay
Department of Psychology
Florida Atlantic University
Fort Lauderdale, FL

Wyndol Furman
Department of Psychology
University of Denver
Denver, CO

Nancy L. Galambos
Department of Psychology
University of Alberta
Edmonton, Alberta, Canada

Gary C. Glick
Department of Psychological Sciences
University of Missouri
Columbia, MO

Christopher A. Hafen
Center for Advanced Study of Teaching and Learning
University of Virginia
Charlottesville, VA

Loes Keijsers
Research Centre Adolescent Development
Faculty of Social and Behavioural Sciences
Utrecht University
Utrecht, The Netherlands

Jan Kornelis Dijkstra
University of Groningen
Groningen, The Netherlands

Lauren Kotylak
Crescent Point Energy Corp
Calgary, Alberta, Canada

Brett Laursen
Department of Psychology
Florida Atlantic University
Fort Lauderdale, FL

Matthew D. Lee
School of Psychology
University of Ottawa
Ottawa, Canada

Wim Meeus
Research Centre Adolescent Development
Faculty of Social and Behavioural Sciences
Utrecht University
Utrecht, The Netherlands

Joel A. Muraco
Family Studies and Human Development
University of Arizona
Tucson, AZ

K. Lee Raby
Institute of Child Development
University of Minnesota
Minneapolis, MN

Holly Roelse
School of Behavioral and Brain Sciences
The University of Texas at Dallas
Richardson, TX

Amanda J. Rose
Department of Psychological Sciences
University of Missouri
Columbia, MO

Stephen T. Russell
Family Studies and Human Development
University of Arizona
Tucson, AZ

Barry H. Schneider
School of Psychology
University of Ottawa
Ottawa, Canada

Rebecca A. Schwartz-Mette
Department of Psychological Sciences
University of Missouri
Columbia, MO

Inge Seiffge-Krenke
Psychologisches Institut
Johannes-Gutenberg-Universität
Mainz, Germany

Lily Shanahan
Department of Psychology
University of North Carolina at Greensboro
Greensboro, NC

Shmuel Shulman
Department of Psychology
Bar Ilan University
Ramat Gan, Israel

Rhiannon L. Smith
Department of Psychological Sciences
University of Missouri
Columbia, MO

Marion K. Underwood
School of Behavioral and Brain Sciences
The University of Texas at Dallas
Richardson, TX

Muriel van Doorn
Research Centre Adolescent Development
Faculty of Social and Behavioural Sciences
Utrecht University
Utrecht, The Netherlands

René Veenstra
University of Groningen
Groningen, The Netherlands

Evelyn B. Waite
Department of Psychology
University of North Carolina at Greensboro
Greensboro, NC

Zhe Wang
Department of Psychology
Virginia Tech
Blacksburg, VA

Ryan J. Watson
Family Studies and Human Development
University of Arizona
Tucson, AZ

Jessica K. Winkles
Department of Psychology
University of Denver
Denver, CO

PART I

Family Relationships

1

Transformations in Close Relationship Networks

Parent–Child Relationships and Their Social Extensions

W. Andrew Collins

K. Lee Raby

José M. Causadias

The ascendance of research on close relationships and their developmental significance springs from both theoretical and empirical roots. Theoretically, socialization and acculturation are now regarded as occurring within interdependent social units marked by bidirectional rather than in the top-down processes assumed in earlier models of rearing by adults (Collins, 2010; Collins & Laursen, 2004). A key implication of this interdependence is that multiple persons of varied ages may become a part of such dyadic units and, as such, contribute to the interpersonal processes of attaining social competence. Empirically, burgeoning research findings in the past decade have shown that close relationships

Preparation of this chapter was supported partly by a grant from the National Institute of Child Health & Human Development (NICHD) to W. Andrew Collins, Byron Egeland, and L. Alan Sroufe.

involving partners other than parents foster the development of social competence in and beyond childhood and adolescence (for reviews, see Aquilino, 2006; Collins & Steinberg, 2006). As a consequence, the research questions now driving both theory and research on socioemotional development have shifted from concerns of *whether* and *how much* particular types of relationship partners to interest in *how* and *under what conditions* relationship partners of different types contribute to functioning and development during significant developmental transitions (Collins, 2010).

Developmental transitions provide rare opportunities to examine changes in close relationships because of the relative density of salient changes in the nature and functions of close relationships. Researchers interested in parent–adolescent relationships first focused on transitional periods to move beyond questions of whether parental influence declined during the social and maturational changes of early adolescence. Research findings consistently showed that although characteristics of interaction and emotional experiences were more variable during early adolescence than before or after, parents remained influential and adolescents generally continued to be connected with parents (Collins, 1995; Collins & Steinberg, 2006; Laursen, Coy, & Collins, 1998). In short, relationships were transformed and, thereafter, the dyadic processes between the two generations continued to play significant roles in the young person's development.

Such functional transformations almost certainly occur in other significant developmental transitions, such as the transition to adulthood. However, research on the continuities and changes in the qualities and functions of relationships *after* adolescence is, if not in its infancy, in its toddlerhood. Even so, an emerging theme in the literature offers a potentially important guidepost for future efforts to identify and examine the distinctive developmental tasks and issues of relationship development in this period. Whereas research on relationships during the transition from childhood to adolescence revealed important patterns in changes within specific categories of relationships (parent–child, friendship, romantic relationships), research on transitions in young adult relationships implies that relationships with parents, friends, and romantic partners increasingly overlap and complement each other as early adulthood approaches (Ainsworth, 1989; Collins & Laursen, 2000). In two recent essays, Collins and Laursen (2000, 2004) have argued that relationships with parents, friends, and romantic partners increasingly overlap and complement each other as early adulthood approaches (Ainsworth, 1989). Thus, understanding the transition to adulthood challenges researchers to understand not only patterns of change within relationships of a given type but also the interplay among the various relationships that are significant in the lives of youth approaching adulthood.

The purpose of this chapter is to take stock of the current status of knowledge about relationships in the transition to adulthood. Thus, the focus is research on the close relationships of individuals ages 19 to 28 (Arnett, 2000; Collins & van Dulmen, 2006). We first review briefly the conceptual hallmarks for research on relationship transformations in early adulthood. Next, we distill the evidence concerning typical changes in relationships with family members, especially parents, friends, and romantic partners. We give particular attention to the interplay among differing types of close relationships. Finally, we point to future research that may lead to a better understanding of the conditions and processes of interplay among relationships during early adult transitions.

⬝⬝ CONCEPTUAL OVERVIEW

Three lines of inquiry converge in research on relationships in early adulthood: (1) the nature of close relationships, (2) the balance and social–psychological implications of continuity and change in the transition to adulthood, and (3) the role of relationships in developmental changes.

Relationships and Relational Processes

The term *relationship* refers to a pair of persons who are *interdependent*, in that each person affects and is affected by the behavior of the other person over time. Interdependence in relationships varies in degree. Some pairs manifest a high degree of mutual impact over a period of years; the involvement and impact of other pairs may be more transitory (Reis, Collins, & Berscheid, 2000). For convenience, in this chapter the terms *close relationships* and *personal relationships* will be used interchangeably to refer to the two most salient types of interdependent relationships outside of the family: friendships and romantic relationships.

Relationships, whether with family members, friends, or romantic partners, vary in the content or kinds of interactions; the patterning, or distribution of positive and negative exchanges; quality, or the degree of responsiveness that each shows to the other; and the cognitive and emotional responses of each individual to events in the relationship (Collins, Welsh, & Furman, 2009; Hinde, 1997). Pairs who consider themselves close also report mostly positive thoughts and feelings (Berscheid, Snyder, & Omoto, 1989; Laursen & Williams, 1997). However, a minority of close relationships are marked by highly interdependent and mutually influential negative behaviors, few mutual positive emotions (e.g., Huston, Niehuis, & Smith, 2001), and by little sense of subjective closeness (Simpson, Collins, Tran, & Haydon, 2007). This negative pattern may be somewhat more likely in familial and romantic relationships than in friendships, although no explicit comparisons have been reported.

Continuity and Change in the Transition to Adulthood

The key premise of a developmental perspective on close relationships during late adolescence and early adulthood is that individuals devote an increasing proportion of time to interactions with others outside of the family. Gradually, these extrafamilial relationships come to serve many of the same functions that appeared exclusive to familial relationships during childhood (Collins & Laursen, 2004; Collins & Steinberg, 2006).

This developmental perspective incorporates a consideration of both continuity and change within and between close relationships, whereas the popular framework associated with the relatively recent concept of emerging adulthood is focused primarily on distinctions between young adult experiences and those of earlier periods. Arnett's (2000) proposal that the years from the late teens to the late 20s constitute a distinctive period of experiences in social relationships stems partly from readily apparent social and demographic changes, rather than from developmental theorizing. As a result, ages 18 to 28 have become a prolonged period of uncertainty and temporizing marked by secular trends toward later marriage and childbearing, longer stints in education and other programs preparatory to career paths, and labor–market changes affecting the availability of long-term employment patterns. Arnett has speculated that this new timetable for assuming adult responsibilities and roles foster intense self-focus, exploring a wide variety of relationships and avoiding commitments to particular partners and lifestyle arrangements (Arnett, 2000, 2004). Although research findings keyed to Arnett's predictions are sparse, his proposal called attention to the need for research on late adolescence and early adulthood. In addition, he raised provocative issues regarding whether the close relationships of 18- to 28-year-olds are developmentally distinct from those of earlier and later periods or a complex combination of continuities from teenage patterns extended into the college and postcollege years along with functional developmental changes appropriate to the incipient developmental challenges of adulthood (Collins & van Dulmen, 2006).

Theoretical Views of Relationships in Developmental Transitions

Theoretical views of adolescent relationships have the common goal of explaining the differentiation of relationships during the second decade of life. Theorists have given particular attention to apparent increases in distance from parents and increased closeness to peers during the second decade of life (Collins & Steinberg, 2006). These views vary, however, in how they account for these complex phenomena and in their implications for the eventual integration of disparate relationships during young adulthood.

One group of theories, *endogenous-change perspectives*, emphasizes biological and motivational pressures toward developmental changes in relationships. Psychoanalytic perspectives (e.g., Blos, 1979), for example, attribute perturbed parent–child relations and increasing orientation toward peers to psychic pressure for individuation from parents and a shift to interpersonal objects appropriate to adult roles. Similarly, evolutionary theorists view changing relationships as fostering autonomy and facilitating the formation of nonfamilial sexual relationships (Steinberg, 1988). Endogenous-change views depict the integration of relationships in young adulthood in terms of increases in the relative dominance of peer and, especially, romantic relationships, at the expense of continued intimacy between parents and offspring.

A second group of theories gives greater weight to exogenous factors in changing adolescent relationships. *Social–psychological perspectives* attribute changes in relationships to pressures associated with age-graded expectations, tasks, and settings, often in combination with maturational changes (Collins & Steinberg, 2006; Hill, 1988). Differences between parent–adolescent and peer relationships thus reflect differing salient contexts and shared activities. This view carries at least two possible implications for relationships during adolescence and for their eventual integration in young adulthood. One possibility is that, during transitions first to adolescence and later to adulthood, the proliferation of contexts and life tasks and the apparently differing demands of families and peers may heighten ambient anxiety and tensions. These negative emotions then may be expressed in conflictual or diminished interactions within the relatively safe confines of familial relationships but not in the more potentially fragile social environment of friendships and romantic experiences. Gradually, emotional perturbations may subside, or individuals may manage emotions more constructively, allowing for improved relationships with family members, as well as with extrafamilial partners. A related possibility is that age-graded expectations give relatively greater emphasis to the importance of success with friends and actual or potential romantic partners; consequently, adolescents and early adults may neglect or even devalue the importance of maintaining positive relationships with family members while investing heavily in harmonious relations with other adolescents. In adulthood, familial expectations may become more finely attuned to the demands of lives beyond the family.

Finally, two formulations emphasize functional similarities even as relationships change over time. Compared to the endogenous- and exogenous-change perspectives, these formulations give relatively greater emphasis to the importance of the history of relationship experiences with which an individual enters a new life period. *Attachment perspectives* hold that specific interactions vary as a function of changing developmental challenges from one age period to the next but are still guided by cognitive representations formed during early life that are essentially stable (Ainsworth, 1989; Allen, 2008; Collins & Sroufe, 1999; Sroufe, Egeland, Carlson, & Collins, 2005). For example, aloof, seemingly shy adolescents both elicit and actively respond to different types of overtures from peers than do more outgoing, relaxed, sociable individuals (Sroufe, Egeland, & Carlson, 1999). At the same time, the relationship histories of interaction partners play a role. Outgoing, relaxed, sociable individuals are mostly likely to manifest these personal characteristics when interacting with others who show similar characteristics or those who appear vulnerable and needy; whereas usually positive, sociable adolescents often appear more tense and conflict-prone when interacting with aloof, unresponsive, or domineering partners (Collins & Sroufe, 1999).

Interdependence perspectives also emphasize the joint patterns in which the actions, cognitions, and emotions of each member of the dyad are significant to the others' reactions. Interdependence, defined in terms of the frequency, diversity, strength, and duration of interactions, reflects the degree of closeness between two persons (Reis et al., 2000). Changes in relationships, such as those during adolescence, thus constitute altered patterns of interdependence. Interdependencies continue within familial relationships but in different forms than in earlier life; whereas interdependencies increase within friendships and romantic relationships. Parents and offspring both adjust expectancies in the service of optimal interdependence (Collins, 1995, 1997). Close peers must develop skills for maintaining interdependence on the basis of shared interests, commitments, and intimacy even when contact is relatively infrequent (Parker & Gottman, 1989). Mismatches between expectancies may precipitate conflicts, which in turn may stimulate adjustments of expectancies that both restore harmony and foster developmental adaptations in the dyad (Collins, 1995). Accounts of interdependence and attachment attempt to explain how the qualities of relationships prior to adolescence are linked to an individual's experiences with others in later life periods.

In contrast to the endogenous-change and social–psychological views, attachment and interdependence perspectives imply that the degree of eventual integration of parent–child, friend, and peer relationships varies across individuals and relationships. For example, histories of positive, supportive relationships with parents and successful relationships with peers portend strong, communal relationships with both parents and peers, including romantic partners, in young adulthood. By contrast, unreliable relationships with parents and peers may be associated with less cohesive patterns of familial and extrafamilial patterns in adulthood (Collins & Sroufe, 1999).

Examining the nature and significance of these developmental adaptations has presented considerable methodological, as well as conceptual, challenges, and researchers have used highly varied methods to meet them. Sociologists have relied almost exclusively on self-report methods, most often using them in cross-sectional surveys (e.g., Sprecher & Felmlee, 1992). Social psychologists, too, have relied almost exclusively on self-report methods but have reported some findings from experimental manipulations (e.g., Regan, Kocan, & Whitlock, 1998). The well-known PAIRS Project (e.g., Huston et al., 2001) is an example of research tracking romantic partnerships from emerging adulthood to later life. Developmental psychologists have relied more extensively on longitudinal studies. In most cases, the methods of choice involve self-report from interviews and questionnaires; in some studies, the reports of other individuals (e.g., teachers, observers) sometimes have been included (e.g., Collins & Sroufe, 1999; Furman, Simon, Shaffer, & Bouchey, 2002). Some ethnographically influenced work consists primarily of informants' open-ended accounts (e.g., Arnett, 2003). Only a minority of studies have included formal observational methods (see Roisman, Madsen, Hennighausen, Sroufe, & Collins, 2001, for an exception). In general, research on the nature and changing features of close relationships requires methods that capture the richness afforded only by a dyadic unit of analysis. The empirical examples described in the remaining sections of the chapter underscore the value of methods that are especially keyed to the study of dyads.

☗ RECENT EMPIRICAL ADVANCES

Research on multiple changing close relationships has burgeoned since the first reviews of the evidence. In this section, we give particular attention to three dominant themes in that research (Collins & Laursen, 2004; Collins, Haydon, & Hesemeyer, 2007): (1) developmental changes in the nature and functional significance of these connections, (2) the expansion and diversification of relationship networks, and (3) increasing interrelations among the significant relationships that typify social connections in late adolescence and early adulthood.

Unfortunately, understanding this transition in parent–child relationships is limited by researchers' heavy reliance on single-informant questionnaires (typically from the child alone), despite the inherently dyadic nature of parent–child relationship (for an exception, see Whiteman, McHale, & Crouter, 2011). Consequently, most current findings testify only to the importance of individuals' perceptions of the relationship quality with their parents. Dyadic measures of interaction such as observations or even reports from both parties are necessary to elucidate the relationship dynamics and processes between parents and children that promote the quality of the child's adaptation during the transition to adulthood.

Changes in Nature and Functional Significance

Just as transitions in relationships between childhood and adolescence involve adapting to often unexpected discrepancies between parental expectations and individual and normative behaviors and attitudes of children (Collins, 1995), transitions during late adolescence and early adulthood involve adapting to new expectations associated with changes in adult social and legal status (Aquilino, 2006; Collins & van Dulmen, 2006).

Parents face pressures to adjust their expectations of control, while continuing to provide emotional and sometimes material support. In turn, offspring must move toward greater autonomy and responsibility while remaining connected to parents (Collins & Steinberg, 2006). Research on the nature and significance of these changes consistently has shown that maintaining functional relationships with parents in late adolescence and early adulthood is both normative and psychologically adaptive (see Aquilino, 2006, for a review).

In contrast to research on earlier transitions, however, research examining changes in nature and functional significance of relationships during late adolescence and early adulthood has revealed that the interplay of parental relationships with extrafamilial relationships often may account more fully for developmental changes than any single relationship does. The interplay may take several forms. For example, despite the stereotype of incompatible or contradictory influences of parents and friends, relationships with parents set the stage for both the selection of friends and the management of these relationships from childhood forward (Collins, Maccoby, Steinberg, Hetherington, & Bornstein, 2000; Collins & Steinberg, 2006). Friends and romantic partners typically are the individuals with whom early adults most like to spend time (proximity-seeking) and with whom they most want to be when feeling down (safe haven function). Parents, however, are just as likely to be the primary source from which early adults seek advice and whom they depend upon (Fraley & Davis, 1997). Representations of romantic relationships are linked to representations of other close relationships, especially relationships with friends, and these interrelated expectancies parallel interrelations in features like support and control (Furman et al., 2002).

It is important to note that these normative transformations within and between relationships are important signs of convergence across differing relationships. Qualities of friendships in middle and late adolescence are associated with concurrent qualities of romantic relationships (Collins et al., 2009; Furman et al., 2002). Working models of friendships and romantic relationships are interrelated as well (Carlivati & Collins, 2007), and displaying safe haven and secure base behaviors with best friends is associated positively with displaying these behaviors with dating partners. This apparently greater coherence among an individual's significant relationships may indicate that the growing importance of romantic relationships makes the common relationship properties across types of relationships more apparent than before. It is also likely, however, that the parallels between early adults' relationships reflect their common similarity to current and prior relationships with parents and peers (Owens et al., 1995).

Links between qualities of friendships and romantic relationships, as well as between familial and romantic relationships, are equally impressive (Collins & van Dulmen, 2006). Relationships with parents, friends, and romantic partners serve overlapping but distinctive functions. Typical exchanges within each of these types of dyads differ accordingly. In comparison to childhood relationships, the diminished distance and greater intimacy in adolescents' peer relationships may satisfy affiliative needs and also contribute to socialization for relations among equals. Intimacy with parents may provide nurturance and support, but may be less important than friendships for socialization to roles and expectations in late adolescence and early adulthood (Collins, 1997; Laursen & Bukowski, 1997).

In a longitudinal study, Beyers and Seiffge-Krenke (2007) documented that even in late adolescence changes occur in the functional significance of relationships with parents, friends, and romantic partners. These authors further showed that the self-reported quality of relationships with friends and romantic partners mediated the links across time between relationships with parents in adolescence and self- and parent reports of internalizing and externalizing behavior at age 17 and self-reported symptoms of psychopathology at age 21. Extrafamilial relationships often show interactive effects, as well. Meeus, Branje, Van der Valk, and De Wied (2007) documented age-related shifts in the relative importance of intimate relationships with romantic partners, relative to best friendships, for individual emotional functioning.

Findings such as these have moved the field forward in two ways. First, they add to evidence of the developmental significance of extrafamilial, as well as familial, relationships. Second, they illustrate the importance of examining jointly the nature and significance of experiences with parents, with friends, and with romantic partners in late adolescence and young adulthood in accounting for the developmental significance of differing categories of close relationships. As an example, findings that romantic relationships were more salient and were differentially related to emotion and behavior in early adulthood compared to adolescence may reflect one or both of two underlying developmental trajectories (Meeus et al., 2007; van Dulmen, Goncy, Haydon, & Collins, 2008). One is that early-adult romantic relationships are likely better quality because developmental capacity for intimate relationships is more advanced at the older ages (Collins & Sroufe, 1999; Collins et al., 2009). The age-related increase in stability of relationship commitment and the associated decline in emotional problems in these findings are consistent with the improve quality hypothesis. The second possibility is that forming intimate relationships in early adulthood is more important to acquiring age-related norms of social roles than in early adolescence. Adhering to developmental norms is generally regarded as an indicator of positive emotional functioning at every age (Sroufe, Duggal, Weinfield, & Carlson, 2000). Together, these findings underscore the need to go beyond simply determining the presence or even the number of relationships in a network by also assessing the quality and content of multiple types of relationships.

Expansion and Diversification of Networks

The importance of multiple social relationships is apparent in research on both human and infrahuman species (Reis et al., 2000). Moreover, varied relationship partners provide overlapping, as well as distinctive, benefits (Laursen & Bukowski, 1997; Reis & Collins, 2004). Recent findings from research on relationships during the transition to adulthood underscore the salience, as well as the significance, of changes in close relationship networks in this period. For example, perceptions of parents as primary sources of support generally decline during adolescence; at the same time, perceived support from friends increases, such that friendships are seen as providing roughly the same or greater support as parental relationships (Furman & Buhrmester, 1992; Helsen, Vollebergh, & Meeus, 2000; Scholte, van Lieshout, & van Aken, 2001). Friends and romantic interests emerge as the individuals with whom early adults prefer to spend time and with whom they most want to be when feeling down (Ainsworth, 1989; Cassidy, 2001; Waters & Cummings, 2000). Although parents are just as likely as friends to be the primary source from which adolescents and early adults seek advice and upon whom they depend (Fraley & Davis, 1997), components of attachment relationships (namely, maintaining proximity, using the other as a safe haven, and using the other as a secure base) also begin to typify relationships with extrafamilial partners (Furman et al., 2002). Thus, not only parental nurturance but also mutual support and intimacy in friendships provide essential training for intimate romantic partnerships. Friendship intimacy may even be relatively more significant than the parent–child relationship in preparing adolescents for social roles and expectations in late adolescence and early adulthood (Collins, 1997; Laursen & Bukowski, 1997). Eventually marriage and formation of new families alter the hegemony of same-gender peer relations to close relationships with intimate partners.

Parent–child relationships also become increasingly egalitarian, with parents more often functioning as a general source of social support, rather than an active guiding agent during the transition to adulthood (see Collins, 1995; Masche, 2008; Nelson, Padilla-Walker, Christensen, Evans, & Carroll, 2011). At the same time, increasingly extensive daily contacts with friends and romantic partners and perceived support from friends and romantic partners rivals and sometimes exceeds that provided by parents (Collins et al., 2009). Indeed, intimacy, mutuality, and self-disclosure between friends intensify during late adolescence, possibly heightening the developmental salience of friendships in the transition to adulthood (Furman & Buhrmester, 1992).

Both familial and extrafamilial relationships contribute significantly to development and functioning during the transition to adulthood. In a longitudinal study, Van Wel and colleagues (Van Wel, Bogt, & Raaijmakers, 2002; Van Wel, Linssen, & Abma, 2000) found that indicators of well-being for young adolescent participants were reliably predicted by the participants' reports of the quality of their bonds with their parents, peers, and romantic partners; the parental bond was not the exclusive predictor of well-being, but it was a stronger predictor than bonds with peers and romantic partners. Significantly, when the follow-up assessment was conducted 3 years later, the parental bond was equivalent to being in a steady relationship with a romantic partner as a predictor of individual well-being, and the same was found in a third assessment after another 3 years. These findings underscore the need for research that addresses simultaneously the possible separate functions of differing types of close relationships and the potential for combined and interactive effects among them in the development of individuals.

Diverse relationship partners provide distinctive, as well as overlapping, benefits (Collins & Steinberg, 2006; Laursen & Bukowski, 1997). For example, the role of friendships as a template for all subsequent close peer affiliations (Connolly, Furman, & Konarski, 2000; Sullivan, 1953) undoubtedly helps to facilitate romantic relationships and pair bonding in early adulthood (Collins & Laursen, 2004). Meeus et al. (2007) further supported this speculation by showing that the transition from best friend to romantic partner as the primary intimate relationship is associated with increased and more stable commitments. The expansion and diversification of relationship networks thus is a gradual elaboration of the less extensive networks of earlier periods.

Functional similarities and differences within social networks may set the stage for considerable influence between close dyadic relationships in the 18- to 28-year-old period. Pertinent evidence comes from research in which the networks of parents and friends significantly influence continuation or dissolution of a romantic relationship. For example, Sprecher and Felmlee (1992) showed that network support for a relationship was associated positively with the quality of the relationship. Numerous other studies have shown that although couples vary in the degree to which they remain integrally involved with their former networks of kin and friends those who do continue close involvements show effects of the support or interference they receive (e.g., Connolly & Goldberg, 1999). Findings like this raise the possibility that involvement in, and qualities of, distinct dyads may moderate the effects of each other.

Normative changes in networks of close relationships should not mask considerable individual differences in the size and scope of relationship networks. Early adults who are romantically uninvolved report greater reliance on friends than their romantically involved peers do. Single adults name friends as their top companions and confidants, and, along with mothers, the primary source for all facets of social support (Carbery & Buhrmester, 1998). Engagement and marriage are both linked to partial withdrawal from friends. Although total social network size remains the same after marriage, single adults have more friends than kin in their social network, whereas married adults report a balance of kin and friends (Fischer, Sollie, Sorrell, & Green, 1989).

As the number of family roles increases, adults depend less on friends to satisfy their social needs. Although this change is most marked between the single and married phases of life, social networks are reorganized again across the transition to parenthood. Both mothers and fathers report a decline in the number of friends in their social networks after the birth of a child, but this decline is greater for fathers. Fathers also report less mutual support in friendship networks and less satisfaction with friendships over time compared to their wives (Bost, Cox, Burchinal, & Payne, 2002).

Increasing Interrelations Among Relationships

The findings already reviewed appear consistent with Collins and Laursen's (2000, 2004) assertion that " . . . affiliations with friends, romantic partners, siblings, and parents unfold along varied and somewhat discrete trajectories for most of the second decade of life, then coalesce during the early twenties into integrated interpersonal structure" (2000, p. 59). Much remains to be learned concerning the implications of increasing interrelations among relationships in the course of development. The theme of interrelations of relationships is especially apparent in the accumulating evidence that friendship quality may either have compensatory or exacerbating effects on adjustment problems, depending on other interpersonal influences. Beyers and Seiffge-Krenke (2007) and Ciairano, Rabaglietti, Roggero, Bonino, and Beyers (2007) identified specific patterns in which friendships both moderate the impact of changing relationships in families and the converse. Larsen, Branje, Van der Valk, & Meeus (2007) focused on similar moderating effects, though with respect to the impact of interparental, rather than parent–adolescent, relationships. To be sure, these findings are complex and, in combination, difficult to interpret. The contradictory picture of the significance of friendship quality vis-à-vis the functioning of other relationships, however, only underscores the importance of acknowledging and examining interrelations among relationships. Similarly, although the particular form of interrelation examined differs across studies, the finding of a normative, clearly functional segue from best friends to romantic partners as primary intimate relationships illuminates the social development process in the years approaching adulthood.

The aggregated findings represent a heretofore relatively neglected line of research in the larger literature on close relationships in the teens and 20s. Most research with adolescent samples has focused on the simple additive effects of relationships. Several exceptions, however, are telling. Wood, Read, Mitchell, & Brand (2004) showed that parental involvement with adolescents moderated peer influences on drinking behavior; Gauze, Bukowski, Aquan-Assee, & Sippola (1996) found that the degree to which mutual friendships are linked positively to adolescents' psychological well-being depends on the degree to which the adolescent also experiences familial cohesion and adaptability. These instances and those reported in the present collection of articles broaden simplistic cause and effect models of the impact of close relationships. Rather than focusing only on the assumption that association with one close relationship partner or another causes the outcomes to which correlational findings commonly link them, this new attention to moderator effects underscores the possibility that relationships contribute to individual development by altering the impact of other sources of influence, even those emanating from other relationships.

⋙ TOWARD FURTHER REJEARCH ON RELATIONJHIPJ NETWORKJ AFTER ADOLEJCENCE

Research on relationships prior to adulthood seeks to describe and explain transformations in relationships under conditions of rapid and extensive changes in participants and in key contexts. Current findings on friendships and romantic relationships in the teens and 20s supplement and extend evidence from earlier periods that adaptations in relationships preserve their functional significance in the midst of change. Social networks expand during adolescence and early adulthood to include an increasing number and diversity of personal relationships, though these extrafamilial bonds also become increasingly interrelated with familial relationships by the late 20s. Although familial relationships often appear to decline in importance in this process, the decline is a relative, rather than an absolute, one. Individual adjustments and reactions by both parties are essential components in this developmental process.

These three themes in the research literature effectively mount the case for continuing to pursue new directions in research on changing networks of close relationships in the second and third decades of life. To be sure, emerging findings admonish future researchers to encompass relationships with parents, friends, and romantic interests—when applicable. Findings from such inclusive designs raise the possibility that adolescents' intensifying involvement in more extensive relationship networks powerfully shapes their future, as well as their current dyadic relationships. An especially significant implication is the importance of looking at the constellation of adolescent close relationships, rather than one type alone, in predicting adjustment.

Consequently, the agenda for filling gaps in research on relationships during early adulthood is a lengthy one. Broader perspectives are needed in research on development and change in relationships. Research largely has been directed toward interpersonal antecedents of deterioration and termination in voluntary adult relationships such as courtship and marriage. Integrating this tradition with perspectives on processes that link individual and relational changes is one possible step toward understanding how relationships are adapted to change in every period of life.

The most compelling accounts would come from longitudinal data sets in which repeated accounts are sought from the same individuals across the three age periods, using standard reporting devices and using standard metrics. Further research on the nature and significance of early adults' close relationships can be pursued most beneficially within the theoretical frameworks of the rapidly growing science of relationships (Reis et al., 2000).

In addition, measurement strategies should be directed toward a broad range of relationship features, moving beyond relationship status to include the content and quality of relationships (Collins et al., 2009). Especially needed are research designs that are sensitive to both similarities and differences between types of relationships and changes in these in the transition to adulthood. New research designs and strategies will be required in this more comprehensive approach to relationships and their developmental significance. Today, the most commonly used statistical approaches often necessitate pitting one relationship against another—that is, controlling the influence of one to test unique contributions of another. In the future, we will need methods that allow us to recognize the nonlinear, nonadditive, dynamic interrelations among parents, peers, and romantic relationships. In rising to these challenges, researchers may gain significant new knowledge of how relationships in every life period both adapt to and influence individual functioning across the life course.

⁂ JUGGEJTED READINGJ

Aquilino, W. S. (2006). Family relationships and support systems in emerging adulthood. In J. J. Arnett & J. Tanner (Eds.), *Emerging adults in America: Coming of age in the 21st century* (pp. 193–217). Washington, DC: American Psychological Association.

Collins, W. A., & van Dulmen, M. (2006). Friendships and romantic relationships in emerging adulthood: Continuities and discontinuities. In J. J. Arnett & J. Tanner (Eds.), *Emerging adults in America: Coming of age in the 21st century* (pp. 219–234). Washington, DC: American Psychological Association.

Meeus, W., Branje, S., Van der Valk, I., De Wied, M. (2007). Relationships with intimate partner, best friends, and parents in adolescence and early adulthood: A study of the saliency of the intimate partnership. *International Journal of Behavioral Development, 31,* 569–580.

Reis, H. T., & Collins, W. A. (2004). Relationships, human behavior, and psychological science. *Current Directions in Psychological Science, 13*(6), 233–237.

van Dulmen, M., Goncy, E., Haydon, K. C., & Collins, W. A. (2008). Distinctiveness of adolescent and emerging adult romantic relationship features in predicting externalizing behavior problems. *Journal of Youth and Adolescence, 37*, 336–345.

▨ REFERENCEƒ

Ainsworth, M. D. S. (1989). Attachments beyond infancy. *American Psychologist, 44*, 709–716.

Allen, J. P. (2008). The attachment system in adolescence. In J. Cassidy & P. R. Shaver (Eds.), *Handbook of attachment: Theory, research, and clinical applications* (Vol. 2, pp. 419–435). New York: Guilford Press.

Aquilino, W. S. (2006). Family relationships and support systems in emerging adulthood. In J. J. Arnett & J. Tanner (Eds.), *Emerging adults in America: Coming of age in the 21st century* (pp. 193–217). Washington, DC: American Psychological Association.

Arnett, J. J. (2000). Emerging adulthood: A theory of development from the late teens through the twenties. *American Psychologist, 54*, 317–326.

Arnett, J. J. (2003). Conceptions of the transition to adulthood among emerging adults in American ethnic groups. *New Directions in Child and Adolescent Development, 100*, 63–75.

Arnett, J. J. (2004). *Emerging adulthood: The winding road from the late teens through the twenties.* New York: Oxford University Press.

Berscheid, E., Snyder, M., & Omoto, A. (1989). The Relationship Closeness Inventory: Assessing the closeness of interpersonal relationships. *Journal of Personality and Social Psychology, 57*, 792–807.

Beyers, W., & Seiffge-Krenke, I. (2007). Are friends and romantic partners the "best medicine"? How the quality of other close relations mediates the impact of changing family relationships on adjustment. *International Journal of Behavioral Development, 31*, 559–568.

Blos, P. (1979). *The adolescent passage.* New York: International Universities Press.

Bost, K. K., Cox, M. J., Burchinal, M. R., & Payne, C. (2002). Structural and supportive changes in couples' family and friendship networks across the transition to parenthood. *Journal of Marriage and the Family, 64*, 517–531.

Carbery, J., & Buhrmester, D. (1998). Friendship and need fulfillment during three phases of young adulthood. *Journal of Social and Personal Relationships, 15*, 393–409.

Carlivati, J., & Collins, W. A. (2007). Adolescent attachment representations and development in a risk sample. In M. Scharf & O. Mayseless (Eds.), Attachment in adolescence. *New Directions For Child and Adolescent Development*, No. 117, 91–106.

Cassidy, J. (2001). Truth, lies, and intimacy: An attachment perspective. *Attachment and Human Development, 3*, 121–155.

Ciairano, S., Rabaglietti, E., Roggero, A., Bonino, S., & Beyers, W. (2007). Patterns of adolescent friendships, psychological adjustment and antisocial behavior: The moderating role of family stress and friendship reciprocity. *International Journal of Behavioral Development, 31,* 539–548.

Collins, W. A. (1995). Relationships and development: Family adaptation to individual change. In S. Shulman (Ed.), *Close relationships and socioemotional development* (pp. 128–154). New York: Ablex.

Collins, W. A. (1997). Relationships and development during adolescence: Interpersonal adaptation to individual change. *Personal Relationships, 4,* 1–14.

Collins, W. A. (2010). Historical perspectives on contemporary research in social development. In C. Hart & P. Smith (Eds.), *Blackwell handbook of childhood social development.* London, England: Blackwell Publishers.

Collins, W. A., Haydon, K. C., & Hesemeyer, P. (2007). Relating relationships: Development, expansion, and interrelations in relationship networks. *International Journal of Behavioral Development, 31*(6), 581–584.

Collins, W. A., & Laursen, B. (2000). Adolescent relationships: The art of fugue. In C. Hendrick & S. Hendrick (Eds.), *Close relationships: A sourcebook* (pp. 59–70). Thousand Oaks, CA: Sage.

Collins, W. A., & Laursen, B. (2004). Changing relationships, changing youth: Interpersonal contexts of adolescent development. *Journal of Early Adolescence, 24,* 55–62.

Collins, W. A., Maccoby, E. E., Steinberg, L., Hetherington, E. M., & Bornstein, M. H. (2000). Contemporary research on parenting: The case for nature and nurture. *American Psychologist, 53,* 218–232.

Collins, W. A., & Sroufe, L. A. (1999). Capacity for intimate relationships: A developmental construction. In W. Furman, B. B. Brown, & C. Feiring (Eds.), *The development of romantic relationships in adolescence* (pp. 125–147). New York: Cambridge University Press.

Collins, W. A., & Steinberg, L. (2006). Adolescent development in interpersonal context. In W. Damon & N. Eisenberg (Eds.), *Handbook of child psychology: Vol. 4. Socioemotional processes* (pp. 1003–1067). New York: Wiley.

Collins, W. A., & van Dulmen, M. (2006). Friendships and romantic relationships in emerging adulthood: Continuities and discontinuities. In J. J. Arnett & J. Tanner (Eds.), *Emerging adults in America: Coming of age in the 21st century* (pp. 219–234). Washington, DC: American Psychological Association.

Collins, W. A., Welsh, D. P., & Furman, W. (2009). Adolescent romantic relationships. *Annual Review of Psychology, 60,* 631–652.

Connolly, J. A., Furman, W., & Konarski, R. (2000). The role of peers in the emergence of heterosexual romantic relationships in adolescence. *Child Development, 71,* 1395–1408.

Connolly, J. A., & Goldberg, A. (1999). Romantic relationships in adolescence: The role of friends and peers in their emergence and development. In W. Furman, B. B. Brown, & C. Feiring (Eds.), *The development of romantic relationships in adolescence* (pp. 266–290). New York: Cambridge University Press.

Fischer, J. L., Sollie, D. L., Sorrell, G. T., & Green, S. K. (1989). Marital status and career stage influences on social networks of young adults. *Journal of Marriage and the Family, 51,* 521–534.

Fraley, R. C., & Davis, K. E. (1997). Attachment formation and transfer in young adults' close friendships and romantic relationships. *Personal Relationships, 4,* 131–144.

Furman, W., & Buhrmester, D. (1992). Age and sex differences in perceptions of networks of personal relationships. *Child Development, 63,* 103–115.

Furman, W., Simon, V. A., Shaffer, L., & Bouchey, H. A. (2002). Adolescents' working models and styles for relationships with parents, friends, and romantic partners. *Child Development, 73,* 241–255.

Gauze, C., Bukowski, W., Asquan-Assee, J., & Sippola, L. K. (1996). Interactions between family environment and friendship and associations with self-perceived well-being in early adolescence. *Child Development, 67*(5), 2201–2216.

Helsen, M., Vollebergh, W., & Meeus, W. (2000). Social support from parents and friends and emotional problems in adolescence. *Journal of Youth and Adolescence, 29,* 319–335.

Hill, J. P. (1988). Adapting to menarche: Family control and conflict. In M. Gunnar & W. A. Collins (Eds.), *Development during the transition to adolescence* (pp. 43–77). Hillsdale, NJ: Lawrence Erlbaum.

Hinde, R. (1997). *Relationships: A dialectical perspective.* Hove, England: Psychology Press.

Huston, T., Niehuis, S., & Smith, S. E. (2001). The early marital roots of conjugal distress and divorce. *Current Directions in Psychological Science, 10*(4), 116–119.

Larsen, H., Branje, S., Van der Valk, I., & Meeus, W. (2007). Friendship quality as a moderator between perception of interparental conflicts and maladjustment in adolescence. *International Journal of Behavioral Development, 31,* 549–558.

Laursen, B., & Bukowski, W. M. (1997). A developmental guide to the organization of close relationships. *International Journal of Behavioral Development, 21,* 747–770.

Laursen, B., Coy, K. C., & Collins, W. A. (1998). Reconsidering changes in parent-child conflict across adolescence: A meta-analysis. *Child Development, 69,* 817–832.

Laursen, B., & Williams, V. (1997). Perceptions of interdependence and closeness in family and peer relationships among adolescents with and without romantic partners. In S. Shulman & W. A. Collins (Eds.), Romantic relationships in adolescence: Developmental perspectives. *New Directions for Child Development, 78,* pp. 3–20.

Masche, G. (2008). Reciprocal influences between developmental transitions and parent–child relationships in young adulthood. *International Journal of Behavioral Development, 32*(5), 401–411.

Meeus, W., Branje, S., Van der Valk, I., & De Wied, M. (2007). Relationships with intimate partner, best friends, and parents in adolescence and early adulthood: A study of the saliency of the intimate partnership. *International Journal of Behavioral Development, 31,* 569–580.

Nelson, L. J., Padilla-Walker, L. M., Christensen, K. J., Evans, C. A., & Carroll, J. S. (2011). Parenting in emerging adulthood: An examination of parenting clusters and correlates. *Journal of Youth and Adolescence 40*(6), 730–743.

Owens, G., Crowell, J., Pan, H., Treboux, D., O'Connor, E., & Waters, E. (1995). The prototype hypothesis and the origins of attachment working models: Adult relationships with parents and romantic partners. In E. Waters, B. Vaughn, G. Posada, & K. Kondo-Ikemura (Eds.), Caregiving, cultural, and cognitive perspectives on secure-base behavior and working models: New growing points of attachment theory and research. *Monographs of the Society for Research in Child Development, 60*(2–3, Serial No. 244), 216–233.

Parker, J. G., & Gottman, J. M. (1989). Social and emotional development in a relational context: Friendship interaction from early childhood to adolescence. In T. J. Berndt & G. W. Ladd (Eds.), *Peer Relationships in Child Development* (pp. 95–131). New York: Wiley.

Regan, P. C., Kocan, E. R., & Whitlock, T. (1998). Ain't love grand! A prototype analysis of romantic love. *Journal of Personal and Social Relationships, 15,* 411–420.

Reis, H. T., & Collins, W. A. (2004). Relationships, human behavior, and psychological science. *Current Directions in Psychological Science, 13*(6), 233–237.

Reis, H. T., Collins, W. A., & Berscheid, E. (2000). Relationships in human behavior and development. *Psychological Bulletin, 126,* 844–872.

Roisman, G. I., Madsen, S. D., Hennighausen, K. H., Sroufe, L. A., & Collins, W. A. (2001). The coherence of dyadic behavior across parent–child and romantic relationships as mediated by the internalized representation of experience. *Attachment & Human Development, 3*(2), 156–172.

Scholte, R. H. J., van Lieshout, C. F. M., & van Aken, M. A. G. (2001). Perceived relational support in adolescence: Dimensions, configurations, and adolescent adjustment. *Journal of Research on Adolescence, 11,* 71–94.

Simpson, J. A., Collins, W. A., Tran, S., & Haydon, K. C. (2007). Attachment and the experience and expression of emotions in romantic relationships: A developmental perspective. *Journal of Personality and Social Psychology, 72*(2), 355–367.

Sprecher, S., & Felmlee, D. (1992). The influence of parents and friends on the quality and stability of romantic relationships: A three-wave longitudinal investigation. *Journal of Marriage and the Family, 54,* 888–900.

Sroufe, L. A., Duggal, S., Weinfield, N., & Carlson, E. A. (2000). Relationships, development, and psychopathology. In A. Sameroff, M. Lewis, & S. Miller (Eds.), *Handbook of developmental psychopathology* (2nd ed., pp. 75–92). New York: Kluwer Academic/ Plenum Press.

Sroufe, L. A., Egeland, B., & Carlson, E. A. (1999). One social world: The integrated development of parent–child and peer relationship. In W. A. Collins & B. Laursen (Eds.), *Relationships as developmental contexts: The 30th Minnesota Symposium on Child Psychology* (pp. 241–262). Hillsdale, NJ: Lawrence Erlbaum.

Sroufe, L. A., Egeland, B., Carlson, E. A., & Collins, W. A. (2005). *The development of the person.* New York: Guilford Press.

Steinberg, L. (1988). Reciprocal relation between parent-child distance and pubertal maturation. *Developmental Psychology, 24,* 122–128.

Sullivan, H. S. (1953). *The interpersonal theory of psychiatry.* New York: Norton.

van Dulmen, M., Goncy, E., Haydon, K. C., & Collins, W. A. (2008). Distinctiveness of adolescent and emerging adult romantic relationship features in predicting externalizing behavior problems. *Journal of Youth and Adolescence, 37,* 336–345.

Van Wel, F., Bogt, T. F. M., & Raaijmakers, Q. (2002). Changes in the parental bond and the well-being of adolescents and young people. *Adolescence, 37*(146), 317–334.

Van Wel, F., Linssen, H., & Abma, R. (2000). The parental bond and the well-being of adolescents and young adults. *Journal of Youth and Adolescence, 29*(3), 307–318.

Waters, E., & Cummings, E. M. (2000). A secure base from which to explore close relationships. *Child Development, 71,* 164–172.

Whiteman, S. D., McHale, S. M., & Crouter, A. C. (2011). Family relationships from adolescence to early adulthood: Changes in the family system following firstborns' leaving home. *Journal of Research on Adolescence 21*(2), 461–474.

Wood, M. D., Read, J. P., Mitchell, R. E., & Brand, N. H. (2004). Do parents still matter? Parent and peer influence on alcohol involvement among recent high school graduates. *Psychology of Addictive Behaviors, 18*(1), 19–30.

2

Transformations in Parent–Child Relationships From Adolescence to Adulthood

Nancy L. Galambos

Lauren A. Kotylak

"There are two lasting bequests we can give our children: One is roots, the other is wings." This aphorism, often credited to American journalist and writer Hodding Carter (1907–1972), reflects the importance of a firm ground to stand on and connectedness to the world as well as the freedom and ability to explore and test that world if children are to develop into responsible and happy adults. These are also major themes in the extensive literature on parent–child relations. Social scientists studying family relations and child development believe that parent–child relationships characterized broadly as supportive, accepting, and warm give rise to roots at the same time that an appropriate amount of autonomy granting gives rise to wings (e.g., Lamborn & Steinberg, 1993; O'Connor, Allen, Bell, & Hauser, 1996). It is in the transition to adulthood, when we expect the emergence of full-fledged mature behavior, that the longer-term importance of the supportive and autonomy-fostering aspects of the parent–child relationship ought to become apparent.

The transition to adulthood involves many changes in context and experience that help to produce a mature and competent adult. Major life experiences at this time generally include leaving home, completing education, finding employment, getting married, and becoming a parent (Fussell & Furstenberg, 2005). In recent decades, these markers of adult maturity have become more variable in sequence with many young people in their 20s moving in and out of their parents' homes, postsecondary training, work situations, and romantic relationships taking longer than previous birth cohorts to complete important life transitions (Cohen, Kasen, Chen, Hartmark, & Gordon, 2003; Goldscheider & Goldscheider, 1999). Differences from person to person in the experience of the transition to adulthood are large, however, with some individuals moving into work or parenthood in their teens and early 20s and others not becoming established in jobs or relationships until their 30s. In short, the transition to adulthood involves many changes, experientially and interpersonally, and in contemporary times it has become less standardized, more individualized, and lengthier (Fussell & Furstenberg, 2005)—so much so that new terms have been devised to label this generation in their 20s who are no longer adolescents but not yet adults. In this chapter, we use the label *emerging adults* to refer to individuals in the general age range of 18 to 29 (Arnett, 2000). We reserve the term *young adults* for people in their early 30s.

Transformations in the parent–child relationship are likely to occur during emerging adulthood (Thornton, Orbuch, & Axinn, 1995). After all, separating from parents and replacing dependence on them with independence from them is a long process, referred to as "individuation," that begins to some extent in childhood and accelerates in the teen years as the adolescent spends increasingly more time away from home and in the company of peers (Laursen & Collins, 2009; O'Connor et al., 1996). With the life transitions that take place in emerging adulthood and the lengthening path to adulthood in contemporary times, the process of individuation continues into the 20s (Frank, Pirsch, & Wright, 1990; Tubman & Lerner, 1994). But what aspects of the parent–child relationship change during the transition to adulthood, how, and for whom?

In this chapter, we attempt to provide some answers to this question by examining empirical evidence for transformations in the relationships between parents and their emerging adult children. First, we briefly outline a broad theoretical approach that guides our thinking on what is important to consider in examining the nature of parent–child relations in the transition to adulthood: the developmental systems perspective. Second, we describe empirical studies that speak to the issue of systematic change as well as stability in parent–child relations during this period. We also describe studies that point to possible correlates or predictors of change in parent–child relations in this transition, including gender and whether the young person has left home. Third, we discuss future directions for research based on what was learned in previous sections of the chapter.

⋙ THEORETICAL OVERVIEW

The Developmental Systems Perspective

To conceptualize issues relevant to understanding how parent–child relations might transform during the transition to adulthood, we turn to the developmental systems perspective on human development. This perspective emphasizes plasticity, or the potential for systematic within-person change across the life span. Individuals at any age, for example, have the potential to alter their attitudes, behaviors, and life choices. A major source of such plasticity lies in interactions between individuals and their social contexts. That is, within-person change can result from ongoing and dynamic interactions between the individual and significant others (e.g., parents, romantic partners). The parent–child relationship is a key potential source of influence on the developing person, but this relationship may also change as a function of parents' and children's behaviors as they move together through the life span. As such, it is important to not only track and describe how the parent–child relationship takes on a different quality over time but to examine how it covaries with changes in the developing child and his or her parents (Lerner, 2004).

The developmental systems perspective also highlights uniqueness and diversity (or differences from person to person) in developmental paths to adulthood linked to life events and experiences (Schulenberg, Maggs, & O'Malley, 2003). Consistent with this perspective is the concept of transition-linked turning points, defined as events or experiences that occur during a transition that may result in the emergence, discontinuation, or alteration of some behaviors (Graber & Brooks-Gunn, 1996b).

Turning points may change the individual's developmental course, presenting opportunities for healthy growth and adaptation—the mark of a successful transition to adulthood (Schulenberg et al., 2003)—as well as risks that can lead to poorer functioning. Timing of experiences is important because it may make the difference between opportunities for optimal development versus risks for unhealthy development. The five markers of adulthood mentioned earlier (leaving home, completing education, finding work, marriage, and parenthood) constitute potential turning points or sources of change in parent–child relations in emerging adults. Furthermore, individual differences in characteristics such as gender and race or ethnicity may not only play a role in how parents and children relate to each other, but they might also affect how a turning point is experienced.

The developmental systems perspective leads to three general questions that organize our consideration of transformations in the parent–child relationship across the transition to adulthood. First, what is the nature of the parent–child relationship upon entering the transition to adulthood, and does it change across the transition? This question asks about continuity in the parent–child relationship in terms of the overall pattern of change in important aspects of the relationship across time. For example, do perceptions of parent support decrease, increase, or remain the same from adolescence into adulthood (Aquilino, 1997; Thornton et al., 1995)? Second, to what extent is there stability between adolescence and through the transition to adulthood in the quality of the parent–child relationship? Although specific aspects of the parent–child relationship (e.g., frequency or intensity of conflict) might increase or decrease, or show improvement or deterioration in an absolute sense, it is more likely than not that parents and children with stronger relationships going into the transition will emerge from the transition in strong positions. Conversely, less healthy parent–child relationships in adolescence are likely to carry over into adulthood (Aquilino, 1997; Belsky, Jaffee, Hsieh, & Silva, 2001; Tubman & Lerner, 1994).

Third, because a developmental systems perspective points to the likelihood of diversity in the way that parent–child relationships change in the transition to adulthood, sources of diversity are important to consider. Such diversity might arise from individual characteristics including gender or ethnicity (Gutman & Eccles, 2007; Smetana, Metzger, & Campione-Barr, 2004; Sneed et al., 2006), family characteristics such as parents' marital status (Aquilino, 2005), and life transitions like leaving home (Seiffge-Krenke, 2006). Thus, we ask the following: To what extent is diversity in the path of parent–child relations during the transition to adulthood attributable to individual and family characteristics as well as choices that make each person's life unique?

A developmental systems perspective suggests that the most effective research design for answering these questions is one that tracks the emerging adult along with his or her parent(s) across time to assess how they and their circumstances (e.g., jobs, educational settings, romantic relationships, housing) change and how these changes covary with shifts in the parent–child relationship. Notably, almost two decades ago, Sherrod, Haggerty, and Featherman (1993) highlighted the importance and scarcity of such longitudinal studies during the transition to adulthood, arguing that the diversity of paths through this period, along with the opportunities and possibilities for change in positive and negative directions (i.e., turning points for the better or worse), make this a prime period for important research on the life course. Undoubtedly, there are more data available today exploring development in emerging adults, but there are still very few published multiwave longitudinal studies tracking parent–child relations for a substantial length of time. In the review to follow, we highlight studies that assessed parent–child relations during at least two points in the transition to adulthood because they arguably have the most to say about how and why transformations in parent–child relationships might occur.

Before turning to the research on transformations in the parent–child relationship in the transition to adulthood, we note that the qualities of these relationships have been assessed using multiple methods (e.g., observations of interactions, interviews of parents and children, responses to questionnaires) to capture a wide variety of parenting behaviors (e.g., psychological and behavioral control); child behaviors when interacting with parents; and parent and child perceptions of diverse aspects of their relationship, including closeness, warmth, trust, support, understanding, respect, conflict frequency and intensity, and behavioral and emotional autonomy. Many different labels have been used to refer to the same or similar construct, and measured constructs have ranged from the very specific to the very global. The literature on parent–child relations in the transition to adulthood is largely based on reports by young people and occasionally by their parents. Typically, the constructs assessed are global, reflecting the dimension of support in the parent–child relationship and to some extent conflict. These are broad constructs that are important because of their impact on psychosocial adjustment (Laursen & Collins, 2009).

⚜ RECENT EMPIRICAL ADVANCES

Change in Parent–Child Relations Across the Transition to Adulthood

Whether the parent–child relationship changes during the transition to adulthood requires an understanding of what that relationship is like in adolescence. A review of the voluminous literature concluded that, in general, parents and adolescents report close, supportive, and warm relationships in adolescence, preceded by similarly positive relations in childhood. This does not mean that there are not some changes in how parents and children relate during adolescence. In fact, amid generally close relations there appears to be a leveling off or decrease in warmth and positive emotion during the teen years that may rebound in late adolescence. Conflict frequency also decreases across adolescence, but negative affect associated with conflict increases between early to middle adolescence and remains at that level through the remaining teen years (Laursen & Collins, 2009; Laursen, Coy, & Collins, 1998). Overall, parent–child relations are generally positive and supportive as children enter the transition to adulthood.

During the emerging and young adult years, young people characterize the parent–child relationship as largely positive and so do their parents (Aquilino & Supple, 1991; Thornton et al., 1995). Still, due to the life transitions and challenges of this period, parent–child relations could improve or deteriorate over time. Insights into possible changes can be gained from an analysis of U.S. college students' responses to a single question about how relationships with parents changed since beginning college (Lefkowitz, 2005). The majority (78%) indicated that relationships had changed, most in a positive direction. Many students felt closer to, more appreciative of, and more open with parents. Some characterized the changing parent–child relationship as more mature and friendship-like. Eleven percent of students indicated that they had grown more independent in the relationship (Lefkowitz, 2005). Are these accounts of improved parent–child relationships reflected in longitudinal data?

Two longitudinal studies suggest that mother–child and father–child relationships improve from the teens into the early 20s, at least on the broad dimension of parental support. A study of mothers and their children assessed at ages 18 and 23 found that at least two thirds of mothers and their children at the age of 18 at assessment reported that respect and understanding "usually" or "always" characterized their relationship. Mothers and their 18-year-olds also enjoyed engaging in mother–child activities, although a larger percentage of mothers "always" enjoyed doing things together (45%) compared to children (29%). Five years later, when children were age 23, mother–child relations had become more positive. For example, 42% of 23-year-olds now enjoyed doing things with their mothers. Children also reported father–child relations as largely positive at ages 18 and 23. In general, the father–child relationship improved between ages 18 and 23 but not as much as did the mother–child relationship (Thornton et al., 1995). In another study that assessed adolescents from ages 13 to 17, and again at 21, increases in mother–child and father–child emotional intimacy were observed (Rice & Mulkeen, 1995). A study examining high school seniors' satisfaction with maternal and paternal relations in Grade 12 and again 2 years later found that maternal relationship satisfaction increased; paternal relationship satisfaction, however, did not change (Levitt, Silver, & Santos, 2007). This study suggests that the apparent increase in support in the mother–child relationship is reflected also in the emerging adult's satisfaction with that relationship.

In research on how much university students believed they mattered to parents, growth trajectories (i.e., patterns of change) across 3 years indicated a significant decline in students' perceptions of mattering to their mothers. Perceived mattering to fathers, however, showed no change. The authors speculated that students slowly came to realize that they were no longer as central in the lives of their mothers as they were in childhood and adolescence or that mothers deliberately encouraged independence—thus promoting the perception of mattering less (Marshall, Liu, Wu, Berzonsky, & Adams, 2010). To the extent that the mattering scale reflects on the quality of the parent–child relationship, this may be the only study suggesting a possible deterioration in the mother–child relationship early in emerging adulthood.

One way in which parents support their children during the transition to adulthood is by providing financial aid. A U.S. national study of parents interviewed once when their children were in adolescence (12 to 18 years old) and again 6 years later (18 to 24 years old) found that at both points, most parents believed that they were obligated to provide economic support to their children, and this belief became stronger between adolescence and emerging adulthood. Parents' beliefs about economic support, however, depended on family structure; two-biological-parent families reported more favorable attitudes toward economic support than did single-parent and stepparent families (Aquilino, 2005).

The amount of contact between parents and children is another aspect of their relationship that is likely to change. Sneed et al. (2006) documented a significant decrease in family contact (face-to-face, telephone, letters, e-mail) between ages 17 and 27, according to retrospective reports of emerging adult children. For example, at 17, the majority of participants (97%) reported daily contact with their parents, but by age 27, the majority (76%) had contact with their parents only twice a week. During the same period, finance and romantic instrumentality (the extent to which young people took full responsibility for their finances and romantic relationships) increased. The findings of increased instrumentality converge with results from two prospective studies following children from early adolescence to age 19 or 20; in both studies, autonomous decision making (without input from parents) increased dramatically after age 15 (Gutman & Eccles, 2007; Wray-Lake, Crouter, & McHale, 2010). Thus, at the same time that parent–child contact is decreasing, there is likely to be an increase in the emerging adult's autonomous behaviors, including making choices about appearance, social life, money, and health-related behaviors.

The evidence on the general quality of and change in parent–child relations in the transition to adulthood leads to the following conclusions. First, emerging adults and their parents perceive the parent–child relationship as warm and supportive. Second, most studies suggest that this relationship improves on average from adolescence into the transition, at least with respect to becoming warmer and more supportive. Third, contact with parents decreases at the same time that personal responsibility and autonomous decision making increase, signs of individuation (i.e., separation from parents) and independence that should occur in the 20s as parents naturally relinquish control. Fourth, parents remain committed to providing some financial assistance to their emerging adult children. Of course, even if parent–child relations are positive and become even more so across the transition to adulthood, every relationship is different and some parent–child dyads will be closer or more conflicted than others. The extent to which the transition to adulthood provides opportunities for improvement in less healthy relationships or risks for deterioration in healthy ones can be gauged by examining stability in parent–child relations.

Stability in Parent–Child Relations Across the Transition to Adulthood

Are parent–child dyads with more positive relationships at the beginning of the transition also more positive at the end? Correlations of scores on the same parent–child relationship dimension at two time points (cross-time stability coefficients) are often used to assess stability. One study showed significant stability in adolescents' attachment to mothers ($r = 0.69$) and fathers ($r = 0.62$) from ages 13 to 15, and from ages 15 to 18 ($r = 0.56$ for attachment to mothers and $r = 0.46$ for attachment to fathers), but conflict ratings were less stable (Smetana et al., 2004). Stability coefficients ranging from the 0.30s to the 0.70s were found for adolescents' reports of support and negative affect in the mother–child and father–child relationship between ages 14 and 17 (Seiffge-Krenke, Overbeek, & Vermulst, 2010) and for adolescents reporting on parental warmth as high school seniors and 1 or 2 years later (Chung, Chen, Greenberger, & Heckhausen, 2009; Levitt et al., 2007). There is also significant stability in adolescents' ratings of satisfaction with mother–child relations and with father–child relations in the 2 years following high school (Levitt et al., 2007). These studies demonstrate significant stability in adolescents' perceptions of a close, warm, and supportive mother–child and father–child relationship during the teen years, but there may be less stability in the conflictual aspect of parent–adolescent relations.

A few studies have examined parent–child relationships between the teens and the 20s, finding that the supportive aspect of parent–child relations is characterized by high stability, as reported by young people and their parents (Aquilino, 1997; Thornton et al., 1995). In a cohort of emerging adults interviewed once when they were ages 20 to 32, and again 2 years later, perceptions of mutual trust were more stable than were perceptions of conflict in the parent–child relationship (Masche, 2008). As in the teens (Smetana et al., 2004), parent–child conflict in the 20s may waver more than does parent–child support.

As much as these studies demonstrate significant stability across adolescence and in the transition to adulthood particularly in the supportive nature of parent–child relations, they are also indicative of the possibility that some parent–child relationships change in a positive or negative direction more than do others. That is, even significant stability coefficients in the high 0.60s show that there is some instability. Although measurement error might account for some of the nonshared variance between the same dimension of parent–child relations measured at two points in time, there are likely important, systematic sources of instability present in the individual or the context that ought to be identified.

Sources of Diversity in Change in Parent–Child Relations

As noted earlier, the way that the parent–child relationship changes in the transition to adulthood is likely related to characteristics of individuals and their parents. Life transitions, such as moving out of the parents' home or getting married, are also possible sources of diversity in the course that the parent–child relationship follows. In this section, we consider gender, ethnicity, family structure, and life transitions as possible influences on change in parent–child relations.

Gender of Parents and Children as Sources of Diversity

There is some evidence that gender of parent and of child may shape the quality of parent–child relations. Many studies document more positive mother–child relationships than father–child relationships in emerging adulthood (Aquilino & Supple, 1991; Levitt et al., 2007; Rice & Mulkeen, 1995; Smetana et al., 2004; Sorokou & Weissbrod, 2005; Thornton et al., 1995). A recent study showed that university students were more likely to relinquish their fathers than their mothers as attachment figures (Rosenthal & Kobak, 2010), and Levitt et al. (2007) suggested that relations with fathers are "tenuous" in the early transition to adulthood years. These findings point to gender of parent effects, with mothers likely to be closer to their emerging adult children than are fathers.

There is also gender of child effects. In a longitudinal study of adolescents' perceptions of family relations measured at four points between ages 13 and 19, Gutman and Eccles (2007) noted that autonomous decision making increased most rapidly between ages 13 and 17 for boys and between ages 15 and 17 for girls. Although this study is limited to the teen years, it is exemplary for using multiwave data to examine growth curves in parent–child relations. According to Sneed et al. (2006), retrospective reports showed that contact with parents fell more rapidly for men than women from ages 17 to 22. Furthermore, whereas higher family contact was associated with lower instrumentality (taking less responsibility for finances and romantic relationships) in adolescence for both men and women, by age 27, higher family contact was related to more instrumentality in men and was less negative for women. Together these studies show that gender of child matters for the paths that parent–child relations follow through emerging adulthood.

Gender composition of the parent–child dyad may affect the nature of parent–child relations in adolescence and emerging adulthood. Some studies suggest, for instance, that mothers and daughters are particularly close (Aquilino & Supple, 1991; Belsky et al., 2001; Smetana et al., 2004). Thus, gender of parent and gender of child together comprise potentially important sources of diversity in parent–child relationship change.

Ethnicity as a Source of Diversity

There is growing attention to ethnicity as a possible source of diversity in transformations in parent–child relations. Chung et al. (2009) found that European American adolescents with higher levels of depressive symptoms at age 18 reported decreased parental warmth 1 year later, but this relationship did not emerge in Hispanic Americans. The authors speculated that the familistic and collectivist orientations associated with the Hispanic culture led Hispanic American parents to remain closer to their children during the transition to adulthood regardless of whether the adolescent evidenced depressive symptoms. Gutman and Eccles (2007) compared adolescents in African and European American families, discovering a number of results involving ethnicity. For example, African American adolescents had less decision making autonomy in middle adolescence compared to European Americans. In the 2 years following high school, however, Levitt et al. (2007) found no differences in change across time in perceived parental support or satisfaction with the parent–child relationship among European, African, and Hispanic Americans when other variables (e.g., college attendance) were controlled. Very few studies examine ethnicity as a source of diversity in parent–child relationship change across the transition to adulthood, leaving this area open for future important research.

Family Structure as a Source of Diversity

Family structure may play a role in shaping the nature of the parent–child relationship. Smetana et al. (2004), for instance, found that father presence in the home was linked to adolescents' perceptions of the father–adolescent relationship as more supportive. In another study, emerging adults in intact families were more satisfied with their relationship with fathers in the 2 years following high school, relative to emerging adults whose parents were not married (Levitt et al., 2007). Aquilino (1997) showed that biological parents perceived the quality of their relationships with their emerging adult children as better compared to stepparents. With respect to financial support, parents in intact families were more likely to feel obligated to provide such support to their emerging adult children than were single parents and stepparents. In fact, between adolescence and emerging adulthood, parental attitudes toward financial support became more negative in stepfamilies in which the parents did not have a child together (Aquilino, 2005). It is clear from these studies that parent–child (and perhaps especially father–child) relationships in single-parent families and stepfamilies face more challenges and may be more strained than parent–child relationships in intact families in emerging adulthood. How these relationships evolve over time, however, and whether they might improve are open questions.

Life Transitions as Sources of Diversity

Of the many life transitions that might influence the course of parent–child relations during emerging adulthood, leaving home has received the most empirical attention perhaps because it is such a clear marker of the process of separating from parents. There is a great deal of variability in the timing of moving away from home, and some young people return home (Mitchell, Wister, & Gee, 2004; Seiffge-Krenke, 2006). Home leaving is thus a complicated process. To examine how home leaving might impact the parent–child relationship, the association between leaving home and parent–child relations has been investigated often in 1st-year university students or in young people in the first couple of years out of high school (e.g., Aseltine & Gore, 1993; Smetana et al., 2004). The bulk of studies tracking young people for 1 or 2 years have found that moving away from parents is related to higher quality (closer, less conflictual, more emotionally supportive) parent–child relationships (Aseltine & Gore, 1993; Dubas & Petersen, 1996; Smetana et al., 2004), particularly among those leaving home to attend a university (Aseltine & Gore, 1993; Furman & Buhrmester, 1992; Larose & Boivin, 1998; Sullivan & Sullivan, 1980). In a few studies, leaving home was not linked to improved relations with parents (Graber & Brooks-Gunn, 1996a; Masche, 2008) or there were both positive and negative changes in parent–child relations (Aquilino, 1997). Although most studies point to positive associations of leaving home and the parent–child relationship, firm conclusions await longitudinal research following people through the teens and well into their 20s.

Just as leaving home might have an impact on the quality of parent–child relations, this relationship might also have an impact on the timing of leaving home. Some young people leave home, for example, because the parent–child relationship is poor to begin with and they wish to escape (Mitchell et al., 2004; Stattin & Magnusson, 1996). Seiffge-Krenke's (2006) study in Germany is perhaps the only study to have tracked adolescents (from ages 14 to 25) and their parents long enough to observe how parent–child relations were related to home-leaving patterns. This study found that young people "still in the nest" (had not left home) up to age 25 had less conflict with and less support for independence from their parents in their teen years compared to "on time" leavers (ages 21 and 23 for women and men, respectively). Thus, the timing of home leaving was related to the nature of the parent–child relationship in adolescence. At age 21, however, the children who did or would leave on time were more securely attached to their parents than were those who remained in the nest, but they also had higher psychological distress. Seiffge-Krenke (2006) argued that parent–child conflict and parent autonomy-granting in adolescence may operate to move the adolescent through the developmental task of leaving home on time but it may also have costs in terms of psychological health. This study demonstrates the value of considering not only how life transitions may transform the parent–child relationship but also how life transitions may be shaped by specific aspects of this relationship.

Emerging adult life transitions other than home leaving may be connected to parent–child relations. Using longitudinal data across two time points 5 years apart, Aquilino (1997) found that parents whose emerging adult children entered college, married, or worked full-time perceived a change from the teen years toward a more positive relationship (e.g., emotional closeness and less conflict). Emerging adults' entrance into parenthood, however, was associated with parents' perceptions of decreases in closeness and increases in conflict, a finding that converges with the observation by Belsky et al. (2001) that parenthood was associated with less closeness and more conflict in the relations of young adults with their own parents. Although there is too little research to draw a firm conclusion, parenthood could be the only normative life transition in emerging adulthood to be associated with worsening relations with parents.

If worsening relations with one's own parents is a possible outcome of the transition to parenthood, it is of interest to speculate on the underlying reasons. Parents of emerging adults likely consider college entrance, marriage, and a full-time job as important symbols of advancing maturity and reason enough to celebrate their children and the parent–child relationship. But while they are probably overjoyed to become grandparents, it is easy to see how the urge to give advice on child rearing, perceptions of obligations to babysit or offer financial support, and short tempers on the part of fatigued and stressed new parents might be sources of conflict and distance in the parent–child relationship. New parents must not only forge a relationship with an infant but they must also negotiate new relationships with their partners as well as with their own parents.

A developmental systems perspective highlights the probability that life transitions and their timing have the potential to be turning points in the parent–child relationship. But consistent with this perspective, the parent–child relationship may affect the timing of life transitions in emerging adulthood (e.g., Seiffge-Krenke, 2006). Indeed, Masche (2008) found that higher perceived mutual trust in the parent–young adult relationship predicted a greater likelihood of marriage and parenthood 2 years later. The parent–child system generally shows continuity from one period of life to the next, but it is also sensitive to and may foreshadow changes in life circumstances.

〢 FUTURE DIRECTIONS

The limited amount of longitudinal research on the transition to adulthood necessarily leads to an incomplete understanding of the nature and sources of transformations in the parent–child relationship brought about during the highly variable and challenging maturational process. Most longitudinal studies examining the transition are limited to the first 1 or 2 years after high school (e.g., Larose & Boivin, 1998; Levitt et al., 2007), yet adulthood may not be reached until the late 20s (Arnett, 2000). On the basis of the literature, we confidently conclude that positive and warm parent–child relations are the norm during the transition to adulthood, and that in general, the parent–child relationship improves (becomes closer and probably less conflicted) in the late teens and early 20s. Furthermore, there is continuity and stability in the quality of the parent–child relationship from adolescence into the early 20s at the same time that there is evidence that these relationships can take a turn for better or worse. Characteristics such as parents' marital status can shape the nature of the parent–emerging adult relationship. Some life transitions, particularly leaving home, are more likely than not to produce improved parent–child relations, but it is possible that other changing circumstances (e.g., parenthood) may produce setbacks. These are not surprising or startling conclusions. In fact, there is more of a story to what we do not know about parent–child relationships during the transition to adulthood than in what we do know.

Specifically, there are too few prospective, multiwave studies (perhaps none) tracking adolescents into and across their 20s to draw clear conclusions about the antecedents, current covariates, and even outcomes of the parent–child relationship during this period. It appears as though gender (of child and parent) and ethnicity might shape the course of parent–child relations through the transition, but it is unknown in what ways and on what dimensions of the parent–child relationship they operate. If prospective research on parent–child relationships through the 20s is lacking in general, even rarer is such research pertaining to special populations. For instance, how does the parent–child relationship change for persons with motor disabilities or chronic physical health conditions as they move toward adulthood? One study found a positive relation between fathers' fostering of autonomy and psychosocial maturity in emerging adults with motor disabilities such as cerebral palsy and spina bifida (Galambos, Magill-Evans, & Darrah, 2008), underscoring the importance of fathers—and understanding more about them—in the transition to adulthood. The nature of the mother–child relationship is important for adherence to treatment regimens in adolescents with Type I diabetes (Berg, Schindler, & Maharaj, 2008), but little is known about how this relationship might change and its impact on the course of physical health in emerging adults. We are not the first to recommend that multiwave longitudinal studies are necessary for understanding the course that the parent–child relationship takes across the lengthy transition to adulthood (see e.g., Sherrod et al., 1993; Smetana et al., 2004).

Another limitation in the literature is the preponderance of studies on university students and small nonrepresentative samples. Although many young people attend universities, representative samples from the general population should be drawn so that we learn about transformations in the parent–child relationship for young people from all walks of life, enabling optimal generalizability. Such samples would ensure that we can examine multiple sources of diversity as well. An interesting and relevant project is underway in Germany. The Panel Analysis of Intimate Relationships and Family Dynamics (pairfam) will follow a random sample of three cohorts (ages 15 to 17, 25 to 27, and 35 to 37) for up to 14 years in annual interviews, including up to three of their parents (biological and stepparents), intimate partners, and some of their own children. Designed to be publicly available to researchers, the data promise to offer the possibility of exceptional insights into short- and long-term changes in parent–child relationships across generations from multiple perspectives (Huinink et al., 2010).

Excellent examples of research examining change in parent–child relationships exist, although they are confined to the earliest part of the transition to adulthood (Gutman & Eccles, 2007; Smetana et al., 2004; Wray-Lake et al., 2010). Seiffge-Krenke's (2006) study is important for associating diverse trajectories in parent–child relationships from ages 14 to 17 with different home-leaving patterns and with attachment to parents and psychological well-being at age 21. It also demonstrated how parent–adolescent relationship trajectories were linked with romantic relationships at ages 21 and 23. Specifically, mother–child relationships that decreased in negativity in middle adolescence were associated with more connectedness in romantic relationships in emerging adulthood, mother–child relationships high in support and low in negative affect across middle adolescence were associated with connectedness and sexual attraction in emerging adult romantic relationships, and increasing mother–child negativity in middle adolescence was associated with lower levels of sexual attraction to romantic partners in the early 20s (Seiffge-Krenke et al., 2010). Ultimately, an important goal of developmental research is to understand not only how the parent–child relationship changes during an important transitional period but to observe how such transformations affect later outcomes, such as romantic and marital relationships, parenting behaviors, psychological well-being, and educational and occupational success.

A better understanding of the complicated ways in which transformations in parent–child relations accompany transitions such as leaving home can be gained through research that examines within-time covariations between one variable (e.g., living with parents or not) and another (e.g., parent–child conflict) as they move together across time. As an example, Galambos and Krahn (2008) used data on a sample of 20- to 29-year-olds tracked for 7 years to show that age moderated the relation between living away from parents (treated as a time-varying covariate) and depressive symptoms. Younger participants, beginning the study as 20-year-olds, had more depressive symptoms in years that they lived away from parents whereas older participants, nearing 30 at study onset, were more depressed in years that they lived with parents. Any life transition and any aspect of the parent–child relationship, as well as possible moderators of their covariation (e.g., ethnicity, gender), could be modeled in a similar manner.

Without a firm grounding in how the parent–child relationship transforms in the transition to adulthood, as well as the early predictors, concurrent covariates, and social and psychological outcomes of particular patterns of change, it is difficult to make serious and specific recommendations about social policy applications. Given that there is continuity between adolescence and emerging adulthood in the general nature of the parent–child relationship, any program that can strengthen families and parent–child relationships prior to emerging adulthood is welcome. Because life transitions such as leaving home and becoming a parent are possible turning points for better or worse in the parent–child relationship, programming that is oriented to easing such transitions may have positive effects. With the high prevalence of leaving home to attend university in the emerging adult population, many universities already have in place orientation programs to make the transition easier. Initial evaluation of one experimental intervention for 1st-year university students, based on the importance of social support during transitional periods, showed promising results (Pratt et al., 2000).

The evidence so far on transformations in the parent–child relationship across the transition to adulthood is positive in the sense that Hodding Carter would most likely appreciate. That is, it appears that today's emerging adults have established their roots, and these roots may even grow deeper as the years pass. The data also suggest that young people in their early 20s have established a healthy sense of separation from their parents, which amidst the connectedness will serve them well as they prepare to take flight and launch their own intimate relationships, families, and careers.

$\gg$ SUGGESTED READINGS

Lefkowitz, E. S. (2005). "Things have gotten better": Developmental changes among emerging adults after the transition to university. *Journal of Adolescent Research, 20,* 40–63.

Seiffge-Krenke, I. (2006). Leaving home or still in the nest? Parent-child relationships and psychological health as predictors or different leaving home patterns. *Developmental Psychology, 42,* 864–876.

Sneed, J. R., Cohen, P., Chen, H., Johnson, J. G., Gilligan, C., Crawford, T. N., et al. (2006). Gender differences in the age-changing relationship between instrumentality and family contact in emerging adulthood. *Developmental Psychology, 42,* 787–797.

REFERENCES

Aquilino, W. S. (1997). From adolescent to young adult: A prospective study of parent–child relations during the transition to adulthood. *Journal of Marriage and the Family, 59,* 670–686.

Aquilino, W. S. (2005). Impact of family structure on parental attitudes toward the economic support of adult children over the transition to adulthood. *Journal of Family Issues, 26,* 143–167.

Aquilino, W. S., & Supple, K. R. (1991). Parent–child relations and parent's satisfaction with living arrangements when adult children live at home. *Journal of Marriage and the Family, 53,* 13–27.

Arnett, J. J. (2000). Emerging adulthood: A theory of development from the late teens through the twenties. *American Psychologist, 55,* 469–480.

Aseltine, R., & Gore, S. (1993). Mental health and social adaptation following the transition from high school. *Journal of Research on Adolescence, 3,* 297–270.

Belsky, J., Jaffee, S. R., Hsieh, K-H., & Silva, P. A. (2001). Child-rearing antecedents of intergenerational relations in young adulthood: A prospective study. *Developmental Psychology, 37,* 801–813.

Berg, C. A., Schindler, I., & Maharaj, S. (2008). Adolescents' and mothers' perceptions of the cognitive and relational functions of collaboration and adjustment in dealing with Type 1 diabetes. *Journal of Family Psychology, 22,* 865–874.

Chung, W. Y., Chen, C., Greenberger, E., & Heckhausen, J. (2009). A cross-ethnic study of adolescents' depressed mood and the erosion of parental and peer warmth during the transition to young adulthood. *Journal of Research on Adolescence, 19,* 359–379.

Cohen, P., Kasen, S., Chen, H., Hartmark, C., & Gordon, K. (2003). Variations in patterns of developmental transitions in the emerging adulthood period. *Developmental Psychology, 39,* 657–669.

Dubas, J. S., & Petersen, A. C. (1996). Geographical distance from parents and adjustment during adolescence and young adulthood. *New Directions for Child Development, 71,* 3–18.

Frank, S. J., Pirsch, L. A., & Wright, V. C. (1990). Late adolescents' perceptions of their relationships with their parents: Relationships among deidealization, autonomy, relatedness, and insecurity and implications for adolescent adjustment and ego identity status. *Journal of Youth and Adolescence, 19,* 571–588.

Furman, W., & Buhrmester, D. (1992). Age and sex differences in perceptions of networks of social relationships. *Child Development, 63,* 103–115.

Fussell, E., & Furstenberg, F. F., Jr. (2005). The transition to adulthood during the twentieth century: Race, nativity, and gender. In R. A. Settersten Jr., F. F., Furstenberg Jr., & R. G. Rumbaut (Eds.), *On the frontier of adulthood: Theory, research, and public policy* (pp. 29–59). Chicago: University of Chicago Press.

Galambos, N. L., & Krahn, H. J. (2008). Depression and anger trajectories during the transition to adulthood. *Journal of Marriage and Family, 70,* 15–27.

Galambos, N. L., Magill-Evans, J., & Darrah, J. (2008). Psychosocial maturity in the transition to adulthood for people with and without motor disabilities. *Rehabilitation Psychology, 53,* 498–504.

Goldscheider, F. K., & Goldscheider, C. (1999). *The changing transition to adulthood: Leaving and returning home.* Thousand Oaks, CA: Sage.

Graber, J. A., & Brooks-Gunn, J. (1996a). Expectations for and precursors of leaving home in young women. *New Directions for Child Development, 71,* 21–52.

Graber, J. A., & Brooks-Gunn, J. (1996b). Transitions and turning points: Navigating the passage from childhood through adolescence. *Developmental Psychology, 32,* 768–776.

Gutman L. M., & Eccles, J. S. (2007). Stage-environment fit during adolescence: Trajectories of family relations and adolescent outcomes. *Developmental Psychology, 43,* 522–537.

Huinink, J., Brüderl, J., Nauck, B., Walper, S., Castiglioni, L., & Feldhaus, M. (2010). *Panel Analysis of Intimate Relationships and Family Dynamics (pairfam): Conceptual framework and design* (Working Paper No. 17). Universities of Bremen, Mannheim, Chemnitz, and Munich. Retrieved from http://www.pairfam.uni-bremen.de/fileadmin/user_upload/redakteur/publis/arbeitspapier_17p.pdf

Lamborn, S. D., & Steinberg, L. (1993). Emotional autonomy redux: Revisiting Ryan and Lynch. *Child Development, 64,* 483–499.

Larose, S., & Boivin, M. (1998). Attachment to parents, social support expectations, and socioemotional adjustment during the high school-college transition. *Journal of Research on Adolescence, 8,* 1–27.

Laursen, B., & Collins, W. A. (2009). Parent-child relationships during adolescence. In R. M. Lerner & L. Steinberg (Eds.), *Handbook of adolescent psychology: Vol. 2. Contextual influences on adolescence development* (3rd ed., pp. 3–42). Hoboken, NJ: Wiley.

Laursen, B., Coy, K. C., & Collins, W. A. (1998). Reconsidering changes in parent-conflict across adolescence: A meta-analysis. *Child Development, 69,* 817–832.

Lefkowitz, E. S. (2005). "Things have gotten better": Developmental changes among emerging adults after the transition to university. *Journal of Adolescent Research, 20,* 40–63.

Lerner, R. M. (2004). Diversity in individual-context relations as the basis for positive development across the life span: A developmental systems perspective for theory, research, and application. *Research in Human Development, 1,* 327–346.

Levitt, M. J., Silver, M. E., & Santos, J. D. (2007). Adolescents in transition to adulthood: parental support, relationship satisfaction, and post-transition adjustment. *Journal of Adult Development, 14,* 53–63.

Marshall, S. K., Liu, Y., Wu, A., Berzonsky, M., & Adams, G. R. (2010). Perceived mattering to parents and friends for university students: A longitudinal study. *Journal of Adolescence, 33,* 367–375.

Masche, J. G. (2008). Reciprocal influences between developmental transitions and parent–child relationships in young adulthood. *International Journal of Behavioral Development, 32,* 401–411.

Mitchell, B. A., Wister, A. V., & Gee, E. M. (2004). The ethnic and family nexus of homeleaving and returning among Canadian young adults. *Canadian Journal of Sociology, 29,* 543–575.

O'Connor, T. G., Allen, J. P., Bell, K. L., & Hauser S. T. (1996). Adolescent–parent relationships and leaving home in young adulthood. *New Directions for Child Development, 71,* 39–52.

Pratt, M., Hunsberger, B., Pancer, S. M., Alisat, S., Bowers, C., Mackey, K., et al. (2000). Facilitating the transition to university: Evaluation of a social support discussion intervention program. *Journal of College Student Development, 41*, 427–441.

Rice, K. G., & Mulkeen, P. (1995). Relationships with parents and peers: A longitudinal study of adolescent intimacy. *Journal of Adolescent Research, 10*, 338–357.

Rosenthal, N. L., & Kobak, R. (2010). Assessing adolescents' attachment hierarchies: Differences across developmental periods and associations with individual adaptation. *Journal of Research on Adolescence, 20*, 678–706.

Schulenberg, J. E., Maggs, J. L., & O'Malley, P. M. (2003). How and why the understanding of developmental continuity and discontinuity is important. In J. T. Mortimer & M. J. Shanahan (Eds.), *Handbook of the life course* (pp. 413–436). New York: Plenum Press.

Seiffge-Krenke, I. (2006). Leaving home or still in the nest? Parent–child relationships and psychological health as predictors of different leaving home patterns. *Developmental Psychology, 42*, 864–876.

Seiffge-Krenke, I., Overbeek, G., & Vermulst, A. (2010). Parent–child relationship trajectories during adolescence: Longitudinal associations with romantic outcomes in emerging adulthood. *Journal of Adolescence, 33*, 159–171.

Sherrod, L. R., Haggerty, F. J., & Featherman, D. L. (1993). Introduction: Late adolescence and the transition to adulthood. *Journal of Research on Adolescence, 3*, 217–226.

Smetana, J. G., Metzger, A., & Campione-Barr, N. (2004). African American late adolescents' relationships with parents: Developmental transitions and longitudinal patterns. *Child Development, 75*, 932–947.

Sneed, J. R., Cohen, P., Chen, H., Johnson, J. G., Gilligan, C., Crawford, T. N., et al. (2006). Gender differences in the age-changing relationship between instrumentality and family contact in emerging adulthood. *Developmental Psychology, 42*, 787–797.

Sorokou, C. F., & Weissbrod, C. S. (2005). Men and women's attachment and contact patterns with parents during the first year of college. *Journal of Youth and Adolescence, 34*, 221–228.

Stattin, H., & Magnusson, C. (1996). Leaving home at an early age among females. *New Directions in Child Development, 71,* 53–69.

Sullivan, K., & Sullivan, A. (1980). Adolescent–parent separation. *Developmental Psychology, 16*, 93–99.

Thornton, A., Orbuch, T. L., & Axinn, W. G. (1995). Parent–child relationships during the transition to adulthood. *Journal of Family Issues, 16*, 538–564.

Tubman, J. G., & Lerner, R. M. (1994). Continuity and discontinuity in the affective experiences of parents and children: Evidence from the New York longitudinal study. *American Journal of Orthopsychiatry, 64*, 112–124.

Wray-Lake, L., Crouter, A. C., & McHale, S. M. (2010). Developmental patterns in decision-making autonomy across middle childhood and adolescence: European American parents' perspectives. *Child Development, 81*, 636–651.

3

Transformations in Sibling Relationships From Adolescence to Adulthood

Lilly Shanahan

Evelyn B. Waite

Timothy W. Boyd II

S iblings are an integral part of most adolescents' lives. Youth typically spend many hours with their siblings (McHale & Crouter, 1996; Updegraff, McHale, Whiteman, Thayer, & Delgado, 2005), and sibling relationships are often a person's most enduring social and familial influence (Cicirelli, 1995). Both parents and youth draw upon siblings as a frame of reference in development, and family dynamics involving siblings are linked to mental health outcomes across the life span (e.g., Waldinger, Vaillant, & Orav, 2007).

Despite the prominence of sibling relationships in most people's lives, changes in the qualities of these relationships from adolescence to young

Acknowledgments: Portions of this work were supported by a New Faculty Grant from the University of North Carolina at Greensboro awarded to Lilly Shanahan. We thank Michael Shanahan and Rebecca Suffness for helpful comments.

adulthood are understudied. Yet, these developmental periods are especially strategic for studying changes in sibling relationships because siblings become increasingly equal in their physical and mental abilities
(e.g., Brody & Stoneman, 1994; Buhrmester & Furman, 1990), with potential implications for changes in their relationship qualities. Moving into
adolescence and young adulthood is also accompanied by multiple normative transitions involving puberty, school, work, and establishing an
independent household. Indeed, the transitions of adolescence and young
adulthood set the stage for potential reorganizations of sibling relationships as youth increasingly take charge of their own lives, including their
sibling relationships, coming to terms with decades of shared and nonshared experiences, and redefining their relationships based on more
egalitarian terms (Cicirelli, 1995).

This chapter focuses on changes in shared sibling time and positive
and negative dimensions of the sibling relationship from adolescence to
young adulthood. We first discuss each of the developmental periods
involved and theories that help understand changes in sibling relationships. The central message from the few extant longitudinal studies is
that mean levels of shared sibling time, sibling intimacy, and sibling
conflict change but that these changes depend on the sex constellation
of sibling dyads, birth order, and contextual factors. More work is needed,
particularly on changes in sibling relationships during the transition to
young adulthood.

CONCEPTUAL OVERVIEW

The development of sibling relationships is inextricably connected to
each sibling's individual development. Thus, both milestones in individual development from adolescence to young adulthood, and theoretical perspectives on relationship development must be considered.
Both siblings in sibling dyads experience multiple transitions during
adolescence and young adulthood, but changes in the sibling relationship are not simply reducible to changes that each sibling experiences
(Hinde, 1979). Indeed, changes in the sibling relationship may have
differential implications for each sibling's subsequent development
depending on when during each sibling's individual development these
changes occur.

Individual Development From Adolescence to Young Adulthood

What types of changes are relevant to the study of sibling relationships in adolescence and young adulthood? At the individual level, puberty is associated with changes in physical appearance that may—temporarily—create new inequalities or permanently close the gap in physical inequality among siblings (Leffert & Petersen, 1996). Pubertal changes are also associated with a peak in the intensity of negative affect in relationships, which may manifest itself in increased bickering with, anger toward, and complaining about siblings—patterns that also hold for parent–child relationships (e.g., Larson, Moneta, Richards, & Wilson, 2002; Laursen, Coy, & Collins, 1998). Adolescents also experience cognitive changes and challenges in the regulation of affect/behavior, potentially disturbing prior equilibria in relationships and resulting in temporary increases in conflict (e.g., Steinberg, 2005; Steinberg & Silk, 2002). Some of these cognitive changes (e.g., advances in metacognition) could, however, also increase adolescents' understanding of social norms and their perspective-taking abilities, with potentially positive implications for sibling relationship qualities.

These individual-level changes of adolescence are accompanied by changes in social contexts. When such changes are stressful, family relationship qualities often decline (Conger, Elder, Lorenz, Simons, & Whitbeck, 1994). School transitions, including to middle and high school, involve reorganizations of social relationships and are stressful for some adolescents (Caspi & Moffitt, 1991). Adolescents also spend less time in family contexts and more time in academic, recreational, and social contexts with peers and romantic partners (Larson, Richards, Moneta, Holmbeck, & Duckett, 1996). This shift from family to peer contexts is also accompanied by greater autonomy for youth, which may, in turn, result in adolescents' increased desire to take the sibling relationship into their own hands, rather than to have it governed by parental rules (Campione-Barr & Smetana, 2010).

The transition to adulthood begins at the end of the second decade of life and is also characterized by multiple transitions, including leaving home, completing education, securing and keeping full-time employment, getting married, and becoming a parent (Mouw, 2005; Shanahan, 2000). Most of these transitions are characterized by making and being responsible for independent decisions and by becoming financially independent from the home of origin (Arnett, 2004; Conger & Little, 2010). Compared to the adolescent transitions (e.g., school transitions), the "transition schedule" for young adults is much more variable (Cohen, Kasen, Chen, Hartmark, & Gordon, 2003; Shanahan, 2000). Each transition by itself (e.g., leaving home versus having children) as well as its timing and position in a sequence of transitions could impact sibling relationship qualities. Indeed, when examining sibling relationships, it may be important not only to take into account the timing of each individual sibling's transition but also how siblings' transitions are timed to one another (Conger & Little, 2010).

Although restructuring family relationships to develop a healthy distance from the family of origin is important in young adulthood, independence needs to be balanced with maintaining close emotional ties and forging a new and more mature understanding with the family of origin (Frank, Avery, & Laman, 1988; O'Connor, Allen, Bell, & Hauser, 1996). As Conger and Little explained (2010), some scholars suggest that sibling relationships become "voluntary" in young adulthood (Aquilino, Arnett, & Tanner, 2006; Stocker, Furman, & Lanthier, 1997), with sibling contact becoming dependent on the rewards involved with sibling exchanges. Others have argued, however, that sibling relationships are never truly voluntary, because of siblings' biological ties (Collins & van Dulmen, 2006) and family obligations (de Munck, 1993; Fuligni et al., 2009).

Taken together, the cumulative changes associated with transitions from adolescence to young adulthood likely also induce changes in sibling relationship qualities. Next, we will review relevant theoretical perspectives on changes in sibling relationships.

Theoretical Perspectives on Changes in Relationships

Several theories are influential in sibling relationship research and can be productively applied to adolescent and young adult transitions. *Family systems theory* conceptualizes families as interrelated subsystems. Each individual has simultaneous membership in multiple subsystems (e.g., in the mother–child dyad, sibling dyad, father–sibling triad), which dynamically influence one another (Whitchurch & Constantine, 1993). Accordingly, changes in sibling relationships take place in the context of the larger family environment (Minuchin, 1974; Minuchin, 1985), and, in turn, reverberate throughout the family system. Family systems are also open systems, meaning that they can be changed by external influences (Whiteman, McHale, & Crouter, 2011). From adolescence to young adulthood, families are increasingly subject to external influences (e.g., school changes), to which they are posited to adapt in dynamic ways. Family systems theory also offers insights on alliances within the family, including between siblings or between parents and select children (e.g., parental differential treatment of siblings).

Although family systems theory is well-known and highly cited, quantitative research examining its central tenants is less common, likely reflecting difficulties in sampling family systems repeatedly over time; measuring shared and nonshared experiences of family members; and longitudinally modeling individual, sibling, and family experiences simultaneously (e.g., McHale, Kim, & Whiteman, 2006). Nevertheless, combined results from past studies support such family systemic dynamics. For example, firstborns' transition to adolescence appears to trigger temporary increases in conflict in their own and in their younger sibling's relationship with parents (Shanahan, McHale, Osgood, & Crouter, 2007), in their parents' marital relationship (Whiteman, McHale, & Crouter, 2007), and, as we describe later, in sibling relationships (Kim, McHale, Osgood, & Crouter, 2006). Thus, changes associated with one family member and his/her involvements in different family subsystems trigger family-wide change.

Attachment theory emphasizes that sibling relationship experiences from adolescence to young adulthood are grounded in children's early experiences (Ainsworth, 1985). Based on early experiences with parents, children form internal working models: representations of themselves and relationships that inform expectations, processing emotions and behaviors that are related to subsequent relationships (Bowlby, 1980). For example, children with responsive caregivers are likely to form a secure, positive attachment with caregivers, with siblings, and, later, with romantic partners (Conger, Ming, Bryant, & Elder, 2000; Hazan & Shaver, 1994). In turn, children with insecure attachments to caregivers are at risk for hostile and conflictual sibling relationships, as has been shown during the childhood years (Teti & Ablard, 1989; Volling & Belsky, 1992). Some work has also focused on sibling attachment in adolescence and young adulthood independent of prior caregiving relationships (e.g., Buist, Dekovi Cacute, Meeus, & Van Aken, 2002). Furthermore, some attachment theorists have focused on the convergence, or similarity of siblings' attachments to their parents considering that siblings are hypothesized to share many of their childhood caregiving experiences (van IJzendoorn et al., 2000).

To date, few sibling studies from adolescence to young adulthood are explicitly rooted in the attachment literature (for an exception, see Buist et al., 2002), but many studies of sibling warmth and support implicitly draw on concepts from this theory, such as the emotional need for an attachment person during times of challenge. Such research shows that under special and adverse circumstances (e.g., twinship, early loss of parents), siblings may serve as primary attachment persons for one another during adolescence and young adulthood (Bank & Kahn, 1997; Stein, Riedel, & Rotheram-Borus, 1999; Tancredy & Fraley, 2006). Taken together, attachment theory predicts that the quality of attachments with parents will transfer to the quality of sibling attachments and that siblings can serve as important attachment persons in development.

Similarities among relationships have also been explained by *social learning theory*, which maintains that siblings, through observation, imitation, and practice, learn interaction styles from parents and from one another (Bandura, 1977). Social learning of relationship qualities may be especially likely when siblings share attributes (e.g., same sex, close in age; see Bussey & Bandura, 1999) or when sibling dyads include a female (Shanahan, Kim, McHale, & Crouter, 2007). *Social coercion* and *social contagion* models also predict similarities in siblings' interaction styles and fall under the umbrella of social learning theory (e.g., Compton, Snyder, Schrepferman, Bank, & Shortt, 2003; Slomkowski et al., 2009).

The *social convoy model* is grounded in social networks theory and describes how relationship partners are organized into inner, middle, and outer circles. As people move through life, the composition of these circles changes (Antonucci, Akiyama, & Takahashi, 2004; Kahn & Antonucci, 1980). The role of siblings in the social convoy is unique: Siblings tend to stay in a person's social convoy throughout life (unlike many same-aged friends), but they do not necessarily stay in the inner circle (unlike parents). Indeed, during adulthood, siblings often move from the inner circle (i.e., people who one cannot imagine living without) to the middle (i.e., people who are not quite as close as those in the inner circle, but who are still very important) or outer (i.e., people who are less close, but still important) circles (Antonucci et al., 2004). Adult transitions, including the loss of a spouse, may also move siblings back into the inner circle (White, 2001). Indeed, " . . . siblings are permanent but flexible members of our social networks, whose roles . . . are renegotiated in light of changing circumstances and competing obligations" (White, 2001, p.557).

Finally, unlike attachment and social learning theories, *sibling differentiation/de-identification theories* focus on divergence in siblings' development. According to these theories, siblings diverge and pick niches in their behavioral, personality, and relationship development in an effort to mitigate sibling competition and conflict and to enhance parental investment (e.g., Ansbacher & Ansbacher, 1956). Differentiation is thought to be especially likely in sibling dyads that are of the same sex, similar in age, and close in birth order rank (e.g., Feinberg & Hetherington, 2000; Schachter, Shore, Feldman-Rotman, Marquis, & Campbell, 1976). Success in de-identification was associated with reductions in sibling conflict and competition in some studies (e.g., Feinberg, McHale, Crouter, & Cumsille, 2003). Sibling differentiation and social learning processes likely occur simultaneously, and both are necessary to understand sibling experiences. Indeed, siblings who are close in age and of the same sex may have strong differentiation pressures, yet their similar environments contribute to making them more similar (Shanahan, Kim, et al., 2007).

Additional theories that have been used with respect to sibling relationships but that cannot be reviewed for reasons of space include psychoanalytic theory, evolutionary perspectives, Adler's theory of individual psychology, ecological theories of development, the confluence model, equity theory, social provisions theory, social comparison theory, several other theories from social psychology, and theories involving siblings' genetic relatedness (for reviews, see East, 2009; Whiteman, Soli, & McHale, in press).

✵ RECENT EMPIRICAL ADVANCES

A limited number of longitudinal studies have examined changes in sibling relationship qualities from adolescence to young adulthood. Despite moderate levels of stability in sibling relationships, these studies also identified mean-level changes (e.g., Kim et al., 2006). Here, we draw on both cross-sectional and longitudinal findings to describe what is currently known about such developmental changes in siblings' shared time and in positive and negative dimensions of sibling relationships (e.g., intimacy, warmth, and acceptance, versus conflict, negativity, hostility). Although other dimensions of sibling relationships are frequently studied—including support, caretaking, perspective-taking, trust, communication, control, and rivalry—we will not review them here because there are even fewer longitudinal studies examining changes in these relationship dimensions. We should also note that the changes described here should not be interpreted as "normative" in development because sibling dynamics differ across the many types of siblings (e.g., full-, half-, step-siblings) and the different ecological contexts in which siblings grow up (McGuire & Shanahan, 2010; McHale et al., 2006).

Changes in Siblings' Shared Time

Adolescence and Young Adulthood

The amount of time that siblings spend together is less frequently studied compared to other dimensions of sibling relationships but may account for some of the changes in sibling relationship qualities described below. Cross-sectional and cross-sequential work shows that shared sibling time declines across adolescence (Buhrmester & Furman, 1990), to an even greater degree than time with parents or extended family (Larson et al., 1996). This decline continues into adulthood (Scharf, Shulman, & Avigad-Spitz, 2005). For example, a study using the nationally representative National Survey for Families and House-holds in the late 1980s and early 1990s showed that the frequency of sibling contact decreased in early adulthood (White, 2001). In addition to the mere amount of time spent together, the types of shared sibling activities also change. Adolescents spend much of their time with sib-lings in outdoor and indoor activities; young adults spend sibling time in emotional exchanges and discussions of personal matters (Scharf et al., 2005).

Taken together, the amount of sibling shared time and frequency of sibling contact generally decreases throughout adolescence and into young adulthood. Such decreases in shared time may allow young people to gain a more mature perspective on their sibling relationships (Scharf et al., 2005).

Changes in Positive Relationship Dimensions

Adolescence

Cross-sectional and short-term longitudinal work has reported lower levels of positive sibling relationship qualities (e.g., intimacy, warmth, acceptance) among adolescent-aged compared to middle childhood-aged siblings (Buhrmester, 1992; Buhrmester & Furman, 1990). Such work also suggested that declines in relationship quality during adolescence may not be purely linear (Cole & Kerns, 2001) and that age-related change in sibling relationships could differ for siblings from different sibling sex constellations (Furman & Buhrmester, 1992; McCoy, Brody, & Stoneman, 1994).

Indeed, a longitudinal study of approximately 400 children from ages 7 to 19 showed quadratic patterns of change in sibling intimacy, but only for mixed-sex sibling dyads (i.e., brother–sister and sister–brother dyads; Kim, et al., 2006), with a decrease in sibling intimacy from late middle childhood through early adolescence, followed by an increase starting in mid-adolescence. Children from same-sex sibling dyads (i.e., sister–sister, brother–brother), however, reported no significant mean changes in sibling intimacy over time (see Figure 3.1). These findings were consistent with findings from a shorter-term longitudinal study with another American sample, which also showed that sibling intimacy increased in middle adolescence, particularly in mixed-sex sibling dyads (Updegraff, McHale, & Crouter, 2002).

Figure 3.1 Changes in Sibling Intimacy From Middle Childhood Through Late Adolescence by Dyad Sex Constellation

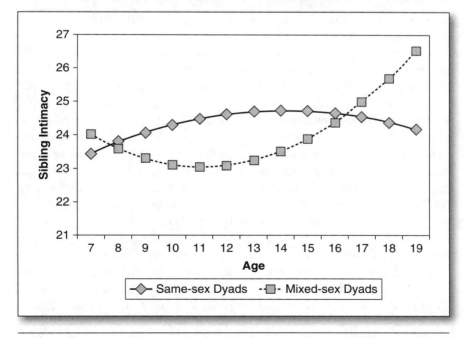

SOURCE: Reprinted with permission from Kim, McHale, Osgood, & Crouter (2006).

Kim and colleagues (2006) explained that the initial decreases in sibling intimacy in mixed-sex dyads may be the consequence of gender segregation in middle childhood (Maccoby, 1998), followed by an increased interest in members of the opposite sex. This interest appears to become particularly strong in late adolescence when levels of intimacy in mixed-sex sibling dyads surpass the level of intimacy that same-sex sibling dyads had from middle childhood on. Late adolescents may seek involvement with and advice and support from a mixed-sex sibling and his/her peers.

Findings of sex-constellation-differential change in sibling positivity are not entirely consistent across the literature and vary depending on the population and exact age-range studied, measures used, and the operationalization of sibling sex constellation (e.g., same- and mixed-sex versus sister–sister, sister–brother, brother–sister, brother–brother). For example, developmental patterns from an accelerated cohort study of approximately 300 Dutch children aged 11 to 17 (Buist et al., 2002) indicated that sister pairs remained at a fairly stable high level of attachment (defined as trust, communication, and lack of alienation) over time, brother–sister pairs showed small increases, sister–brother pairs showed no increases, and brother pairs reported the greatest increases in attachment over time, reaching levels of sibling attachment similar to that of sister pairs by age 17.

Reports of high levels/increases in sibling positivity for brother pairs are an exception: These pairs typically report the lowest levels of sibling intimacy. In contrast, sisters generally report the highest levels of sibling intimacy (Cole & Kerns, 2001; Dunn, Slomkowski, & Beardsall, 1994; Kim et al., 2006; Updegraff et al., 2002). Warm and intimate relationships tend to have greater significance in females' than in males' lives from childhood into adulthood (e.g., Maccoby, 1998). Males may place less emphasis on self-disclosure to and seeking support, advice, and endorsement from siblings. Nevertheless, they may value their sibling affiliations and express their positive relationships in ways that are less well captured by traditional measures of positive sibling relationships (Camarena, Sarigiani, & Petersen, 1990), including companionship in activities and conversations that do not involve emotional exchanges.

In addition to the sex constellation of the sibling dyad, contextual variables may influence the developmental course of sibling intimacy during adolescence, including attendance at similar or different schools. Buist and colleagues (2002), for example, showed that sibling attachment increased sharply in almost all sibling dyads when siblings changed from being in different schools (when the younger sibling was 11 years old) to being in the same school (when the younger sibling was 12 years old). Indeed, only sister–sister dyads, who already reported the highest levels of sibling attachment throughout development, did not increase in sibling attachment when siblings began attending the same school.

Taken together, these findings suggest that adolescence is characterized by both declines and increases in sibling intimacy, which depend on the sex constellation of the sibling dyad and other contextual variables such as attendance at the same or different schools. Importantly, toward the end of adolescence, siblings appear to have levels of intimacy that are at least the same, if not higher than they were at the beginning of adolescence (Buist et al., 2002; Kim et al., 2006; Updegraff et al., 2002).

Young Adulthood

Few sibling studies have explicitly focused on the transition to young adulthood, with preliminary work suggesting that high levels of sibling intimacy in late adolescence may be quite stable until the college ages (Buhrmester, 1992). Indeed, a cross-sectional study in Israel showed that three raters (respondents, their sibling, and mothers) rated sibling intimacy as higher in young adulthood (average age 24 years old) than in adolescence (average age 16 years old; Scharf et al., 2005). The sample was heterogeneous in terms of young adult transitions, however, and the majority of young adults still resided at home with their parents and siblings. Findings could differ in a sample in which the majority of young adults have left the parental home.

Addressing this criticism, Whiteman, McHale, et al. (2011) followed up the sample studied by Kim and colleagues (2006) and used 8 years of data from this prospective-longitudinal study to examine changes in sibling relationships for firstborns who were leaving home for the first time and their next-youngest sibling. Analyses indicated small but significant increases in sibling intimacy for both firstborns and second-borns as firstborns left home. Perhaps, as they no longer interact daily and even miss each other, siblings gain a new appreciation of one another. These findings are in contrast, however, to some cross-sectional work in young adulthood that reported increased distance and decreased affect intensity in the sibling relationship (Shortt & Gottman, 1997; Stocker et al., 1997; White, 2001). This cross-sectional work was not limited to the period immediately following firstborns' transition out of the home, however. It may be that as the family rallies to support the firstborn's first young adult transition family closeness temporarily increases. Perhaps only later, when subsequent young adult transitions occur for firstborns or when later-born siblings make this transition, does the sibling relationship grow more distant.

Thus, studies suggest that sibling intimacy may be higher in early young adulthood than in adolescence. During later young adulthood, for example when siblings form their own families of procreation, sibling relationships may, at least temporarily, grow more distant (White, 2001).

Changes in Negative Relationship Dimensions

Adolescence

Adolescents report having more conflict with siblings than with parents, grandparents, teachers, or friends—perhaps because of the many hours they spend with siblings and the special, ambivalent nature of their relationship (Furman & Buhrmester, 1985). Some initial cross-sectional work suggested lower negativity, including major and minor conflicts, antagonism, and competition among older as compared to younger adolescent- or middle childhood-aged siblings (Buhrmester & Furman, 1990; Cole & Kerns, 2001). Thus, similar to parent–child conflict (Shanahan, McHale, Osgood, et al., 2007), the trajectory of sibling conflict may be characterized by only temporary perturbations during adolescence, followed by declines in sibling conflict.

Somewhat consistent with this idea, longitudinal work shows continuity in mean levels of the frequency of sibling conflict in middle childhood, followed by an accelerated decline in adolescence (Kim et al., 2006). The decline in sibling conflict began at approximately age 13 for firstborns and at approximately age 10 for second-borns (see Figure 3.2). This birth-order-differential pattern makes sense: These siblings were spaced approximately 3 years apart and were both part of the same sibling relationship. Thus, most likely, siblings reported decreases in sibling conflict at the same time (but at different ages), because their conflict with each other decreased simultaneously.

There are several potential reasons for the relatively high levels of sibling conflict in late-middle childhood and early adolescence (see also Kim et al., 2006). First, temporary increases in parent–child conflict may spill over to the larger family system, including to sibling relationships (Shanahan, McHale, Osgood, et al., 2007). Second, as their physical and developmental differences decline, siblings may use conflict as a means of renegotiating the

Figure 3.2 Changes in Sibling Conflict From Middle Childhood Through Late Adolescence by Birth Order

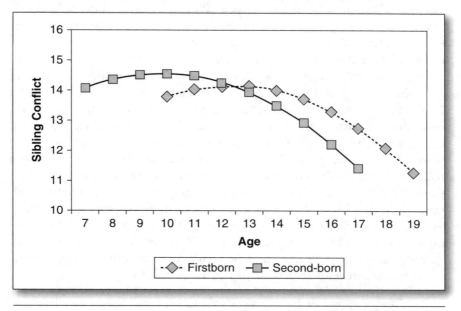

SOURCE: Reprinted with permission from Kim, McHale, Osgood, & Crouter (2006).

power differential between them and establishing more symmetry (Brody & Stoneman, 1994). Furthermore, because of increased developmental similarities, siblings may engage in more social comparisons, which can be associated with negative sibling relationship qualities (Shanahan, McHale, Crouter, & Osgood, 2008). Finally, because of challenges in self-regulation (Steinberg, 2005), adolescent siblings may have difficulties when it comes to managing disagreements in their relationships.

In addition to late adolescents' enhanced social-cognitive understanding and conflict resolution abilities (Laursen, Finkelstein, & Betts, 2001), there are several other potential explanations for the subsequent decreases in sibling conflict. For example, siblings may spend less time together, decreasing their opportunities for conflict (note, however, that decreases in sibling conflict are not always accounted for by decreases in joint sibling time; Cole & Kerns, 2001). Furthermore, youth may be less stressed by later rather than by initial adolescent transitions (Band & Weisz, 1988), and such reductions in stress tend to have a positive impact on relationship qualities.

In sum, longitudinal research reported no changes in the mean levels of sibling conflict frequency from late-middle childhood to early adolescence, followed by decreases in conflict in later adolescence. These decreases began at different ages for firstborns and second-borns. Some notable differences for findings regarding changes in sibling conflict versus intimacy emerged. First, Kim and colleagues (2006) reported sex constellation-differential changes in sibling intimacy but not in conflict, a finding consistent with longitudinal work on parent–child relationships (Shanahan, McHale, Crouter, & Osgood, 2007; Shanahan, McHale, Osgood, et al., 2007). Second, and also consistent with the parent–child literature, birth order only moderated trajectories of conflict but not of intimacy. That is, changes in sibling conflict took place simultaneously for both siblings, when they differed in age. In contrast, changes in sibling intimacy took place at different waves of assessment for the two siblings but when they were of the same age. Perhaps conflict is mostly a bilateral relationship dimension that can only change simultaneously for the people involved. Sibling intimacy could be a comparatively more unilateral relationship dimension. Changes in intimacy may be more subtle and subjective and do not necessarily have to be matched with corresponding changes in the relationship partner's perception of the relationship.

Young Adulthood

Cross-sectional studies suggest less sibling conflict and competition in young adulthood compared to adolescence (Stewart et al., 2001). Scharf and colleagues (2005), for example, found that young adult-aged respondents (and their siblings, and mothers) reported less sibling conflict compared to adolescent-aged respondents. In their longitudinal study, Whiteman, McHale, et al. (2011) also reported declines in sibling negativity after the firstborn left home, especially for brothers. Firstborns' transitions out of their home also had indirect family-systemic consequences: Second-borns now reported increases in parent–child conflict frequency, perhaps because of the increased parental focus on the second-born after the firstborn had left home (Whiteman, McHale, et al., 2011).

Declines in sibling conflict in early adulthood may be explained by several factors. Young adults who have left the home may have fewer occasions to fight with a sibling and may, for the first time, have the option to spend less time with siblings with whom they do not get along (Conger & Little, 2010; Stocker et al., 1997). Similarly, the most common sources triggering sibling conflict may have simply disappeared, including the invasion of personal space, such as borrowing something without permission, fighting over time in the bathroom or the choice of TV programs, copying one another, and teasing (Campione-Barr & Smetana, 2010). It is worth noting that, although sibling conflict may generally decrease, sibling competition may be deep-seated and episodically resurface whenever opportunities for conflict and competition arise in adult life (Boll, Ferring, & Filipp, 2005).

Summarizing the section on empirical advances, sibling intimacy decreases during early adolescence but then increases for mixed-sex sibling dyads (Kim et al., 2006). Sibling conflict decreases simultaneously for both siblings starting in mid-adolescence. Depending on the dimension of the sibling relationship studied, overall change trajectories can be qualified by the sibling sex constellation, birth order, and contextual factors, highlighting the importance of a nuanced view on changes in sibling relationships.

⟋⟍ FUTURE DIRECTIONS

Most youth in the United States have at least one sibling, and sibling relationships in adolescence and young adulthood may set the stage for how siblings cope with future joint tasks, including taking care of aging parents, dividing parental assets, and preserving family connections after parents die. How can future research further enhance our understanding of changes in sibling relationships from adolescence to young adulthood?

Adolescence

Although we understand changes in sibling conflict during the adolescent transitions to some extent (e.g., sibling shared time typically decreases; intimacy temporarily decreases in some dyads; conflict initially does not change but then declines; birth order and sex constellation modify the course of sibling relationships; changes in sibling relationship qualities covary with parent–child and marital relationship qualities; e.g., Kim et al., 2006), there are also nuances that we do not yet understand. For example, does the course of sibling relationship qualities vary depending on earlier qualities of that relationship and depending on each sibling's personal characteristics including their temperament/ personality and psychological adjustment, as has been shown for parent–child relationships (Hafen & Laursen, 2009; Laursen, DeLay, & Adams, 2010)? Influences on sibling relationship qualities have been reviewed elsewhere (e.g., East, 2009; McHale, et al., 2006), but many of these influences now need to be examined with respect to *changes* in sibling relationship qualities.

Young Adulthood

Compared to adolescence, the transition to young adulthood is currently much less studied. The study by Whiteman, McHale, et al. (2011) is seminal in charting the course of sibling relationships from adolescence until after firstborns' leaving home. Additional research is needed on young adult siblings who do not leave home or who undergo other young adult transitions, including completing one's education, getting a job, marriage, and childbearing (Conger & Little, 2010). Importantly, each of these transitions represents an opportunity to mentor and support a less experienced sibling and can be a potential turning point for sibling relationship qualities. For example, pursuing higher education and entering the workforce could afford siblings new opportunities for connecting with one another but could also trigger sibling competition, including for high achievements and parental financial resources (Behrman, Pollak, & Taubman, 1982; Conley, 2000). Furthermore, the transition to marriage brings new spouses into sibling dynamics, which, depending on the new marital dynamics, could increase or decrease the emotional distance between siblings. Moreover, the transition to parenthood involves new family roles and responsibilities. This transition may encourage siblings to recall and review their shared childhood experiences, but may also revive old rivalries—for example, if siblings' parents replicate old patterns of differential treatment with their grandchildren.

In addition to charting sibling relationships across all of these transitions, research is needed on how siblings maintain contact during adulthood (e.g., Conger & Little, 2010). E-mail, texting, social networking, and videoconferencing websites have removed barriers to keeping in close contact with siblings despite geographical distance, perhaps allowing siblings to remain close and actively provide emotional support for one another. Indeed, new research shows that just hearing a trusted person's voice has a physiologically effect similar to the effect derived from being physically close to that person (Seltzer, Ziegler, & Pollak, 2010). A related line of research should explore what role parents play directly or indirectly in connecting young adult siblings—for example, by hosting family holidays or by sharing information about a sibling's life. Direct parental involvement in sibling conflict during childhood has been linked to negative implications for sibling relationship qualities (McHale, Updegraff, Tucker, & Crouter, 2000). What is the role of parental involvement in the sibling relationship and continued parental differential treatment in young adulthood, and what strategies might young adult siblings use to counteract potentially negative influences of parental involvement?

Prospectively longitudinal research is also needed to understand how children's reports of their sibling experiences during childhood correspond to their recalled childhood sibling experience once they are adults. How do young adults reconstruct, interpret, and scaffold their earlier sibling experiences, including disappointing sibling experiences? Do siblings, who are often assumed to have shared childhood family experiences, actually recall similar family experiences or do their retrospective reports vary widely? Such prospectively longitudinal studies could also inform which childhood factors, including each sibling's temperament, parental differential treatment, and parental marital dynamics have long-lasting effects on sibling relationship qualities (e.g., Brody & Stoneman, 1994).

Across Developmental Periods

Several aspects of sibling relationships deserve increased attention across development. First, most of the sibling research reviewed here focused on sibling dyads, and we need to better understand how sibling dynamics work beyond the dyad. Second, most of the research reviewed here focused on siblings with fairly narrow age gaps. Sibling dynamics may differ, however, for siblings with larger age gaps. For example, much older siblings may have important caretaking responsibilities for younger siblings, with even more dramatic effects on family dynamics when the older sibling leaves the home. Third, much of the research discussed in this chapter was based on white, middle-class, two-parent families, and changes in sibling relationships need to be better understood in understudied contexts, including ethnically and structurally diverse family contexts (McGuire & Shanahan, 2010). Changes in sibling relationship qualities may differ, for example, in families from cultures that emphasize loyalty and support among family members (e.g., McHale, Updegraff, Shanahan, Crouter, & Killoren, 2005).

Fourth, consistent with studies reviewed here, we mostly focused on different dimensions of sibling relationships separately; in reality, siblings' shared time, conflict, and intimacy do not exist in isolation and instead co-occur and interact at any given time. Indeed, person-oriented cross-sectional approaches have identified subgroups of youth who are relatively homogeneous in terms of their configurations of different sibling relationship dimensions. Such subgroups were characterized, for example, by high-negativity, high-warmth, emotional distance, or intense sibling affect (e.g., McGuire, McHale, & Updegraff, 1996; McHale, Whiteman, Kim, & Crouter, 2007; Sherman, Lansford, & Volling, 2006; Whiteman & Loken, 2006). Little is known, however, about whether and how such groupings of different sibling relationship dimensions change over time.

Finally, abuse and violence in sibling relationships has been understudied but has potentially long-lasting influences on development. Many forms of physical aggression between siblings, including hitting and pushing are viewed as normative by most parents and communities (Emery & Laumann-Billings, 1998). Indeed, 80% or more of children experience violence from a sibling or perpetrate violence toward a sibling at some point in their lives (Straus, Gelles, & Steinmetz, 1980), and young adults report more sibling violence than dating violence (Reese-Weber, 2008). Yet, youth, parents, and communities often tolerate forms of violence among siblings that they would reprimand when committed among peers or romantic partners (Finkelhor & Dziuba-Leatherman, 1994; Martin & Ross, 1995). Thus, serious forms of violence are committed among siblings, an area of research that deserves further study.

In sum, transitions from adolescence to young adulthood are filled with opportunities for change in sibling relationships, but research on these changes is needed, especially in diverse contexts and during the young adult transitions. Many of the gaps in research can only be addressed with prospectively longitudinal studies with sufficient sample sizes to test for differences among the four sibling sex constellations. Considering the mostly uncharted territory with respect to sibling relationships during the young adult transitions, both quantitative and qualitative methods should be used to capture sibling experiences (Whiteman & Christiansen, 2008).

ⅢⅢ JUGGEJTED READINGJ

Buist, K. L., Dekovi Cacute, M., Meeus, W., & Van Aken, M. A. G. (2002). Developmental patterns in adolescent attachment to mother, father and sibling. *Journal of Youth and Adolescence, 31*(3), 167–176.

East, P. L. (2009). Adolescents' relationships with siblings. In R. M. Lerner & L. Steinberg (Eds.), *Handbook of adolescent psychology, Vol 2. Contextual influences on adolescent development* (3rd ed., pp. 43–73). Hoboken, NJ: Wiley.

Kim, J., McHale, S. M., Osgood, D. W., & Crouter, A. C. (2006). Longitudinal course and family correlates of sibling relationships from childhood through adolescence. *Child Development, 77*(6), 1746–1761.

Scharf, M., Shulman, S., & Avigad-Spitz, L. (2005). Sibling relationships in emerging adulthood and in adolescence. *Journal of Adolescent Research, 20*(1), 64–90.

Whiteman, S. D., McHale, S. M., & Crouter, A. C. (2011). Family relationships from adolescence to early adulthood: Changes in the family system following firstborns' leaving home. *Journal of Research on Adolescence 21*(2), 461–474

ⅢⅢ REFERENCEJ

Ainsworth, M. D. (1985). Attachments across the life span. *Bulletin of the New York Academy of Medicine, 61*(9), 792–812.

Ansbacher, H. L., & Ansbacher, R. R. (1956). *The individual psychology of Alfred Adler.* New York: Basic Books.

Antonucci, T., Akiyama, H., & Takahashi, K. (2004). Attachment and close relationships across the life span. *Attachment & Human Development, 6*(4), 353–370.

Aquilino, W. S., Arnett, J. J., & Tanner, J. L. (2006). Family relationships and support systems in emerging adulthood. In J. J. Arnett & J. L. Tanner (Eds.), *Emerging adults in America: Coming of age in the 21st century* (pp. 193–217). Washington, DC: American Psychological Association.

Arnett, J. J. (2004). *Emerging adulthood: The winding road from the late teens through the twenties.* New York: Oxford University Press.

Band, E. B., & Weisz, J. R. (1988). How to feel better when it feels bad: Children's perspectives on coping with everyday stress. *Developmental Psychology, 24*(2), 247–253.

Bandura, A. (1977). *Social learning theory.* Englewood Cliffs, NJ: Prentice Hall.

Bank, S. P., & Kahn, M. D. (1997). *The sibling bond.* New York: Basic Books.

Behrman, J. R., Pollak, R. A., & Taubman, P. (1982). Parental preferences and provision for progeny. *The Journal of Political Economy, 90*(1), 52–73.

Boll, T., Ferring, D., & Filipp, S. (2005). Effects of parental differential treatment on relationship quality with siblings and parents: Justice evaluations as mediators. *Social Justice Research, 18*(2), 155–182.

Bowlby, J. (1980). *Attachment and loss.* New York: Basic Books.

Brody, G. H., & Stoneman, Z. (1994). Forecasting sibling relationships in early adolescence from child temperaments and family processes in middle childhood. *Child Development, 65*(3), 771–784.

Buhrmester, D. (1992). The developmental courses of sibling and peer relationships. In F. Boer & J. Dunn (Eds.), *Children's sibling relationships: Developmental and clinical issues* (pp. 19–40). Hillsdale, NJ: Lawrence Erlbaum.

Buhrmester, D., & Furman, W. (1990). Perceptions of sibling relationships during middle childhood and adolescence. *Child Development, 61*(5), 1387–1398.

Buist, K. L., Dekovi Cacute, M., Meeus, W., & Van Aken, M. A. G. (2002). Developmental patterns in adolescent attachment to mother, father and sibling. *Journal of Youth and Adolescence, 31*(3), 167–176.

Bussey, K., & Bandura, A. (1999). Social cognitive theory of gender development and differentiation. *Psychological Review, 106*(4), 676–713.

Camarena, P. M., Sarigiani, P. A., & Petersen, A. C. (1990). Gender-specific pathways to intimacy in early adolescence. *Journal of Youth and Adolescence, 19*(1), 19–32.

Campione-Barr, N., & Smetana, J. G. (2010). "Who said you could wear my sweater?" Adolescent siblings' conflicts and associations with relationship quality. *Child Development, 81*(2), 464–471.

Caspi, A., & Moffitt, T. E. (1991). Individual differences are accentuated during periods of social change: The sample case of girls at puberty. *Journal of Personality & Social Psychology, 61*(1), 157–168.

Cicirelli, V. G. (1995). *Sibling relationships across the life span.* New York: Plenum Press.

Cohen, P., Kasen, S., Chen, H., Hartmark, C., & Gordon, K. (2003). Variations in patterns of developmental transmissions in the emerging adulthood period. *Developmental Psychology, 39*(4), 657–669.

Cole, A., & Kerns, K. A. (2001). Perceptions of sibling qualities and activities of early adolescents. *Journal of Early Adolescence, 21*(2), 204–227.

Collins, A., & van Dulmen, M. (2006). Friendships and romance in emerging adulthood: Assessing distinctiveness in close relationships. In J. J. Arnett & J. L. Tanner (Eds.), *Emerging adults in America: Coming of age in the 21st century* (pp. 219–234). Washington, DC: American Psychological Association.

Compton, K., Snyder, J., Schrepferman, L., Bank, L., & Shortt, J. W. (2003). The contribution of parents and siblings to antisocial and depressive behavior in adolescents: A double jeopardy coercion model. *Development and Psychopathology, 15*(1),163–182.

Conger, K. J., & Little, W. M. (2010). Sibling relationships during the transition to adulthood. *Child Development Perspectives, 4*(2), 87–94.

Conger, R. D., Elder, G. H., Jr., Lorenz, F. O., Simons, R. L., & Whitbeck, L. B. (1994). *Families in troubled times: Adapting to change in rural America.* Hawthorne, NY: Aldine de Gruyter.

Conger, R. D., Ming, C., Bryant, C. M., & Elder, G. H., Jr. (2000). Competence in early adult romantic relationships: A developmental perspective on family influences. *Journal of Personality & Social Psychology, 79*(2), 224–237.

Conley, D. (2000). Sibship sex composition: Effects on educational attainment. *Social Science Research, 29*(3), 441–458.

de Munck, V. C. (1993). The dialectics and norms of self interest: Reciprocity among cross-siblings in a Sri Lankan Muslim community. In C. W. Nuckolls (Ed.), *Siblings in South Asia: Brothers and sisters in cultural context* (pp. 143–162). New York: Guilford Press.

Dunn, J., Slomkowski, C., & Beardsall, L. (1994). Sibling relationships from the preschool period through middle childhood and early adolescence. *Developmental Psychology, 30*(3), 315–325.

East, P. L. (2009). Adolescents' relationships with siblings. In R. M. Lerner & L. Steinberg (Eds.), *Handbook of adolescent psychology, Vol 2. Contextual influences on adolescent development* (3rd ed., pp. 43–73). Hoboken, NJ: Wiley.

Emery, R. E., & Laumann-Billings, L. (1998). An overview of the nature, causes, and consequences of abusive family relationships. *American Psychologist, 53*, 121–135.

Feinberg, M. E., & Hetherington, E. M. (2000). Sibling differentiation in adolescence: Implications for behavioral genetic theory. *Child Development, 71*(6), 1512–1524.

Feinberg, M. E., McHale, S. M., Crouter, A. C., & Cumsille, P. (2003). Sibling differentiation: Sibling and parent relationship trajectories in adolescence. *Child Development, 74*(5), 1261–1274.

Finkelhor, D., & Dziuba-Leatherman, J. (1994). Victimization of children. *American Psychologist, 49*, 173–183.

Frank, S. J., Avery, C. B., & Laman, M. S. (1988). Young adults' perceptions of their relationships with their parents: Individual differences in connectedness, competence, and emotional autonomy. *Developmental Psychology, 24*(5), 729–737.

Fuligni, A. J., Telzer, E. H., Bower, J., Irwin, M. R., Kiang, L., & Cole, S. W. (2009). Daily family assistance and inflammation among adolescents from Latin American and European backgrounds. *Brain, Behavior & Immunity, 23*(6), 803–809.

Furman, W., & Buhrmester, D. (1985). Children's perceptions of the personal relationships in their social networks. *Developmental Psychology, 21*(6), 1016–1024.

Furman, W., & Buhrmester, D. (1992). Age and sex differences in perceptions of networks of personal relationships. *Child Development, 63*(1), 103–116.

Hafen, C. A., & Laursen, B. (2009). More problems and less support: Early adolescent adjustment forecasts changes in perceived support from parents. *Journal of Family Psychology, 23*(2), 193–202.

Hazan, C., & Shaver, P. R. (1994). Attachment as an organizational framework for research on close relationships. *Psychological Inquiry, 5*(1), 1–22.

Hinde, R. A. (1979). *Towards understanding relationships.* Ontario/London: Academic Press.

Kahn, R. L., & Antonucci, T. C. (1980). Convoys over the life course: Attachment, roles and social support. In P. B. Baltes & O. G. Brim (Eds.), *Life-span development and behavior.* San Diego, CA: Academic Press.

Kim, J., McHale, S. M., Osgood, D. W., & Crouter, A. C. (2006). Longitudinal course and family correlates of sibling relationships from childhood through adolescence. *Child Development, 77*(6), 1746–1761.

Larson, R. W., Moneta, G., Richards, M. H., & Wilson, S. (2002). Continuity, stability, and change in daily emotional experience across adolescence. *Child Development, 73*(4), 1151–1165.

Larson, R. W., Richards, M. H., Moneta, G., Holmbeck, G., & Duckett, E. (1996). Changes in adolescents' daily interactions with their families from ages 10 to 18: Disengagement and transformation. *Developmental Psychology, 32*(4), 744–754.

Laursen, B., Coy, K. C., & Collins, W. A. (1998). Reconsidering changes in parent–child conflict across adolescence: A meta-analysis. *Child Development, 69*(3), 817–833.

Laursen, B., DeLay, D., & Adams, R. E. (2010). Trajectories of perceived support in mother–adolescent relationships: The poor (quality) get poorer. *Developmental Psychology, 46*(6), 1792–1798.

Laursen, B., Finkelstein, B. D., & Betts, N. T. (2001). A developmental meta-analysis of peer conflict resolution. *Developmental Review, 21*(4), 423–449.

Leffert, N., & Petersen, A. C. (1996). Biology, challenge, and coping in adolescence: Effects on physical and mental health. In M. H. Bornstein & J. L. Genevro (Eds.), *Child development and behavioral pediatrics* (pp. 129–154). Mahwah, NJ: Lawrence Erlbaum.

Maccoby, E. E. (1998). *The two sexes: Growing up apart, coming together.* Cambridge, MA: Belknap/Harvard University Press.

Martin, J. L., & Ross, H. S. (1995). The development of aggression within sibling conflict. *Early Education and Development, 6,* 335–358.

McCoy, J. K., Brody, G. H., & Stoneman, Z. (1994). A longitudinal analysis of sibling relationships as mediators of the link between family processes and youths' best friendships. *Family Relations, 43*(4), 400–408.

McGuire, S., McHale, S. M., & Updegraff, K. (1996). Children's perceptions of the sibling relationship in middle childhood: Connections within and between family relationships. *Personal Relationships, 3*(3), 229–239.

McGuire, S., & Shanahan, L. (2010). Sibling experiences in diverse family contexts. *Child Development Perspectives, 4*(2), 72–79.

McHale, S. M., & Crouter, A. C. (1996). The family contexts of children's sibling relationships. In G. H. Brody (Ed.), *Sibling relationships: Their causes and consequences* (pp. 173–195). Westport, CT: Ablex Publishing.

McHale, S. M., Kim, J., & Whiteman, S. D. (2006). Sibling relationships in childhood and adolescence. In P. Noller & J. A. Feeney (Eds.), *Close relationships: Functions, forms and processes* (pp. 127–149). New York: Psychology Press/Taylor & Francis.

McHale, S. M., Updegraff, K. A., Shanahan, L., Crouter, A. C., & Killoren, S. E. (2005). Siblings' differential treatment in Mexican American families. *Journal of Marriage and Family, 67*(5), 1259–1274.

McHale, S. M., Updegraff, K. A., Tucker, C. J., & Crouter, A. C. (2000). Step in or stay out? Parents' roles in adolescent siblings' relationships. *Journal of Marriage & the Family, 62*(3), 746–760.

McHale, S. M., Whiteman, S. D., Kim, J., & Crouter, A. C. (2007). Characteristics and correlates of sibling relationships in two-parent African American families. *Journal of Family Psychology, 21*(2), 227–235.

Minuchin, P. (1985). Families and individual development: Provocations from the field of family therapy. *Child Development, 56*(2), 289–302.

Minuchin, S. (1974). *Families & family therapy.* Cambridge, MA: Harvard University Press.

Mouw, T. (2005). Sequences of early adult transitions: A look at variability and consequences. In R. A. Settersten Jr., F. F. Furstenberg Jr., & R. G. Rumbaut (Eds.), *On the frontier of adulthood: Theory, research, and public policy* (pp. 256–291). Chicago: University of Chicago Press.

O'Connor, T. G., Allen, J. P., Bell, K. L., & Hauser, S. T. (1996). Adolescents' parent relationships and leaving home in young adulthood. In J. A. Graber & J. S. Dubas (Eds.), *Leaving home: Understanding the transition to adulthood* (pp. 39–52). San Francisco: Jossey-Bass.

Reese-Weber, M. (2008). A new experimental method assessing attitudes toward adolescent dating and sibling violence using observations of violent interactions. *Journal of Adolescence*, 31(6), 857–876.

Schachter, F. F., Shore, E., Feldman-Rotman, S., Marquis, R. E., & Campbell, S. (1976). Sibling deidentification. *Developmental Psychology*, 12(5), 418–427.

Scharf, M., Shulman, S., & Avigad-Spitz, L. (2005). Sibling relationships in emerging adulthood and in adolescence. *Journal of Adolescent Research*, 20(1), 64–90.

Seltzer, L. J., Ziegler, T. E., & Pollak, S. D. (2010). Social vocalizations can release oxytocin in humans. *Proceedings of Biological Sciences*, 277(1694), 2661–2666.

Shanahan, L., Kim, J., McHale, S. M., & Crouter, A. C. (2007). Sibling similarities and differences in time use: A pattern-analytic, within-family approach. *Social Development*, 16(4), 662–681.

Shanahan, L., McHale, S. M., Crouter, A. C., & Osgood, D. W. (2007). Warmth with mothers and fathers from middle childhood to late adolescence: Within- and between-families comparisons. *Developmental Psychology*, 43(3), 551–563.

Shanahan, L., McHale, S. M., Crouter, A. C., & Osgood, D. W. (2008). Linkages between parents' differential treatment, youth depressive symptoms, and sibling relationships. *Journal of Marriage & Family*, 70(2), 480–494.

Shanahan, L., McHale, S. M., Osgood, D. W., & Crouter, A. C. (2007). Conflict frequency with mothers and fathers from middle childhood to late adolescence: Within- and between-families comparisons. *Developmental Psychology*, 43(3), 539–550.

Shanahan, M. J. (2000). Pathways to adulthood in changing societies: Variability and mechanisms in life course perspective. *Annual Review of Sociology*, 26(1), 667–692.

Sherman, A. M., Lansford, J. E., & Volling, B. L. (2006). Sibling relationships and best friendships in young adulthood: Warmth, conflict, and well-being. *Personal Relationships*, 13(2), 151–165.

Shortt, J. W., & Gottman, J. M. (1997). Closeness in young adult sibling relationships: Affective and physiological processes. *Social Development*, 6(2), 142–164.

Slomkowski, C., Conger, K. J., Rende, R., Heylen, E., Little, W. M., Shebloski, B., et al. (2009). Sibling contagion for drinking in adolescence: A micro process framework. *European Journal of Developmental Science*, 3(2), 161–174.

Stein, J. A., Riedel, M., & Rotheram-Borus, M. J. (1999). Parentification and its impact on adolescent children of parents with AIDS. *Family Process*, 38(2), 193–208.

Steinberg, L. (2005). Cognitive and affective development in adolescence. *Trends in Cognitive Sciences*, 9(2), 69–74.

Steinberg, L., & Silk, J. S. (2002). Parenting adolescents. In M. H. Bornstein (Ed.), *Handbook of parenting, Vol. 1. Children and parenting* (2nd ed., pp. 103–133). Mahwah, NJ: Lawrence Erlbaum.

Stewart, R. B., Kozak, A. L., Tingley, L. M., Goddard, J. M., Blake, E. M., & Cassel, W. A. (2001). Adult sibling relationships: Validation of a typology. *Personal Relationships*, 8(3), 299–324.

Stocker, C. M., Furman, W., & Lanthier, R. P. (1997). Sibling relationships in early adulthood. *Journal of Family Psychology*, 11(2), 210–221.

Straus, M. A., Gelles, R. J., & Steinmetz, S. (1980). *Behind closed doors: Violence in the American family*. New York: Doubleday.

Tancredy, C. M., & Fraley, R. C. (2006). The nature of adult twin relationships: An attachment-theoretical perspective. *Journal of Personality and Social Psychology*, 90(1), 78–93.

Teti, D. M., & Ablard, K. E. (1989). Security of attachment and infant-sibling relationships: A laboratory study. *Child Development, 60*(6), 1519–1528.

Updegraff, K. A., McHale, S. M., & Crouter, A. C. (2002). Adolescents' sibling relationship and friendship experiences: Developmental patterns and relationship linkages. *Social Development, 11*(2), 182–204.

Updegraff, K. A., McHale, S. M., Whiteman, S. D., Thayer, S. M., & Delgado, M. (2005). Adolescent sibling relationships in Mexican American families: Exploring the role of familism. *Journal of Family Psychology, 19*(4), 512–522.

van IJzendoorn, M. H., Moran, G., Belsky, J., Pederson, D., Bakermans-Kranenburg, M. J., & Kneppers, K. (2000). The similarity of siblings' attachments to their mother. *Child Development, 71*(4), 1086–1098.

Volling, B. L., & Belsky, J. (1992). The contribution of mother–child and father–child relationships to the quality of sibling interaction: A longitudinal study. *Child Development, 63*(5), 1209–1222.

Waldinger, R. J., Vaillant, G. E., & Orav, E. J. (2007). Childhood sibling relationships as a predictor of major depression in adulthood: A 30-year prospective study. *The American Journal of Psychiatry, 164*(6), 949–954.

Whitchurch, G. G., & Constantine, L. L. (1993). Systems theory. In P. G. Boss, W. J. Doherty, R. LaRossa, W. R. Schumm & S. K. Steinmetz (Eds.), *Sourcebook of family theories and methods: A contextual approach* (pp. 325–355). New York: Plenum Press.

White, L. (2001). Sibling relationships over the life course: A panel analysis. *Journal of Marriage & Family, 63*(2), 555–569.

Whiteman, S. D., & Christiansen, A. (2008). Processes of sibling influence in adolescence: Individual and family correlates. *Family Relations, 57*(1), 24–34.

Whiteman, S. D., & Loken, E. (2006). Comparing analytic techniques to classify dyadic relationships: An example using siblings. *Journal of Marriage & Family, 68*(5), 1370–1382.

Whiteman, S. D., McHale, S. M., & Crouter, A. C. (2007). Longitudinal changes in marital relationships: The role of offspring's pubertal development. *Journal of Marriage and Family, 69*(4), 1005–1020.

Whiteman, S. D., McHale, S. M., & Crouter, A. C. (2011). Family relationships from adolescence to early adulthood: Changes in the family system following firstborns' leaving home. *Journal of Research on Adolescence, 21*(2), 461–474.

Whiteman, S. D., Soli, A. R., & McHale, S. M. (in press). Theoretical perspectives on sibling relationships. *Journal of Family Theory and Review.*

PART II

Friendships and Friend Networks

4

Transformations in Friend Relationships Across the Transition Into Adolescence

Christopher A. Hafen

Brett Laursen

Dawn DeLay

E arly adolescence, the period from about 10 to 13 years old, is a time of growth and new experiences. As children enter into early adolescence, they spend more time with peers and less time with parents and other adults. They are also beginning the lengthy process of identity development and so may be preoccupied with doubts about who they are and how they fit into their expanding social world. Withdrawal from parents and uncertainty about the definition of self may leave the individual vulnerable to new sources of influence. Friends often step into this void. Consistent with this claim is evidence that the likelihood of being influenced by one's peers is strongest in early adolescence (Engels, Knibbe, de Vries, Drop, & Van Breukelen, 1999). Influence experiences

Support for the preparation of this chapter was provided to Brett Laursen from the U.S. National Science Foundation (0923745).

are vital to forming stronger bonds and closer relationships, but susceptibility to peer influence can also serve as a risk factor for the escalation of negative behaviors.

Deviant behavior increases during adolescence, even among well-adjusted youth (Moffitt, 1993). The mechanisms responsible for this increase are not entirely clear. To be sure, adolescents seek to be recognized as adults and some norm-breaking behaviors during early adolescence are simply a matter of status offenses that encompass behaviors reserved for adults. Others involve emulation of peers whose deviant behaviors accord them greater status, which is equated with autonomy and maturity. But this cannot account for all changes in deviant behavior during early adolescence. We know little, for instance, about the mechanisms whereby friends influence one another. This chapter summarizes theory and research concerning changes in peer influence across the transition to early adolescence, with a particular emphasis on individual characteristics and friendship contexts that are most likely to be associated with heightened susceptibility to peer influence.

CONCEPTUAL OVERVIEW

A discussion of friend influence during early adolescence must necessarily include a discussion of parent influence during the same period. This is because theories addressing the growing influence of friends are intimately bound to theories concerning the declining influence of parents (Laursen & Collins, 2009). Indeed, most models that address change in friend influence do so in the context of explaining alterations in parent–adolescent relationships. Changes in peer relationships are invoked as both a cause and a consequence of changes in parent–adolescent relationships. We organize these theories under two headings: (1) changes linked to individual adolescent development and (2) changes linked to the rise of peer culture.

The earliest theories embraced a hydraulic model of influence. In this view, the amount of influence that an adolescent receives is fixed; developmental changes arise in the allocation of this finite commodity (Bowerman & Kinch, 1959). Parents and peers represent opposing spheres of influence, with adolescents buffeted between them. Increases in peer influence must necessarily result in decreases in parent influence and vice versa. As youth approach adulthood, they should grow increasingly immune to pressure from outside sources. This means that parents and peers vie for a shrinking measure of power across the adolescent years (Laursen & Collins, 2004). Nuanced versions of this model hold that developmental changes may be domain specific (Kandel & Lesser, 1972). Different developmental patterns may arise for different outcomes. Peer influence over attire may grow at the expense of parents, but parents may retain their position of importance over matters such as career aspirations.

Hydraulic models captured the popular imagination, but research scientists thought them to be too rigid. Influence need not necessarily be a zero-sum proposition, and peer influence is not necessarily tied to parent influence (Brittain, 1963). If absolute levels of influence are unrelated across adolescence, then change in influence accorded to one relationship does not necessarily prompt change in influence accorded to another. When peers become more influential, parents do not necessarily become less influential. In other words, the influence of parents may not decline in absolute terms over the course of early adolescence, although it may decline relative to that of peers. Peers and parents are not assumed to be opposing sources of influence. Instead, peers and parents are more likely to be complementary influences who offer a consistent message about expected behavior (Berndt, 1999). Some have suggested that these complementarities increase across adolescence, such that parents and peers start off as unique sources of influence that eventually become integrated as young adulthood approaches (Collins & Laursen, 2000).

Changes in Friend Influence Linked to Individual Development

Models with very different conceptual foundations often come to similar conclusions about changes in friend influence associated with puberty. Psychoanalytic theorists assumed that hormonal changes at puberty foster unwelcome Oedipal urges, which creates anxiety about relationships with parents that is manifest in rebelliousness and contentiousness (A. Freud, 1958; S. Freud, 1921/1949). Physical and emotional separation from parents reduces anxiety, as does the identification of a peer who can serve as an appropriate alternative love object. Evolutionary views also emphasize the role that puberty plays in transforming parent–child relationships (e.g., Steinberg, 1989). Adolescent maturation threatens parental dominance, which strains relationships with parents. This prompts youth to turn away from their family to be comforted by peers who are experiencing similar relationship disruptions. Separation from the family follows, which encourages the selection of a mate from outside of the family. Both accounts emphasize how adolescents increasingly need friends to weather difficulties at home and to assist in the search for lovers and mates. Presumably this gives friends greater influence over individual behavior, although this part of the formulation is usually left unstated.

Related theories emphasize adolescent autonomy striving and ego identity development as reasons for parent–child distance. In this view, adolescents go through a period of de-identification from parents, highlighting parental fallibility that serves to promote separation from the family (Blos, 1979). Rejecting the identity of parents, adolescents are forced to create a new, unique sense of self. Identity development is a slow, gradual process that extends across adolescence, with opportunities to explore options without making final commitments (Erikson, 1968). The early stages of this process are marked by an influence vacuum; parental values are rejected but have not yet been replaced with a value set of one's own. Early adolescents are especially vulnerable to peer pressure during the process of identity formation because, in the absence of a clear sense of self, they look to friends for guidance (Devereux, 1970). It follows that susceptibility to peer pressure should decline with a rise in independent, autonomous thought.

Cognitive advances spur changes in conceptions about friendship. The importance of intimacy and loyalty increases as youth come to understand reciprocity and mutuality as the foundation of relationships between equals (Selman, 1980). Adolescents come to place the needs of the relationship above the needs of the individual, which suggests that friends should place a special value on conformity and uniformity (Laursen & Hartup, 2002). Recent theories about brain maturation come to much the same conclusion (Steinberg, 2008). Alterations to the dopaminergic system during early adolescence give rise to increased reward seeking, particularly in the presence of peers; these changes are eventually followed later in adolescence and in young adulthood by developments in areas responsible for cognitive control, gradually improving self-regulatory capabilities. Adolescents are thought to be particularly susceptible to peer pressure when the former system lacks the restraint of the latter.

Some peers are undoubtedly more influential than others, but theory is largely silent on this point. At the group level, select cliques are instrumental in defining normative values and behaviors. Coleman (1961) referred to these cliques as "leading crowds." These groups take it upon themselves to not only define standards of behavior but also to enforce them. Youth who care about the opinions of members of the leading crowd, particularly those who wish to join the leading crowd, may be especially vulnerable to pressure to conform exerted by members of the leading crowd. This suggests that influence within a friendship might cleave along lines of perceived popularity. Other theories imply other differences. Investment theory holds that relationship commitment varies as a function of available alternatives (Rusbult, 1980). Individuals with fewer alternatives to their current relationship partner are more committed to the relationship than those with many alternatives. Better accepted youth, who have more potential options for friends, should be more influential than less accepted youth, who have fewer friendship choices. Finally, there are theories that emphasize the maturity gap (Moffitt, 1993). In this view, adolescents seek tokens of maturity and adult status during the long and awkward transition from childhood to adulthood. Deviant peers who display more autonomy are perceived to be more adultlike. As a consequence, some deviant peers may influence nondeviant peers who aspire to receive the respect and behavioral latitude accorded to adults.

Changes in Friend Influence
Linked to the Rise of Peer Culture

Structural changes in schools heighten the significance of friendships during the adolescent years. As children move from primary school, to middle school, to secondary school, they increasingly occupy a world that is dominated by age-mates (Coleman, 1961). During their long days at school and in their extensive extracurricular and leisure activities, youth find themselves isolated from adult society. The values and priorities of the adolescent peer culture are perpetuated through the institutions dedicated to educating and socializing youth, to the point where adult values concerning the importance of achievement hold little sway when compared to peer values that emphasize the importance of sports and popularity. It is not just that adolescents increasingly lead lives apart from adults. It is also that the school structure becomes increasingly impersonal. As schools get larger and contact with teachers becomes more superficial, young adolescents band together to form their own culture (Bronfenbrenner, 1970). Social pressures to conform to the group increase, which means that a greater emphasis is placed on values that facilitate the smooth functioning of the group.

The rise of the peer culture gives rise to new relationships needs. Sullivan (1953) argued that different developmental periods are dominated by different social needs. Preadolescence and early adolescence are dominated by the need for interpersonal intimacy. During this "chumship" phase, same-sex friends occupy a new position of importance because they satisfy new needs for companionship, intimacy, and acceptance. In a world increasingly dominated by peers, an individual needs a mate to confide in, hang out with, and watch your back. During early adolescence, friends occupy a new place in the network of close relationships, because the demands of the social world now require new skills and new competencies that can only be acquired through interactions with friends (Furman, 1989). The more youth need their friends, the more influential these friends become.

Peer influence and peer pressure are assumed to be synonymous. Both imply that friends persuade individuals to act in a manner consistent with that of other members of the group. In other words, influence implies conformity, and conformity implies that friends look and behave similarly. But how best to operationalize the construct? Although it is tempting to assume that friend similarity is an exclusive product of friend influence, the origins of similarity are more complicated. Homophily (literally, "love of the same") captures the varied processes that give rise to similarity (Lazarsfeld & Merton, 1954). Selection refers to the tendency of youth to select similar others as friends. The first portion of dyadic similarity is due to preexisting similarities that form the basis of a friendship. *Deselection* refers to the tendency of youth to stop being friends with those who are different. The second portion of dyadic similarity is due to the fact that dissimilar friendships tend to be unstable. *Socialization* refers to the tendency of youth to become more similar to their friends over time. The third portion of dyadic similarity is due to friend influence and peer pressure to conform. Theories addressing the rise of peer culture often ascribe changes in friendship during early adolescence to socialization pressures from friends; they rarely acknowledge the possibility that changes in friendship may be a product of changes in how early adolescents select friends.

⊗ RECENT EMPIRICAL ADVANCES

The increasing developmental significance of friendships across the transition into adolescence can be traced to changes in three overlapping domains. The first concerns the process of identity formation that begins to take shape in early adolescence. The second concerns the nature of friendship homophily during early adolescence. The third concerns increases in susceptibility to peer influence that arise during early adolescence. In this section, we will selectively review recent empirical studies that describe changes in individuals and in friendships that give rise to the outsized influence that friends exert over individual behavior during early adolescence.

Changes in Identity

Friends play a critical role in adolescent identity development. Friends offer insight into characteristics and values that others possess, with a perspective that cannot be obtained in other relationships. The development of friendships during the transition to adolescence is in large part characterized by the emergence and growth of intimacy and emotional support (Hartup, 1996). Some of these characteristics have origins in parent–child relationships, most notably with attachment-based interactions. The extent to which adolescent friendships are characterized by increased intimacy and emotional support owes much to experiences gained in relationships during childhood with parents (Allen, Hauser, O'Connor, & Bell, 2002). Close friends may even serve as attachment figures (Buhrmester, 1992).

Close relationships with friends are enhanced by the shared experience of identity formation. Early adolescence is a period of self-reflective analysis and self-evaluation that in its most successful form leads to the establishment of a clear and integrated identity (Erikson, 1968). To form this integrated sense of self, the child must have experiences and connections that allow him or her to experiment with different identities. This requires intimacy and trust, unique features that set horizontal relationships with friends apart from vertical relationships with parents (Laursen & Bukowski, 1997). Strong evidence suggests that there is a sharp rise in friendship intimacy and connectedness during the transition into adolescence (Berndt, 1982).

Autonomy and separation from parents often accompany identity development. Those who successfully manage this transition are able to balance needs for growing autonomy with an independent identity while still maintaining a positive relationship with parents (Allen, Hauser, Eickholt, Bell, & O'Connor, 1994). Youth who are able to balance family relationships and new, more intimate peer relationships tend to be successful in the development of close relationships during late adolescence and early adulthood (Sroufe, Egeland, & Carlson, 1999). Youth who fail to develop a unique identity outside of the family relationship are more likely to succumb to peer pressure (Fuligni & Eccles, 1993). Thus, experiences in the home during early adolescence set the stage not just for the formation of identity but also for the ability to function independently with peers.

Friends take on new significance during the process of adolescent identity development. Greater importance is given to finding friends who have similar interests, values, and beliefs and who will generally be supportive and understanding during the process of separate from the family and exploration of self (Youniss & Smollar, 1985). Concerns about finding the right friend are well grounded: The success and stability of early adolescent friendships have been linked to self-esteem and life satisfaction (Keefe & Berndt, 1996). Indeed, friendship support uniquely predicts adolescent self-worth over and above the contributions made by parents and romantic partners (Laursen, Furman, & Mooney, 2006). The role of friendships in identity formation is not well understood, but it is thought to hinge on finding a partner who shares similar experiences and so can validate one's own behaviors and beliefs.

Changes in Homophily

Similarity during adolescence is of particular concern because of worries that youth are especially susceptible to pressure from peers during a period when more time is spent in the company of age-mates than adults. Selection similarity in early adolescence begins with a preference for same-sex and same-race peers, but is also evident for behavioral attributes such as overall delinquency and alcohol use (Brown & Klute, 2003). After a friendship is formed, reciprocity is the basis for homophilic tendencies. The processes of selection and socialization are typically studied under the premise that deviant attitudes and behaviors are the means by which adolescents look for relationships (selection); once in a friendship, participants begin to influence each other's behavior (socialization). Spending time with friends that engage in deviant behaviors makes it more likely that an individual will engage in deviant behaviors (Kobus, 2003). Adolescents with deviant friends are more apt to display deviant behaviors than those with nondeviant friends. Because deviance can be a sign of status or maturity, deviant peers may be particularly influential and adolescents may be susceptible to the effects of exposure to antisocial peers.

Similarity between friends can be traced to both selection and socialization (Cohen, 1977; Kandel, 1978). This suggests that peers who select one another to be friends may share some salient characteristics, which should grow as the friendship deepens. The first studies to examine these processes used large samples in which students identified their friends and described their own behaviors and attitudes at two time points during the school year. Selection was measured in terms of Time 1 similarity for individuals who were not friends at Time 1 but who were friends at Time 2. Socialization was measured in terms of changes in similarity for youth who were friends at both Time 1 and Time 2. The results of these studies indicated that selection and socialization contributed to homophily, but that selection accounted for considerably more similarity than socialization in domains ranging from minor delinquency to drug use.

Recent studies extended this work in new directions. In studies focusing exclusively on selection effects, there is evidence that early adolescents seek friendships with others who are similar on a wide range of delinquent behaviors. In one example, sixth and eighth graders were found to be similar to prospective or future friends on minor delinquent behavior, alcohol use, and cigarette use (Urberg, Değirmencioğlu, & Tolson, 1998). In another example, data from adolescents ages 13 to 16 provided evidence of strong selection effects on cigarette smoking behavior (de Leeuw, Scholte, Harakeh, van Leeuwe, & Engels, 2008).

Newer studies suggest that socialization plays a greater role than previously thought in the development of friendship similarity. In studies that control for selection and focus exclusively on socialization, there is evidence to indicate that affiliation with friends who engage in delinquent behaviors heightens the risk of subsequent increases in delinquent behaviors (Aseltine, 1995; Vitaro, Brendgen, & Tremblay, 2000). Two studies highlight this process. These studies describe self-reports of classroom disruption among sixth- and seventh-grade friends (Berndt & Keefe, 1995) and self-reports of cigarette and alcohol use among sixth- and eighth-grade friends (Urberg, Değirmencioğlu, & Pilgrim, 1997). After controlling for initial similarity, both studies found evidence that stable friends grew more similar on problem behaviors. Socialization effects are not an artifact of age group increases in similarity that arise as problem behaviors normatively grow across adolescence. Increases in similarity at the population level did not account for socialization between friends. Early adolescents are more likely to become sexually active and to exhibit binge drinking if their stable friends reported the same behaviors (Jaccard, Blanton, & Dodge, 2005).

Few studies have simultaneously measured selection and socialization in the same analyses. Those that have tend to confirm earlier findings about the relative importance of selection. In one such study, Engels, Vitaro, Den Exter Blokland, de Kemp, and Scholte (2004) found strong selection effects, with adolescents' choosing as new friends those who had similar smoking habits. Socialization effects were modest. Other studies have similarly concluded that selection effects are as strong if not stronger than socialization effects, at least when it comes to similarity of alcohol consumption (Bullers, Cooper, & Russell, 2001; Engels et al., 1999).

Findings suggest that similarity plays a key role in the success of a friendship. But can friendships survive in the absence of homophily? One study suggests not. In a sample of 6th, 8th, and 10th graders, adolescents who were not friends at Time 1 but would be friends 1 year later reported significantly similar levels of engaging in minor delinquency, cigarette smoking, and drinking behavior (Urberg et al., 1998). Furthermore, adolescents who remained friends from Time 1 to Time 2 were more similar on cigarette use, participation in adult organized activities, and participation in sports activities than friends who terminated their friendships after Time 1. This study supports the notion that friendships with a lack of similarity are not destined to last.

One important limitation of this work is its focus on friendships in school. Most delinquent youth tend to affiliate with peers who are not classmates, and most deviant activities take place in settings other than school. This limits conclusions we can draw about the degree to which similarity on deviant activities is a prerequisite for friendship success. To address these limitations, we recently examined friendship similarity in a large community-based sample of Swedish adolescents in middle school and in upper school (Hafen, Laursen, Burk, Kerr, & Stattin, in press). We sought to determine whether similarity on drinking behavior, delinquency, achievement motivation, and self-esteem predicts subsequent friendship stability. Estimates of dyadic similarity were adjusted for age group similarity. Stable friendships lasted from 1 academic year to the next. One year before the friendship began, stable friendships were found to be more similar than unstable friendships on delinquency but not on drinking behavior, achievement motivation, and self-esteem. During the first year of the relationship, stable friendships were more similar than unstable friendships on drinking behavior, delinquency, and achievement motivation but not on self-esteem. Stable and unstable friends were also contrasted against randomly paired dyads. Stable friends differed from these random affiliates on every dimension—before and after the start of the friendship. Unstable friends, however, did not differ from random peers in terms of their similarity. The finding suggests that partners who build on initial similarity with subsequent gains in similarity through influence and socialization are those who are most likely to remain friends over time.

Changes in Susceptibility to Peer Influence

Clearly, socialization promotes similarity, which enhances the stability of adolescent friendships. But the precise mechanisms of socialization influence are unclear. We know that friends become more similar over the course of their relationships, but we do not know which partner changes to resemble the other. Who is influencing whom?

Parents and mental health professionals know that peers have the potential to adversely influence peers development. Recent research suggests that susceptibility peaks during the early adolescent years. In separate studies of the development of resistance to peer influence among youth from 10 to 18 years old, results suggested that early adolescents were most prone to be influenced by peers. In the first study, participants were drawn from several large cities on the East and West Coast of the United States, and adolescents were assessed using a measure designed to capture an individual's ability to resist peer influence (Steinberg & Monahan, 2007). The results suggest that there is little growth in resistance to peer influence during the early adolescent years, but that during middle adolescence there is significant growth in this capacity. In a similar study with Dutch adolescents (Sumter, Bokhorst, Steinberg, & Westenberg, 2009), results again suggested that early adolescence is characterized by low levels of resistance to peer influence. As adolescents develop, they undergo increases in this ability. Taken together, these studies suggest that early adolescence is a period of heightened susceptibility to peer influence.

Peer influence is not necessarily negative. Positive effects have been documented (Allen & Antonishak, 2008). Nevertheless, most studies focus on detrimental outcomes, such as heightened susceptibility to problems in domains such as delinquency, drinking behaviors, and drug use (Hawkins, Catalano, & Miller, 1992; Rodgers & Rowe, 1993).

The concept of peer pressure implies that friends entice one another into engaging in risky behaviors by sanctions, such as teasing or threats to social standing. Although this certainly occurs in some instances, alternative explanations have received more support. Primary among these is modeling—the notion that problems are acquired by example—and reinforcement—the notion that peers adopt problem behaviors because it carries rewards in the form of praise, admiration, or status (Urberg, Shyu, & Liang, 1990). A more recent formulation emphasizes peer contagion (Dishion & Dodge, 2005). Peer contagion is mutual influence that occurs between peers undermining healthy development. This peer contagion often takes the form of deviancy training in which peers mutually discuss or model deviant behaviors and then reinforce this behavior through positive expressions such as laughter (Dishion & Tipsord, 2011). This process helps to explain the negative influence that exposure to deviant peers has on an individual.

Peer influence is not uniform. Some groups of individuals are more apt to respond to influence attempts than others. For instance, susceptibility to peer influence is typically higher among boys than among girls (Berndt, 1979; Brown, Clasen, & Eicher, 1986). This is likely due to a delayed development in resistance to peer influence, which is seen in studies of early and middle adolescence (Sumter et al., 2009). A host of characteristics have been identified that might foster heightened susceptibility to peer influence, including popularity (Allen, Porter, McFarland, Marsh, & McElhaney, 2005), authoritarian parenting (Mounts & Steinberg, 1995), and poor relationships with parents (Savin-Williams & Berndt, 1990). Popular adolescents are more likely to adapt behaviors and attitudes that help them receive approval from peers, adolescents from authoritarian households are more likely to be influenced by well adjusted friends, and adolescents who experience poor relationships with parents are more likely to be influenced by poorly adjusted peers. But speculation has outpaced research; there are few empirical studies of individual differences in susceptibility to peer influence.

Two studies suggest that adolescents who have initiated deviant behaviors in the past may be more susceptible to doing so again. In one study, adolescents exhibiting moderate levels of behavioral disturbance were more likely to be influenced by delinquent peers than adolescents exhibiting either high or low levels of the same behavioral disturbance (Vitaro, Tremblay, Kerr, Pagani, & Bukowski, 1997). In another study, early adolescents who reported higher concurrent levels of substance use, sexual behavior, and externalizing behaviors were more susceptible to peer influence in a laboratory task than adolescents with lower concurrent levels of these behaviors (Allen et al., 2005). These findings support the hypothesis that individuals who have succumbed to negative peer pressure in the past are likely to do so again in the future.

Reasoned action theory suggests that higher status individuals are particularly influential because they establish, model, and enforce social norms (Fishbein & Azjen, 2010). Applied to friendships, this suggests that influence within the dyad may be apportioned unevenly. It also implies that the extent to which an individual may be susceptible to influence from a friend may depend on the characteristics of the friend or on how the individual compares to the friend on a given attribute. Recent studies have suggested that socialization effects may be moderated by peer social status, calculated as a social preference score by subtracting negative (liked least) nominations received from classmates from positive (liked most) nominations (Bot, Engels, Knibbe, & Meeus, 2005). The findings indicated that adolescents with high status friends were more likely to adopt their friend's drinking behavior than adolescents with low status friends.

Another study found that friendship influence varies with relative age (Popp, Laursen, Kerr, Stattin, & Burk, 2008). During the establishment of a friendship, older friends influenced the degree to which younger friends drank to intoxication at a subsequent time period, but younger friends did not influence older friends. After the friendship was established, both partners influence each other, but the relatively older friend continues to exert more influence over the relatively younger friends. Unpublished findings from the same data set reveal a similar pattern of results for delinquency: Older friends influenced subsequent delinquency reported by younger friends during the establishment of the friendship; both partners influenced subsequent delinquency after the friendship was established.

New work examines whether friend influence also differs as a function of relative partner acceptance (Laursen, Hafen, Kerr, & Stattin, in press). In this 3-year study of Swedish youth, friend dyads were divided according to acceptance, defined as the relative number of positive (liked most) nominations each partner received. The findings suggest that influence is not reserved for the highest status members of the group. Instead, the effect of status is evident at all levels of peer acceptance, where influence is reserved for the more popular member of the dyad. Specifically, high status friends exert considerable influence over subsequent drinking and delinquency reported by low status friends but only in friendships that lasted at least 1 year. In unstable friendships, neither partner influenced the subsequent behavior of the other.

These findings have important implications for understanding the rise of problem behaviors in early adolescence and the contexts in which susceptibility to friend influence are heightened. They suggest that influence is accorded to the individual with more options for friends. The influence mechanism is stark: Either the less liked member of a dyad conformed to the behavior of the better liked member or the relationship was discontinued. Given that the latter option may be a hardship for the youth with few choices for new friends, it is not surprising that these youth are particularly susceptible to influence from their better accepted friends.

❙ FUTURE DIRECTIONS

Research on peer influence during the transition to adolescence has a long history. Nevertheless, several important questions remain unanswered. The first concerns the role of parents in susceptibility to peer influence. Do parents help youth resist peer pressure? We know that increases in peer influence are not balanced by decreases in parental influence (Chassin, Presson, Sherman, Montello, & McGrew, 1986). In contrast, recent research demonstrates that parent–child influence works in concordance with peer influence, as parent–child relationships set the stage for both the maintenance and management of friendships during the adolescent years (Collins & Laursen, 2004). One promising line of inquiry involves characteristics of parents or parent–child relationships as moderators of deviant peer influence.

Recent work has demonstrated, for example, that binge drinking peer effects may be specific to adolescents who are dissatisfied with their maternal relationships (Jaccard et al., 2005). There is evidence that parents and peers both exert influence over the short term on the choice to abstain from antisocial behaviors, but over the long term, adolescents rely increasingly more on parents and increasingly less on peers (Cook, Buehler, & Henson, 2009). Needed are studies that apply person-oriented perspectives to the problem to complement the rapidly expanding variable oriented literature (Laursen & Hoff, 2006). For instance, we know that friends with divergent perspectives on their relationship have different quality friendships than those who see their relationship similarly (Burk & Laursen, 2005). It is not clear, however, if these discrepancies are related to relative levels of friend influence. Studies of this nature will help to identify constellations of relationship properties that are unique to youth who are especially susceptible or especially resistant to peer influence.

Mediated and moderated models of relationship influence on adolescent outcomes also suggest the importance of contextual factors (e.g., neighborhood distress, socioeconomic status, cultural factors) in predicting adolescent outcomes. In these models, developmental pathways may vary as a function of contextual demands (Collins, Maccoby, Steinberg, Hetherington, & Bornstein, 2000). For example, similar types of interactions may produce different adolescent outcomes, varying as a function of context. A transactional developmental model proposes that reciprocal influences among adolescent dispositions, contextual factors, and life experiences interact in a series of recursive iterations across time to predict the development of antisocial behaviors during adolescence (Dodge & Pettit, 2003). The association of place-based social network quality, or the quality of the social interactions in an adolescent's routine locations, has also been determined to play an important role in adolescent substance use (Mason et al., 2010). Certain social networks are protective while others are destructive. It is important to consider how sociocultural mechanisms interact with ecological factors to produce developmental outcomes during the adolescent years. Finally, research should strive to account for the intersection between dyadic relationships and group relationships. Modeling techniques such as the actor–partner interdependence model (APIM) have advanced current research in the study of dyadic relationships during adolescence (Laursen, Popp, Burk, Kerr, & Stattin, 2007; Popp et al., 2008) and multilevel modeling methods have been used to more effectively examine peer group relations (Kiuru, Burk, Laursen, Salmela-Aro, & Nurmi, 2010), but they are not without their limitations. One limitation of these approaches is that individuals are restricted to unique, nonoverlapping relationship dyads or groups. By definition, these methods exclude some relational information from the analyses. The interactive nature of dyadic relationships, group relationships, and an adolescent's larger social network makes it necessary to account for the effect of these interactions simultaneously. The future of relational research during adolescence may then need to consider these relationship processes in the context of complete data from the social network (Veenstra & Steglich, 2011). Considering the larger social network will allow future research to account for the associations between important relationships at the dyadic and group level while simultaneously accounting for the effects of the adolescent's larger social network. Several studies suggest that in some domains the group exerts more influence over the individual than the dyad, whereas in other domains, the reverse is true (e.g., Ennett et al., 2006; Urberg, 1992). Disentangling group from dyadic effects within particular domains is an important challenge awaiting future scholars.

⚞ SUMMARY

During the transition into adolescence, individuals experience a period of identity confusion and exploration during which friends exert as much if not more influence than parents. At the same time this identity exploration is occurring, early adolescents experience a rise in negative behavior such as drinking, using drugs, and performing other forms of delinquent acts. As a result, initial conclusions suggested that negative peer influence in the form of peer pressure is to blame. A review of the empirical literature suggests that the landscape of early adolescent development is not that simple. The research reviewed in this article suggests that early adolescents are influenced in both positive and negative ways by friends and that certain characteristics and the context of a friendship help explain which adolescents are more susceptible to influence. Continued research on friend relationships across the transition to adolescence is needed to better understand the nature of this influence.

⚞ SUGGESTED READINGS

Chen, X., French, D. C., & Schneider, B. H. (Eds.) (2006). *Peer relationships in cultural context*. New York: Cambridge University Press.

Prinstein, M. J., & Dodge, K. A. (Eds.) (2008). *Understanding peer influence in children and adolescents*. New York: Guilford Press.

Rubin, K. H., Bukowski, W. M., & Laursen, B. (Eds.) (2009). *Handbook of peer interactions, relationships, and groups*. New York: Guilford Press.

⚞ REFERENCES

Allen, J. P., & Antonishak, J. (2008). Adolescent peer influences: Beyond the dark side. In M. J. Prinstein & K. A. Dodge (Eds.), *Understanding peer influence in children and adolescents*. New York: Guilford Press.

Allen, J. P., Hauser, S. T., Eickholt, C., Bell, K., & O'Connor, T. G. (1994). Autonomy relatedness in family interactions as predictors of expressions of negative adolescent affect. *Journal of Research on Adolescence, 4,* 535–552.

Allen, J. P., Hauser, S. T., O'Connor, T. G., & Bell, K. (2002). Prediction of peer-rated adult hostility from autonomy struggles in adolescent-family interactions. *Development and Psychopathology, 14,* 123–137.

Allen, J. P., Porter, M. R., McFarland, F. C., Marsh, P., & McElhaney, K. B. (2005). The two faces of adolescents' success with peers: Adolescent popularity, social adaptation, and deviant behavior. *Child Development, 76,* 747–760.

Aseltine, R. H. (1995). A reconsideration of parental and peer influences on adolescent deviance. *Journal of Health and Social Behavior, 36,* 103–121.

Berndt, T. J. (1979). Developmental changes in conformity to peers and parents. *Developmental Psychology, 15,* 608–616.

Berndt, T. J. (1982). The features and effects of friendship in early adolescence. *Child Development, 53,* 1447–1450.

Berndt, T. (1999). Friends' influence on children's adjustment to school. In W. A. Collins & B. Laursen (Eds.), *Relationships as developmental contexts: The Minnesota Symposia on Child Psychology* (Vol. 30, pp. 85–107). Mahwah, NJ: Lawrence Erlbaum.

Berndt, T. J., & Keefe, K. (1995). Friends' influence on adolescents' adjustment to school. *Child Development, 66,* 1312–1329.

Blos, P. (1979). *The adolescent passage.* New York: International Universities Press.

Bot, S. M., Engels, R. C. M. E., Knibbe, R. A., & Meeus, W. H. J. (2005). Friend's drinking behaviour and adolescent alcohol consumption: The moderating role of friendship characteristics. *Addictive Behaviors, 30,* 929–947.

Bowerman, C. E., & Kinch, J. W. (1959). Changes in family and peer orientation of children between the 4th and 10th grades. *Social Forces, 37,* 206–211.

Brittain, C. (1963). Adolescent choices and parent–peer cross pressures. *American Sociological Review, 28,* 385–391.

Bronfenbrenner, U. (1970). Reaction to social pressure from adults versus peers among Soviet day school and boarding school pupils in the perspective on an American sample. *Journal of Personality and Social Psychology, 15,* 179–189.

Brown, B. B., Clasen, D. R., & Eicher, S. A. (1986). Perceptions of peer pressure, peer conformity dispositions, and self-reported behavior among adolescents. *Developmental Psychology, 22,* 521–530.

Brown, B. B., & Klute, C. (2003). Friendships, cliques, and crowds. In G. R. Adams & M. D. Berzonsky (Eds.), *Blackwell Handbook of Adolescence.* Malden, MA: Blackwell Publishing.

Buhrmester, D. (1992). The developmental courses of sibling and peer relationships. In F. Boer & J. Dunn (Eds.), *Children's sibling relationships: Developmental and clinical issues.* Hillsdale, NJ: Lawrence Erlbaum.

Bullers, S., Cooper, M. L., & Russell, M. (2001). Social network drinking and adult alcohol involvement: A longitudinal exploration of the direction of influence. *Addictive Behaviors, 26,* 181–191.

Burk, W. J., & Laursen, B. (2005). Adolescent perceptions of friendship and their associations with individual adjustment. *International Journal of Behavioral Development, 29,* 156–164.

Chassin, L., Presson, C. C., Sherman, S. J., Montello, D., & McGrew, J. (1986). Changes in peer and parent influence during adolescence: Longitudinal versus cross-sectional perspectives on smoking initiation. *Developmental Psychology, 22,* 327–334.

Cohen, J. M. (1977). Sources of peer group homophily. *Sociology of Education, 50,* 227–241.

Coleman, J. S. (1961). *The adolescent society: The social life of the teenager and its impact on education.* New York: Free Press.

Collins, W. A., & Laursen, B. (2000). Adolescent relationships: The art of fugue. In C. Hendrick & S. S. Hendrick (Eds.), *Close relationships: A sourcebook* (pp. 59–69). Thousand Oaks, CA: Sage.

Collins, W. A., & Laursen, B. (2004). Changing relationships, changing youth: Interpersonal contexts of adolescent development. *Journal of Early Adolescence, 24,* 55–62.

Collins, W. A., Maccoby, E., Steinberg, L., Hetherington, E. M., & Bomstein, M. (2000). Contemporary research on parenting: The case for nature *and* nurture. *American Psychologist, 55,* 218–232.

Cook, E. C., Buehler, C., & Henson, R. (2009). Parents and peers as social influence to deter antisocial behavior. *Journal of Youth and Adolescence, 38,* 1240–1252.

De Leeuw, R. N. H., Scholte, R. H. J., Harakeh, Z., Van Leeuwe, J. F. J., & Engels, R. C. M. E. (2008). Parental smoking-specific communication, adolescents' smoking behavior and friendship selection. *Journal of Youth and Adolescence, 37,* 1229–1241.

Devereux, E. (1970). The role of peer group experience in moral development. In J. Hill (Ed.), *The Minnesota Symposia on Child Psychology: Vol. 4* (pp. 94–140). Minneapolis: University of Minnesota Press.

Dishion, T. J., & Dodge, K. A. (2005). Peer contagion in interventions for children and adolescents: Moving towards an understanding of the ecology and dynamics of change. *Journal of Abnormal Child Psychology: An Official Publication of the International Society for Research in Child and Adolescent Psychopathology, 33,* 395–400.

Dishion, T. J., & Tipsord, J. M. (2011). Peer contagion in child and adolescent social and emotional development. *Annual Review of Psychology, 62,* 189–214.

Dodge, K. A., & Pettit, G. S (2003). A biopsychosocial model of the development of chronic conduct problems in adolescence. *Developmental Psychology, 29,* 349–371.

Engels, R. C. M. E., Knibbe, R. A., De Vries, H., Drop, M. J., & van Breukelen, G. J. P. (1999). Influences of parental and best friends' smoking and drinking on adolescent use: A longitudinal study. *Journal of Applied Social Psychology, 29,* 337–361.

Engels, R. C. M. E., Vitaro, F., Den Exter Blokland, E., de Kemp, R., & Scholte, R. H. J. (2004). Influence and selection processes in friendships and adolescent smoking behaviour: The role of parental smoking. *Journal of Adolescence, 27,* 531–544.

Ennett, S. T., Bauman, K. E., Hussong, A., Faris, R., Foshee, V. A., Cai, L., et al. (2006). The peer context of adolescent substance use: Findings from social network analysis. *Journal of Research on Adolescence, 16,* 159–186.

Erikson, E. H. (1968). *Identity: Youth and crisis.* New York: Norton.

Fishbein, M., & Azjen, I. (2010). *Predicting and changing behavior: The reasoned action approach.* New York: Psychology Press.

Freud, A. (1958). Adolescence. In R. Eissler, A. Freud, H. Hartman, & M. Kris (Eds.), *Psychoanalytic study of the child* (Vol. 13, pp. 255–278). New York: International Universities Press.

Freud, S. (1949). *Group psychology and the analysis of the ego.* New York: Bantam. (Original work published 1921)

Fuligni, A. J., & Eccles, J. S. (1993). Perceived parent–child relationships and early adolescents' orientation toward peers. *Developmental Psychology, 29,* 622–632.

Furman, W. (1989). The development of children's social networks. In D. Belle (Ed.), *Children's social networks and social supports.* New York: Wiley.

Hafen, C. A., Laursen, B., Burk, W. J., Kerr, M., & Stattin, H. (2011). Homophily in stable and unstable adolescent friendships: Similarity breeds constancy. *Personality and Individual Differences, 51*, 607–612.

Hartup, W. W. (1996). The company they keep: Friendships and their developmental significance. *Child Development, 67*, 1–16.

Hawkins, J. D., Catalano, R. F., & Miller, J. Y. (1992). Risk and protective factors for alcohol and other drug problems in adolescence and early adulthood: Implications for substance abuse prevention. *Psychological Bulletin, 112*, 64–105.

Jaccard, J., Blanton, H., & Dodge, K. A. (2005). Peer influences on risk behavior: An analysis of the effects of a close friend. *Developmental Psychology, 41*, 135–147.

Kandel, D. B. (1978). Homophily, selection, and socialization in adolescent friendships. *American Journal of Sociology, 84*, 427–436.

Kandel, D. B., & Lesser, G. S. (1972). *Youth in two worlds.* San Francisco: Jossey-Bass.

Keefe, K. & Berndt, T. J. (1996). Relations of friendship quality to self-esteem in early adolescence. *The Journal of Early Adolescence, 16*, 110–129.

Kiuru, N., Burk, W. J., Laursen, B., Salmela-Aro, K., & Nurmi, J.-E. (2010). Pressure to drink but not to smoke: Disentangling selection and socialization in adolescent peer networks and peer groups. *Journal of Adolescence, 33*, 801–812.

Kobus, K. (2003). Peers and adolescent smoking. *Addiction, 98*, 37–55.

Laursen, B., & Bukowski, W. M. (1997). A developmental guide to the organisation of close relationships. *International Journal of Behavioral Development, 21*, 747–770.

Laursen, B., & Collins, W. A. (2004). Parent–child communication during adolescence. In A. Vangelisti (Ed.), *Handbook of family communication* (pp. 333–348). Mahwah, NJ: Lawrence Erlbaum.

Laursen, B., & Collins, W. A. (2009). Parent–child relationships during adolescence. In R. Lerner & L. Steinberg (Eds.), *Handbook of adolescent psychology: Vol. 2. Contextual influences on adolescent development* (3rd ed., pp. 3–42). New York: Wiley.

Laursen, B., Furman, W., & Mooney, K. S. (2006). Predicting interpersonal competence and self-worth from adolescent relationships and relationship networks: Variable-centered and person-centered perspectives. *Merrill-Palmer Quarterly, 52*, 572–600.

Laursen, B., Hafen, C. A., Kerr, M., & Stattin, H. (in press). Friend influence over adolescent problem behaviors as a function of relative peer acceptance: To be liked is to be emulated. *Journal of Abnormal Psychology.*

Laursen, B., & Hartup, W. W. (2002). The origins of reciprocity and social exchange in friendships. In B. Laursen & W. G. Graziano (Eds.), *Social exchange in development: New directions for child and adolescent development* (No. 95), 27–40.

Laursen, B., & Hoff, E. (2006). Person-centered and variable-centered approaches to longitudinal data. *Merrill-Palmer Quarterly, 52*, 377–389.

Laursen, B., Popp, D., Burk, W., Kerr, M., & Stattin, H. (2007). Incorporating interdependence into developmental research: Examples from the study of homophily and homogeneity. In N. A. Card, T. D. Little, & J. P. Selig (Eds.), *Modeling dyadic and interdependent data in developmental research.* Mahwah, NJ: Lawrence Erlbaum.

Lazarsfeld, P., & Merton, R. K. (1954). Friendship as a social process: A substantive and methodological analysis. In M. Berger, T. Abel, & C. H. Page (Eds.), *Freedom and control in modern society* (pp. 18–66). New York: Van Nostrand.

Mason, M. J., Valente, T. W., Coatsworth, J. D., Mennis, J., Lawrence, F., & Zelenak, P. (2010). Place-based social network quality and correlates of substance use among urban adolescents. *Journal of Adolescence, 33*, 419–427.

Moffitt, T. E. (1993). Adolescence-limited and life-course persistent antisocial behavior: A developmental taxonomy. *Psychological Review, 100,* 674–701.

Mounts, N. S., & Steinberg, L. (1995). An ecological analysis of peer influence on adolescent grade point average and drug use. *Developmental Psychology, 31,* 915–922.

Popp, D., Laursen, W. J., Kerr, M., Stattin, H., & Burk, W. J. (2008). Modeling homophily over time with an actor-partner interdependence model. *Developmental Psychology, 4,* 1028–1039.

Rodgers, J. L., & Rowe, D. C. (1993). Social contagion and adolescent sexual behavior: A developmental EMOSA model. *Psychological Review, 100,* 479–510.

Rusbult, C. E. (1980). Commitment and satisfaction in romantic relationships: A test of the investment model. *Journal of Experimental Social Psychology, 16,* 172–186.

Savin-Williams, R. C., & Berndt, T. J. (1990). Friendship and peer relations. In S. S. Feldman & Elliot G. R. (Eds.), *At the threshold: The developing adolescent.* Cambridge, MA: Harvard University Press.

Selman, R. (1980). *The development of interpersonal understanding.* New York: Academic Press.

Sroufe, L. A., Egeland, B., & Carlson, E. A. (1999). One social world: The integrated development of parent–child and peer relationships. In W. A. Collins & B. Laursen (Eds.), *Relationships as developmental contexts: The Minnesota symposia on child psychology* (Vol. 30, pp. 241–261). Mahwah, NJ: Laurence Erlbaum.

Steinberg, L. (1989). Pubertal maturation and parent–adolescent distance: An evolutionary perspective. In G. R. Adams, R. Montemayor, & T. Gullotta (Eds.), *Advances in adolescent development* (pp. 71–97). Newbury Park, CA: Sage.

Steinberg, L. (2008). A social-neuroscience perspective on adolescent risk-taking. *Developmental Review, 28,* 78–106.

Steinberg, L., & Monahan, K. (2007). Age differences in resistance to peer influence. *Developmental Psychology, 43,* 1531–1543.

Sullivan, H. S. (1953). *The interpersonal theory of psychiatry.* New York: Norton.

Sumter, S. R., Bokhorst, C. L., Steinberg, L., & Westenberg, P. M. (2009). The developmental pattern of resistance to peer influence in adolescence: Will the teenager ever be able to resist? *Journal of Adolescence, 32,* 1009–1021.

Urberg, K. A. (1992). Locus of peer influence: Social crowd and best friend. *Journal of Youth and Adolescence, 21,* 439–450.

Urberg, K. A., Değirmencioğlu, S. M., & Pilgrim, C. (1997). Close friend and group influence on adolescent cigarette smoking and alcohol use. *Developmental Psychology, 33,* 834–844.

Urberg, K. A., Değirmencioğlu, S. M., & Tolson, J. M. (1998). Adolescent friendship selection and termination: The role of similarity. *Journal of Social and Personal Relationships, 15,* 703–710.

Urberg, K. A., Shyu, S., & Liang, J. (1990). Peer influence in adolescent cigarette smoking. *Addictive Behaviors, 15,* 247–255.

Veenstra, R., & Steglich, C. (2011). Actor-based model for network and behavior dynamics: A tool to examine selection and influence processes. In B. Laursen, T. D. Little, & N. A. Card (Eds.), *Handbook of developmental research methods.* New York: Guilford Press.

Vitaro, F., Brendgen, M., & Tremblay, R. E. (2000). The influence of deviant friends on delinquency: Searching for moderator variables. *Journal of Abnormal Child Psychology:*

An official publication of the International Society for Research in Child and Adolescent Psychopathology, 28, 313–325.

Vitaro, F., Tremblay, R. E., Kerr, M., Pagani, L., & Bukowski, W. M. (1997). Disruptiveness, friends' characteristics, and delinquency in early adolescence: A test of two competing models of development. *Child Development, 68,* 676–689.

Youniss, J., & Smollar, J. (1985). *Adolescent relations with mothers, fathers, and friends.* Chicago: University of Chicago Press.

5

Transformations in Friend Relationships Across the Transition Into Adulthood

Chong Man Chow

Holly Roelse

Duane Buhrmester

Marion K. Underwood

Intimate exchanges of self-disclosure and support represent the central features of friendship during adolescence and young adulthood (Berndt, 1982; Buhrmester & Furman, 1987; Fehr, 2004). Through intimate conversations, best friends share their secrets, problems, and feelings, as well as provide each other with validation and emotional support. Indeed, there is considerable research demonstrating that close

---

This is dedicated to Duane Buhrmester, our dearest mentor, colleague, and friend.

friends are among the most common partners adolescents and young adults turn to when distressed (Fraley & Davis, 1997; Trinke & Bartholomew, 1997) and that receiving social support from friends has important implications for multiple domains of individual and social adjustment (Friedlander, Reid, Shupak, & Cribbie, 2007). Given the significance of intimate friendships, it is not surprising that the dynamics and development of friendship have attracted considerable attention from both developmental and social psychologists.

Existing studies on adolescent and young adult friendships are broadly organized by two approaches: (1) *developmental* and (2) *individual differences*. Researchers who adopt a developmental approach are typically interested in *how* and *why* intimate friendship changes over the course of adolescence and young adulthood. This body of literature focuses on developmental changes in perceived closeness and intimacy, self-disclosure, and social support that occur in friendships over time. Developmental research also emphasizes that the developmental changes that occur in friendships over time are partially explained by changing social needs and involvement in different relational roles. Researchers who adopt an individual differences approach, in contrast, are typically interested in the different levels of disclosure and support/validation that occur between friends, as well as the behavioral interdependence of disclosure and support in friendships. Together, the developmental and individual differences approaches offer distinctive, yet complementary perspectives on friendship intimacy in adolescence and young adulthood by addressing the overall changes that typically occur in adolescent friendships as well as the interactions that occur between the specific individuals in a friendship.

The focus of this chapter is on intimate friendships during adolescence and early adulthood (Arnett, 2000; Smetana, Campione-Barr, & Metzger, 2006), where friendship intimacy is broadly defined as subjective perceptions of closeness and intimacy, as well as the intimate behavioral exchanges of self-disclosure and coping/support (Reis & Shaver, 1988). The chapter is divided into three sections. The first section outlines the major theories that pertain to the development of and individual differences in friendship intimacy during adolescence and young adulthood. The second section highlights existing research that resides within the developmental and individual differences frameworks. Last, the third section provides suggestions for future directions in friendship research based on existing approaches.

𝕎 CONCEPTUAL APPROACHEſ TO FRIENDſHIP INTIMACY

Developmental Approaches to Friendship Intimacy

Developmental approaches to friendship intimacy focus on the changes that occur in friendships over the course of adolescence and young adulthood. Developmental theorists are often concerned with how and why friendships change during this important period in life. The most prominent theoretical perspectives on the development of intimate friendships are Harry Stack Sullivan's (1953) interpersonal theory and those of writers who have elaborated on his seminal work (e.g., Buhrmester & Furman, 1986; Youniss, 1980). According to Sullivan, early adolescence is an important turning point when the *need for intimate exchange* begins to emerge. This is a period when adolescents are motivated to establish social relationships beyond family bonds in order to fulfill their intimacy needs. The egalitarian nature of adolescent friendship provides an ideal context for the expression of intimacy, where the mutual disclosure of feelings, secrets, and personal vulnerabilities becomes the prominent dyadic process.

Coupled with increased self-disclosure, friends are also expected to take on a support-giving (or caregiving) role with each other. As Sullivan (1953) contended, rather than the egotistical attitude of "what should I do to get what I want," adolescents begin to develop an attitude of "what should I do to contribute to the happiness or to support the prestige and feeling of worth-whileness of my chum" (p. 245). Friends are asked to be sensitive and compassionate to their friends' needs in times of distress and are even called upon to sacrifice altruistically personal needs for the sake of their friends. Sullivan believed that mature, intimate friendships involve a mutual form of love where partners reciprocally provide support to and seek support from one another.

Although Sullivan's (1953) framework (Buhrmester & Furman, 1986) provides a rich account of the development of same-sex friendships during early and middle adolescence, this perspective does not adequately address the transitional period from late adolescence to early adulthood (i.e., 17 to 25 years). In contrast, contemporary theorists have begun to address the developmental pathways of friendship through early adulthood (e.g., Carbery & Buhrmester, 1998; Johnson & Leslie, 1982), focusing on changes in the features and functions of friendship that parallel changes in social role involvement.

One notable perspective is Carbery and Buhrmester's (1998) *family role involvement* perspective. Unlike Sullivan's (1953) theory that focuses on chronological maturation, this perspective suggests that features and functions of friendships are integrally connected to the broader organization of adolescents' and young adults' networks of close relationships, including those with parents, romantic partners, and even their own children. According to this perspective, the transition from adolescence to young adulthood is a period of considerable change in the organization of social networks, which is reflected by individuals' participation in different relational roles. Thus, the nature and functional significance of friendships is better understood in relation to that of other significant relationships.

Borrowing ideas from sociological work (e.g., Fischer & Oliker, 1983), Carbery and Buhrmester's (1998) perspective considered three major phases of family role involvement that are likely to occur in the transitional period from late adolescence to young adulthood: (1) the single uncommitted phase, (2) the married-without-children phase, and (3) the married-with-young-children phase. They sought to explain how young adults' time and emotional investment in friendships, as well as the functional significance of their friendships, may vary depending on their involvement in other relational roles. According to this perspective, different family role commitments are likely to affect the amount of time and emotional energy available to invest in friendships, which in turn, influence the degree of interdependence and intimacy between friends. In addition, taking on new family roles (e.g., spouse, parent) can create new sources of support, thereby reducing the pragmatic necessity of friends for the fulfillment of intimacy needs (e.g., disclosure, support). Similar arguments have also been offered by Johnson and Leslie's (1982) *Dyadic Withdrawal* hypothesis such that when individuals become more involved in romantic relationships, less emotional and physical investment will be put into friendships. Taken together, these role involvement perspectives on friendships differ from Sullivan's (1953) developmental theory in two major ways. First, these perspectives do not have a rigid definition of development stages. Unlike Sullivan's definition of stages based on age differences, these perspectives emphasize shifts in different relational roles that may occur in the transition to young adulthood but at different times for different individuals.

Second, these perspectives emphasize the transformation of friendships in relation to other social networks, describing the roles of friends in relation to other significant social relationships.

Individual Differences Approaches to Friendship Intimacy

Individual differences approaches focus on describing intimate friendship in terms of perceived intimacy and closeness, as well as the behavioral exchanges of disclosure and support that occur between friends (Chow & Buhrmester, in press; Grabill & Kerns, 2000; Shulman, 1993). Attachment theory serves as the most prominent approach to describing individual differences in friendship intimacy (Furman & Wehner, 1994; Kerns, 1996). Friendship researchers utilize insights from traditional attachment theory (e.g., Bowlby, 1982) in order to describe different orientations toward self-disclosure and support-giving and how these orientations are systematically driven by relational views, or mental representations, that adolescents derive from past and current relationship experiences. For instance, Furman and Wehner (1994) argued that individual differences in self-disclosure and caregiving behaviors (e.g., compassion and responsiveness) that are expressed in friendships can be conceptualized by a classification system similar to the categorical system utilized by attachment researchers. More specifically, they suggest that these behaviors can be conceptualized in a manner similar to the secure, dismissing (avoidant), and preoccupied (ambivalent) attachment classifications of individuals denoted by attachment researchers. Adolescents with a secure orientation of friendships feel comfortable seeking comfort and support from friends in times of distress; as caregivers, they are also expected to be more sensitive and responsive to their friends' needs. Adolescents with a dismissing orientation, in contrast, will be uncomfortable with closeness and reluctant to seek for support from friends in times of distress; as caregivers, they are not sensitive to their friends' feelings and tend to be aloof and cold when their friends are in need of comfort or support. Finally, adolescents with a preoccupied orientation have an intense need for attachment and closeness; as caregivers, they tend to be emotionally overinvolved in their friends' distress.

Some theories further describe friendship intimacy by considering individual differences in self-disclosure and support that occur between friends at the dyadic level. For instance, Shulman (1993) drew on family systems theory and characterized friend dyads based on their closeness and intimacy. This approach views a dyadic friendship as a system that includes two interdependent individuals. Three types of friendship systems have been proposed: (1) *interdependent,* (2) *disengaged,* and (3) *enmeshed.* Interdependent friends are close to each other; however, although intimacy is emphasized in interdependent friendships, it is achieved without costing either friend their autonomy. Disengaged friends emphasize individuality; these friends prefer compulsive self-reliance and are unable to form collaborative and interdependent relationships with each other. Enmeshed friends overly emphasize intimacy and closeness; such tendencies lead friends to insist on each other's availability in all circumstances.

Through the integration of attachment theory and coping/support research (Furman & Wehner, 1994; Kunce & Shaver, 1994; Mikulincer & Florian, 2001), another dyadic model of friendship has emerged. Chow and Buhrmester (in press) recently proposed the Coping-Support Interdependence Model (CSIM) for characterizing how young adult friend dyads jointly respond to stressful events. Much like Furman and Wehner's (1994) conceptualization, the CSIM has identified three prototypic ways of coping that are likely to occur between friends: (1) *distancing,* (2) *adaptive,* and (3) *overwhelmed.* The first prototypic way of coping involves a distancing pattern that focuses on controlling the primary appraisal of a stressor (through selective inattention, minimization, denial, suppression, distraction, and escape) in order to short-circuit the perception of threat. The second prototypic pattern of adaptive coping involves the realistic appraisal of stressors, problem-focused coping efforts, and a willingness to turn to partners for assistance in dealing with the problem and any accompanying emotional distress. The adaptive pattern is characterized by the sharing of emotions and the seeking of comfort, reassurance, sympathy, advice, and tangible assistance. Finally, the overwhelmed pattern involves intense and prolonged emotional experiences in response to stressful situations and a tendency to ruminate and self-blame. In response to a distressed friend, three prototypic ways of offering support are likely to occur: (1) *disengaged,* (2) *responsive,* and (3) *overinvolved.* The disengaged prototypic pattern is characterized by discomfort and disinterest in helping a partner and typically involves withdrawal, limited involvement, and the rejection of neediness. In contrast, the responsive prototypic support-giving pattern is characterized by empathetic sensitivity and by a willingness to provide comfort, reassurance, and affection. Finally, the overinvolved prototypic pattern is characterized by a self-focused need for excessive involvement in the partner's problems and typically involves criticism, controlling behavior, overinvolvement, and enmeshment.

The important distinction between Furman and Wehner's (1994) conceptualization and the CSIM is that the latter emphasizes the behavioral dependency of coping and support-giving between friends (Chow & Buhrmester, in press). This framework further characterizes friend dyads based on joint-coping exchanges. Specifically, the characterization of dyads in terms of their coping/support patterns yields a 3x3 matrix typology of dyadic pairings that capture the important patterns manifest in intimate friendships (see Figure 5.1). The vertical axis of Figure 5.1 describes Friend 1's prototypic coping at the individual level whereas the horizontal axis describes Friend 2's prototypic support at the individual

Figure 5.1 Chow and Buhrmester's Coping-Support Interdependence Model (CSIM)

		Friend 2 Support-Giving		
		Disengaged	**Responsive**	**Overinvolved**
Friend 1 Coping	**Distancing**	*Distancing Disengaged*	Distancing Responsive	Distancing Overinvolved
	Adaptive	Adaptive Disengaged	*Adaptive Responsive*	Adaptive Overinvolved
	Overwhelmed	Overwhelmed Disengaged	Overwhelmed Responsive	*Overwhelmed Overinvolved*

SOURCE: Chow & Buhrmester (in press).

level. The combinations of both friends' behaviors constitute the dyadic interdependent patterns of coping and support-giving, which are useful for characterizing intimate friendships in adolescence and young adulthood. Although nine combinations have been proposed, this model predicts that five major patterns of interaction are particularly prominent and frequent. The first three (shown in bold italics in Figure 5.1) are *corresponding* pairings: (1) *distancing–disengaged*, (2) *adaptive–responsive*, and (3) *overwhelmed–overinvolved*. The distancing–disengaged pairing occurs when one friend copes with stress by utilizing distancing strategies (e.g., denial, compulsive self-reliance) and their friend is rather aloof or uncaring in his/her support-giving. The adaptive–responsive pairing occurs when one friend copes with stress effectively through the use of problem solving strategies or social support-seeking and their friend reacts sensitively and supportively in his/her support-giving. The overwhelmed–overinvolved pairing occurs when one friend is emotionally overwhelmed and unable to cope constructively and their friend is also affected emotionally (empathic distress) and is unable to offer adequate support. Although these descriptions are of coping-support interactions, the dyadic dynamics are similar to Shulman's (1993) conceptualization of the disengaged, interdependent, and enmeshed typologies of friendships.

Chow and Buhrmester (in press) further proposed that there are *noncorresponding* dyadic friendship pairings. Two of these noncorresponding pairings, shown in bold in Figure 5.1, are of particular interest because, at least in theory, they represent incompatible demand–withdraw patterns of coping with stress (Christensen, 1988). The overwhelmed–disengaged pairing occurs when one person responds to stress by becoming overwhelmed (e.g., ruminating, excessive reassurance seeking) while their partner is disengaged in their support-giving (i.e., uncaring, detached); the pressing nature of the overwhelmed person's response may prove especially inconsistent with (or even aversive to) the disengaged partner's desire to avoid involvement, which might exacerbate his/her disengagement. The distancing–overinvolved pairing seems equally problematic. The stressed person's distancing style (e.g., denial, behavioral disengagement from stressors) seems evasive to the overinvolved partner, which may spurn the latter to heighten efforts to get the person to "face up to" the problem and deal with unexpressed feelings.

░ EMPIRICAL STUDIES OF FRIENDSHIP INTIMACY

The Developmental Approach

Research on Change in Friendship in Early and Mid-Adolescence

Most of the existing research on normative change in friendship during adolescence focuses on developmental changes in friendship intimacy—typically assessed with changes in disclosure and support—that occur with age. Research on development in early and mid-adolescent friendships appears to be relatively consistent, suggesting that mutuality, self-disclosure, and intimacy increase markedly during adolescence (e.g., Berndt, 1982; Buhrmester & Furman, 1987; De Goede, Branje, & Meeus, 2009; Furman & Buhrmester, 1992; Poulin & Pedersen, 2007). Not only do adolescents disclose more to and become more dependent on their friends for support but they also become more supportive of their friends. The overall perceived quality of friendship also improves from early to mid-adolescence (Way & Greene, 2006). These findings support Sullivan's (1953) notion that adolescents begin to utilize friendships as a means to fulfill their needs for intimate exchange and that friendships provide an ideal context for the intimate exchange of self-disclosure, support, and validation.

Research on Change in Friendship in Late Adolescence and Young Adulthood

Whereas the research on friendship development during early and mid-adolescence appears to be relatively consistent, the research on friendships in late adolescence and early adulthood seems to be mixed. For instance, some studies indicate that late adolescents and young adults engage in more self-disclosure (Radmacher & Azmitia, 2006), become more supportive (De Goede et al., 2009), and experience more intimacy in their friendships (Reis, Lin, Bennett, & Nezlek, 1993) compared to their younger counterparts. Other studies, however, suggest that intimacy (Updegraff, McHale, & Crouter, 2002), as well as commitment and satisfaction (Oswald & Clark, 2003) in friendships, decreases during the transition to late adolescence. Borrowing ideas from Carbery and Buhrmester (1998), there are two possible reasons for this discrepancy in the literature. First, friendship is typically studied in isolation from other types of relationships (e.g., De Goede et al., 2009; Poulin & Pedersen, 2007; Radmacher & Azmitia, 2006). Thus, findings typically offer limited insight into how young adults' friendships change when additional social roles (e.g., involvement in a romantic relationship) become more prominent. Second, life stages are often loosely defined in terms of chronological maturation rather than by shifts in social role participation, which may not coincide perfectly with age. Thus, these studies may fail to detect the consistent patterns of change in friendships in late adolescence and young adulthood. In other words, what might be perceived as inconsistency in the literature may just be a failure to detect how other relationships (e.g., romantic relationships) differentially affect intimacy, support, disclosure, and satisfaction in friendships depending upon the extent to which an individual is involved in these other relationships.

In order to address the possibility that friendship development is dependent upon individuals' involvement in other relationships, contemporary researchers have argued that a broader social network of relationships should be considered, in order to better understand friendship development in late adolescence and young adulthood (e.g., Carbery and Buhrmester, 1998; Johnson & Leslie, 1982; Laursen & Williams, 1997; Meeus, Branje, van der Valk, & de Wied, 2007). Because both friendships and romantic relationships are generally thought of as the most prominent relationships during late adolescence and young adulthood (e.g., Collins & Madsen, 2006), a handful of studies have addressed the nature of friendships in adolescence in relation to the nature of concurrent romantic relationships (Carbery & Buhrmester, 1998; Connolly & Johnson, 1996; Johnson & Leslie, 1982; Laursen & Williams, 1997; Reis et al., 1993; Seiffge-Krenke, 2003). Overall, these studies suggest that when late adolescents and young adults become involved in romantic roles, the necessity of friends for the fulfillment of intimacy needs is lessened, and romantic partners emerge as the major figure of intimacy. For example, adolescents with romantic partners spend significantly less time with family and friends than adolescents without romantic relationships (Laursen & Williams, 1997). Additionally, upon entering young adulthood, the proportion of individuals who choose romantic partners as their closest friends nearly doubles, whereas the proportion of participants who choose nonromantic friends as their closest friends significantly declines (Pahl & Pevalin, 2005). Late adolescents and young adults also rate intimacy with romantic partners as significantly higher than intimacy with friends (Salas & Ketzenberger, 2004), emotional closeness in romantic relationships as more important than in friendships (Fuhrman, Flannagan, & Matamoros, 2009), and relational commitment as stronger in romantic relationships than friendships (Meeus et al., 2007). Late adolescents and young adults also mention intimacy and support more often as rewards of romantic relationships than of friendships (Hand & Furman, 2009) and report that they are more likely to utilize a romantic partner or parent as an attachment figure (i.e., a person whom they can seek comfort in when distressed, count on always, and see and talk to regularly) than they are a best friend (Trinke & Bartholomew, 1997). In general, these findings suggest that as late adolescents and young adults become involved in romantic relationships, they become less involved and intimate with friends, possibly because they are fulfilling their needs for intimacy with their romantic partners and because they now have less time to spend with friends.

Surprisingly, some studies suggest that romantic involvement in itself has little impact on friendship quality (e.g., Connolly & Johnson, 1996; Reis et al., 1993). For instance, Connolly and Johnson (1996) found that late adolescents do not differ in the amount of social support received from their best friend depending on whether they are romantically involved or not. Similarly, Reis et al. (1993) found that married and single adults do not differ in their perception of friendship intimacy. These inconsistent findings may be attributable to the fact that the classifications of "involved" versus "not involved" may oversimplify the conceptualization of romantic status; instead, degree of involvement in a romantic relationship (e.g., duration, commitment) may be more indicative of changes in friendship intimacy (Johnson & Leslie, 1982). For example, a study examining the association between different levels of romantic involvement (e.g., from casual dating to marriage) and friendship qualities found that when compared to less romantically committed young adults (e.g., casual daters), young adults who were highly committed to their partner (e.g., married) perceived of existing friendships as less important, and disclosed less to friends about personal matters (Johnson & Leslie, 1982). These findings suggest that as adolescents and young adults become more involved and committed in their romantic relationships, they become less intimate in their friendships because their romantic involvement begins to take the place of their friendship involvement.

Studies that focus on the stage of young adulthood in which individuals get married and begin to have children are also supportive of the *family role involvement* perspective (Carbery & Buhrmester, 1998) in that they suggest that as individuals begin to have children with their spouses, friendships decrease in number and importance. For instance, from the period of pregnancy to postpartum, women report a decrease in the number of friends and an increase in the number of family members in their primary social network; they also rate their emotional and instrumental support from friends as lower and their support from family as higher (Gameiro, Boivin, Canavarro, Moura-Ramos, & Soares, 2010). Similarly, new parents report a decline in their number of friends after the birth of a child, and they report spending more time with family members and spouses (Bost, Cox, Burchinal, & Payne, 2002). These findings may be due to a change in relational needs in that new parents may need help and advice raising their child, which may be more available from their spouses, parents, and other family members (Gameiro et al., 2010). Additionally, as individuals have children, they experience a change in the number of roles that they must take on as new parents, which may prohibit them from maintaining friendships to the same extent and number as before they had children (Carbery & Buhrmester, 1998). These findings are supportive of the notion that as young adults enter into marriage and early parenthood, their social networks undergo an important reorganization because their new responsibilities as spouses and parents leave them less time for friendship. Additionally, friendships have less to offer these young adults in terms of support for dealing with emotional stressors that accompany marriage and parenthood or in terms of relational intimacy, which can now be found by confiding in their spouse.

The Individual Differences Approach

Attachment Styles and Individual Differences in Friendship Intimacy

Attachment research typically focuses on adolescents' and young adults' perceptions of their friendship intimacy, which is often defined by levels of disclosure and social support. According to attachment theory, highly anxious individuals are preoccupied by needs for intimacy; such tendencies lead them to perceive friends as less supportive and to perceive their relationships as less intimate (Fraley & Shaver, 2000). Existing studies on adolescents' and young adults' friendships, however, have provided mixed findings for this proposition. Whereas some researchers find that attachment anxiety is associated with perceptions of lower relationship intimacy or closeness (Bauminger, Finzi-Dottan, Chason, & Har-Even, 2008), others have failed to find such an association (Fraley & Davis, 1997; Furman, 2001; You & Malley-Morrison, 2000). One possible explanation for these mixed findings is that individuals who are high in attachment anxiety hold complex views of their partner (Mikulincer, Shaver, Bar-On, & Ein-Dor, 2010). On the one hand, anxiously attached individuals may perceive that their partner hardly meets their intense desires for proximity, and this lack of fulfillment leads them to perceive of their relationship as less close and intimate. On the other hand, anxiously attached individuals also tend to focus on the potential rewards of intimacy and, thus, hold positive and hopeful attitudes toward their relationships. Therefore, these conflicting relational views and attitudes, or *relational ambivalence*, toward partners quite possibly explain the mixed findings in the literature.

In contrast to preoccupied individuals, avoidant individuals tend to feel uneasy with intimate relationships and actively suppress their needs for support or comfort from their attachment figure, placing emphasis on independence and interpersonal distance (Furman & Wehner, 1994). Self-report studies that have examined the association between attachment avoidance and intimacy in friendship suggest that adolescents who possess avoidant internal working models of friendships (as opposed to secure working models of friendship) tend to describe their friendship experiences as less warm and supportive and feel less intimate with their best friend (Bauminger et al., 2008; Furman, 2001; Zimmermann, 2004). Results from a longitudinal study examining adolescents from Grade 6 to Grade 12 further suggest that avoidant attachment and friendship intimacy are reciprocally related (Chow, Roelse, & Buhrmester, 2010). Specifically, avoidant attachment is predictive of subsequent friendship intimacy whereas friendship intimacy is also predictive of the emergence of avoidant attachment.

Characterizing Friend Dyads by Individual Differences in Friendship Intimacy

Contemporary researchers have argued that it is important to consider friendship intimacy at the dyadic level. Emphasizing interdependence in friendships, this line of research focuses on characterizing friendships based on the intimate exchanges that occur within the dyad. For instance, borrowing ideas from family systems theory, Shulman (1993) suggested that there are three major types of adolescent friendships: (1) *disengaged,* (2) *interdependent,* and (3) *enmeshed.* In order to investigate this assumption, studies have observed adolescents' behavioral interactions during a problem solving task, examining the extent to which the proposed dyadic friendship types manifest themselves behaviorally (Shulman, 1993; Shulman, Laursen, Kalman, & Karpovsky, 1997). Partially supporting Shulman's hypothesis, two major types have emerged: (1) interdependent and (2) disengaged. Interdependent dyads are characterized by high levels of coordination and joint effort when engaging in the problem-solving task.

In contrast, disengaged dyads are characterized by high levels of individuality and a lack of coordination, even when they have been explicitly encouraged to consult with each other (Shulman, 1993; Shulman et al., 1997). These two types of friendship can be further distinguishable by their concepts of intimacy. Specifically, when compared to disengaged dyads, interdependent dyads' concepts of intimacy involve a better balance of closeness and individuality (Shulman, 1993), as well as higher levels of emotional closeness and respect (Shulman et al., 1997). Overall, these observational studies suggest that interdependent friendships that are characterized by joint effort and closeness as well as disengaged friendships that are characterized by individuality and a lack of coordination can both be found in adolescence.

Although the enmeshed friendship type did not emerge in Shulman's studies (1993; Shulman et. al., 1997), another line of friendship research has provided tentative support for this typology. Specifically, Rose (2002) observed a tendency for co-rumination between some friends. This co-rumination can be conceptualized as a dyadic phenomenon in which friends extensively discuss and revisit their problems, with a focus on their negative feelings. Co-rumination appears to resemble the features of enmeshed friendship described by Shulman's (1993) theory. Because Shulman (1993; Shulman et al., 1997) assessed friendship typologies with a problem-solving task, it is possible that the nature of this task may not have been "emotionally driven" enough to capture enmeshed friendship, which involves excessive levels of emotional intimacy.

Attachment researchers also examined different pairings of friendships based on their attachment styles and how these different pairings are reflective of friendship intimacy. For instance, using a categorical approach for measuring attachment styles, Weimer, Kerns, and Oldenburg (2004) identified three types of friendship pairings based on the attachment styles of the individuals in a friendship: (1) secure–secure, (2) secure–insecure, and (3) insecure–insecure. They examined the extent to which these different pairings differed in terms of their closeness and their intimate behavioral exchanges. They found that the three pairings did not differ in terms of their self-reported friendship closeness. However, when compared to dyads in which one or both of the friends were insecure, the secure–secure dyads tended to display more behaviors that are likely to promote a sense of connection within the friendship, such as higher levels of intimate disclosure and supportiveness, as well as lower levels of superficial disclosure when engaging in discussions. A study assessing attachment styles through the use of two attachment dimensions (avoidance and anxiety) found similar results (Grabill & Kerns, 2000). Specifically, dyads in which both friends were high in attachment avoidance reported lower self-disclosure in their friendship; individuals within this type of dyad reported feeling as though they were not validated or supported by their friend. Contrary, dyads in which both friends were high in attachment anxiety reported greater self-disclosure than dyads not as high in attachment anxiety. Taken together, this body of literature suggests that the different pairings of attachment styles present in friend dyads may have important effects on the intimacy and closeness in these friendships.

A separate line of research also discusses the dynamics of intimate behavioral exchanges between friends, focusing on the interdependence of self-disclosure as well as support-seeking and support-giving in close friendships. For instance, Chow and Buhrmester (in press) examined the interdependence of coping and support among young adult friends. This study found a strong association between the extent to which one friend sought emotional/instrumental support and the extent to which the other friend responded with sensitive support. Consistent with Reis and Shaver's (1988) intimacy model, this study suggests that individuals who routinely experience sensitive and responsive support from friends are more confident about their friends' availability and are, therefore, more comfortable relying on them for instrumental and emotional support.

Interestingly, Chow and Buhrmester (in press) also found a positive association between individuals' distancing coping and their friends' disengaged support-giving. These findings suggest that the avoidance of support-givers in times of distress is an emotion regulation strategy (i.e., compulsive self-reliance and suppression of attachment needs) used to cope with an uncaring/unsupportive friend. It is equally possible, however, that when an individual copes with stress by denying or dismissing the importance of the stressor, his/her avoidance puts little direct impetus on the partner to provide a supportive response. That is, if the friend does not want to acknowledge that he/she has a problem, the partner is, to an extent, implicitly asked not to offer support. Thus, it is equally possible that a person's distancing coping may cause their friend to react with disengagement or that a friend's disengaged support-giving may cause an individual to utilize avoidance as a coping strategy.

Chow and Buhrmester's (in press) study also provides insight into another type of coping-support dynamic: the overwhelmed–overinvolved pairing. This pattern closely resembles the enmeshed pattern of friendship (Shulman, 1993) as well as the co-rumination dynamics Rose (2002) observed in friendships (especially those of females). Interestingly, Chow and Buhrmester (in press) found that overwhelmed coping was associated with disengaged support-giving behaviors. One possible interpretation of this finding involves the evolving process of coping and support-giving between friends. That is, when faced with a friend who is overwhelmed and not readily consoled, a friend may sequentially engage in more than one way of providing support. For instance, the friend may begin by offering support, but once they realize that the friend is unreceptive to the support, they may disengage.

Empirical studies that investigate individual differences in friendship intimacy using a dyadic approach suggest it is important to consider the characteristics and roles of both individuals involved in the friendship. For instance, although traditional research has consistently found an individual-level link between attachment security and friendship intimacy (Furman, 2001), more recent research also suggests that it is crucial to consider how different pairings of attachment security between friends may have an impact on perceptions of intimacy within the dyad (Weimer et al., 2004). Furthermore, research also suggests that individual differences in the expression of intimate behaviors (e.g., disclosure, support) are heavily dependent on another's friend's characteristics (Chow & Buhrmester, in press), arguing that friendship intimacy is established by the intimate behavioral exchanges between two friends.

〰 FUTURE DIRECTIONS

Research from the developmental and individual differences perspectives of friendship development has revealed important features of friend relations in adolescence and young adulthood, but to understand real transformations in this developmental period, more work is needed on the time course of friendships, both chronologically and developmentally. Illuminating these transformations will require an integration of the developmental and individual differences perspectives.

Understanding the course that friendships take in real, chronological time requires knowledge of where, when, and how individuals find friends. As emerging adults move beyond compulsory schooling and are no longer forced into daily interaction with large numbers of peers, how do young adults initiate friendships? Where do they find friends, and what strategies do they use to initiate contact with new potential friends? In addition to these questions, future research should examine the different types of social overtures that might be effective in initiating and strengthening friendships. Similarly, research should consider the different interactional processes that contribute to the strength and satisfaction of dyadic friendships, as well as the strategies that young adults use to offer support and companionship to friends as the commitments to marriage and parenthood make daily contact with friends less likely. Another interesting perspective on friendships that has not been extensively considered is the manner in which adolescent and young adult friendships come to an end. Do serious conflicts erupt that cause friends to "break up" as at earlier ages, or do problematic friendships in young adulthood slowly degrade and eventually break apart with time?

Future work should also examine transformations in relationship processes that occur developmentally. As individuals mature into young adulthood, are they more likely to have the capacity for interdependent friendships as opposed to enmeshed or disengaged relationships? Do young adults learn from their experiences in friend relationships and become more likely to engage in solve and solace type interactions when in distress, as opposed to dismiss or escape interactions? In light of Chow and Buhrmester's (in press) model, as a result of maturation, increased skill in emotion regulation, and experience in relationships, it seems quite plausible that young adults would become more likely to engage in adaptive coping with friends as they mature, as opposed to distancing or overwhelmed coping.

We concur with Carbery and Buhrmester (1998) that studying age differences in young adult friendships may be far less revealing than studying friendships in relation to other close relationships that accompany the major transition points in early adulthood, such as marriage and becoming a parent. Adults' friendships likely continue to evolve as the transitions continue. For individuals who become parents, children's changing social ecologies likely influence parents' relationships, as children begin school and bring their parents into contact with new networks, as older children become intensely involved in extracurricular activities, and as older adolescent children move away from home and parents find renewed energy and more time for friendships. Additionally, almost all adults experience transformations in relationships related to employment; new social challenges arise from moving to a new community to start a new job, being promoted and being asked to supervise peers, and losing a job.

Developmental psychopathologists studying risk and resilience have argued that for children resilience may be fostered by the "ordinary" magic of adaptive relationships (Masten, 2001). Friendships for young adults may be part of the ordinary magic that allows some to thrive in the face of adversity; these relationships may also be a source of pleasurable companionship and support. However, it is important to remember that the ordinary magic of friend relationships is not available to everyone. Both the developmental and individual differences theories seek to account for characteristics of existing friendships. Additional theoretical and empirical work will be important for understanding how exactly adolescents and young adults form and strengthen friendships, how friendships sometimes dissolve, and how young adults create the ordinary magic of friend relationships through the major transitions of adulthood.

SUGGESTED READINGS

Buhrmester, D., & Furman, W. (1986). The changing functions of children's friendships: A neo-Sullivanian perspective. In V. Derlega & B. Winstead (Eds.), *Friendships and social interaction* (pp. 41–62). New York: Springer.

Carbery, J., & Buhrmester, D. (1998). Friendship and need fulfillment during three phases of young adulthood. *Journal of Social and Personal Relationships, 15*(3), 393–409.

Chow, C. M., & Buhrmester, D. (in press). Interdependent patterns of coping and support among close friends. *Journal of Social and Personal Relationships.*

Furman, W., & Wehner, E. A. (1994). Romantic views: Toward a theory of adolescent romantic relationships. In R. Montemayor, G. R. Adams, & G. P. Gullota (Eds.), *Advances in adolescent development: Volume 6. Relationships during adolescence* (pp. 168–195). Thousand Oaks, CA: Sage.

Reis, H., Lin, Y., Bennett, M., & Nezlek, J. (1993). Change and consistency in social participation during early adulthood. *Developmental Psychology, 29*(4), 633–645.

REFERENCES

Arnett, J. (2000). Emerging adulthood: A theory of development from the late teens through the twenties. *American Psychologist, 55*(5), 469–480.

Bauminger, N., Finzi-Dottan, R., Chason, S., & Har-Even, D. (2008). Intimacy in adolescent friendship: The roles of attachment, coherence, and self-disclosure. *Journal of Social & Personal Relationships, 25*(3), 409–428.

Berndt, T. (1982). The features and effects of friendship in early adolescence. *Child Development, 53*(6), 1447.

Bost, K., Cox, M., Burchinal, M., & Payne, C. (2002). Structural and supportive changes in couples' family and friendship networks across the transition to parenthood. *Journal of Marriage & Family, 64*(2), 517–531.

Bowlby, J. (1982). *Attchment and loss: Vol 1. Attachment.* New York: Basic Books.

Buhrmester, D., & Furman, W. (1986). The changing functions of children's friendships: A neo-Sullivanian perspective. In V. Derlega & B. Winstead (Eds.), *Friendships and social interaction* (pp. 41–62). New York: Springer.

Buhrmester, D., & Furman, W. (1987). The development of companionship and intimacy. *Child Development, 58*(4), 1101–1113.

Carbery, J., & Buhrmester, D. (1998). Friendship and need fulfillment during three phases of young adulthood. *Journal of Social and Personal Relationships, 15*(3), 393–409.

Chow, C. M., & Buhrmester, D. (in press). Interdependent patterns of coping and support among close friends. *Journal of Social and Personal Relationships.*

Chow, C. M., Roelse, H. B., & Buhrmester, D. (2010). *Reciprocal associations between attachment security and friendship intimacy and exclusion during adolescence.* Manuscript submitted for publication.

Christensen, A. (1988). Dysfunctional interaction patterns in couples. In P. Noller & M. A. Fitzpatrick (Eds.), *Perspectives on marital interaction* (pp. 31–52). Clevedon, Avon, UK: Multilingual Matters.

Collins, W. A., & Madsen, S. D. (2006). Personal relationships in adolescence and early adulthood. In D. Perlman & A. Vangelisti (Eds.), *Handbook of personal relationships* (pp. 191–209). New York: Cambridge University Press.

Connolly, J., & Johnson, A. (1996). Adolescents' romantic relationships and the structure and quality of their close interpersonal ties. *Personal Relationships, 3*(2), 185–195.

De Goede, I., Branje, S., & Meeus, W. (2009). Developmental changes and gender differences in adolescents' perceptions of friendships. *Journal of Adolescence, 32*(5), 1105–1123.

Fehr, B. (2004). Intimacy expectations in same-sex friendships: A prototype interaction-pattern model. *Journal of Personality and Social Psychology, 86*(2), 265–284.

Fischer, C. S., & Oliker, S. J. (1983). A research note on friendship, gender, and the life cycle. *Social Forces, 62*, 124–133.

Fraley, R., & Davis, K. (1997). Attachment formation and transfer in young adults' close friendships and romantic relationships. *Personal Relationships, 4*, 131–144.

Fraley, R., & Shaver, P. (2000). Adult romantic attachment: Theoretical developments, emerging controversies, and unanswered questions. *Review of General Psychology, 4*, 132–154.

Friedlander, L., Reid, G., Shupak, N., & Cribbie, R. (2007). Social support, self-esteem, and stressor as predictors of adjustment to university among first-year undergraduates. *Journal of College Student Development, 48*(3), 259–274.

Fuhrman, R., Flannagan, D., & Matamoros, M. (2009). Behavior expectations in cross-sex friendships, same-sex friendships, and romantic relationships. *Personal Relationships, 16*(4), 575–596.

Furman, W. (2001). Working models of friendships. *Journal of Social & Personal Relationships, 18*(5), 583.

Furman, W., & Buhrmester, D. (1992). Age and sex differences in perceptions of networks of personal relationships. *Child Development, 63*(1), 103–115.

Furman, W., & Wehner, E. A. (1994). Romantic views: Toward a theory of adolescent romantic relationships. In R. Montemayor, G. R. Adams, & G. P. Gullota (Eds.), *Advances in adolescent development: Volume 6. Relationships during adolescence* (pp. 168–195). Thousand Oaks, CA: Sage.

Gameiro, S., Boivin, J., Canavarro, M., Moura-Ramos, M., & Soares, I. (2010). Social nesting: Changes in social network and support across the transition to parenthood in couples that conceived spontaneously or through assisted reproductive technologies. *Journal of Family Psychology, 24*(2), 175–187.

Grabill, C., & Kerns, K. (2000). Attachment style and intimacy in friendship. *Personal Relationships, 7*(4), 363–378.

Hand, L. S., & Furman, W. (2009). Rewards and costs in adolescent other-sex friendships: Comparisons to same-sex friendships and romantic relationships. *Social Development, 18*(2), 270–287.

Johnson, M., & Leslie, L. (1982). Couple involvement and network structure: A test of the dyadic withdrawal hypothesis. *Social Psychology Quarterly, 45*(1), 34–43.

Kerns, K. A. (1996). Individual differences in friendship quality: Links to child–mother attachment. In W. M. Bukowski, A. F. Newcomb, & W. W. Hartup (Eds.), *The company they keep: Friendship in childhood and adolescence* (pp. 137–157). New York: Cambridge University Press.

Kunce, L. J. & Shaver, P. R. (1994). An attachment-theoretical approach to caregiving in romantic relationships. In K. Bartholomew & D. Perlman (Eds.), *Advances in personal relationships: Vol 5. Attachment processes in adulthood* (pp. 205–237). London, UK: Jessica Kingsley Publishers.

Laursen, B., & Williams, V. A. (1997). Perceptions of interdependence and closeness in family and peer relationships among adolescents with and without romantic partners. In S. Shulman & W. A. Collins (Eds.), *Romantic relationships in adolescence: Developmental perspectives* (pp. 3–20). San Francisco: Jossey-Bass.

Masten, A. (2001). Ordinary magic: Resilience processes in development. *American Psychologist, 56*, 227–238.

Meeus, W., Branje, S., van der Valk, I., & de Wied, M. (2007). Relationships with intimate partner, best friend, and parents in adolescence and early adulthood: A study of the saliency of the intimate partnership. *International Journal of Behavioral Development, 31*(6), 569–580.

Mikulincer, M., & Florian, V. (2001). Attachment style and affect regulation: Implications for coping with stressor and mental health. In G. J. O. Fletcher & M. S. Clark (Eds.), *Blackwell handbook of social psychology: Interpersonal processes* (pp. 537–557). Malden, MA: Blackwell Publishing.

Mikulincer, M., Shaver, P., Bar-On, N., & Ein-Dor, T. (2010). The pushes and pulls of close relationships: Attachment insecurities and relational ambivalence. *Journal of Personality and Social Psychology, 98*, 450–468.

Oswald, D., & Clark, E. (2003). Best friends forever?: High school best friendships and the transition to college. *Personal Relationships, 10*(2), 187–196.

Pahl, R., & Pevalin, D. (2005). Between family and friends: A longitudinal study of friendship choice. *British Journal of Sociology, 56*(3), 433–450.

Poulin, F., & Pedersen, S. (2007). Developmental changes in gender composition of friendship networks in adolescent girls and boys. *Developmental Psychology, 43*(6), 1484–1496.

Radmacher, K., & Azmitia, M. (2006). Are there gendered pathways to intimacy in early adolescents' and emerging adults' friendships? *Journal of Adolescent Research, 21*(4), 415–448.

Reis, H., Lin, Y., Bennett, M., & Nezlek, J. (1993). Change and consistency in social participation during early adulthood. *Developmental Psychology, 29*(4), 633–645.

Reis, H., & Shaver, P. R. (1988). Intimacy as an interpersonal process. In S. Duck (Ed.), *Handbook of research in personal relationships* (pp. 367–389). London, UK: Wiley.

Rose, A. J. (2002). Co-rumination in the friendships of girls and boys. *Child Development, 73*, 1830–1843.

Salas, D., & Ketzenberger, K. (2004). Associations of sex and type of relationship on intimacy. *Psychological Reports, 94*(3), 1322–1324.

Seiffge-Krenke, I. (2003). Testing theories of romantic development from adolescence to young adulthood: Evidence of a developmental sequence. *International Journal of Behavioral Development, 27*, 519–531.

Shulman, S. (1993). Close friendships in early and middle adolescence: Typology and friendship reasoning. *Close friendships in adolescence* (pp. 55–71). San Francisco: Jossey-Bass.

Shulman, S., Laursen, B., Kalman, Z., & Karpovsky, S. (1997). Adolescent intimacy revisited. *Journal of Youth and Adolescence, 26*(5), 597–617.

Smetana, J. G., Campione-Barr, N., & Metzger, A. (2006). Adolescent development in interpersonal and societal contexts. In *Annual Review of Psychology* (Vol. 57, pp. 255–284). Palo Alto, CA: Annual Review Press.

Sullivan, H. (1953). *The interpersonal theory of psychiatry.* New York: Norton.

Trinke, S., & Bartholomew, K. (1997). Hierarchies of attachment relationships in young adulthood. *Journal of Social and Personal Relationships, 14*(5), 603–625.

Updegraff, K., McHale, S., & Crouter, A. (2002). Adolescents' sibling relationship and friendship experiences: Developmental patterns and relationship linkages. *Social Development, 11*(2), 182–204.

Way, N., & Greene, M. (2006). Trajectories of perceived friendship quality during adolescence: The patterns and contextual predictors. *Journal of Research on Adolescence, 16*(2), 293–320.

Weimer, B., Kerns, K., & Oldenburg, C. (2004). Adolescents' interactions with a best friend: Associations with attachment style. *Journal of Experimental Child Psychology, 88*(1), 102–120.

You, H., & Malley-Morrison, K. (2000). Young adult attachment styles and intimate relationships with close friends: A cross-cultural study of Koreans and Caucasian Americans. *Journal of Cross-Cultural Psychology, 31*(4), 528–534.

Youniss, J. (1980). *Parents and peers in social development.* Chicago: University of Chicago Press.

Zimmermann, P. (2004). Attachment representations and characteristics of friendship relations during adolescence. *Journal of Experimental Child Psychology, 88*(1), 83.

6

Adolescent Friendship Bonds in Cultures of Connectedness

Barry H. Schneider

Matthew D. Lee

Ibis Alvarez-Valdivia

☰ CONCEPTUAL OVERVIEW

The virtues of friendship have been extolled since ancient times in philosophic writings within the Judeo-Christian belief system that underlies the majority cultures of North America and Western Europe (Cairn, 2009; Entralgo, 1985). From Aristotle and Cicero through St. Augustine to C. S. Lewis, these writings contain reflections about why individuals might choose to enter into the voluntary dyadic relationship of friendship, about what their obligations are to their friends (as opposed to obligations to any fellow human), and about what benefits friends derive from the friendship bond. The development function of adolescent friendship as preparation for intimate relationships during the adult years

Acknowledgments: The authors would like to thank Dr. Chiaki Konishi for providing valuable insight, comments, and suggestions. The authors would also like to thank Masako Tsusaka for her indispensable assistance and tireless support.

was articulated most clearly by the American psychiatrist Harry Stack Sullivan (1953). His views were certainly shaped by his life experiences growing up in small-town upstate New York, then moving to New York City and serving in the U.S. military (Perry, 1982). In this chapter, we consider the nature and functions of adolescent friendship in cultures very different from the majority culture of North America and Western Europe.

Emphasis on interdependence, social harmony, and strong in-group identification is what distinguishes collectivistic from individualistic nations (Markus & Kitayama, 1991). Accordingly, adapting to diverse social settings, displaying self-restraint, and empathizing with others are social skills that are valued in collectivistic, interdependent cultures. In contrast, the predominant cultures of *individualistic* nations, such as those of North America and Western Europe, emphasize the development of an independent and unique self; self-assertion and autonomy are valued. These cultural differences, which affect the cognitions and motivations of the individual participant in the society, are believed to affect a variety of developmental and social outcomes, including the formation and maintenance of peer and friend relations (Markus & Kitayama, 1991; Rothbaum, Pott, Azuma, Miyake, & Weisz, 2000; Takahashi, Ohara, Antonucci, & Akiyama, 2002). Individualism/collectivism has emerged as the most important distinction among the world's cultures (Oyserman, Coon, & Kemmelmeier, 2002). Many authorities maintain that friendship bonds in collectivistic cultures might be particularly close, reflecting the general interdependence of members of collectivistic societies, although individuals might chose to develop close friendships with a relatively small number of peers (Triandis, Bontempo, Villareal, Asai, & Lucca, 1988). Empirical evidence for this is limited and inconsistent, with some data indicating exactly the opposite, such as the findings by French, Lee and Pidada (2006) regarding young people in collectivistic Indonesia.

Features of cultures other than individualism/collectivism are often ignored, including several features that may be reflected in adolescent friendship. One such feature is the parenting provided to young people in different cultures. As will be detailed later in this chapter, *filial piety*, the respect and obligation owed by young people to their parents, is a fundamental precept of East Asian culture. This may extend to school or religious authorities in societies characterized by high *power distance*, which are characterized by reverence for people in authority (Hofstede, 2001). In such cultures, parents and/or teachers may have extensive control over adolescents' choices of friends and over the activities that they may share with their friends. In addition to emphasis on filial piety, the religious or philosophical beliefs of different cultures may prescribe expectations for relationships with others. Only occasionally do these teachings apply specifically to friendship.

The organization of school and work life in different cultures may affect the opportunities available adolescents to initiate and maintain relationships with each other. In some countries, school is an important and often stressful feature of adolescents' lives. Teachers may share with parents some degree of authority over adolescents' personal development and their exchanges with friends. School life may provide extensive opportunities for meeting prospective friends. In other countries, as in much of Western Europe, secondary school is more of a businesslike academic enterprise (Hirsch, 1997), which is not to say that school does not remain an important place for potential friends to meet. Secondary schools in many European cities are often not in session for a full day, with most of the schooltime devoted to highly structured academic lessons. As well, the schools do not provide the array of extracurricular activities that may catalyze friendship as do North American schools. Furthermore, in many cultures other than those of North America, Europe, and the Far East, some or most adolescents do not have the privilege of attending school. At work, their social contact is not usually concentrated on young people their own age.

Another feature of culture that may affect friendship relations is *masculinity/femininity* (Hofstede, 2001). This term is somewhat confusing because it does not refer primarily to sexuality or self-presentation but to the degree to which gender roles are distinct. Importantly, a culture is considered "feminine" if there is extensive concern with interpersonal relationships, intimacy, and expression of feelings.

Given the many ways in which the core values of a society may be reflected in the relationships between its adolescents and their friends, it is not surprising that the basic understanding of the concept of "friend" may not be the same across cultures. This issue is examined in depth by Krappman (1996).

In this chapter, we do not present a compendium of the research in which the friendships of young people of different cultures are compared. We have elected to provide a more comprehensive description of the societal context surrounding the friendships of adolescents in two societies that, in our opinion, provide revealing examples of the processes already mentioned, namely those of Japan and Cuba. We make reference to both literature and empirical research from both countries; much less empirical research has been conducted in Cuba than in Japan.

∭ YŪJŌ: FRIENDſHIP AMONG JAPANEſE ADOLEſCENTſ

At the end of the 19th century, scholar and Japanophile Lafcadio Hearn (or Koizumi Yakumo as he is known in Japan) documented the modernization of Japan. He described a nation that benefited from many of the economic and technological advances enjoyed in the West but preserved a distinct social and cultural identity that he dubbed *emotional life* (Hearn, 1972). More than a century later, Japan continues to offer intriguing prospects for developmental research because of its highly educated population living within an affluent, open, and democratic society that continues to remain culturally, philosophically, and demographically distinct from the West.

Japan, along with neighboring Asian countries, is frequently cited as a prototypical example of collectivistic culture (Markus & Kitayama, 1991). However, because the findings of research frequently emphasize differences between cultures, similarities between Japan and more individualistic nations may be overlooked. In a meta-analysis of individualism/collectivism studies, Oyserman et al. (2002) found there to be fewer differences between Japan and North America than between North America and other Asian nations, such as China. Cross-national findings of peer relations researchers provide a useful example: Park, Killen, Crystal and Watanabe (2003) found that the response patterns of Japanese youth more closely resembled those of U.S. youth than those of Korean youth when deciding to exclude an atypical peer. Contradictory results such as these have caused some theorists to suggest that each culture, regardless of where it might rest on the individualism/collectivism spectrum, may have context-specific situations that elicit individualistic or collectivistic responses (Crystal, 2000; Triandis, 1989). For instance, Kitayama and Uchida (2003) suggested that North Americans and Asians do not differ in overall individualistic and collectivistic behaviors but rather in the *variety* and *number of situations* that call for individualist or collectivist behavior. Thus, given the proper social conditions, North Americans can be found to engage in typically collectivistic behavior, such as calling on others for support or adopting a self-critical attitude. As well, Japanese can be found to exhibit self-reliance and to express positive self-evaluations in certain situations (Crystal, Kakinuma, DeBell, Azuma, & Miyashita, 2008; Kitayama & Uchida, 2003). Indeed, the results of the meta-analysis conducted by Oyserman et al. (2002) revealed that when reliable scales are used North Americans actually report more collectivistic behavior than do Japanese! These authors posit that when measures of collectivism include concepts such as in-group belonging and help seeking, the differences between North American and traditionally collectivistic countries such as Japan are diminished.

Adolescence in Japan

Japanese and Western societies share many concepts regarding adolescence. Several ethnographers (LeTendre, 2000; White, 1993) and social theorists (Rothbaum et al., 2000; Salamon, 1977) suggested that the development of self-control and volition as well as positive peer relations are important developmental goals during adolescence in both societies. Consistent with Western theorists such as Sullivan (1953), the Japanese consider relationships during adolescence as a valuable stage for learning the skills required to successfully form and maintain adult relationships (White, 1993). Nonetheless, there are some notable differences. For instance, the development of a unique personal identity that is separate from that of parents and peers is considered to be a sign of maturity by many Western parents, teachers, and developmental theorists (Erikson, 1968). In Japan, the goal of self-fulfillment is not seen as incongruent with the goal of integrating into the larger society (White & LeVine, 1986). As will be explored in further detail later, adolescence is a critical period during which Japanese young people are expected to learn to balance their personal and social selves (LeTendre, 2000; White, 1993). Among collectivist societies, the ability to control inner feelings in order to adapt to a variety of social situations and maintain social cohesion is an important marker of maturity, whereas excessive self-assurance attests to immaturity (Markus & Kitayama, 1991).

Japanese Values Regarding Close Relationships

In their germinal review of the literature on the development of close relationships in Japan and the United States, Rothbaum et al. (2000) identified two different foci that characterize Japan and the United States. The Japanese focus, on empathy and propriety (i.e., respect for rules and compliance with social conventions), is labeled *accommodation*. The U.S. focus, comprised of autonomy, expressiveness, and exploration, is labeled *individuation*. These culturally distinct ways of looking at interpersonal interaction give rise to two distinct developmental pathways for close relationships. *Symbiotic harmony* is the dominant path in Japan and is characterized by the "continual pull toward adapting the self to fit the needs of others" resulting in social relationships that are stable and continuous (Rothbaum et al., 2000, p. 1123). *Generative tension* is the path typical to U.S. relationships and is characterized by the tension that results within the family as adolescents, eager to assert their individuality and autonomy, transfer their allegiances from parents to peers. In Japan, it is expected that adolescents will continue to maintain the strong bonds developed with parents while fostering new relationships with peers. This is typified by the relative lack of conflict between adolescents and their parents and by satisfaction with family and friendship relations.

There are both ethnographic and empirical data that support the Japanese elements of this theory. Based on interviews with teenagers, parents, teachers, and psychologists in Japan over the course of 3 years, White (1993) reported that, in comparison to U.S. teens, Japanese teens show less opposition toward adults and report more feelings of respect and gratitude toward their parents. This may be because in Japan traditional beliefs regarding filial piety result in Japanese adolescents continuing to hold their parents in high regard and because Japanese parents actively encourage strong relationships with friends (Salamon, 1977; White, 1993). Adolescents who maintain a positive understanding with parents report greater intimacy with friends (Okamoto & Uechi, 1999). Lansford (2004) examined the parallels between friendship quality (e.g., positive affect, negative affect, and instrumental aid) and family-relationship quality among individuals aged 13 to 93 in Japan and the United States. Associations between friendship and family relationship quality were more pervasive and stronger in the Japanese sample than the U.S. sample, suggesting that the importance assigned to family harmony in Japan does not come at all at the expense of rich, rewarding friendships with peers. In fact, Rothbaum et al. (2000) posited that in Japan the constancy between family and friend expectations make it easier for adolescents to transition between both groups.

Concepts of Friendship in Japan

Melos, Run! by Ozamu Dazai (1989) is a classic Japanese retelling of a legend that illustrates the virtues of fidelity and personal sacrifice associated with a friendship of high quality. First published in the 1940s, it is still widely read in junior high schools in Japan (C. Konishi, personal communication, November 17, 2010). The plot concerns the plight of Melos, who must make an arduous 10-league journey on foot in 1 day in order to save the life of his friend, Selinunteus. Over the course of his voyage, Melos must overcome obstacles both physical and mental, which threaten to overwhelm him. Yet, driven on by devotion for his friend and the trust that they share, Melos perseveres.

In addition to fidelity and personal sacrifice, Japanese research has revealed other core features of friendship such as intimacy, desire for exclusivity, support, mutual understanding, and security (Enomoto, 1999; Ochiai & Satoh, 1996; Yoshioka, 2001). These are congruent with Western notions of friendship. Japanese also appear to have some expectations of friends that are different from those traditionally found in the Western societies. For instance, conformity and equitable treatment of others have emerged as primary elements of friendship in Japan (Killen, Crystal & Watanabe, 2002; Ochiai & Satoh, 1996). These factors appear to be manifestations of the social expectations of harmony, obedience, and interdependence of the surrounding society that reflected in friendship.

Importantly, the terms used by researchers for friendship in English and Japanese may not really be equivalent. For instance, the term *friend* is often translated as tomodachi or the more formal y jin. Namba (2005) found that these terms referred to general friendships of varying levels of intimacy. Takahashi et al. (2002) suggested that the Japanese term *tomodachi* may be broader and more inclusive than the word *friend*. This is consistent with observations made by White (1993), who found that *tomodachi*, when used by adolescents, included acquaintances. This could lead to the erroneous interpretation that Japanese have friendships of lower quality than do North Americans.

Nakama is the term generally used to refer to a specific group of companions or playmates, a clique or gang. Nakama are commonly composed of four to eight members who are all friends, but broader, more loosely knit groups can include acquaintances. During adolescence, time spent with nakama provides opportunities to learn how to behave appropriately within a group. With nakama, there exists the expectation that individuals within the group will behave in a way that will please others and maximize group cohesion, even when this might go against an individual's personal beliefs. In Japan, this is an important context for learning the distinction between *tatemae*, which is the convention-directed, socially-oriented self, and *honne*, which is the private and often hidden inner-self (Kim, 1994).

In interviews with adolescents, Namba (2005) found that adolescents choose nakama based on common goals. Sharing a common goal is a feature of the nakama relationship that distinguishes it from friendship and best friendship. This feature is also reflected in the Japanese language; many different types of nakama exist. During adolescence, one might have *benkyonakama* (study friends) or *asobinakama* (pal-around friends). In adulthood, these groups of friends can become increasingly distinct and specialized, such as *shigotonakama* (work friends) or *nominakama* (drinking buddies), each group serving a different purpose. Learning to identify the goal of a group and facilitate achieving that goal is an important developmental step.

Whereas the nakama relationship compels a friend to consider group atmosphere, to self-censor, and to conform in relationships with *shinyū*, friends are free from group obligations. The term *shinyū* is commonly associated with dyadic, same-gender close friendship of high quality (Krappman, 1996; Namba, 2005; White, 1993). Salamon (1977) described the shinyū relationship as one "in which there are no barriers; one withholds nothing and is never suspicious of another's motives" (p. 813). Moreover, Salamon (1977) claimed the shinyū relationship is more intimate than that of family because close friends are devoid of the watchfulness and obligation characteristic of familial ties.

Thus, the shinyū relationship provides respite from the more demanding social exertions required of nakama, or even early romantic relationships. Shinji Iwai's (Iwai & Maeda, 2004) *Hana and Alice* provides a modern cinematic depiction of the importance of shinyū to adolescents transitioning from middle to high school. The main plotline concerns the best friendship of the two female leads, Hana and Alice, and Hana's attempts to fabricate a romantic relationship with a gullible senior student, Masashi. To accomplish this, Hana presses upon Masashi an outrageous lie that she and Masashi had been romantically involved, but that Masashi suffers from amnesia and can no longer recall their relationship. Hana enlists Alice's support to carry out the ruse. However, things begin to fall apart for Hana when Masashi begins to "recall" false memories of his love for Alice. Despite the complications of a burgeoning love triangle, the friendship between the girls endures. One scene in particular symbolizes the steadfast nature of the bond between shinyū: Moments before she is to present a monologue before the student body at a school festival,

Hana tearfully confesses her deception to Masashi. Emotionally drained, Hana takes to the stage only to discover that the spectators have all left— all save for Alice, who tells her, "I'm still here."

School as a Context for Friendship

The school environment influences the burgeoning social lives of Japanese youth by providing opportunities for positive social interaction and limiting the social influence from those outside school. Unlike U.S. students, who are as likely to interact with friends in school as outside of it, the social interactions of Japanese adolescents take place predominantly at school (Fuligni & Stevenson, 1995). However, the growing popularity of social networking technologies among youth worldwide may increase the likelihood of Japanese youth making friends outside of school. Nationwide guidelines set out by the Japanese Ministry of Education emphasize the balance between academic and personal development (Ministry of Education, Culture, Sports, Science and Technology [MEXT], 2008). This policy is reflected in the predominantly social nonacademic activities, such as culture festivals, sports days, art shows, field trips, and club activities hosted by schools throughout the year. The purpose of these activities is to emphasize group cohesion and identification, mutual participation, and social values such as role performance and personal sacrifice (Fukuzawa & LeTendre, 2001). School club activities provide one of the main settings for social interaction with friends among Japanese middle and high school students. Interviews conducted by Fukuzawa and LeTendre (2001) revealed that 80% of middle school students participated in clubs and spent an average of 7.5 hours a week participating. Many students look forward to this time as it allows them not only a brief respite from the rigors of class but an opportunity to socialize with friends in an atmosphere that is relaxed and fun.

Schoolteachers in Japan play an active role in shaping the social lives of students. Japanese society holds teachers responsible not only for the academic but also the social development of students. It is not uncommon for homeroom teachers to discourage students from spending time in places where they might make friends with delinquent youth, as in video arcades, and to patrol these places for students who skip class. Most Japanese schools prohibit students from taking on part-time employment, as this might distract them from their studies. Thus, opportunities to meet and form friendships with adolescents outside of school and beyond the supervision of adults are limited.

Selection of Friends

In Japan, adolescents who disrupt group harmony by hurting the feelings of others, being argumentative, or speaking badly about or showing a lack or care for others risks being labeled as a *warui ko* (bad kid) by their peers (Crystal & Stevenson, 1995). As many Japanese adolescents value conformity (Killen et al., 2002), these "bad kids" may be less likely than their peers who conform to the basic expectations of the school and society to be chosen as friends by other youths. Japanese youth are more likely than U.S. youth to endorse excluding a peer who displays a melancholy disposition or an unconventional appearance. In Japan, an adolescent who is withdrawn, brooding, or gloomy may be labeled *kurai* (dark) by peers (Fukuzawa & LeTendre, 2001; White, 1993).

The need for forming friendships with peers who are similar to oneself, a hallmark of friendship in the West, appears less important to Japanese adolescents than the need for intimacy (Yoshioka, 2001) and affiliation (Enomoto, 2000), particularly among older adolescents (Crystal, Watanabe, & Chen, 2000). Choosing a friend who is different from oneself may be mutually beneficial to the personal development of both friends. For instance, Crystal et al. (2000) found that Japanese adolescents give more mastery- and cognitive-based explanations for their preference for diversity among a hypothetical peer group. Thus, Japanese youths may prefer friends from whom they can learn or who will introduce them to new ideas (Crystal et al., 2000). Consistent with the concept of nakama, where a common goal is stressed, Japanese youth may be more forgiving of personal differences in the interest of being able to pursue a mutual goal.

Developmental Changes in the Friendships of Japanese Adolescents

With age, societal obligations and emotional maturity combine to influence the quantity and quality of friendships an adolescent maintains. Ochiai and Satoh (1996) summarized the typical friendship pattern of middle school students as broad (many friends) and shallow (little intimacy) and that of high school students as restrictive (few friends) and deep (considerable intimacy). Intimacy, that is the sharing of close personal feelings between friends, is considered as the most important positive feature of friendship in adolescence (Schneider, 2000; Sullivan, 1953).

In early adolescence, youths may be more concerned with acceptance than intimacy; simply making and maintaining a friendship is paramount. In middle school, having fun is often the goal of being with friends. Enomoto (1999, 2000) found that, in comparison to high school students, middle school students spend more time with friends doing things that are fun and casual. Affiliation with friends provides young adolescents with a sense of safety and belonging. Consequently, middle school adolescents may not risk behaviors that could alienate them, such as voicing one's private thoughts. For instance, Ochiai and Satoh (1996) found that compared with high school students, middle school students' relationships with friends are characterized by a greater desire to conform and less concern for mutual understanding.

Transition to high school marks the high point of academic and nonacademic commitments for many Japanese students. As time is at a premium, Japanese youths may become more selective in terms of whom they chose to be with and what they chose to do together. In high school, youths increasingly seek to spend time in private, one-on-one activities (White, 1993) in which they may develop a mutual understanding of one another (Enomoto, 1999, 2000). Expectations of openness, trust, and intimacy in friendship are greater in high school than in middle school (Yoshioka, 2001). Friendships in high school have a greater potential for intimacy than those formed in middle school, as youth are more amenable to self-disclosure (Ochiai & Satoh, 1996). Older adolescents report greater reliance on friends and less reliance on parents as a source of support than do younger adolescents (Omi, 1999), particularly when they need cheering up and or help with schoolwork (Crystal et al., 2008). At this stage in adolescent development, students seek support and cooperation rather than competition from friends. Enomoto (1999, 2000) found that high school students generally report lower levels of rivalry and conflict with friends than middle school students.

In conclusion, Japanese society has emphasized for centuries the maintenance of harmony and social cohesion and the importance of differentiating between a public and a private self. Participation in group and dyadic friendships during adolescence is recognized as a means of developing these disparate roles.

☰ WHEN A YOUNG PIONEER NEEDS A FRIEND

Cuban society is characterized by highly collectivistic community life, reflecting the general collectivism of Latin American countries, the psychological importance of the extended family in Hispanic society, and the collectivistic ideology of the communist political system. De la Torre-Molina (2001), in well-documented historical and sociological treatise on identity formation in Cuba over the course of history, cited the combined influences of the family, of circles of friends, of work colleagues, of neighbors and of national institutions in promoting a highly collectivistic value system. Núñez (2003), a social psychologist, emphasized the intensity of interpersonal communication in Cuba, which reflects the pressures to participate daily in collective life and "to feel and be a part of" the collective group.

Concept of Friendship

It is often maintained that dyadic friendship relationships are damaging to the social organization of societies and groups that are very highly collectivistic on all levels. This has been articulated systematically and consistently by Lieblich, who based her reflections on the narrative accounts of people in highly collectivistic societies as diverse as the Israeli kibbutz in the era of comprehensive economic collectivism (Lieblich, 1981) and groups of prisoners from the same country interned together at prisoner-of-war camps (Lieblich, 1995). Nevertheless, there is a distinct role for friendship in highly collectivistic Cuba, as detailed in the next few pages.

The importance of friendship in Cuban culture can be traced to the writings of José Martí (1853–1895), journalist, poet, political theorist, and hero of the fight for Cuba's independence from Spain. His many poems and essays are revered by contemporary Cubans and studied in great detail. The theme of friendship emerges in many places in Martí's writings. At several places in the 46 poems in his *Versos Sencillos* (Martí, 2005), he extolled the value of friendship, reiterating that friendship is more valuable than a king's treasure or any other prized possession. For an example, see the following:

> *I have obtained,*
> *the pick of the jeweller's trove,*
> *A good friend is what I've gained,*
> *And I have put aside love.*

In another poem, Martí commented on the support best provided by a friend:

> The leopard has found its den
> In the forest, brown and dry,
> More than the leopard have I,
> A good friend's the best haven.
>
> As on a toy, she lies to rest
> The geisha on the maple cushion:
> I also rest and can attest,
> A friend is like no other cushion.
>
> . . . The President, they contend,
> Has a garden with a fountain,
> And rich stores of gold and grain
> I have more, I have a friend.

Contemporary Cuban culture contains a number of graphic representations of friendship, no less reverent than those of Martí. Probably the most well-known depiction of friendship between young people to emerge in recent years is the successful 2005 film *Viva Cuba* by J. Cremata (2005). The plot of this film centers on the friendship of Malu and Jorgito, fellow pupils in a school in Havana. Their relationship depicts in a very clear and loving manner the prototypical patterns of interaction between adolescent friends in Cuba. During their everyday interactions at school and in the neighborhood, Malu and Jorgito enjoy some common pastimes but also have some conflicts. Their parents fan the flames, accentuating any differences between them because neither mother wants her child to befriend the other. The parents' desire to end the young people's friendship stems from the deep ideological differences between the families. One family is strongly devoted to Fidel and communist ideology, and the other is devoted to the Roman Catholic religion, the practice of which was discouraged during the early years of communism.

Rivalries and petty conflicts between the two friends must be set aside when an external threat to their relationship appears. Malu's mother has applied to leave the country and needs only the signature of her estranged ex-husband on a consent form for Malu to leave the country. Once the two friends find out that the form has been mailed to the father, a lighthouse keeper at the distant Eastern tip of the island, they decide to go see the father and persuade him not to sign. Police are called; citizens across the island help locate the two missing young habaneros. All protagonists reunite at the lighthouse. In the closing scene, Malu and Jorgito share a private outburst of laughter in the foreground as in the background all the adults in their lives verbally attack. As the adults look even more juvenile than they have throughout the film, the two young people, strengthened by their common challenge and the intensification of their relationship, have matured and brought opposing sides together. This final scene symbolizes not only the strength of young people's friendship in Cuba but also an important function of their friendship. Surrounded by intense pressures to be cooperative, successful and exemplary in many ways, friendship provides a refuge in which to express individual identity and individual desires, including some desires that adults may not wish to see fulfilled.

The friendship context may also provide a relief from the intense stimulation of the typical calle (street) in urban neighborhoods where there is constant communication among neighbors—borrowing and sharing, trading of neighborhood news—and the perpetual background rhythm of Latin music. A somewhat similar notion was proposed by Sutton (1981) with regard to African American neighborhoods in the United States. These authors commented that there is so much stimulation in the family and neighborhood settings that some young people become overstimulated and need to withdraw. They may seek some privacy and tranquility on their own. However, the need to step back from the intensity of group interaction may also lead them to seek out the companionship of a friend who will listen more intently to them than will acquaintances. A possibly crucial difference between the friendship context and the adult-dominated social work that surrounds it is that the adolescent friends have some role in determining whom they will befriend and how the relationship will proceed.

Distinction Between a Friend and Any Other Compañero (Comrade)

Because of the intensity of group interaction at all levels, intimate relationships in Cuba are probably much more likely than in most other places to be incubated in large groups. This is depicted in the 1985 film *Una Novia Para David (A Girlfriend for David)*, which takes place in a public boarding school for adolescents in Havana. The group of male students encourages individual members to make sexual advances, which is certainly not unique to Cuba. David's closest friend is made responsible for taking care of David by making sure he finds a girlfriend. David subsequently becomes a friend of some of his new girlfriend's friends, including the newly elected head of the students' association. This film illustrates the degree to which friendship at the dyadic level is nested within the interactions of the larger group but has its own specific functions.

David's girlfriend would probably not have the prerogative to initiate a "conquest." Although one of the major objectives of the Cuban Revolution has been to promote women's rights, sexism in adolescents' romantic relationships appears to continue, as confirmed in a doctoral thesis by Alvarez-Marante (2002). It confirms that boys are still likely to take the initiative in adolescent romantic relationships although girls indicated that they would like to.

Time Available to Associate With Friends

Cuban society provides its adolescents with ample and mandatory opportunities to associate with each other at the group level but not necessarily at the dyadic level. All young people participate in the Pioneers, a Scout-like group organized by the school and by the Communist party, which has clear responsibilities for character education. As a way of achieving this, the Pioneers of a community may jointly be assigned to help needy people or to implement hygienic measures. Cooperative learning experiences are provided in school and are organized outside of school by teachers. For example, many teachers organize study groups that meet in pupils' homes after school, consistent with national policy that emphasizes individual citizens' obligations to each other (Ministerio de Educación [MINED], 2010).

School-directed interaction among pupils intensifies with the onset of adolescence. Whether they attend day school or boarding school, which is public, all Cuban adolescents participate in residential escuelas del campo (country schools) together with their school classmates. At the escuelas del campo, all take part in agricultural work and learn the value of labor. Despite such intensive interaction in large groups and equally intensive interaction in neighborhoods and among members of extended family members, dyadic friendships between Cuban adolescents exist and are important to them even though there is essentially no dedicated time for dyadic friendship in Cuba. Cuban adolescents, who are in school for at least 6 hours a day and who participate in many collective activities outside of school, probably have less time than their counterparts in most other countries to orchestrate individual activities with friends. Nevertheless, the fact that dyadic friendship emerges and is valued is an intriguing affirmation of the cross-cultural adaptive significance of friendship.

Influences of Adults on the Selection of Friends or Their Activities

Most Cuban parents and teachers probably believe that they are instilling in their children the prosocial values and behaviors that will help them form and maintain relationships at any level, including friendships and romantic relations. Parents in Cuba probably have no more or less to say about the friendships of their adolescent sons and daughters than do parents in North America or Europe. Accordingly, as depicted in the film *Viva Cuba*, Cuban parents may try to discourage friendships of which they do not approve. They certainly do not have the same degree of authority over their children's selection of friends as do parents in Japan, for example.

Criteria Used by Adolescents to Select Friends; Characteristics of the Ideal Friend

Schneider, Woodburn, Udvari, and Soteras del Toro (2005), studying patterns of friendship, liking, and disliking by adolescents in Cuba, Canada, and Costa Rica, found that relationships between friends in Cuba are at least as close as those in the other countries. Both Cuban and Costa Rican participants refrained from competing with their friends; this did not apply to Canadian participants. Furthermore, competing with a friend in Cuba or Costa Rica but not in Canada (especially for males) predicted the termination of the friendship.

A study by Santana-Gonzales, Moreno-Silot, and Schneider (2004) illustrates the permeability of the boundary between friendship and comradeship. These researchers asked Cuban and Canadian early adolescents to write short essays about their expectations of their friends, stating how their expectations would differ from what they expect of any other comrade. One frequent Cuban response, probably reflective of the pervasiveness of character education in Cuba, was admiration of the friend's character; this was totally absent from the Canadian protocols. One adolescent in Santiago de Cuba, Cuba's second largest city, responded as follows: "First of all, I would like my best friends to be likeable, honest, noble, and responsible, ready to lay down their lives for other people, for the country and for the liberty of all men."

Other responses emphasized the readiness of the friends to help each other, either in tangible ways or by providing emotional support. The researchers complemented the analysis of the frequencies of individual categories in the participants' reasoning with a stage scoring based on Piaget's model. The Cuban adolescents' reasoning about their friendships was significantly more likely than the Canadian data to reach the stage of reciprocal exchange and concern for the friend. Cooperation and mutual help might characterize both expectations of a friend and of any other comrade. However, responses indicating expectations of intimacy and personal loyalty—hallmarks of friendship—were essentially as frequent in Cuba as in Canada. In a study by Pérez- Luján, Vergel, and Rodríguez (2007), who interviewed a somewhat younger group of participants (9–10 years old) in Santa Clara, Cuba, the respondents indicated most frequently that they chose friends who would help them and keep their secrets.

In summary, friendship in Cuba appears both to mirror the intensive and rich interaction of communal life and to provide refuge from it. Despite the radical social transformations in Cuba since its independence in the late 19th century, friendship appears to have survived and adapted to the surrounding collectivistic context but not to have lost its importance to Cubans.

☙ GENERAL CONCLUSION

The cases of Japan and Cuba do not necessarily represent all collectivistic, familistic societies, but studying the role of friendship within them does permit meaningful reflection about the role of friendship in such cultures. In both countries, most dyadic friendships are likely to emerge from interactions within a larger and organized peer group—probably much more so than in the Anglo-Saxon countries. There is no doubt that friendship does exist in both Cuba and Japan and that having good friends is considered important by adolescents in those countries. Research clearly shows that adolescent friendships in Japan and Cuba are close and of psychological importance. In neither of these countries do adolescents rely on their friends for social support in the ways that their U.S. counterparts do, given the other sources of social support available to Cuban and Japanese young people. Nevertheless, there appear to be distinct situations in which young people in collectivistic societies need their friends despite the family support available to them. Furthermore, in both Cuba and Japan, the supportive dyadic friendship seems to serve the valuable function of allowing some degree of respite from the intensity of highly collective communal and family life. The counterpoint to collective living that is provided by dyadic friendship does not seem at all to create conflict with family and community life in either country. Only longitudinal research will be able to determine if friendship among adolescents in these cultures of relatedness provides preparation for intimacy in relationships during the adult years.

As different as they are, the cases of Cuba and Japan do share at least one important feature other than societal collectivism: the critical importance of education. School and extracurricular activities based in school are the meeting ground of friends. The pressure to do well is often the substance of the issues for which adolescents need support from their friends. Therefore, future researchers who are able to might profitably explore the dynamics of adolescent friendship in societies where school plays a less central role in adolescent development.

Methodological issues temper somewhat our confidence in the impressions obtained from the research conducted in both Japan and Cuba. The way an adolescent is perceived by others is vitally important to young people in both Cuba and Japan, surely much more so than in North America, which is not to say that self-presentation is not important there. As noted earlier, when responding to social situation, Japanese tend toward self-criticism rather than self-enhancement (Kitayama, Markus, Matsumoto, & Norasakkunkit, 1997). In Cuba, an adolescent's character is evaluated regularly in school and in his or her peer group. This must influence the way adolescents in both countries respond to self-report questionnaires about themselves; such questionnaires are the mainstay of the research we have discussed in this chapter. As well, it is important to remember that, however careful a researcher has been in translating questionnaires, translations are never exact. Precision in using language and determining how terms are understood by adolescents are necessary in the specific case of the word *friend*, most particularly in an era when even Facebook contacts are called "friends."

Japan and Cuba continue to undergo many significant changes, such as economic slowdown and absence of population growth. Families are getting smaller. This may have an influence on how children choose and interact with friends. Many of the world's nations are similarly undergoing rapid change. Moreover, the technological revolution that is changing the way in which youth relate to one another is as vibrant in Japan as anywhere although it only beginning to reach Cuba. Some of the research included in this summary dates from many years ago and may no longer be an accurate reflection of modern Japanese and Cuban youth. New research is necessary if researchers hope to document the evolution of the friendship bond and its link with the emotional lives of members of collectivistic cultures.

※ SUGGESTED READINGS

Chen, X., French, D., & Schneider, B. H. (2006). *Peer relationships in cultural context.* New York: Cambridge University Press.

French, D. C., Pidada, S., & Victor, A. (2005). Friendships of Indonesian and United States youth. *International Journal of Behavioral Development, 29,* 304–313.

Gummerum, M., & Keller, M. (2008). Affection, virtue, pleasure, and profit: Developing an understanding of friendship closeness and intimacy in Western and Asian societies. *International Journal of Behavioral Development, 32,* 218–231.

Schneider, B. H., Woodburn, S., Soteras del Toro, M., & Udvari, S. J. (2005). Cultural and gender differences in the implications of competition for early adolescent friendship. *Merrill-Palmer Quarterly, 51,* 163–191.

※ REFERENCES

Alvarez-Marante, A. (2002). *Courtship and gender identity in early adolescence.* Nijmegen, Netherlands: Drukkerij.

Cairn, B. (2009). *Friendship: A history.* London: Equinox.

Cremata, J. (Director). (2005). *Viva Cuba* [Motion Picture]. Cuba: DDC Films LLC, TVC. ICRT—Instituto Cubano de Radio y Televisión.

Crystal, D. S. (2000). Concepts of deviance in children and adolescents: A comparison between the United States and Japan. *International Journal of Psychology, 35,* 207–218.

Crystal, D. S., & Stevenson, H. W. (1995). What is a bad kid? Answers of adolescents and their mothers in three cultures. *Journal of Research on Adolescents, 5,* 71–91.

Crystal, D. S., Kakinuma, M., DeBell, M., Azuma, H., & Miyashita, T. (2008). Who helps you? Self and other sources of support among youth in Japan and the USA. *International Journal of Behavioral Development, 32,* 496–508.

Crystal, D. S., Watanabe, H., & Chen, R. S. (2000). Preference for diversity in competitive and cooperative contexts: A study of American and Japanese children and adolescents. *International Journal of Behavioural Development, 24,* 348–355.

Dazai, O. (1989). *Crackling mountain and other stories* (Jans O'Brien, Trans.). Tokyo: Charles E. Tuttle.

De la Torre-Molina, C. (2001). *Las identidades. Una mirada desde la Psicología* [Identities. A view from Psychology]. Havana, Cuba: Centro de Investigación y Desarrollo de la Cultura Cubana Juan Marinello.

Enomoto, J. (1999). Socio-emotional development of friendship among adolescents: Activities with friends and the feeling for friends. *Japanese Journal of Educational Psychology, 47,* 180–190.

Enomoto, J. (2000). Friendship among adolescents: Needs and their relations to emotions and activities. *Japanese Journal of Educational Psychology, 48,* 444–453.

Entralgo, J. (1985). *Sobre la amistad (About friendship)*. Madrid: Austral.

Erikson, E. H. (1968). *Identity: Youth and crisis.* New York: Norton.

French, D. C., Lee, O. & Pidada, S. U. (2006). Friendships of Indonesian, South Korean, and U.S. youth: Exclusivity, intimacy, enhancement of worth, and conflict. In X. Chen, D. C. French & B. H. Schneider (Eds.), *Peer relationships in cultural context* (pp. 379–402). New York: Cambridge University Press.

Fukuzawa, R. E., & LeTendre, G. K. (2001). *Intense years: How Japanese adolescents balance school, family and friends.* New York: Routledge Falmer.

Fuligni, A. J., & Stevenson, H. W. (1995). Time use and academic achievement among American, Chinese, and Japanese high school students. *Child Development, 66,* 830–842.

Hearn, L. (1972). *Kokoro: Hints and echoes of Japanese inner life.* Boston: Tuttle.

Hirsch, D. (1997). Schooling for the middle years: Developments in Europe. In R. Takanishi & D. A. Hamburg (Eds.), *Preparing adolescents for the twenty-first century: Challenges facing Europe and the United States.* New York: Cambridge University Press.

Hofstede, G. H. (2001). *Culture's consequences: Comparing values, behaviors, institutions, & organizations across nations.* Thousand Oaks, CA: Sage.

Iwai, S. (Director/Producer), & Maeda, K. (Producer). (2005). *Hana and Alice* [Motion picture]. Japan: Rockwell Eyes.

Killen, M., Crystal, D. S., & Watanabe, H. (2002). Japanese and American children's evaluations of peer exclusion, tolerance of differences, and prescriptions for conformity. *Child Development, 73,* 1788–1802.

Kim, U. (1994). Individualism and collectivism: Conceptual clarification and elaboration. In U. Kim, H. C. Triadis, C. Kagitcibas, S. Choi, & G. Yoon (Eds), *Individualism and collectivism: Theory, methods and applications* (pp. 19–40). Thousand Oaks, CA: Sage.

Kitayama, S., Markus, H. R., Matsumoto, H., & Norasakkunkit, V. (1997). Individual and collective processes in the construction of the self: Self-enhancement in the United States and self-criticism in Japan. *Journal of Personality and Social Psychology, 72,* 1245–1267.

Kitayama, S., & Uchida, Y. (2003). Explicit self-criticism and implicit self-regard: Evaluating self and friend in two cultures. *Journal of Experimental Social Psychology, 39,* 476–482.

Krappman, L. (1996). Amicitia, drujba, shin-yu, philia, freundschaft, friendship: On the cultural diversity of a human relationship. In W. M. Bukowski, A. F. Newcomb, & W. W. Hartup (Eds.), *The company they keep: Friendship in childhood and adolescence* (pp. 19–40). New York: Cambridge University Press.

Lansford, J. E. (2004). Links between family relationships and best friendships in the United States and Japan. *International Journal of Aging and Human Development, 59,* 287–304.

LeTendre, G. K. (2000). *Learning to be adolescent: Growing up in US and Japanese middle schools.* New Haven, CT: Yale University Press.

Lieblich, A. (1981). *Kibbutz makom.* New York: Pantheon.

Lieblich, A. (1995). *Seasons of captivity: The inner world of POWs.* New York: New York University Press.

Markus, H., & Kitayama, S. (1991). Culture and the self: Implications for cognition, emotion, and motivation. *Psychological Review, 98,* 224–253.

Martí, J. (2005). *Versos sencillos/Simple verses: A dual-language edition* (A. Fountain, Trans.). Jefferson, NC: McFarland & Company.

Ministerio de Educación (2010). *Portal Educativo Cubano.*

Ministry of Education, Culture, Sports, Science and Technology–Jaban (2008). *Basic plan for the promotion of education.* Retrieved from http://www.mext.go.jp/english/reform/1260281.htm

Namba, K. (2005). The concept of nakama (peer groups) in Japanese adolescence: Its position within peer relationships compared with friends and best friends. *Japanese Journal of Developmental Psychology, 16,* 276–285.

Núñez, C. (2003). Para sentirse y ser parte. In R. Portal Moreno, H. Saladriga Medina, & M. Recio Silva (Eds). *Selección de lecturas sobre comunicación social* (pp. 90–93). La Habana: Servigraf.

Ochiai, Y., & Satoh, Y. (1996). The developmental change of friendship in adolescence. *Japanese Journal of Educational Psychology, 44,* 55–65.

Okamoto, K., & Uechi, Y. (1999). Adolescents' relations with parents and friends in the second individuation process. *Japanese Journal of Educational Psychology, 47,* 248–258.

Omi, Y. (1999). A cross-sectional study of the social support networks of children and adolescents. *Japanese Journal of Educational Psychology, 47,* 40–48.

Oyserman, D., Coon, H., & Kemmelmeier, M. (2002). Rethinking individualism and collectivism: Evaluation of theoretical assumptions and meta-analyses. *Psychological Bulletin, 128,* 3–73.

Park, Y., Killen, M., Crystal, D. S., & Watanabe, H. (2003). Korean, Japanese and US students' judgements about peer exclusion: Evidence for diversity. *International Journal of Behavioral Development, 27,* 555–565.

Pérez- Luján, D., Vergel, A. E., & Rodríguez, C. E. (2007). La influencia de la amistad en la formación de cualidades morales en escolares cubanos de 9 y 10 años. *Revista Iberoamericana de Educación, 42.* Retrieved from www.rieoei.org/deloslectores/1450Perez.pdf

Perry, H. D. (1982). *Psychiatrist of America: The life of Harry Stack Sullivan.* Cambridge: Belknap.

Rothbaum, F., Pott, M., Azuma, H., Miyake, K., & Weisz, J. (2000). The development of close relationships in Japan and the US: Pathways of symbiotic harmony and generative tension. *Child Development, 71,* 1121–1142.

Salamon, S. (1977). Family bounds and friendship bonds: Japan and West Germany. *Journal of Marriage and Family, 39,* 807–820.

Santana-Gonzales, Y., Silot-Moreno, D., & Schneider, B. (2004). Friendship expectations of early adolescents in Cuba and Canada. *Journal of Cross-Cultural Psychology, 35*(4), 436–445.

Schneider, B. H. (2000). *Friends and enemies: Peer relations in childhood.* London: Arnold.

Schneider, B. H., Woodburn, S., Udvari, S., & Soteras del Toro, M. P. (2005). Cultural and gender differences in the implications of competition for early adolescent friendship. *Merrill-Palmer Quarterly, 51*(2), 163–191.

Sullivan, H. S. (1953). *The interpersonal theory of psychiatry*. New York: Norton.

Sutton, S. E. (1981). *African American youth as actors in community change*. Aspen, CO: Aspen Institute.

Takahashi, K., Ohara, N., Antonucci, T. C., & Akiyama, H. (2002). Commonalities and differences in close relationships among the Americans and Japanese: A comparison by the individualism/collectivism concept. *International Journal of Behavioral Development, 26*, 453–465.

Triandis, H. C. (1989). The self and social behavior in differing cultural contexts. *Psychological Review, 96*, 506–520.

Triandis, H. C., Bontempo, R., Villareal, M. J., Asai, M., & Lucca, N. (1988). Individualism and collectivism: Cross-cultural perspectives on self-ingroup relationships. *Journal of Personality and Social Psychology, 54*, 323–338.

White, M. (1993). *The material child: Coming of age in Japan and America*. New York: Free Press.

White, M., & LeVine, R. (1986). What is ii ko (good child)? In H. Stevenson, H. Azuma, & K. Hakuta (Eds.), *Child development and education in Japan* (pp. 55–62). New York: Freeman.

Yoshioka, K. (2001). The satisfaction in peer relationships in terms of self-acceptance and the discrepancies between ideal and real peer relationships. *Japanese Journal of Adolescent Psychology, 13*, 13–30.

7

Transformations in Adolescent Peer Networks

René Veenstra

Jan Kornelis Dijkstra

Transformations in peer networks concern the dynamics of both the network and behaviors. Beginning in early childhood, children sort themselves nonrandomly into friendships, selecting peers who are similar to themselves in important ways. In turn, the processes of creating and keeping friendships influence the behavior and attitudes of individuals. Thus, the interplay between dynamics in behaviors and networks is captured by two distinct processes: (1) selection processes and (2) influence processes.

Selection processes comprise the formation and dissolution of relationships and, thus, changes in the network. The best-known example of a selection process may be the assortative pairing process: the formation of a relationship based on the similarity of two individuals (McPherson, Smith-Lovin, & Cook, 2001), also known as preferential attraction.

Influence processes refer to the observation that individuals change their behavior or attitudes in accordance with the peers they affiliate with. A prominent example is the assimilation process, by which socially connected individuals become increasingly similar over time (Friedkin, 1998). Because assortative pairing and assimilation result in the same empirical phenomenon (similarity of connected individuals), developmental researchers have known for a long time that the study of influence requires consideration of selection and that the study of selection requires consideration of influence (Billy & Udry, 1985; Cohen, 1977; Ennett & Bauman, 1994; Kandel, 1978).

In this chapter, we discuss the importance of social networks for understanding selection and influence processes in behaviors. If selection results in similarity, it suggests that behavior remains similar but relationships change. By contrast, influence processes suggest that relations remain stable but behavior changes. The sequence of changes in the network and in the behavior, reacting on each other, generates a mutual dependence between the network dynamics and the behavior dynamics. It is thus necessary to examine behavior and network dynamics simultaneously. For that reason, we focus in this chapter on research into selection and influence as joint or co-occurring processes.

⁂ THEORETICAL OVERVIEW

Selection and Influence Processes

The idea that people acquire friends on the basis of preexisting similarities can be traced back to the work of Lazarsfeld and Merton (1954) and Homans (1961), among others. People select similar others because those who are similar in behaviors, characteristics, and attitudes understand each other better. The similarity-attraction theory (Byrne, 1971) states that similarity increases trustworthiness and predictability, enabling individuals to communicate with less effort and with shared feelings of understanding and belongingness, which makes these relationships more rewarding and stable. This increased predictability and these positive feelings are suggested to enhance selection of similar friends and reduce conflicts. In addition to providing a basis for mutual approval, shared characteristics provide a source of validation for development and reinforcement of social identity (Hallinan, 1980).

The selection of peers is not only steered by preferences but also depends upon the social composition of the pool of available others (Blau, 1977; George & Hartman, 1996; Verbrugge, 1977). The composition of such a pool structures and restricts choices among possible friends. For instance, within a school, the network members tend to have much more in common, such as socioeconomic status, ethnicity, or intelligence, than in society at large. As schools tend to be more homogenous in composition, the chances of meeting and affiliating with similar peers are considerably higher than in places where people have distinct backgrounds. Feld (1982) has noted that social settings that structure a person's actions and interactions increase the likelihood of similarity in behavior. Thus, similarity may be a result of the opportunity to meet similar others, also called propinquity (see also Osgood & Anderson, 2004).

Opportunities for affiliation also have an impact on the idea that similarity between actors in networks is due to influence processes in which actors adopt behaviors and attitudes of their peers in the network. The importance of social relationships as socializing agents can be traced back to Durkheim (1897). He argued that all types of behavior are influenced by social norms and that norm conformity is enforced through membership and integration in social groups. Thus, similarity may be a result of influence or socialization, referring to the tendency of individuals to grow more similar to one another in response to behaviors or attitudes of others in the network.

Shortcomings of Most Studies on Selection and Influence

A large number of studies have documented substantial similarity between adolescents' behavioral repertoires and those of their friends. However, most research initially relied on cross-sectional data, which did not allow researchers to disentangle selection from influence effects. These processes can only be untangled using longitudinal data that allow researchers to examine whether similarity results from a mutual selection process based on preexisting similarity or an influence process in which already connected individuals become more similar. Another limitation of both cross-sectional and longitudinal studies has been that the assessments of peer characteristics usually came from the focal respondent (referring to that respondent's report on characteristics of his or her friends), a strategy that potentially inflates the magnitude of peer effects owing to exaggeration of similarity to friends in behavior, the so-called assumed similarity or false consensus bias.

Until the recent development of statistical models to examine co-occurring network and behavior processes, studies that included data provided by focal respondents as well as their friends also suffered several limitations. These limitations restricted the ability to make firm statements about the underlying process responsible for similarity among befriended peers (Steglich, Snijders, & Pearson, 2010). First, changes in behavior and social relations that occurred between observations were not modeled. For example, at the first observation, the focal respondent (ego) might consider another network member (alter) as a friend. If at the second observation, the focal respondent had changed his or her behavior and became similar to alter, this change was considered to be influence. However, what happened between the two observations was unobserved and, therefore, remained unclear. It is possible that after the initial friendship between the two peers the relationship ended and ego changed his or her behavior in the absence of a relationship with alter. After ego changed his or her behavior, ego might again have formed a friendship with alter, which was observed at the second observation. Based on the two observations, changes in the behavior of ego were attributed to the friendship with alter and as such were considered to reflect influence. However, as is clear in this example, the change in behavior occurred when the relationship between ego and alter was absent. As a consequence, the influence of alter on the behavior of ego might be overestimated. Therefore, a true test of selection and influence effects should take such unobserved changes into account to avoid overestimation of both effects.

A second limitation of previous models is a failure to control for the effect of the network structure on both network and behavior dynamics. Several structural (network-inherent) selection processes are known to play a role in the dynamics of friendship networks (Steglich et al., 2010). For example, friendships are more likely to be established when persons share a common friend (Davis, 1970). Hence, such a transitivity effect rather than similarity in behavior might account for friendship formation between network members. Thus, when friendship formation between two smoking adolescents occurs via a third shared friend (transitivity), leaving out an estimate for transitivity for this friendship selection would cause one to incorrectly attribute it to their smoking behavior. Not controlling for such structural network tendencies in the analyses can lead to overestimation of selection effects, which, in turn, affects the estimates for influence by failing to rule out selection effects in a statistically sound way (Steglich et al., 2010).

A third limitation is the failure to use complete networks. In order to identify the determinants of selection, it does not suffice to know who was selected as network partner; it is also necessary to know who was not selected. Likewise, for identifying peer influence effects, it needs to be known what the absence of influence looks like, referring to how behavior changes in the absence of opportunities for influence. In earlier studies

(Ennett & Bauman, 1994; Kandel, 1978), this was typically acknowledged by comparing a sample of dyads in which the individuals were (and stayed) connected to each other in the network with a matched sample of dyads in which the individuals were (and stayed) unconnected. However, use of the crucially important control for selection processes is impossible in this approach (Veenstra & Steglich, 2011). To unravel selection and influence processes, network data have to be used. Because many dependencies exist between actors in networks, it is not warranted to apply many commonly used statistical procedures. It is necessary to apply special procedures in which network dependencies are explicitly acknowledged and part of the modeling.

Longitudinal Social Network Analysis

To overcome these shortcomings, the Simulation Investigation for Empirical Network Analyses (SIENA) program was developed (Snijders, Steglich, & Schweinberger, 2007). Within the SIENA program (see http://stat.gamma.rug.nl/siena.html), the estimations of behavioral changes and network changes (changes in the absence or presence of a relation) are modeled simultaneously. Therefore, the program allows researchers to test both selection and influence effects while controlling each for the other (Burk, Steglich, & Snijders, 2007; Steglich et al., 2010). SIENA was used in most of the recent empirical studies reported on in this chapter (these studies are asterisked in the reference list).

The model in Figure 7.1 expresses that, in response to the current network structure and the current behavior of the other individuals in the network, individuals can change either their peer network (make a new friend or break a relationship) or their behavior (increase or decrease in behavior) between two time points. It is assumed that changes may occur continuously between discrete time points. A simulation procedure is used to estimate the likelihood of changes in behavior and networks in response to the current network structure and behavior of others. The longitudinal social network model interprets discrete time series of data as the cumulative result of an unobserved sequence of elementary changes, resulting from decisions taken by the actors between observation moments. The unobserved change process is assumed to take place as gradually as possible, in so-called microsteps that consist of either a network tie being broken or created or a unit change in behavior

(Veenstra & Steglich, 2011). The dependencies at the beginning of an unobserved period are taken as the starting value of the change process, and later changes naturally depend on these and the occurrence of earlier changes in the sequence. By repeatedly imputing sequences of microsteps, the model allows differentiation of the strengths of multiple contributing mechanisms to observed longitudinal patterns. Due to the unobserved nature of the exact sequence of changes connecting observation moments, simulation-based inference is necessary for estimating the model parameters (Snijders, 2001, 2005; Snijders et al. 2007, 2010).

Figure 7.1 Representation of Selection and Influence Effects

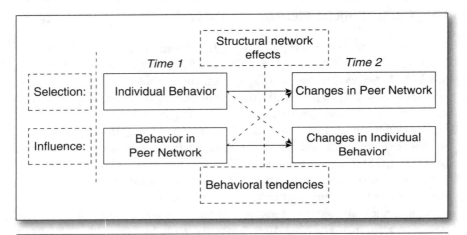

NOTE: The solid lines in Figure 7.1 express that individuals can change their peer network (selection) and behavior (influence) between two time points. The dashed lines express that selection and influence effects are estimated while the network structure and behavior at Time 1, the structural network effects (e.g., reciprocity, transitivity), and behavioral tendencies are taken into account.

Analyses using the actor-based model yield different types of parameters. First, *structural network effects* such as reciprocity and transitivity are controlled to avoid overestimation of other network-related estimates and influence effects; see Figure 7.1. In addition to these structural network effects, changes in the peer network represent *selection effects:* the extent to which individuals tend to form new friendships on the basis of preexisting similarities in behavior; see Figure 7.1.

Another set of estimates indicates the extent to which behavior changes over time, referred to as behavior dynamics. Most important is the *influence effect,* which indicates the extent to which participants change their behavior in accordance with their friends' behavior. Influence effects manifest themselves in behavioral change; see Figure 7.1. Finally, *behavioral tendencies* are taken into account to model the distribution and likelihood of changes in the behavior under investigation; see Figure 7.1. These tendencies provide a valuable insight into the likelihood of low or high values of the behavior occurring and into whether the behavior of respondents tends to regress to the mean (self-correcting mechanism) or to the extremes of the scale (polarization or self-reinforcing mechanism).

⚡ RECENT EMPIRICAL ADVANCES

A growing body of researchers use longitudinal social network data to simultaneously investigate network and behavior dynamics among adolescents (Snijders et al., 2007; Veenstra & Steglich, 2011). Social network data have been used to examine a range of behaviors among adolescents, such as externalizing problems (e.g., aggression, delinquency, weapon carrying), internalizing problems (e.g., anxiety, depression, loneliness), and substance use (e.g., alcohol, cannabis, cigarettes). The main research questions of these studies were whether adolescents *select* friends based on similarity in behavior and whether adolescents are *influenced* (socialized) by their friends' behavior.

Selection and influence processes have been investigated with respect to, for example, externalizing problem behavior. Dishion, Patterson, and Griesler (1994) have described the operation of peer selection processes through preferential attraction for children who also display antisocial behavior as well as through peer rejection of antisocial youth by others (see also Baerveldt, Völker, & Van Rossem, 2008; Burk, Kerr, & Stattin, 2008). Consequently, antisocial adolescents may have fewer opportunities to establish friendships. In addition, peer influences toward higher rates of antisocial behavior have been found to occur through an active process in which antisocial behavior is reinforced by antisocial peers. Using longitudinal social network modeling, Sijtsema et al. (2010) found that adolescents with relationally or instrumentally aggressive friends became, respectively, more relationally and instrumentally aggressive themselves over time. In addition, the influence effect of delinquency was absent in studies that looked at the effects of classmates (Knecht, Snijders, Baerveldt, Steglich, & Raub, 2010; Light & Dishion, 2007) but was found in studies that looked at the effects of grade-mates or town mates (Baerveldt et al., 2008; Burk et al., 2008). This suggests that the behavior of out-of-class friends influences delinquency more than the behavior of classmates.

Mercer and DeRosier (2010) argued that similar selection and influence mechanisms contribute to similarity in anxiety, depression, or loneliness. The findings of previous studies have shown that young people with such characteristics are more likely to experience peer rejection and engage in solitary play (Altmann & Gotlib, 1988; Connolly, Geller, Marton, & Kutcher, 1992; Gazelle & Ladd, 2003; Joiner, 2001). Consequently, children with internalizing problems have fewer opportunities to establish friendships. In a test of preferential attraction, Mercer and DeRosier (2010) reported that lonely children were more likely to select other lonely children as friends. Van Zalk, Kerr, Branje, Stattin, and Meeus (2010) found the same for depressed adolescents. Thus, there is support for a greater likelihood of friendship formation among children with similar levels of internalizing problems. However, the greater likelihood may be the result of fewer overall opportunities for friendship formation due to peer rejection and of active searching for similar friends.

Application of the longitudinal social network model has yielded insight into transformation in peer networks. The default in models of network dynamics is that breaking a tie is simply the opposite of creating one. This is not always a good representation of reality. It is conceivable, for example, that the loss when terminating a reciprocal tie is greater than the gain in creating one. Van Zalk and colleagues (2010) tested hypotheses about deselection processes in relation to adolescent depressive symptoms. Based on the theory of social corrosion (Coyne, 1976), they hypothesized that individuals prone to depressive symptoms lack the social skills necessary to provide support and closeness, which, in turn, triggers dissatisfaction and even deselection by the nondepressive dyadic partner in the relationship and therefore increases the chances of a close relationship ending (see also Borelli & Prinstein, 2006). In contrast, they hypothesized that interactions between two depressive friends are characterized by mutual feelings of understanding and high self-disclosure, which seem to increase closeness and intimacy between these friends (Rose, 2002). This, in turn, is suggested to lead to fewer endings of relationships between two depressive friends. The findings of Van Zalk et al. (2010) were in line with these ideas. Deselection offered an alternative explanation for why adolescents tend to be similar to their peers.

Influence processes offer an alternative explanation for why adolescents are similar to their peers in internalizing symptoms. Anxious and depressive feelings and thoughts may increase through reinforcement of negative cues in interactions with friends with internalizing symptoms (Prinstein, Cheah, & Guyer, 2005; Rudolph, Hammen, & Burge, 1994). This may be an active process in which adolescents with internalizing symptoms engage in co-rumination, referring to the tendency of such youth to dwell on negative affect and repetitively discuss, rehash, and speculate about problems (Rose, 2002). Mercer and DeRosier (2010) indeed reported that friends' anxiety, depression, and loneliness influenced children's own internalizing problems. These peer influence processes regarding depressive symptoms turned out to be stronger for girls than boys (Van Zalk et al., 2010). The underlying mechanism may be that girls are more sensitive than boys to stressful events occurring within peer relationships. Further, girls may experience, encode, and interpret negative exchanges within friendships more than boys do (Hankin & Abramson, 2001).

All studies on network dynamics report clear sex similarity in friendships. Voluntary sex segregation begins in early childhood, peaks in middle childhood, and is to some extent still present in adolescence (see also Maccoby, 1998). Several studies also report selection similarity for age and ethnicity and thus a preference for same-age and same-ethnic friends.

Beyond the question of whether similarity is due to selection or influence, application of these models has given greater insight into the *mechanisms* underlying network and behavior dynamics. In an exemplary study, Kiuru, Burk, Laursen, Salmela-Aro, and Nurmi (2010) compared selection and influence mechanisms for alcohol use and smoking. It turned out that selection played a greater role than influence for explaining similarity in the smoking behavior of friends (see also Mercken, Snijders, Steglich, & De Vries, 2009), whereas both selection and influence played a significant role in explaining similarity in drinking behavior. This finding is consistent with the idea that tobacco use is addictive and that once adolescents have started smoking the social influence on smoking may become less important for smoking progression. Thus, peer influence plays less of a role for dynamics in smoking behavior. Spatial segregation of smokers may provide an explanation for the selection effect: Society separates smokers from nonsmokers (referring to smoking designated areas), creating an opportunity structure in which smokers are more likely to establish new contacts with other smokers and then affiliate with each other. In addition, Kiuru et al. (2010) found that adolescents with a high level of smoking tended to receive more peer nominations than those who did not smoke, and smoking was accordingly seen as cool.

In another exemplary study, Dijkstra and colleagues (2010) compared selection and influence mechanisms for weapon carrying. They found that in early adolescence, weapon carrying was quite stable over a 1-year period. Using social network data of 207 Latino male adolescents in New Jersey, they found no support for a selection mechanism on the basis of weapon carrying. However, associating with friends who carry weapons increased the level of weapon carrying over the course of a year. Thus, selection plays no role, whereas influence does for the development of weapon carrying. In addition, Dijkstra et al. (2010) found that adolescents with a high level of problem behavior tended not only to be more popular, referring to the number of nominations received, than others with a low level of problem behavior but also to be more restrictive in the number of friendship nominations they gave to others. Thus, weapon carriers were seen by others as popular and were more selective than others in the number of friendships that they mentioned.

Moderating Effects

Examining moderating effects in peer influence processes also adds to our understanding of dynamics in the peer context. Influence effects can be moderated by characteristics of individuals (e.g., impulsivity), peers (e.g., status), the dyadic relationship (e.g., friendship quality), and the context (e.g., density of the network) (Prinstein, 2007). As far as we know, it has not been tested whether influence effects depend on contextual characteristics. The empirical evidence for the other types of moderation is scarce, too.

Moderating effects of individual characteristics have been tested in some studies. It was found that boys are more sensitive to the influence of delinquent friends (Burk et al., 2007) and that girls are more sensitive to the influence of depressed friends (Van Zalk et al., 2010). Impulsive youth were found to be more susceptible to the influence of friends' alcohol use (Burk et al., 2008; see also Snyder et al., 2010). With regard to involvement in externalizing behaviors, the role of self-control has been considered essential (Gottfredson & Hirschi, 1990). Although it has been shown that self-control is directly linked to involvement in externalizing behaviors (Pratt & Cullen, 2000), it has also been revealed that low self-control increases the chances of affiliation with deviant peers (Creemers et al., 2010). This suggests that individuals with low self-control are more likely to select deviant peers as friends, which can lead to contagion effects.

Other interesting moderating effects may be that adolescents who are intelligent may be low in susceptibility to certain influence attempts or that adolescents who are anxious and unassertive may be more susceptible to friends' influence (Caspi, 2006; Cohen & Prinstein, 2006). Furthermore, the importance of the group to the individual may also moderate sensitivity to the influence of friends (Kiesner, Cadinu, Poulin, & Bucci, 2002). In addition, parental characteristics may affect susceptibility to peer influence. For instance, the positive impact of a friend's academic achievement is stronger among adolescents whose parents are more authoritative, whereas the negative impact of friends' drug use is stronger among adolescents whose parents are less authoritative (Mounts & Steinberg, 1995).

It is also relevant to examine who is more influential when referring to the influence of peer characteristics. So far, this has not been examined in longitudinal social network models. It is likely that people will be more influenced by high-status peers (Dijkstra, Lindenberg, & Veenstra, 2008). For example, Cohen and Prinstein (2006) found that peer influence was more likely to occur when peers' status ranked high (see also Harvey & Rutherford, 1960). In an experimental study, participants believed they were interacting with fellow students in a chat room, but in reality they were e-confederates. The status of the focal e-confederate was manipulated in the study. When the focal e-confederate was given a high status, participants were more likely to exclude a fellow student without any apparent personal benefit other than the opportunity to obtain the approval of high-status peers.

It is also possible that popular adolescents become more trapped in deviant behaviors in order to maintain their status in the peer group. A cross-sectional study by Haynie (2001) showed that centrality and popularity in the peer network strengthened similarity in delinquency, suggesting that these adolescents are more prone to resemble their peers' behavior.

It is also likely that relative age moderates influence processes. Popp, Laursen, Kerr, Stattin, and Burk (2008) found that older peers in a network influence drinking behavior more than younger peers do.

Research on how relationship characteristics affect influence processes is scarce. On the one hand, it is possible that influence effects are stronger for close, intimate friends because frequent interaction and communication create numerous opportunities for influence (Piehler & Dishion, 2007; Stevens & Prinstein, 2005). On the other hand, adolescents with unreciprocated friendships may feel greater pressure to adapt their behavior in an attempt to persuade a disinterested peer or to gain additional emotional intimacy (see also Sandstrom, 2011). Overall, there is no consistent evidence in social network models that mutual friends have a stronger influence than unilateral friends (see for two exceptions Burk et al., 2007; Ojanen, Sijtsema, Hawley, & Little, 2010). Other measures for closeness or intimacy of friendships have not been included in actor-based models of behavior dynamics so far. For now, there is no evidence that the more adolescents value particular affiliations, the more they are willing to accede to influence attempts in order to maintain or enhance their friendships.

Age Effects

It is also important to examine whether selection and influence processes differ according to age. Monahan, Steinberg, and Cauffman (2009) suggested that the early years of adolescence are marked by young people selecting themselves into peer groups. If peer groups are better established by the time people have entered late adolescence, it stands to reason that changes in similarity among friends would have to be due to the impact that friends have on each other (Monahan et al., 2009). The influence of friends might wane in adulthood, because individuals' ability to resist peer influence is stronger in (emerging) adulthood than in adolescence (Gardner & Steinberg, 2005; Steinberg & Monahan, 2007). However, Berndt and Murphy (2003) consider it a myth that friends' influence peaks in middle adolescence. They argue that consistent age changes in the strength of friends' influence have not been found. Hypotheses about developmental changes in friends' influence may deserve consideration if future research reveals consistent age changes in influence effects on behavior dynamics.

Mediation Effects

Longitudinal social network models also allow researchers to examine mediation processes that help explain why adolescents change their network or their behavior. For instance, with regard to internalizing problems, the process of co-rumination might account for the influence processes in which adolescents contaminate their peers.

Potential influence mechanisms on externalizing problem behavior may involve encouragement, mutual participation, and attention (Dishion & Tipsord, 2011). The concept of deviancy training, introduced by Dishion, Spracklen, Andrews, and Patterson (1996), might also provide an understanding of the mechanisms underlying peer influence processes. In an experimental setting, they showed that involvement in deviant behavior was predicted by positive reactions of peers to deviancy. This suggests that the influence of peers can (partially) be explained by reinforcement processes.

The idea of social reinforcement of deviant behaviors also relates to the role of cognitions in peer influence processes (Scheier & Botvin, 1997). Adolescents might imitate their peers for expected outcomes, such as status and social bonding. Incorporating concepts such as deviancy training and expectancies in a longitudinal social network design might enhance our understanding of why and how peers influence each other.

FUTURE DIRECTIONS

Observations of similarity between friends in behaviors or attitudes have led scholars to examine friendship selection and influence processes. Examination of both network and behavior dynamics enables us to understand the processes of why and how adolescents display certain characteristics.

Future research on similarity in behaviors needs to incorporate not only selection and influence processes but also deselection processes. Van Zalk et al. (2010) were the first to show that nondepressive adolescents "filter out" depressive peers from their peer relationships. As a result, adolescents with high levels of depression mainly remained friends with other depressed adolescents.

Future research should also examine the extent to which not only similarity but also complementarity underlies the formation and continuation of relationships (Farmer, 2007), referring to people's seeking not only friends with similar characteristics but also friends who complement their own characteristics. The findings of some studies have shown that similarity is important during the initial phase of friendship formation—when individuals choose potential friends (Aboud & Mendelson, 1996). In later phases, when long-lasting friendships are established, the provision of social and emotional resources such as companionship, emotional support, help, and self-validation becomes more important and may allow for more dissimilarity in behavior.

The findings of other studies have also shown that similarity is only half the story. For example, a landmark study by Kupersmidt, DeRosier, and Patterson (1995) revealed that the likelihood of being friends increased linearly with the number of similar attributes. Still, even when children had seven similar attributes, the chances of being best friends were only 10% and of being school friends 50%. This suggests that a substantial part of peer affiliations remains unexplained by similarity in characteristics. The question is whether a lack of similarity reflects complementarity. Bukowski, Sippola, and Newcomb (2000) argued from a features perspective that certain characteristics are seen as valuable by peers and, therefore, attract peers who lack these characteristics. A striking example is that of popular adolescents who are considered attractive due to behaviors and characteristics that deviate from those of "normal" peers and signal maturity (Dijkstra, Lindenberg, Verhulst, Ormel, & Veenstra, 2009). However, attraction to certain peers does not necessarily imply complementarity. Future research is needed to reveal under what conditions similarity, attraction, and complementarity are helpful to understanding the formation of peer relations.

In a unique study with preschool children, Schaefer, Light, Fabes, Hanish, and Martin (2010) aimed to observe the principles that drive social network development. They argued that for many children the preschool classroom is the first opportunity to interact regularly with a large number of age-mates. Moreover, the diverse array of classmates allows children to exercise choice in their regular play partners. It was found in that study that reciprocity effects peaked early in the school year. As children began to sort themselves into relationships, the effects of reciprocity remained constant while other network processes became relatively more important. As relationships strengthened and their distribution solidified, children became more likely to seek and maintain relationships with popular peers. Popularity peaked in importance midway through the school year. From that point on, children became increasingly likely to form relationships with the most socially involved peers in the classroom. Unlike popularity, triadic closure increased in importance over the entire course of the school year, peaking in the final period. Presumably, as the interactions underlying relationships became more consistent, children were increasingly exposed to other children with whom their friends were playing. Beyond mere propinquity, this selective exposure may provide children with the opportunity to learn to infer relationships between other children in the class (Schaefer et al., 2010). Future research should also examine the principles that affect social networks in adolescence. An ideal case for that is the period after the transition to secondary education.

Broadening the focus of research on processes in peer networks has provided a more complete picture of the social landscape that children are part of (Gifford-Smith & Brownell, 2003). Beginning in early childhood, children sort themselves nonrandomly into friendships, selecting peers who are similar to themselves in important ways. In turn, the processes of creating and keeping friendships influence the behavior and attitudes of individuals. We have recently seen a growth in the number of studies in which network and behavior dynamics were examined simultaneously. These findings are very promising. To build a solid knowledge base of selection and influence processes, it is necessary for these findings to be replicated and tested in different contexts, with different age groups, and with different behaviors. It has to be made clear in which contexts, at which ages, and for which behaviors selection and influence play a role.

⦚ SUMMARY

Transformations in peer networks, referring to the dynamics of both the network and behaviors, are key elements in understanding development in adolescence. Advances in social network techniques enable researchers to address adequately selection and influence processes as mechanisms that steer these transformations. Social network models allow the examination of selection and influence processes simultaneously, while taking into account network and behavioral tendencies. Building on pioneering work on peer relations as well as valuable insights from experimental studies, a growing number of longitudinal social network studies have enhanced our understanding of the extent to which selection and influence contribute to (dis)similarity in peer networks and also of the mechanisms underlying these processes.

Despite this progress, a lot of work still needs to be done. The theoretical underpinning of the dynamics in networks and behaviors by specific mechanisms—and its integration in longitudinal social network modeling—has only just started. Questions about mediation and moderation effects that shed light on why and under what conditions adolescents change their behaviors and networks are open to investigation.

Empirically, social network analysis puts high demands on data. Not only do data need to comprise complete networks with information about the behaviors and characteristics of all participants but the same data are also required over time in order for changes in behaviors and networks to be modeled. Moreover, the questions to be addressed using longitudinal social network analyses define the type of data to be collected. Information on networks in classrooms is easily collected but does not provide the opportunity to examine peer influence effects from grade-mates, schoolmates, or town mates. The collection of network data on out-of-school friendships is challenging but probably needed (Kiesner, Poulin, & Nicotra, 2003).

The theoretical incorporation of mechanisms that explain why and under what conditions behaviors and networks change as well as the collection of the rich data necessary to address these processes will be a challenge for years to come.

☰ SUGGESTED READINGS

Burk, W. J., Steglich, C. E. G., & Snijders, T. A. B. (2007). Beyond dyadic interdependence: Actor-oriented models for co-evolving social networks and individual behaviors. *International Journal of Behavioral Development, 31,* 397–404.

Steglich, C., Snijders, T. A. B., & Pearson, M. (2010). Dynamic networks and behavior: Separating selection from influence. *Sociological Methodology, 41,* 329–393.

Veenstra, R., & Steglich, C. (2012). Actor-based model for network and behavior dynamics: A tool to examine selection and influence processes. In B. Laursen, T. D. Little, & N. A. Card (Eds.), *Handbook of developmental research methods.* New York: Guilford Press.

☰ REFERENCES

NOTE: The asterisks denote SIENA was used.

Aboud, F. E., & Mendelson, M. J. (1996). Determinants of friendship selection and quality: Developmental perspectives. In W. M. Bukowski, A. F. Newcomb, & W. W. Hartup (Eds.), *The company they keep. Friendships in childhood and adolescence* (pp. 87–112). Cambridge, UK: Cambridge University Press.

Altmann, E. O., & Gotlib, I. H. (1988). The social behavior of depressed children: An observational study. *Journal of Abnormal Child Psychology, 16,* 29–44.

*Baerveldt, C., Völker, B., & Van Rossem, R. (2008). Revisiting selection and influence: An inquiry into the friendship networks of high school students and their association with delinquency. *Canadian Journal of Criminology and Criminal Justice, 50,* 559–587.

Berndt, T. J., & Murphy, L. M. (2003). Influences of friends and friendships: Myths, truths, and research recommendations. *Advances in Child Development and Behavior, 30,* 275–310.

Billy, J. O. G., & Udry, R. (1985). Patterns of adolescent friendship and effects on sexual behavior. *Social Psychology Quarterly, 48*, 27–41.

Blau, P. M. (1977). A macrosociological theory of social structure. *American Journal of Sociology, 83*, 26–54.

Borelli, J. L., & Prinstein, M. J. (2006). Reciprocal, longitudinal associations among adolescents' negative feedback-seeking, depressive symptoms, and peer relations. *Journal of Abnormal Child Psychology, 34*, 159–169.

Bukowski, W. M., Sippola, L. K., & Newcomb, A. F. (2000). Variations in patterns of attraction of same- and other-sex peers during early adolescence. *Developmental Psychology, 36*, 147–154.

*Burk, W. J., Kerr, M., & Stattin, H. (2008). The co-evolution of early adolescent friendship networks, school involvement, and delinquent behaviors. *Revue Française de Sociologie, 49*, 499–522.

*Burk, W. J., Steglich, C. E. G., & Snijders, T. A. B. (2007). Beyond dyadic interdependence: Actor-oriented models for co-evolving social networks and individual behaviors. *International Journal of Behavioral Development, 31*, 397–404.

Byrne, D. E. (1971). *The attraction paradigm*. New York: Academic.

Caspi, A. (2006). Personality development. In N. Eisenberg (Ed.), *Handbook of child psychology: Vol. 3. Social, emotional, and personality development* (pp. 300–365). New York: Wiley.

Cohen, G. L., & Prinstein, M. J. (2006). Peer contagion of aggression and health risk behavior among adolescent males: An experimental investigation of effects on public conduct and private attitudes. *Child Development, 77*, 967–983.

Cohen, J. M. (1977). Sources of peer group homogeneity. *Sociology of Education, 50*, 227–241.

Connolly, J., Geller, S., Marton, P., & Kutcher, S. (1992). Peer responses to social interaction with depressed adolescents. *Journal of Clinical Child Psychology, 21*, 365–370.

Coyne, J. C. (1976). Depression and the response of others. *Journal of Abnormal Psychology, 85*, 186–193.

Creemers, H. E., Dijkstra, J. K., Vollebergh, W. A. M., Ormel, J., Verhulst, F. C., & Huizink, A. C. (2010). Predicting frequent cannabis use in adolescence; the roles of temperament and peer substance use: The TRAILS study. *Addiction, 105*, 699–708.

Davis, J. A. (1970). Clustering and hierarchy in interpersonal relations: Testing two graph theoretical models on 742 sociomatrices. *American Sociological Review, 35*, 843–851.

Dijkstra, J. K., Lindenberg, S., & Veenstra, R. (2008). Beyond the class norm: Bullying behavior of popular adolescents and its relation to peer acceptance and rejection. *Journal of Abnormal Child Psychology, 36*, 1289–1299.

*Dijkstra, J. K., Lindenberg, S., Veenstra, R., Steglich, C., Isaacs, J., Card, N. A., et al. (2010). Influence and selection processes in weapon carrying during adolescence: The roles of status, aggression, and vulnerability. *Criminology, 48*, 187–220.

Dijkstra, J. K., Lindenberg, S., Verhulst, F. C., Ormel, J., & Veenstra, R. (2009). The relation between popularity and aggressive, destructive, and norm-breaking behaviors: Moderating effects of athletic abilities, physical attractiveness, and prosociality. *Journal of Research on Adolescence, 19*, 401–413.

Dishion, T. J., Patterson, G. R., & Griesler, P. C. (1994). Peer adaptations in the development of antisocial behavior: A confluence model. In L. R. Huesmann (Ed.), *Aggressive behavior: Current perspectives* (pp. 61–95). New York: Plenum.

Dishion, T. J., Spracklen, K. M., Andrews, D. W., & Patterson, G. R. (1996). Deviancy training in male adolescent friendships. *Behavior Therapy, 27*, 373–390.

Dishion, T. J., & Tipsord, J. M. (2011). Peer contagion in child and adolescent social and emotional development. *Annual Review of Psychology, 62,* 189–214.

Durkheim, E. (1897). *Suicide: A study in sociology.* London: Routledge.

Ennett, S. T., & Bauman, K. E. (1994). The contribution of influence and selection to adolescent peer group homogeneity: The case of adolescent cigarette smoking. *Journal of Personality and Social Psychology, 67,* 653–663.

Farmer, T. W. (2007). Studying the individual within the peer context: Are we on target? *New Directions for Child and Adolescent Development, 118,* 101–108.

Feld, S. L. (1982). Social structural determinants of similarity among associates. *American Sociological Review, 47,* 797–801.

Friedkin, N. E. (1998). *A structural theory of social influence.* Cambridge, UK: Cambridge University Press.

Gardner, M., & Steinberg, L. (2005). Peer influence on risk taking, risk preference, and risky decision making in adolescence and adulthood: An experimental study. *Developmental Psychology, 41,* 625–635.

Gazelle, H., & Ladd, G. W. (2003). Anxious solitude and peer exclusion: A diathesis-stress model of internalizing trajectories in childhood. *Child Development, 74,* 257–278.

George, T. P., & Hartman, D. P. (1996). Friendship networks of unpopular average, and popular children. *Child Development, 67,* 2301–2316.

Gifford-Smith, M. E., & Brownell, C. A. (2003). Childhood peer relationships: Social acceptance, friendships, and peer networks. *Journal of School Psychology, 41,* 235–284.

Gottfredson, M. R., & Hirschi, T. (1990). *A general theory of crime.* Stanford, CA: Stanford University Press.

Hallinan, M. T. (1980). Patterns of cliquing among youth. In H. C. Foot, A. J. Chapman, & J. R. Smith (Eds.), *Friendship and social relations in children* (pp. 321–342). Chichester, UK: Wiley.

Hankin, B. L., & Abramson, L. Y. (2001). Development of gender differences in depression: An elaborated cognitive vulnerability-transactional stress theory. *Psychological Bulletin, 127,* 773–796.

Harvey, O. J., & Rutherford, J. (1960). Status in the informal group: Influence and influencibility at differing age levels. *Developmental Psychology, 31,* 377–385.

Haynie, D. L. (2001). Delinquent peers revisited: Does network structure matter? *American Journal of Sociology, 106,* 1013–1057.

Homans, G. C. (1961). *Social behaviour: Its elementary forms.* London: Routledge.

Joiner, T. E., Jr. (2001). Defensiveness predicts peer rejection of depressed children. *Behaviour Research and Therapy, 39,* 929–938.

Kandel, D. B. (1978). Homophily, selection, and socialization in adolescent friendship pairs. *American Journal of Sociology, 48,* 427–436.

Kiesner, J., Cadinu, M., Poulin, F., & Bucci, M. (2002). Group identification in early adolescence: Its relation with peer adjustment and its moderator effect on peer influence. *Child Development, 73,* 196–208.

Kiesner, J., Poulin, F., & Nicotra, E. (2003). Peer relations across contexts: Individual-network homophily and network inclusion in and after school. *Child Development, 74,* 1328–1343.

*Kiuru, N., Burk, W., Laursen, B., Salmela-Aro, K., & Nurmi, J.-E. (2010). Pressure to drink but not to smoke: Disentangling selection and socialization in adolescent peer networks and peer groups. *Journal of Adolescence, 33,* 801–812.

*Knecht, A., Snijders, T. A. B., Baerveldt, C., Steglich, C. E. G., & Raub, W. (2010). Friendship and delinquency: Selection and influence processes in early adolescence. *Social Development, 19,* 494–514.

Kupersmidt, J. B., DeRosier, M. E., & Patterson, C. P. (1995). Similarity as the basis for children's friendships: The roles of sociometric status, aggressive and withdrawn behavior, academic achievement and demographic characteristics. *Journal of Social and Personal Relationships, 12,* 439–452.

Lazarsfeld, P. F., & Merton, R. K. (1954). Friendship as social process: A substantive and methodological analysis. In M. Berger, T. Abel, & C. H. Page (Eds.), *Freedom and control in modern society* (pp. 18–66). New York: Van Nostrand.

*Light, J. M., & Dishion, T. J. (2007). Early adolescent antisocial behavior and peer rejection: A dynamic test of a developmental process. *New Directions for Child and Adolescent Development, 118,* 77–89.

Maccoby, E. E. (1998). *The two sexes: Growing up apart, coming together.* Cambridge, MA: Belknap.

McPherson, M., Smith-Lovin, L., & Cook, J. M. (2001). Birds of a feather: Homophily in social networks. *Annual Review of Sociology, 27,* 415–444.

*Mercer, S. H., & DeRosier, M. (2010). Selection and socialization of internalizing problems in middle childhood. *Journal of Social and Clinical Psychology, 29,* 1032–1059.

*Mercken, L., Snijders, T. A. B., Steglich, C. E. G., & De Vries, H. (2009). Dynamics of adolescent friendship networks and smoking behavior: Social network analyses in six European countries. *Social Science & Medicine, 69,* 1506–1514.

Monahan, K. C., Steinberg, L., & Cauffman, E. (2009). Affiliation with antisocial peers, susceptibility to peer influence, and antisocial behavior during the transition to adulthood. *Developmental Psychology, 45,* 1520–1530.

Mounts, N. S., & Steinberg, L. (1995). An ecological analysis of peer influence on adolescent grade point average and drug use. *Developmental Psychology, 31,* 915–922.

*Ojanen, T., Sijtsema, J. J., Hawley, P. H., & Little, T. D. (2010). Intrinsic and extrinsic motivation in early adolescents' friendship development: Friendship selection, influence, and prospective friendship quality. *Journal of Adolescence, 33,* 837–851.

Osgood, D. W., & Anderson, A. L. (2004). Unstructured socializing and rates of delinquency. *Criminology, 42,* 519–549.

Piehler, T. F., & Dishion, T. J. (2007). Interpersonal dynamics within adolescent friendships: Dyadic mutuality, deviant talk, and patterns of antisocial behavior. *Child Development, 78,* 1611–1624.

Popp, D., Laursen, B., Kerr, M., Stattin, H., & Burk, W. J. (2008). Modeling homophily over time with an actor-partner interdependence model. *Developmental Psychology, 44,* 1028–1039.

Pratt, T. C., & Cullen, F. T. (2000). The empirical status of Gottfredson and Hirschi's general theory of crime: A meta-analysis. *Criminology, 38,* 931–964.

Prinstein, M. J. (2007). Moderators of peer contagion: A longitudinal examination of depression socialization between adolescents and their best friends. *Journal of Clinical Child and Adolescent Psychology, 36,* 159–170.

Prinstein, M. J., Cheah, C. S. L., & Guyer, A. E. (2005). Peer victimization, cue interpretation, and internalizing symptoms: Preliminary concurrent and longitudinal findings for children and adolescents. *Journal of Clinical Child Psychology, 34,* 11–24.

Rose, A. J. (2002). Co-rumination in the friendships of girls and boys. *Child Development, 73,* 1830–1843.

Rudolph, K. D., Hammen, C., & Burge, D. (1994). Interpersonal functioning and depressive symptoms in childhood: Addressing the issues of specificity and comorbidity. *Journal of Abnormal Child Psychology, 22,* 355–371.

Sandstrom, M. J. (2011). The power of popularity: Influence processes in childhood and adolescence. In A. H. N. Cillessen, D. Schwartz, & L. Mayeux (Eds.), *Popularity in the peer system.* New York: Guilford Press.

*Schaefer, D. R., Light, J. M., Fabes, R. A., Hanish, L. D., & Martin, C. L. (2010). Fundamental principles of network formation among preschool children. *Social Networks, 32,* 61–71.

Scheier, L. M., & Botvin, G. J. (1997). Expectancies as mediators of the effects of social influences and alcohol knowledge on adolescent alcohol use: A prospective analysis. *Psychology of Addictive Behaviors, 11,* 48–64.

*Sijtsema, J. J., Ojanen, T., Veenstra, R., Lindenberg, S., Hawley, P. H., & Little, T. D. (2010). Forms and functions of aggression in adolescent friendship selection and influence: A longitudinal social network analysis. *Social Development, 19,* 515–534.

Snijders, T. A. B. (2001). The statistical evaluation of social network dynamics. *Sociological Methodology, 31,* 361–395.

Snijders, T. A. B. (2005). Models for longitudinal network data. In P. J. Carrington, J. Scott, & S. Wasserman (Eds.), *Models and methods in social network analysis* (pp. 215–247). New York: Cambridge University Press.

Snijders, T. A. B., Steglich, C., & Schweinberger, M. (2007). Modeling the coevolution of networks and behavior. In K. Van Montfort, J. Oud, & A. Satorra (Eds.), *Longitudinal models in the behavioral and related sciences* (pp. 41–71). Mahwah, NJ: Lawrence Erlbaum.

Snijders, T. A. B., Van de Bunt, G. G., & Steglich, C. E. G. (2010). Introduction to stochastic actor-based models for network dynamics. *Social Networks, 32,* 44–60.

Snyder, J., McEachern, A., Schrepferman, L., Just, C., Jenkins, M., Roberts, S. et al. (2010). Contribution of peer deviancy training to the early development of conduct problems: Mediators and moderators. *Behavior Therapy, 27,* 317–328.

*Steglich, C., Snijders, T. A. B., & Pearson, M. (2010). Dynamic networks and behavior: Separating selection from influence. *Sociological Methodology, 41,* 329–393.

Steinberg, L., & Monahan, K. C. (2007). Age differences in resistance to peer influence. *Developmental Psychology, 43,* 1531–1543.

Stevens, E. A., & Prinstein, M. J. (2005). Peer contagion of depressogenic attributional styles among adolescents: A longitudinal study. *Journal of Abnormal Child Psychology, 33,* 25–37.

*Van Zalk, M. H. W., Kerr, M., Branje, S. J. T., Stattin, H., & Meeus, W. H. J. (2010). It takes three: Selection, influence, and de-selection processes of depression in adolescent friendship networks. *Developmental Psychology, 46,* 927–938.

Veenstra, R., & Steglich, C. (2011). Actor-based model for network and behavior dynamics: A tool to examine selection and influence processes. In B. Laursen, T. D. Little, & N. A. Card (Eds.), *Handbook of developmental research methods.* New York: Guilford Press.

Verbrugge, L. M. (1977). The structure of adult friendship choices. *Social Forces, 56,* 576–597.

PART III

Romantic Relationships

8

Transformations in Heterosexual Romantic Relationships Across the Transition Into Adolescence

Inge Seiffge-Krenke

Shmuel Shulman

For a long time, romantic relations during adolescence have been ignored by researchers. The first book on this issue was published in 1999 (Furman, Brown, & Feiring, 1999). Since then, theories on romantic development have been developed, and numerous studies were conducted (see Collins, Welsh, & Furman, 2009, for a review), including various methods such as interviews, questionnaires, observations of couple interactions, and longitudinal studies, which studied romantic couples over an extended time span. Once considered to be trivial and transitory, romantic relationships have become increasingly regarded as potentially meaningful relationships that have a significant impact on subsequent romantic relationships in adulthood (Gottman, Coan, Carrere, & Swanson, 1998).

In this chapter, we present individual, familial, and cultural aspects that play a role in the development and sustainment of romantic relations.

Theoretical models that guide our perspective on romance will be highlighted, and the links between romantic relationships and other close relationships such as those with friends and parents discussed. In addition, the impact of romantic relations on health will be analyzed.

⦚⦚ ARE ROMANTIC RELATIONS TRIVIAL AND TRANSITORY?

The emergence of romantic relationships is a central feature of social development. Following pubertal development, adolescents start to experience cravings for sexual gratification and to fantasize about emotional union with a partner. Through peer activities, adolescents learn to meet and interact with romantic partners and to become involved in sustained relationships. Recent research has shown that common prejudices of adults about adolescents' romances (e.g., that they are trivial and transitory) are not justified (Collins, 2003). Although differing from adult partnerships, adolescent romantic relationships become steady and exclusive, and individuals experience a high level of intimacy and concern for their partner. However, a closer inspection of the emergence and development of romantic relationships suggests that there is some ground for the popular beliefs. During early adolescence, romantic feelings and cravings may remain on the imaginary level or may be expressed through short-lived encounters; it is only during the latter stages of adolescence that romantic connections become steady, intimate, and committed (Shulman, Connolly, & McIsaac, in press).

From the Emergence of Romantic Interests to Romantic Relationships

Throughout the years of elementary school, children's activities and friendships are strongly separated by gender. By late childhood, other-gender classmates start to become targets of great interest, while direct interactions are rare and proscribed by peers. However, indirect ways of cross-gender interactions start to appear, consisting of short-lived episodes of taunting, teasing, name calling, and chasing games between boys and girls. Despite the seemingly outspoken disavowal of interest, anyone who observes such interactions cannot miss the high level of interest and excitement that characterize them.

Hormonal changes that are part of pubertal development lead to the growing interest in the other gender, as well as to the emotional arousal and mood fluctuations that characterize adolescents' initial romantic interests (Fisher, 2006). Moreover, adolescents start to experience cravings for sexual gratification as well as for emotional union with a partner. As part of this process, early adolescents need first to become aware of their sexual cravings, accept themselves as sexual beings, and learn how to express these feelings in an accepted manner. Considering the novelty of these experiences and unfamiliarity in interacting with the other gender, adolescents' strong feelings and cravings are initially likely to stay within the private domain and not be directly expressed behaviorally.

For some individuals starting in the early adolescent years, fantasizing emerges about a romantic experience one would like to have while in reality he or she has rarely or never spoken to the admired one. The excitement accompanying romantic fantasies may be a rewarding experience in itself (Tuval-Mashiach, Walsh, Harel, & Shulman, 2008). The need for a safe territory to cope with romantic awakening partly explains the role of the close friends and same-aged peers in the early romantic involvements (Brown, 1999; Connolly & Johnson, 1996). Within the familiar and comfortable context of same-gender friendship cliques, young adolescents feel safe enough to discuss issues of sexuality, attraction, and passion; share dreams and fantasies; and learn what is allowed and what is prohibited (Brown, 1999; Connolly & Johnson, 1996).

Later, participation in mixed-gender groups becomes common and provides comfortable and safe opportunities for associations with the other gender. Initially, activities may not necessarily, at least explicitly, focus on dating but bring boys and girls together in activities like two boys and three girls going to a movie. Some adolescents may participate in the mixed-gender interactions only indirectly by observation, whereas others are more active. Yet within these mixed-gender contexts adolescents have the opportunity to meet potential partners. Gradually, mixed-gender groups become populated by pairings of adolescents who are romantically connected to each other. These emergent relationships are fragile, rarely long-lasting, and more casual than serious in the eyes of the adolescents (Connolly, Craig, Goldberg, & Pepler, 1999).

Contingent upon the accumulating experiences of transient romantic encounters, meaningful romantic relationships start to emerge—particularly among older adolescents. Characteristic of these relationships is their increased stability and durability. Uppermost, these relationships are intimate and emotionally supportive for both partners (Furman & Wehner,

1997; Shulman & Scharf, 2000). Coinciding with this new level of intimacy, consolidated romantic relationships also bring challenges to adolescents as to how to maintain a sufficient level of personal identity and independence from their romantic partner.

Taken together, the transition to romantic involvements and relationships is a new experience for adolescents. Individuals need to become aware of their sexuality and sexual attraction and learn the proper ways to express these emerging wishes and fantasies. Through group facilitation, adolescents learn how to interact with potential partners. Gradually, with age, they become involved in more stable relationships that start to resemble those of adult partners.

⧸⧸ DURATION AND QUALITY OF ROMANTIC RELATIONSHIPS

A number of studies have documented the increasing importance of romantic attraction and relationships during adolescence. They demonstrated that with time and experience, the quality of romantic encounter shifts from more superficial relationships based on infatuation and status to relationships characterized by intimacy and commitment.

Frequency and Duration

Nearly all early adolescents (ages 13–14) report on romantic fantasies and express an interest in dating, but these do not necessarily match their actual experience (Tuval-Mashiach et al., 2008). In contrast, by late adolescence (ages 17–19), most individuals have experienced some kind of romantic relationship (Collins et al., 2009; Connolly et al., 1999; Feiring, 1996). More than half of U.S. adolescents report having had a romantic relationship in the past 18 months (Carver, Joyner, & Udry, 2003), and the frequency of dating and romantic involvement in Canadian (Connolly, Craig, Goldberg, & Pepler, 2004), German (Seiffge-Krenke, 2003), Italian (Connolly, Friedlander, Pepler, Craig, & Laporte, 2010), and Israeli adolescents (Shulman & Scharf, 2000) is similarly high.

The duration of romance increases substantially from about 3 months in early adolescent couple relationships (Feiring, 1996) to between 1 and 2 years at middle and late adolescence (Creasey, 2002). These individual frequencies match with research on couples, which show that by late adolescence 40% of all couples were together for more than 12 months (Bucx & Seiffge-Krenke, 2010). The age differences between male and female partners of a couple were small (Galliher, Welsh, Rotosky, & Kawaguchi, 2004); males are approximately 3 years older then females (Seiffge-Krenke & Burk, 2010), though females are more likely to start earlier to become involved in longer lasting relationships (Shulman, Walsh, Weisman, & Schleyer, 2009). Increasing frequency and duration demonstrate that a romantic affair has become more enduring and committed by late adolescence.

Different Components of Romantic Love

Initial romantic overtures are characterized by attraction aimed at focusing and selecting a potential partner. Attraction is characterized by elation, heightened energy, mood swings, focused attention, obsessive thinking about a partner, and craving for an emotional union with him or her (Fisher, 2006). Adolescents tend to describe their romantic encounters in terms such as uniqueness, absolutes, and idealism (Fischer & Alapack, 1987). However, despite the intense nature of adolescent romance, it is brief (Feiring, 1996) and likely to dissolve after a short period of time. These short-lived attractions characterizing the first stage of a romantic involvement are typical among early adolescents where short-term fascinations are less likely to evolve into sustained relationship (Feiring, 1996; Shulman et al., 2009). Of note, recent findings from our studies show that even among older adolescents romantic attraction tends to decrease within less than a year after they had started (Shulman, Appel, & Swain, 2010).

Classical theories and models of love have conceptualized three distinguishable components: (1) *intimacy*, (2) *commitment*, and (3) *passion* (Sternberg, 1986) to characterize romantic love. Intimacy involves complex motivational, emotional, and behavioral aspects that emerge through interaction with other persons such as parents and close friends (Collins & Sroufe 1999; Feldman, Gowen, & Fisher, 1998). During adolescence, intimacy becomes increasingly important, and intimacy perceived in friendships is gradually transferred to romantic partners (Scharf & Mayseless, 2001). Commitment refers to the desire to stay involved in one's romantic relationship and to maintain a potential long-term relationship. Sternberg's third component, passion, refers to feelings of romance, attraction, and sexuality. As we have discussed, passion and attraction characterizes the initial stage of a romantic relationship. Yet, once interactions are sustained, interchanges become rule governed and regulated. Passion, then, needs to be integrated within the other relational components like intimacy and commitment.

Nonetheless, both common experience and empirical research show that disagreements and conflicts are also integral to romantic relationships (McIsaac, Connolly, McKenney, Pepler, & Craig, 2008). The mere presence of conflict, therefore, reveals less about the quality of a relationship than does the way in which the conflict is handled. Self-reports as well as observations have shown that the ability to negotiate differences and even using distraction to avoid direct confrontation can be helpful in the maintenance of a relationship, while direct aggression and contempt are likely to lead to dissolution (Shulman, Tuval-Mashiach, Levran, & Anbar, 2006; Tuval-Mashiach & Shulman, 2006). The ability to resolve disagreements can be helpful for negotiating closeness and individuality and may contribute to mutually satisfying solutions and subsequent intensification of the relationship.

⦚ DIFFERENT TYPES OF ROMANTIC LOVE AND CHANGES OVER TIME

After having described the overall developmental sequence from the first romantic encounters during early adolescence to more sustained, committed relationships in late adolescence, we need now to differentiate between different types of romantic love at a given time point. Although the overall developmental sequence may be valid for most adolescents, it is noticeable that at each phase of romantic development there is considerable diversity how both partners experience the relationship. This diversity partly resulted from the fact that romantic relations evolve out of friendships and are initiated and sustained in the friendship network.

Fluidity in Boundaries Between Romantic and Affiliative Experiences

In this respect, it is useful to differentiate between romantic experiences that describe physical attraction, infatuation, and sexual preoccupation and nonromantic, or affiliative, experiences, which describe platonic aspects of the relationship, such as companionship, trust, and friendship. Studies on the prevalence and patterns of romantic relationships suggest considerable fluidity in the boundaries between adolescents' romantic and nonromantic experiences (Connolly & McIsaac, 2008). There are romantic couple relationships that may resemble friendships, and there are adolescents who have sex with someone other than their boyfriend or girlfriend (hookups) (Manning, Giordano, & Longmore, 2006). Affiliative experiences with a romantic partner sometimes develop into enduring passionate romances, while others develop into friendships (Connolly & McIsaac, 2008). Other romantic relationships have been passionate but turn after a break into friendship, with the romantic partner being integrated into the peer network (Connolly, Furman, & Konarski, 2000).

Our research on late adolescent couples suggests that there is considerable diversity in the features of enduring romantic relations (Seiffge-Krenke & Burk, 2010). Altogether, we distinguished several different types with varying degrees of romantic or affiliative qualities. We found 35% of couples whose relationships had a strong romantic quality—for example, characterized by physical attraction, infatuation, and sexual preoccupation—and only a small proportion—16% of couples—in which males and females described their relationships predominantly by affiliative components such as companionship, trust, and friendship. A further group of 28% of the couples showed a similarly high quality of both romantic and affiliative components in their relationships. Finally, roughly one fourth of all couples were highly interdependent and mutually influential, but the partners feel neither positive nor close to each other. This finding may be understandable, given the fact that having a romantic partner increases peer group status (Brown, 1999). Alternatively, these may be nonromantic sexual relationships (Giordano, Longmore, & Manning, 2006). The different types of romance were not depending on duration, suggesting that even among late adolescent couples, who have been together since quite a time, affiliative components and a nonlove quality may be quite frequent. Noteworthy, in most couples, males and females share more similar than dissimilar perspectives on their romance.

Gendered socialization and different interactional histories may impact male and female adolescents' interpretations and experiences of their romantic relationships (Galliher et al., 2004), with females reporting a higher level of affective intensity in their romantic relationships and placing more value on closeness and caring in their romantic relationships than males (Shulman & Scharf, 2000). The higher investment of girls can also explain the greater impact of their behavior on the partner and the dyad once disagreements are negotiated (McIsaac et al., 2008).

Changes in the Quality of Romantic Relations

Both normative maturation and ongoing experiences in the romantic arena contribute to relationship changes. Unlike early adolescent romantic relationships, which are often transient and capricious (Feiring, 1996), and middle to late adolescent romance, which is highly passionate and sometimes idealistic (Connolly & McIsaac, 2008), romantic relationships at the latter stages of adolescence are in general less idealistic and often freighted with a "pragmatic perspective" (Brown, 1999). Similarly, longer-term romantic relationships commonly manifest higher levels of intimacy, passion, and commitment than do relationships of shorter duration.

As adolescents grow older, their ability to resolve disagreements and conflicts also increases (Laursen, Finkelstein, & Betts, 2001). Younger couples tended more to downplay disagreement as if they were afraid that any discord would lead to a breakup. In contrast, older adolescent couples were more capable of sorting out their disagreement, understanding each other better, and arriving at solutions that balance better the needs of both partners (Tuval-Mashiach & Shulman, 2006). As could be assumed, the negotiating between romantic partners on issues of self and the relationship leads to higher quality relationships—for example, to an increase in commitment and intimacy (Seiffge-Krenke, 2003).

Taken together, though romantic involvements can be expressed in different forms, in general they evolve from romantic attraction to intimacy and commitment. Within this process, partners must learn how to negotiate differences in order to solidify their relationship.

THEORETICAL MODELS DESCRIBING ROMANTIC AFFAIRS DURING ADOLESCENCE

With burgeoning interest in romantic activity, several theories have been developed to describe the developmental sequence of romantic relations and the impact of other close relationship (e.g., with parents and peers) on romantic development. Several of these models have been supported by research on adolescent couples.

Developmental Models About the Sequence of Romantic Phases

Referring to a developmental-contextual perspective, Brown (1999) proposed a heuristic model of a four-phase sequence through which adolescents pass in their development of romantic interests, skills, and relationship experiences. This developmental sequence is neither fixed nor inevitable or unrepeatable. Brown (1999) has proposed that each phase is characterized by the specific nature of romantic activity and by key features. The *initiation phase* symbolizes a turning point in adolescent social activities. After having played in strongly gender segregated groups during childhood, the early adolescent needs to become reoriented to and reacquainted with the opposite gender. The basic objectives in this first phase are to broaden one's self-concept and to gain confidence in one's ability to relate to potential partners in a romantic way. Thus, the focus is on the self, not on the romantic relationship. Romantic dating occurs in the context of and with the assistance of same-sex peers. During the second phase, the *status phase,* adolescents are confronted with the pressure of having the "right kinds" of romantic relationships. Dating the "wrong" people can seriously damage the adolescents' standing in the group. Romantic relationships may thus be used to obtain or increase peer acceptance and, as such, may hinder the establishment of a mutually rewarding romantic relationship. The third phase, the *affection phase,* is characterized by a shift of focus from the context in which the relationship exists toward the romantic relationship itself. Romance becomes a personal and relational affair, and the relationship becomes exclusive and dyadic. At the same time, the influence of the peer group wanes. Partners in affection-oriented relationships generate deeper feelings of commitment to their relationship, express deeper levels of caring for each other, and typically engage in more extensive sexual activity. The adolescent's peer network in this phase is reduced from a large crowd of same-sex peers to a smaller circle of mixed-sex friends or adolescents couples. Finally, during the fourth phase of romantic development, the *bonding phase,* individuals are expected to maintain the depth of relationships typical for the affection phase yet adopt a more pragmatic perspective. Central issues of this phase concern the possibilities of remaining together with a romantic partner for a lifetime. Typically, while the romantic partners consider themselves to be inseparable as a couple, they remain distinctive personalities. As such, questions of identity may also rise again. Brown (1999) has claimed that this phase may be characteristic for the transition between adolescence and young adulthood.

Brown's (1999) model highlights the importance of peers in the romantic development. This perspective is taken up and broadened by family relationships and biological perspectives in the model by Furman & Wehner (1997). According to the theory of romantic development they put forth, romantic relationships involve the integration of attachment, affiliative, caregiving, behavioral systems as well as the sexual reproductive system. Mature attachments to romantic partners are unlikely to emerge in early adolescence, when romantic relationships are casual and short-lived. Early adolescents' romantic partners are primarily companions and friends. At a later stage, a partner is sought out in times of distress and is expected to provide support, comfort, and care. When sexual desires begin to emerge following puberty, the individual turns to the romantic partner for sexual fulfillment as well. In meeting these different needs, the romantic partner becomes a major figure in late adolescence. As the relationship develops, the romantic partner gradually assumes a higher position in the adolescent's social hierarchy, thereby replacing parents and peers. These models emphasize the role of social relations in shaping and regulating individual development within the romantic domain. Yet, as previously indicated, the role of pubertal development in the emergence of romantic and sexual interests cannot be overlooked (Fisher, 2006).

Psychoanalytic Conceptualizations

The psychoanalytic theories have pointed to the role of puberty and sexuality in adolescent development at large and adolescent romantic involvement specifically. Within this framework, Anna Freud (1958) described the reawakening of an incestuous tension that leads to increased distance between children and parents. Blos (1967) and Gray and Steinberg (1999) have proposed that the development of romantic interests is inherently linked to the task of separation and individuation from the family. The emergence of romantic activity can thus be understood as part of a more general process of the development of emotional autonomy, first taking place in the family context and later on, as the quality of romances changes from casual to more committed, in the peer context.

Other thinkers within the psychoanalytic school have paid even more attention to the direct impact of body and sexual changes that characterize puberty and adolescence. In their work, Laufer and Laufer (1984) described the difficulties in integrating sexual drives and genitals into the body concept and selecting a heterosexual nonincestuous love object. Though their tenets are based on their clinical work, we can understand the complexity of integrating pubertal changes and develop a mature sexual organization (which includes the physical mature body and fantasies or real interactions with a new partner) that each adolescent has to cope with.

Erikson's theory links identity development with the development of intimacy in partnerships (Erikson, 1982). His theory of life span development suggests that in Stage 5, adolescents try to figure out what is unique or distinctive about them. Erikson strongly argued that adolescents who fail to find a suitable identity may have difficulty forming and maintaining long-lasting close relationships with romantic partners. In Stage 6, young adulthood, according to Erikson, the focus is on developing such close, intimate relationships. Erikson added that difficulties during this phase may stem from an earlier failure to develop a strong identity. Thus, the development of the self is posited as a key aspect in the development of interpersonal intimacy (Erikson, 1968).

Although each theory makes a distinct contribution, with Brown focusing on the peer status ramifications of partner choice, Furman on the affiliation and intimacy provisions of romantic relationships, and the neopsychoanalytic theorists on individuation processes, a number of consistent themes is evident across these conceptualizations. First, each theory connects the development of romantic relationships to individuation from the family and to increasing connectedness to peers. Second, the need to achieve mature forms of sexuality, autonomy, affiliation, and intimacy, namely balancing needs of self and partner is the central goal of this developmental progression. Finally, involvement in romantic increases an individual's capacity for mature relationships, thus serving as a model and training ground for adult romantic relationships (Connolly & McIsaac, 2009).

Empirical Support for the Different Theoretical Tenets

Empirical studies evaluating the phase models have indeed shown that the focus changes from romantic wishes and fantasies (Tuval-Mashiach et al., 2008) through romantic activity being embedded in peer group activities and romantic quality sometimes resembling friendships (Connolly et al.,

2004; Seiffge-Krenke & Burk, 2010) to more dyadic, exclusive, and intimate encounters between the couple in love (Seiffge-Krenke, 2003; Shulman & Scharf, 2000). This research has further revealed that the early phases of romantic involvement can be motivated by individual needs like status seeking or companionship while the needs and wishes of the romantic partner may not yet be in the focus (Connolly & McIsaac, 2009). Thus, true intimacy (as the balance between autonomy and connectedness) has not yet developed, and affiliation is more important than intimacy. But, as detailed earlier, there is considerable diversity in couple relationships with even late adolescent couples in relationships of considerable duration being characterized by different qualities of romance versus affiliation.

Further research has substantiated evidence for the developmental ordering of identity and intimacy as outlined by Erikson. These studies suggest that younger individuals are more concerned with identity than intimacy issues and, further, that older individuals who show mature identity levels also have high levels of intimacy with partners (Lacombe & Gay, 1998; Montgomery, 2005). Studies following the romantic development over several years (Beyers & Seiffge-Krenke, 2010) suggest that Erikson's tenets are still valid today, as differences in identity during adolescence predicted different growth in intimacy with romantic partners when the individuals became young adults. However, whereas we have quite substantial support for the contribution of peers, earlier romantic partners and identity for romantic development, not many studies to date have examined the importance of the maturing body (Seiffge-Krenke, Shulman, & Klessinger, 2001) and how sexuality is integrated and develops with adolescent romantic relationships (Davila et al., 2009; Shulman et al., 2009; Shulman et al., in press).

⋙ "WITH A LITTLE HELP FROM MY FRIENDS": THE IMPACT OF PARENTS AND PEERS

The growing interest and investment in a romantic partner occurs in the context of other close relationships with family and friends. In most Western societies, an individuation process is noticeable away from parents and toward the peer context in which new behaviors, such as intimacy, can be practiced (Overbeek, Vollebergh, Engels, & Meeus, 2003).

Besides, and as outlined in several theoretical conceptualizations, the quality of relationships with parents and friends are pivotal for adolescents' romantic relationship quality.

Internal Working Models and the Impact of Family Functioning

In line with attachment theory, relational patterns experienced in earlier relationships with parents were carried forward and thought to influence later romantic relationships (Hazan & Shaver, 1987). Accordingly, earlier experiences of closeness and basic trust with parents were internalized and carried forward into future romantic relationships (Collins & van Dulmen, 2006; Seiffge-Krenke et al., 2001), suggesting a continuity of internal working models.

There are also indications for a transgenerational perspective in which the romantic experiences of parents and their offspring is interdependent. In a recent study, we have been able to show how adolescent daughters' emerging romantic activities become a mirror for mothers who see, or remember, themselves in the same situation, activate their attitudes and behavior toward their offspring, and sometimes were unable to distinguish between their own and their daughters' experiences (Crittenden, Lang, Claussen, & Partridge, 2000). Based on their own less favorable past histories, some mothers reacted in patterns that were not adaptive, neither for their daughters nor for themselves and impacted their daughters' romantic behavior (Shulman, Scharf, & Shahar-Shapira, in press).

The carryover of relational patterns from the family to romantic relations can be also understood from a social learning perspective (Bandura, 1977; Conger, Cui, Bryant, & Elder, 2000). Interactions with their primary caregivers may help children learn important social skills, which form the basis for close relationships with other people. In particular, communication patterns (Whitton et al., 2008) between parents and their adolescent children served as a mechanism to be transferred in later adolescents' romantic interactions. Conflict with a romantic partner may replicate discord within one's family. Studies have shown that adolescents tend to use the same strategies that they employ in their conflicts with parents—be they integrative, avoidant, or coercive—to manage the disagreements that they have with their romantic partners (Reese-Weber & Bartle-Haring, 1998; Reese-Weber & Khan, 2005).

High family discord and conflictual family interactions had a negative impact on romantic development of the offspring. When parental marital relationships were characterized by high discord, it was likely that the romantic involvements of their children will be marked by elevated levels of hostility (Scharf & Mayseless, 2001). It was repeatedly found that individuals from divorced families tend to hold less favorable views about romantic relationships and marriage (Giuliani, Lafrate, & Rosnati, 1998; van Schaick & Stolberg, 2001) and were more likely to experience romantic breakups, compared to adolescents in two-parent families.

The quality of family relations has not only long-term implications; the impacts of relationships with fathers and mothers differ. It seems that the earlier quality of relationships with mothers impacted more the emotional tone of later romantic quality, whereas father–child relationships impacted more the closeness versus distant quality of later romantic relationships. We found that mother–child relationships were linked with later connectedness and sexual attraction, whereas distant father–child relationships during adolescence were linked with the child's later anxious love (Seiffge-Krenke, Overbeek, & Vermulst, 2010). Interestingly, for both sons and daughters, the relational skills involved in interacting with opposite-gender romantic partners seems to be learned during early interactions with the opposite-gender parent (Bucx & Seiffge-Krenke, 2010). Apparently, adolescents look toward their opposite-gender parent for information about how to interact with romantic partners. When the quality of the relationship with the opposite-gender parents in an overall attachment context is low, adolescents may lack specific opportunities for learning how to behave in heterosexual romantic relationships. Conversely, a too-strong bonding to the parents may interfere with a child's progression toward romantic love, resulting in less investment in the romantic partner (Seiffge-Krenke, 2006).

The Many Functions of Close Friends

During adolescence, friendships partly replace the family as the primary socializing agent and parents become less important, at least in Western societies, triggering a temporarily decline in parent–adolescent relationship quality (Granic, Hollenstein, Dishion, & Patterson, 2003).

As outlined earlier, peers and close friends serve important functions in the process of mate selection, forming and maintaining romantic relations.

In addition, closeness, trust, and openness that are experienced with close friends are carried forward into romantic involvements (Connolly & Johnson, 1996; Seiffge-Krenke, 2000). More specifically, Furman and Wehner (1997) theorized that friendships would contribute to adolescents' ability to express intimacy in romantic relationships. During adolescence, intimacy becomes increasingly important in adolescent's friendships, and intimacy perceived in friendships is gradually transferred to romantic partners (Scharf &Mayseless, 2001), a phenomenon particularly visible in female's romantic relationships (Brown, 1999).

Despite the interrelatedness between relationships with parents, friends, and romantic partners, each relationship has its distinctive qualities (Furman & Simon, 2006). In contrast to hierarchical parent–adolescent relationships, adolescents can practice egalitarian interactions with friends, which are more comparable to interactions with romantic partners (Overbeek et al., 2003). In a similar vein, adolescents reported more support and less negative interactions with romantic partners than in relationships with mothers (Furman & Shoemaker, 2008). In contrast, adolescents were observed to engage in more conflict and express less positive affectivity with romantic partners than with friends (Furman & Shoemaker, 2008). It would be reasonable then to conclude that distinctive patterns of interaction are learned in each respective relationship and individuals probably learn what is appropriate in each relationship.

A comparison of the family and peer-romantic relationships associations among younger and older adolescents, however, points to an important developmental distinction. Studies conducted on younger adolescents show that peer relationships, in comparison to family relations, were more likely to impact the quality of the relationship with a romantic partner (Shulman & Scharf, 2000). In contrast, studies on older adolescents consistently reveal the greater role of parents in shaping their offspring's romantic lives (Seiffge-Krenke et al., 2001). A probable turning point is around the age of 16 when the role of peers begins to recede and the role of parents comes into the forefront. These shifts in influence are in line with the developmental differences between romance in early and later adolescence. As detailed earlier, early romantic involvement is located in the peer group, and therefore it is more likely to be linked with other peer experiences. As adolescents grow older, their romantic relations mature and start to resemble adult dyadic relationships and therefore, the links to parents as model figures become more evident.

﹨ STRESS, CONFLICT RESOLUTION, AND ROMANTIC BREAKUPS

Conflicts in adolescent romantic couples are not frequent, and they may be particularly downplayed at early stages of romance, as they are threatening to the growing, yet fragile, relationship. Nevertheless, relationship problems and romantic quarrels are an important characteristic of spontaneous descriptions of romantic couples in early and late adolescence likewise (Shulman & Kipnis, 2001). Further, romantic relations are novel experiences and as such are quite stressful. However, the stress perceived in romantic relationships is only partly related to the romantic affair as such; its origin lies in the diverse functions romantic relationships serve for adolescents—for example separating from the family (Gray & Steinberg, 1999). In particular, in early and mid-adolescence, the increasing involvement in romantic partnerships sparks conflict between adolescents and their parents but also between adolescents and their close friends. Research on conflict management strategies has demonstrated the increasing importance of negotiation between romantic partners for stability and commitment in partnerships (Seiffge-Krenke & Nieder, 2001; Shulman et al., 2006).

Different Stressors and Different Conflict Resolutions Strategies

The awakening of romantic and sexual desires is accompanied by strong physiological, cognitive, and emotional components that can lead to mood swings and intensive focusing on a desired partner. Managing a romantic affair while at the same time maintaining other social relationships can be stressful. Becoming involved in a relationship exposes the adolescent to additional stress because the inevitable relational challenges raise the need to find a compromise between self and partner wishes. However, disagreement between romantic partners provides also an opportunity for partners to define their relationship and learn more about themselves and their partners.

Romantic experiences are novel and adolescents need to develop the means of coping with them. In observing interactions with different partners, Furman & Shoemaker (2008) found that there was much more reciprocation of positive affect with romantic partners as with peers. Moreover, though conflicts are integral components of romantic relationships, partners were more likely to report positive feelings after a conflict, and the conflict has little or no long-term impact on the relationships. In addition, some gender differences in handling and responding to conflict were found; males showed more denial, behavioral disengagement, and self-blame than females (Powers & McArdle, 2003). Finally, coping effectively with disagreement is associated with the quality and longevity of a relationship. Adolescent couples who competently solve relationship conflicts (e.g., by integrating the divergent perspective and by compromising) stayed together for a longer time (Shulman et al., 2006). Thus, conflict management is an important indicator for relationship functioning and duration.

〰 CHANGEſ IN ROMANTIC ſTREſſORſ AND INCREAſING COMPETENCE OVER TIME

Overall, most studies showed an increasing competence in coping with romantic stressors. Early adolescents' conflicts with romantic partners were much more concrete, brief, and superficial (Tuval-Masiach & Shulman, 2006), whereas older adolescents were able to use compromising as a means of conflict resolution in romantic dyads much more often (Feldman & Gowen, 1998).

Studies following adolescent couples over an extended time span highlight the importance of an adaptive capacity for solving romantic conflicts on later relationship quality. Based on their study of dating couples' daily diaries, Downey, Freitas, Michaelis, and Khouri (1998) found that conflict management skills during earlier phases were important determinants of later relationship quality. That adaptive coping style and relationship quality are interdependent and influence each other over the course of 4 years, was and substantiated in the longitudinal study by Seiffge-Krenke and Nieder (2001). During early phases of romantic development, when romantic relationships are more casual, comparably high levels of stress occurred and were related to identity concern, the peer context, and the romantic relationship itself. At these early stages, the adolescents were not very active in coming to terms with these stressors. The most frequent coping strategy was trying to solve the problems with the help of friends or seeking support by peers, illustrating the aforementioned importance of the peer context for beginning romantic relationships. At the same time, subjectively perceived intimacy and affection in romantic relationships was low. In the following years, as the romantic relationship became more exclusive and enduring, negotiating closeness and individuality in the romantic relationship was perceived as quite stressful by the adolescents, whereas the potential impact on peer relationships was no longer a salient stressor. Compared to earlier phases, the adolescents employed the most active coping modes during this phase, such as discussing the issue with the romantic partner. At the same time, high levels of intimacy and affection were experienced. Overall, these findings show that as the relationship develops over time, romantic stress decreases and adolescents deal with them in a increasingly competent way.

Precursors of Adaptive and Maladaptive Conflict Regulation Strategies in Partnerships

The conflict management strategies an adolescent employs in a romantic encounter are learned in the family of origin and may be carried forward. Adolescents from families with higher family discord do lack adaptive conflict management strategies. Generally, interparental conflict is associated with low quality in offspring's romantic relationships. (Rodrigues & Kitzmann, 2007). Conger and colleagues (2000) reported that parental hostility and coercion when the child was an adolescent predicted lower warmth and higher hostility during later conflict discussions with a romantic partner. Further, maladaptive conflict resolution styles in adolescent couples tend to mirror their parents' marital conflict style (Dadds, Atkinson, Turner, Blums, & Lendich, 1999).

There are indications in family violence research (Fosco, DeBoard, & Grych, 2007) for a spillover of appraisal in one relationship to stress perception in other close relationships. Adolescents in families with high discord and violence may become overly vigilant to signs of anger and conflicts in relationships outside the family. When they begin dating, highly sensitized youth may be overly vigilant to signs of anger, may avoid conflict in their relationship, and thus undermine a healthy development of intimacy. The pathways from early family violence to later aggressive and maladaptive coping styles in partnerships, however, are far from clear, because not all adolescents witnessing a violent family situation became later victims or perpetrators of partner violence.

Windle & Mrug (2009) found that parents exhibiting harsh and inconsistent discipline and being together with deviant peers all contribute to dating violence in adolescent couples. Similarly, in Linder & Collins' (2005) longitudinal study, individuals who experienced higher levels of inadequate parenting (i.e., boundary violation, seductive and role reversal behavior) when they were early adolescents reported higher levels of physical perpetration and victimization in their later romantic relationships. Parental border-violating behavior predicted less adaptive coping styles in romantic conflicts, but delinquent friendship quality at age 16 contributed over and above familial predictors.

A similar spillover was found between peer and romantic relations. Levels of conflicts and hostility with friends were correlated with conflict levels among romantic partners (Furman, Simon, Shaffer, & Bouchey, 2002). Furthermore, negative peer tendencies crystallized into stable patterns of bullying carried over into romantic relationships (Connolly, Pepler, Craig, & Taradash, 2000). Taken together, deficient skills in handling the relationship and managing conflicts that origins rooted in family and peer experiences may be repeated in romantic relationships and may even foster victimhood.

Romantic Breakups

Most individuals report at least one breakup during their adolescent years (Connolly & McIsaac, 2009). The increasing emotional investment in a relationship and its idealization is likely to turn a breakup into a highly stressful experience. The initial distress following the dissolution of a romantic relationship can be high but then subsides as time passes. By this, adolescents learn to cope with relational difficulties and understand breakups within the broader context of relationships and their development.

Inability to overcome a separation and continued rumination regarding a dissolved relationship may indicate additional problems that become more visible during a dissolution (Hankin & Abramson, 2001; Joyner & Udry, 2000). Adolescents who report a larger number of relationship beginnings and terminations are likely to experience accumulating feelings of loss that eventually overwhelm their coping resources and mood states. Of note, dissolution of a relationship can become highly stressful for highly sensitive individuals (Rizzo, Daley, & Gunderson, 2006) and even increase the risk of onset of a depressive reaction.

As in the other relational processes, some gender differences in response to a breakup have been documented. Females, who often invest more emotionally in their relationships and tend to be more committed than males, feel more loss and distress once a breakup had occurred. Males, in contrast, are generally less affected and are more likely to cope effectively when a relationship dissolves.

※ IΓ IT THE ΓAME EVERYWHERE? PLACING ROMANTIC EXPERIENCEΓ IN A BROADER ΓOCIETAL AND CULTURAL CONTEXT

Although work on romantic relationships has substantially expanded in recent years (for reviews, see Collins, 2003; Collins et al., 2009; Connolly & McIsaac, 2009), little research has focused on how different contexts influence romantic development. To date, we have treated romantic relationships as if they were a relatively homogeneous phenomenon, regardless of culture, ethnicity, or sexual orientation. Research on nonheterosexual youth suggested that the process of mate selection is particularly challenging and difficult (see also Russell, Watson, & Muraco, 2011 or Chapter 10 in this volume). Until very recently, it was unclear whether adolescents from other parts of the world assign the same significance to romantic relationships as those who have participated in North American and European studies.

Differences in Importance and Prevalence?

Romantic relationships in adolescence are highly normative in Western countries (Collins, 2003), but there is reason to query the extent to which our current knowledge of romantic development might generalize to non-Western cultures. This relates to the importance and functions of romantic relations for the adolescent, the views of the appropriateness of adolescent romance, the age at which such experiences are to be encouraged, and the supervision of romantic activity by parents.

Regarding importance, Seiffge-Krenke and colleagues (2010) analyzed adolescents in 17 countries and found that for adolescents in several regions of the world (Southern Europe, Middle East, Africa, South America, and Asia) identity- related stressors are of far greater concern than romantic issues. Most Western adolescents are commonly characterized by a strongly individualistic cultural orientation (Dion & Dion, 1996). For these adolescents, the context of romantic relationships means valuing the freedom to seek partners who gratify their own personal development without parental interference. In contrast, for adolescents from Arabic, African, or Asian countries who live in a predominantly collectivist culture, romantic relationships are defined in terms of interconnectedness and interdependence with the family.

Cultural norms also affect the activities that are expected and approved within dating relationships and the amount of parental monitoring. There are reports showing that Asian adolescents are less involved in dating than Canadian adolescents (Zhi Hong, Connolly, Depeng, Pepler, & Craig, 2010) and that Latino girls are considerably less involved in dating than Latino boys (Milbrath, Ohlson, & Eyre, 2009) and were more closely supervised by their parents. Gendered behaviors and sex role stereotypes are stronger in some cultures than in others even within the same region. For example, gender differences in attitudes about sex are stronger in Southern than in Middle Europe (Giannotta, Ciairano, Spruijt, & Spruijt-Metz, 2009).

Different Functions and Expectations

Not only might Western and non-Western cultures vary with respect to the importance and occurrence of adolescent romantic involvement but they might also alter the linkages among peer, family, and romantic experiences. The short duration of early romantic relationships found in Western cultures underscore their function as "training exercises" and pawns in a game of gaining social status rather than as a deep and meaningful relationship between two individuals (Brown, 1999). Role experimentation, either with different types of romantic partners or with different ways of behaving in a relationship, were considered as normative during these early stages, at least in North American and European samples. It is, however, an open question whether the focus on achieving social status or being accepted by peers is as important for adolescents in other regions of the world.

That romantic relationships at earlier stages may be used to obtain autonomy from parents and to increase peer acceptance is a tenet underlying most studies that reflect an individualistic orientation (Dion & Dion, 1996). In contrast, in a collectivistic orientation, parents may be the prime socialization force for adolescent romance, and the transmission of cultural knowledge about romantic love may stress the respect for the family of origin, the importance of responsibility, of having children, and perhaps a double standard in attitudes about sexual relationships for male and female adolescents (Milbrath et al., 2009). Such different cultural models in romance impose different stressors in the romantic arena for adolescents from different regions of the world (Seiffge-Krenke et al., 2010). For adolescents from Southern European countries, who leave home later than Northern and Mid European youth, having a romantic partner is of high importance in order to signal independence from parents. In contrast, adolescents from South America and the Middle East experience lower romantic stress, as family rules offer more guidance in the romantic arena. Further studies are necessary to analyze whether the sequence beginning with casual, short-term encounters and leading to exclusive, long-term, and bonded relationships found in North American and European samples (Collins et al., 2009; Seiffge-Krenke, 2003) is characteristic for adolescents living in other cultural contexts.

Taken together, sociocultural values, norms, and expectations form the background within which adolescent romance develops (Nelson, Nelson, Hart, Yang, & Jin, 2006). This has consequences for adolescents from predominantly individualistic or collectivistic cultures but is also important for adolescents who migrated with their families into a culture different from their culture of origin (Ha, Overbeek, de Greef, Scholte, & Engels, 2010).

╲╲ NETWORKING AND ROMANCE VIA THE INTERNET

The overall developmental context has changed both in Western and non-Western countries. In particular, new media have changed life dramatically and impacted all domains of close relationships. Consequently, they may change the models of adolescent romantic relationships and subsequently the frequency of contact, communication style, and perhaps also the quality of romantic relations.

New media offer new opportunities to make contact or stay in contact, for example via e-mailing or Facebook. Gross & Acquisti (2005) analyzed the e-mails of 13- to 16-year-old adolescents and found "fairly ordinary yet intimate topics (friends, gossip)," including also messages about romantic partners (between same sex friends) or with romantic partners. Users of the largest and the fast growing social online network Facebook found that their portrayals describe them accurately and that these were mainly positive (Schonfeld, 2008). Profile visitors were high school friends (93%), people in the same classes (86%), people who met at parties (70%), and even people from the same town who didn't know each other (69%) (Lampe, Ellison, & Steinflied, 2006). Virtual and real social interactions are strongly interwoven, as romantic partners may post information, pictures, and videos about their relationship online for their friends and other profile visitors. Nosko, Wood, & Molema (2010) found that a large portion of members in traditional online communities are rather lurkers than active posters. This suggests that observing (and social comparison) is quite important and may help in the new arena of romance where the adolescent feels less comfortable. Of note, peer pressure can be a reason for adolescents to join Facebook and create a profile, as adolescents share information and send invitations for all kinds of events and parties. If someone does not join the social network, he or she is—at least partially—excluded from social life (Cassidy, 2006). Lampe and colleagues (2006) stated that Facebook is largely employed to learn more about people adolescents already met offline rather than initiate new contacts.

Other websites like Parship24.de or Gayromeo.com do more directly serve the function of establishing contact to potential heterosexual or nonheterosexual partners. Again, a profile has to be created, and in order to select potential partners, up to 22 different characteristics were compared in order to find out potential partners with a good match. Further, users express some anxieties about privacy given that exchanges could be read by different groups of friends and possibly broadcast to the whole network (Rau, Gau, & Ding, 2008). Although the new media certainly can be considered as a positive contribution, broadening the potential network for romantic partners, potential dangers lie in the different time perspective (no delay between messages, particularly with instant messaging), the elevated levels of (pseudo) intimacy, and favoring online relationships instead off offline relationships, perhaps because of social anxiety (Pierce, 2009).

⑅ HEALTH CONSEQUENCES: RISK FACTORS AND TIMING

The emergence of romantic interests is a major developmental marker of adolescent development. Yet a growing number of studies also point to possible negative impacts of romantic experiences, as evidenced by increases in problem behaviors and emotional distress, particularly among girls for whom romance is often associated with depressive mood (Davila, Steinberg, Kachadourian, Cobb, & Fincham, 2004; Joyner & Udry, 2000; Shulman et al., 2009).

Despite their developmental appropriateness, romantic activities and romantic relationships can, by their very nature, become a source of stress: the need to integrate sexual desires and relationships, the challenge of handling an emotionally intensive relationship, balancing self and partner needs, and finally coping with breakups. The first romantic explorations conducted within a peer context can be very helpful as they guide and support individual behavior. This can explain why early dating has widely been described to have negative consequences. The combination of early dating with early pubertal maturation may further exacerbate the negative effects of early dating. Early dating exposes the adolescent to increased stress. Early adolescents might be more concerned about their body image and lack the skills to cope with the demands of handling a relationship (Graber, Brooks-Gunn, & Petersen, 1996; Welsh, Grello, & Harper, 2003). Early dating is also highly likely not to be accepted by a normative group of peers (Young & d'Arcy, 2005). There is evidence connecting early dating to externalizing behaviors such as delinquency, risk taking, and substance abuse (van Dulmen, Goncy, Haydon, & Collins, 2008; Zimmer-Gembeck, Siebenbruner, & Collins, 2001).

A normative perspective contends that with age, healthy romantic involvements shift to more sustained and intimate relationships. In contrast, persisting in casual encounters or nonintimate relationships might be an expression of some degree of psychological turmoil among older adolescents. Empirical findings support this contention. For example, as early as in middle adolescence, problem behaviors increased with more frequent casual dating and multiple relationships, whereas problem behaviors and emotional distress declined as dating resolved toward steady relationships (Zimmer-Gembeck et al., 2001). Similarly, a number of studies showed that engaging in sexual behavior within a steady romantic relationship was not associated with increased depressive symptoms (Grello, Welsh, Harper, & Dickson, 2003), whereas sexual activity in casual, less intimate relationships was related to increased levels of depressive symptoms (Shulman et al., 2009). Of note, the association between casual encounters and increased depressive affect was mainly found among girls but not among boys.

Two related mechanisms can explain the link. The first refers to individuals' relational vulnerabilities and the second points to preceding depressive affect that leads individuals to unhealthy relationships. Relationally vulnerable individuals tend to fear rejection and feel as if their romantic needs are not being met and as a result experience more dysphoric mood over time. Fear of rejection may also lead to self-silencing behavior, giving in to a partner, and to be involved in unhealthy relationships (Downey et al., 1998; Harper & Welsh, 2007). With the hope that the relationship and support of the partner will reduce depressive affect, individuals tend to give in order to placate a partner and secure the relationship (Longmore, Manning, Giordano, & Rudolph, 2004; Shulman et al., 2009). Unfortunately, their elevated but insecure investment in the relationship is likely to be counterproductive, leading more often to relationship dissolution, which in turn further increases their sense of hopelessness and depression.

It is also plausible that increased involvement in nonhealthy relationships is due to a preceding higher depressive symptomatology (Grello et al., 2003). A meta-analysis conducted on studies with adult samples provides some evidence that negative affect is associated with subsequent increased sexual risk behavior (Crepaz & Marks, 2001). In addition, assessment of daily sexual behavior among adolescents has shown that preceding negative mood was associated with a decreased ability to cope with relationship stress among college students (Tolpin, Cohen, Gunthert, & Farrehi, 2006). With the hope of alleviating negative mood, adolescents may become involved in nonadaptive romantic relationships, which in turn become a source of further stress (Shulman et al., 2009).

⚜ SUMMARY AND FINAL COMMENTS

On the basis of the accumulated data and theories, we have demonstrated how the perception of the importance and the impact of adolescents' romance on subsequent development changed. Once considered to be trivial and transitory (Collins, 2003), adolescent romantic relationships were found to be frequent, complex in function and significant in their impact on later relationships development, for example for couple development and marriages (Gottman et al., 1998). Moreover, these early romantic experiences form not only the basis for other, more committed romantic relationships later in life but are of importance for individuals' mental well-being likewise (Joyner & Udry, 2000; Overbeek, Stattin, Vermulst, Ha, & Engels, 2007). In this chapter, based on the evolving theories and research findings on adolescent romantic behavior, we discussed individual, familial, and cultural aspects, which may play a role in the development and sustainment of romantic relations. Theoretical models that guide our perspective on romance have been highlighted, and a developmental sequence for romantic affairs has been demonstrated. Of note, a transgenerational perspective and the interrelatedness of close relationships with romantic partners, friends, and parents became apparent. The existing research also offered a rich picture of the diversity of adolescent couples, including highly intensive and passionate relationships, couples who integrate friendship and love, and couples who experience an emotionally less intensive but comparable stable relationship.

The nature and quality of these relationships provides opportunities for positive growth during the adolescent years as well as important preparation for the mature relationships of adulthood. However, despite their developmental importance, romantic involvements can also become a source of increased stress and were found to be associated in some contexts with increased negative affect. In particular for females, negative health outcomes such as depression are of concern for health professionals.

Our overview also points to the powerful role of societal expectations, of economic conditions, and of the culture the adolescents and their families live in. Adolescent romantic relationships are mainly found in Western societies. It is important for future research to better understand how families, peers, and culture at large impact romantic involvements during the adolescent time span in different societies. Finally, it is important to learn about the mechanisms that can differentiate between adolescents whose romantic behaviors are expressions of normal, healthy development and those whose expressions and behavior of romance are symptomatic of psychological turmoil. It will be also important to understand the limits and implications of romantic relationships within an increasingly complex world so that parents, teachers, and youth themselves can productively engage in healthy relationships.

ℕ JUGGEJTED READINGJ

Collins, W. A., Welsh, D. P., & Furman, W. (2009). Adolescent romantic relationships. *The Annual Review of Psychology, 60,* 631–652.

Fisher, H. E. (2004). *Why we love: The nature and chemistry of romantic love.* New York: Henry Holt.

Seiffge-Krenke, I., Bosma, H., Chau, C., Cok, F., Gillespie, C., Loncaric, D., et al. (2010). All they need is love? Placing romantic stress in the context of other stressors: A 17-nation study. *International Journal of Behavioral Development, 34,* 106–112.

〟 REFERENCEſ

Bandura, A. (1977). *Social learning theory.* New York: General Learning Press.

Beyers, W., & Seiffge-Krenke, I. (2010). Does identity precede intimacy? Testing Erikson's theory on romantic development in emerging adults of the 21st century. *Journal of Adolescent Research, 25,* 387–415.

Blos, P. (1967). The second individuation process of adolescence. *Psychoanalytic Study of the Child, 22,* 162–185.

Brown, B. B. (1999). "You're going out with who?": Peer group influences on adolescent romantic relationships. In W. Furman, B. B. Brown, & C. Feiring (Eds.), *The development of romantic relationships in adolescence* (pp. 291–329). Cambridge, UK: Cambridge University Press.

Bucx, F., & Seiffge-Krenke, I. (2010). Romantic relationships in intra-ethnic and inter-ethnic adolescent couples in Germany: The role of attachment to parents, self-esteem, and conflict resolution skills. *International Journal of Behavioral Development, 34,* 128–135.

Carver, K., Joyner, K., & Udry, J. R. (2003). National estimates of adolescent romantic relationships. In P. Florsheim (Ed.), *Adolescent romantic relations and sexual behaviour: Theory, research, and practical implications* (pp. 23–56). Mahwah, NJ: Lawrence Erlbaum.

Cassidy, J. (2006). Me media. How hanging out on the internet became big business. *The New Yorker, 82,* 50.

Collins, W. A. (2003). More than myth: The developmental significance of romantic relationships during adolescence. *Journal of Research on Adolescence, 13,* 1–24.

Collins, W. A., & Sroufe, L. A. (1999). Capacity for intimate relationship: A developmental construction. In W. Furman, B. B. Brown, & C. Feiring (Eds.), *The development of romantic relationships in adolescence* (pp. 125–147). New York: Cambridge University Press.

Collins, W. A., & van Dulmen, M. (2006). "The course of true love(s) . . .": Origins and pathways in the development of romantic relationships. In A. C. Crouter & A. Booth (Eds.), *Romance and sex in adolescence and emerging adulthood: Risks and opportunities* (pp. 63–86). Mahwah, NJ: Lawrence Erlbaum.

Collins, W. A., Welsh, D. P., & Furman, W. (2009). Adolescent romantic relationships. *The Annual Review of Psychology, 60,* 631–652.

Conger, R. D., Cui, M., Bryant, C. M., & Elder, G. H., Jr. (2000). Competence in early adult romantic relationships: A developmental perspective on family influences. *Journal of Personality and Social Psychology, 79,* 224–237.

Connolly, J., Craig, W., Goldberg, A., & Pepler, D. (1999). Conceptions of cross-sex friendships and romantic relationships in early adolescence. *Journal of Youth and Adolescence, 28,* 481–494.

Connolly, J.A., Craig, W., Goldberg, A., & Pepler, D. (2004). Mixed-gender groups, dating, and romantic relationships in early adolescence. *Journal of Research on Adolescence, 14,* 185–207.

Connolly, J. A., Friedlander, L., Pepler, D., Craig, W., & Laporte, L. (2010). The ecology of adolescent dating aggression: Attitudes, relationships, media use, and socio-demographic risk factors. *Journal of Aggression, Maltreatment & Trauma, 19,* 469–491.

Connolly, J. A., Furman, W., & Konarski, R. (2000). The role of peers in the emergence of heterosexual romantic relationships in adolescence. *Child Development, 71,* 1395–1408.

Connolly, J. A., & Johnson, A. M. (1996). Adolescents' romantic relationships and the structure and quality of their close ties. *Personal Relationships, 3,* 185–195.

Connolly, J. A., & McIsaac, C. (2008). Adolescent romantic relationships: Beginnings, endings, and psychosocial challenges. *Newsletter of the International Society for the Study of Behavioural Development, 32,* 1–5.

Connolly, J. A., & McIsaac, C. (2009). Romantic relationships in adolescence. In R. M. Lerner & L. Steinberg (Eds.), *Handbook of adolescent psychology, Vol 2: Contextual influences on adolescent development* (3rd ed., pp. 104–151). Hoboken, NJ: Wiley.

Connolly, J., Pepler, D., Craig, W., & Taradash, A. (2000). Dating experiences of bullies in early adolescence. *Child Maltreatment, 5,* 299–310.

Creasey, G. (2002). Associations between working models of attachment and conflict management behavior in romantic couples. *Journal of Counseling Psychology, 49,* 365–375.

Crepaz, G., & Marks, N. (2001). Are negative affective states associated with HIV sexual risk behaviors?: A meta-analytic review. *Health Psychology, 20,* 291–299.

Crittenden, P. M., Lang, C., Claussen, A. H., & Partridge, M. F. (2000). Relations among mothers' procedural, semantic, and episodic internal representational models of parenting. In P. M. Crittenden & A. H. Claussen (Eds.), *The organization of attachment relationships: Maturation, culture, and context* (pp. 214–233). New York: Cambridge University Press.

Dadds, M. R., Atkinson, E., Turner, C., Blums, G. J., & Lendich, B. (1999). Family conflict and child adjustment: Evidence for a cognitive-contextual model of intergenerational transmission. *Journal of Family Psychology, 13*(2), 194–208.

Davila, J., Steinberg, S., Kachadourian, L., Cobb, R., & Fincham, F. (2004). Romantic involvement and depressive symptoms in early and late adolescence: The role of a preoccupied relational style. *Personal Relationships, 11,* 161–178.

Davila, J., Steinberg, S. J., Miller, M. R., Stroud, C. B., Starr, L. R., & Yoneda, A. (2009). Assessing romantic competence in adolescence: The romantic competence interview. *Journal of Adolescence, 32,* 55–75.

Dion, K. K., & Dion, K. L. (1996). Cultural perspectives on romantic love. *Personal Relationships, 3,* 5–17.

Downey, G., Freitas, A. L., Michaelis, B., & Khouri, H. (1998). The self-fulfilling prophecy in close relationships: Rejection sensitivity and rejection by romantic partners. *Journal of Personality and Social Psychology, 75,* 545–560.

Erikson, E. H. (1968). The problem of ego identity. *Journal of the American Psychoanalytic Association, 4,* 56–121.

Erikson, E. H. (1982). *Identität und Lebenszyklus.* Frankfurt, Germany: Suhrkamp.

Feiring, C. (1996). Lovers as friends. Developing conscious views of romance in adolescence. *Journal of Research in Adolescence, 7,* 214–224.

Feldman, S. S., & Gowen, L. K. (1998). Conflict negotiation tactics in romantic relationships in high school students. *Journal of Youth and Adolescence, 27,* 691–717.

Feldman, S. S., Gowen, L. K., & Fisher, L. (1998). Family relationships and gender as predictors of romantic intimacy in young adults: A longitudinal study. *Journal of Research on Adolescence, 8,* 263–268.

Fischer, C. T., & Alapack, R. A. (1987). A phenomenological approach to adolescence. In L. van Hassellt (Ed.), *Handbook of adolescence psychology* (pp.91–109). New York: Wiley.

Fisher, H. E. (2004). *Why we love: The nature and chemistry of romantic love.* New York: Henry Holt.

Fisher, H. E. (2006). Broken hearts: The nature and risks of romantic rejection. In A. Booth & C. Crouter (Eds.). *Romance and sex in adolescence and emerging adulthood: Risks and opportunities* (pp. 3–29). Mahwah, NJ: Lawrence Erlbaum.

Fosco, G. M., DeBoard, R. L., & Grych, J. H. (2007). Making sense of family violence: Implications of children's appraisals of interparental aggression for their short- and long-term functioning. *European Psychologist, 12*(1), 6–16.

Freud, A. (1958). On adolescence. *Psychoanalytic Study of the Child, 13,* 255–278.

Furman, W., Brown, B. B., & Feiring C. (1999). *The development of romantic relationships in adolescence.* New York: Cambridge University Press.

Furman, W., & Shoemaker, L. B. (2008). Patterns of interactions in adolescent romantic relationships: Distinct features and links to other close relationships. *Journal of Adolescence, 31,* 771–788.

Furman, W., & Simon, V. (2006). Actor and partner effects of adolescents' romantic working models and styles on interactions with romantic partners. *Child Development, 77,* 588–604.

Furman, W., Simon, V. A., Shaffer, L., & Bouchey, H. A. (2002). Adolescents' working models and styles for relationships with parents, friends, and romantic partners. *Child Development, 73,* 241–255.

Furman, W., & Wehner, E. A. (1997). Adolescent romantic relationships: A developmental perspective. In S. Shulman, & W. A. Collins (Eds.), *Romantic relationships in adolescence: Developmental perspectives* (pp. 168–195). San Francisco: Jossey-Bass.

Galliher, R. V., Welsh, D. P., Rostosky, S. S., & Kawaguchi, M. C. (2004). Interaction and relationship quality in late adolescent romantic couples. *Journal of Social and Personal Relationships, 21,* 203–216.

Giannotta, F., Ciairano, S., Spruijt, R., & Spruijt-Metz, D. (2009). Meanings of sexual intercourse for Italian adolescents. *Journal of Adolescence, 32,* 157–169.

Giordano, P. C., Longmore, M. A., & Manning, W. D. (2006). Adolescent romantic relationships: An emerging portrait of their nature and developmental significance. In A. C. Crouter & A. Booth (Eds.), *Romance and sex in adolescence and emerging adulthood* (pp. 127–150). Mahwah, NJ: Lawrence Erlbaum.

Giuliani, C., Iafrate, R., & Rosnati, R. (1998). Peer-group and romantic relationships in adolescents from intact and separated families. *Contemporary Family Therapy, 20,* 93–105.

Gottman, J. M., Coan, J., Carrere, S., & Swanson, C. (1998). Predicting marital happiness and stability from newlywed interactions. *Journal of Marriage and the Family, 60,* 5–22.

Graber, J. A., Brooks-Gunn, J., & Petersen, A. C. (Eds.) (1996). *Transitions through adolescence: Interpersonal domains and context.* Mahwah, NJ: Lawrence Erlbaum.

Granic, I., Hollenstein, T., Dishion, T. J., & Patterson, G. R. (2003). Longitudinal analysis of flexibility and reorganization in early adolescence: A dynamics systems study of family interactions. *Developmental Psychology, 39*(3), 606–617.

Gray, M. R., & Steinberg, L. (1999). Adolescent romance and the parent–child relationship: A contextual perspective. In C. Feiring, W. Furman, & B. B. Brown (Eds.), *The development of romantic relationships in adolescence* (pp. 235–262). New York: Cambridge University Press.

Grello, C. M., Welsh, D. P., Harper, M. S., & Dickson, J. W., (2003). Dating and sexual relationship trajectories and adolescent functioning. *Adolescent & Family Health, 3,* 103–112.

Gross, R., & Acquisti, A. (2005). Information revelation and privacy in online social networks. *Proceedings of the 2005 ACM Workshop on Privacy in the Electronic Society, 2005,* 71–80.

Ha, T., Overbeek, G., de Greef, M., Scholte, R., & Engels, R. C. M. E. (2010). The importance of relationships with parents and best friends for adolescents' romantic relationship quality: Differences between indigenious and ethnic Dutch adolescents. *International Journal of Behavioral Development, 34,* 121–127.

Hankin, B. L., & Abramson, L. Y. (2001). Development of gender differences in depression: An elaborated cognitive vulnerability-transactional stress theory. *Psychological Bulletin, 127,* 773–796.

Harper, M. S. & Welsh, D. P. (2007). Keeping quiet: Self-silencing and its association with relational and individual functioning among adolescent romantic couples. *Journal of Social and Personal Relationships, 24,* 99–116.

Hazan, C., & Shaver, P. (1987). Romantic love conceptualized as an attachment process. *Journal of Personality and Social Psychology, 52,* 511–524.

Joyner, K., & Udry, J. R. (2000). You don't bring me anything but down: Adolescent romance and depression. *Journal of Health and Social Behavior, 41,* 369–391.

Lacombe, A. C., & Gay, J. (1998). The role of gender in adolescent identity and intimacy decisions. *Journal of Youth and Adolescence, 27,* 795–802.

Lampe, C., Ellison, N., & Steinflied, C. (2006). A face(book) on the crowd: Social searching vs. social browsing. In *Proceedings of the 2006 20th Anniversary Conference on Computer Supported Cooperative Work* (pp. 167–170).

Laufer, M. L., & Laufer, E. (1984). Adolescence and developmental breakdown. New Haven, CT: Yale.

Laursen, B., & Williams, V. A. (1997). Perceptions of interdependence and closeness in family and peer relationships among adolescents with and without romantic partners. In S. Shulman & W. A. Collins (Eds.), *Romantic relationships in adolescence: Developmental perspectives* (pp. 3–20). San Francisco: Jossey-Bass.

Laursen, B., Finkelstein, B. D., & Betts, N. T. (2001). A developmental meta-analysis of peer conflict resolution. *Developmental Review, 21,* 423–449.

Linder J. R., & Collins, A. W. (2005). Parent and peer predictors of physical aggression and conflict management in romantic relationships in early adulthood. *Journal of Family Psychology, 19,* 252–262.

Longmore, M. A., Manning, W. D., Giordano, P. C., & Rudolph, J. L. (2004.). Self-esteem, depressive symptoms, and adolescents' sexual onset. *Social Psychological Quarterly, 67,* 279–295.

Manning, W. D., Giordano, P. C., & Longmore, M. A. (2006). Hooking up: The relationship contexts of "non-relationship" sex. *Journal of Adolescent Research, 21*(5), 459–483.

McIsaac, C., Connolly, J., McKenney, S., Pepler, D., & Craig, W. (2008). Conflict negotiation and autonomy processes in adolescent relationships: An observational study of interdependency in boyfriend and girlfriend effects. *Journal of Adolescence, 31,* 691–707.

Milbrath, C., Ohlson, B., & Eyre, S. (2009). Analyzing cultural models in adolescent accounts of romantic relationships. *Journal of Research on Adolescence, 19,* 313–351.

Montgomery, M. J. (2005). Psychosocial intimacy and identity: From early adolescence to emerging adulthood. *Journal of Adolescent Research, 20,* 346–374.

Nelson, D. A., Nelson, L. J., Hart, C. H., Yang, C., & Jin, S. (2006). Parenting and peer-group behavior in cultural context. In X. Chen, D. French, & B. Schneider (Eds.), *Peer relations in cultural context* (pp. 213–246). New York: Cambridge University Press.

Nosko, A., Wood, E., & Molema, S. (2010). All about me. Disclosure in online networking profiles: The case of Facebook. *Computers in Human Behavior, 26,* 406–418.

Overbeek, G., Stattin, H., Vermulst, A., Ha, T., & Engels, R. C. M. E. (2007). Parent–child relationships, partner relationships, and emotional adjustment: A birth-to-maturity prospective study. *Developmental Psychology, 43*(2), 429–437.

Overbeek, G., Vollebergh, W. A. M., Engels, R. C. M. E., & Meeus, W. H. J. (2003). Parental attachment and romantic relationships: Associations with emotional disturbance during late adolescence. *Journal of Counseling Psychology, 50,* 1–12.

Pierce, T. (2009). Social anxiety and technology: Face-to-face communication versus technological communication among teens. *Computers in Human Behavior, 25,* 1367–1372.

Powers, S., & McArdle, E. T. (2003). Coping strategies moderate the relation of hypothalamus-piuitary-adrenal axis reactivity to self-injurious behavior. *Annuals of the New York Acadamy of Science, 1008,* 285–288.

Rau, P.-L. P., Gao, Q., & Ding, Y. (2008). Relationship between the level of intimacy and lurking in online social network services. *Computers in Human Behavior, 24,* 2757–2770.

Reese-Weber, M., & Bartle-Haring, S. (1998). Conflict resolution styles in family subsystems and adolescent romantic relationships. *Journal of Youth and Adolescence, 27,* 735–752.

Reese-Weber, M., & Khan, J. H. (2005). Familial predictors of sibling and romantic-partner conflict resolution: Comparing late adolescents from intact and divorced families. *Journal of Adolescence, 28,* 479–493.

Rizzo, C. J., Daley, S. E., & Gunderson, B. H. (2006). Interpersonal sensitivity, romantic stress, and the prediction of depression: A study of inner-city, minority adolescent girls. *Journal of Youth and Adolescence, 35,* 469–478.

Rodrigues, L., & Kitzmann, K. (2007). Coping as a mediator between interparental conflict and adolescents' romantic attachment. *Journal of Personal and Social Relationships, 24,* 423–429.

Russell, S. T., Watson, R., & Muraco, J. A. (2011). The development of same-sex intimate relationships during adolescence. In B. Laursen & W. A. Collins (Eds.), *Relationship pathways: From adolescence to young adulthood.* Thousand Oaks, CA: Sage.

Scharf, M., & Mayseless, O. (2001). The capacity for romantic intimacy: Exploring the contribution of best friend and marital and parental relationships. *Journal of Adolescence, 24,* 379–399.

Schonfeld, E. (2008). *Facebook is not only the world's largest social network, it is also the fastest growing.* Retrieved from www.TechCrunch.com

Seiffge-Krenke, I. (2000). Diversity in romantic relations of adolescents with varying health status: Links to intimacy in close friendships. *Journal of Adolescent Research, 15,* 611–636.

Seiffge-Krenke, I. (2003). Testing theories of romantic development from adolescence to young adulthood: Evidence of a developmental sequence. *International Journal of Behavioral Development, 27,* 519–531.

Seiffge-Krenke, I. (2006). Leaving home or still in the nest? Parent-child relationships and psychological health as predictors of different leaving home patterns. *Developmental Psychology, 42,* 864–876.

Seiffge-Krenke, I., Bosma, H., Chau, C., Cok, F., Gillespie, C., Loncaric, D., et al. (2010). All they need is love? Placing romantic stress in the context of other stressors: A 17-nation study. *International Journal of Behavioral Development, 34,* 106–112.

Seiffge-Krenke, I., & Burk, W. J. (2010). *"Friends" or "lovers"? Similarity in affiliative and romantic experiences in adolescent couples and its impact on relationship functioning.* Manuscript submitted for publication.

Seiffge-Krenke, I., & Nieder, T. (2001). Coping with stress in different phases of romantic development. *Journal of Adolescence, 24,* 297–311.

Seiffge-Krenke, I., Overbeek, G., & Vermulst, A. (2010). Parent–child relationship trajectories during adolescence: Longitudinal associations with romantic outcomes in emerging adulthood. *Journal of Adolescence, 33,* 159–171.

Seiffge-Krenke, I., Shulman, S., & Klessinger, N. (2001). Adolescent precursors of romantic relationships in young adulthood. *Journal of Social and Personal Relationships, 18,* 327–346.

Shulman, S., Appel, I., & Swain, J. (2010). *Romantic attraction: Scale construction and construct validation.* Manuscript submitted for publication.

Shulman, S., Connolly, J. A., & McIsaac, J. C. (in press). Romantic relationships. In B. B. Brown & M. Prinstein (Eds.), *Encyclopedia of Adolescence.*

Shulman, S., & Kipnis, O. (2001). Adolescent romantic relationships: A look from the future. *Journal of Adolescence, 24,* 337–351.

Shulman, S., & Scharf, M. (2000). Adolescent romantic behaviors and perceptions: Age- and gender-related differences, and links with family and peer relationships. *Journal of Research on Adolescence, 10,* 99–118.

Shulman, S., Scharf, M., & Shahar-Shapira, L. (in press). The intergenerational transmission of adolescent romantic relationships. In P. Kerig, D. Schulz, & S. Hauser (Eds,) *Close relationships in adolescence and beyond.* New York: Oxford University Press.

Shulman, S., Tuval-Mashiach, R., Levran, E., & Anbar, S. (2006). Conflict resolution patterns and longevity of adolescent romantic couples: A 2-year follow-up study. *Journal of Adolescence, 29,* 575–588.

Shulman, S., Walsh, S. D., Weisman, O., & Schleyer, M. (2009). Romantic contexts, sexual behavior, and depressive symptoms among adolescent males and females. *Sex Roles, 61,* 850–863.

Sternberg, R. J. (1986). A triangular theory of love. *Psychological Review, 93,* 119–135.

Tolpin, L., Cohen, L., Gunthert, K., & Farrehi, A. (2006). Unique effects of depressive symptoms and relationship satisfaction on exposure and reactivity to daily romantic relationship stress. *Journal of Social and Clinical Psychology, 25,* 565–583.

Tuval-Mashiach, R., & Shulman, S. (2006). Resolution of disagreements between romantic partners, among adolescents and young adults: Qualitative analysis of interaction discourses. *Journal of Research on Adolescence, 16,* 561–587.

Tuval-Mashiach, R., Walsh, S., Harel, S., & Shulman, S. (2008). Romantic fantasies, cross gender friendships, and romantic experiences in adolescence. *Journal of Adolescent Research, 23,* 471–478.

van Dulmen, M. H. M., Goncy, E. A., Haydon, K. C., & Collins, W. A. (2008). Distinctiveness of adolescent and emerging adulthood romantic relationship features in predicting externalizing behavior problems. *Journal of Youth and Adolescence, 37,* 336–345.

van Schaick, K., & Stolberg, A. L. (2001). The impact of paternal involvement and parental divorce on young adults' intimate relationships. *Journal of Divorce & Remarriage, 36,* 99–122.

Welsh, D. P., Grello, C. M., & Harper, M. S. (2003). When love hurts: Depression and adolescent romantic relationships. In P. Florsheim (Ed.), *Adolescent romantic relations and sexual behavior: Theory, research, and practical implications* (pp. 185–211). Mahwah, NJ: Lawrence Erlbaum.

Whitton, S. W., Waldinger, R. J., Schulz, M. S., Allen, J. P., Crowell, J. A., & Hauser, S. T. (2008). Prospective associations from family-of-origin interactions to adult marital interactions and relationship adjustment. *Journal of Family Psychology, 22,* 274–286.

Windle, W., & Mrug, S. (2009). Cross-gender violence perpetration and victimization among early adolescents and associations with attitudes toward dating conflict. *Journal of Youth and Adolescence, 38*(3), 429–439.

Young, A. M., & d'Arcy, H. (2005). Older boyfriends of adolescent girls: The cause or a sign of the problem? *Journal of Adolescent Mental Health, 36,* 410–419.

Zhi Hong, L., Connolly, J., Depeng, J., Pepler, D., & Craig, W. (2010). Adolescent romantic relationships in China and Canada: A cross-national comparison. *International Journal of Behavioral Development, 34,* 113–120.

Zimmer-Gembeck, M., Siebenbruner, J., & Collins, W. A. (2001). The divergent influences of romantic involvement on individual and social functioning from early to middle adolescence. *Journal of Adolescence, 24,* 313–336.

9

Transformations in Heterosexual Romantic Relationships Across the Transition Into Adulthood

"Meet Me at the Bleachers . . . I Mean the Bar"

Wyndol Furman

Jessica K. Winkles

O ne of the most striking differences between adolescence and early adulthood is the change in romantic relationships. In most Western cultures, romantic relationships first appear in adolescence, but they become increasingly interdependent and committed in

This research was supported by Grant 50106 from the National Institute of Mental Health (NIMH) (W. Furman, principal investigator [PI]) and Grant HD049080 from the National Institute of Child Health and Human Development (NICHD (W. Furman, PI).

early adulthood. In the present chapter, we review the theories and existing empirical literature on changes in heterosexual romantic relationships and experiences from adolescence to early adulthood, and outline directions for subsequent research.

For the sake of brevity, we use the term *romantic relationships*, but we are primarily referring to heterosexual romantic relationships. Most of the existing literature is based on samples of predominantly or exclusively heterosexual relationships. Some findings on heterosexual relationships may apply to same-sex relationships, and some findings on same-sex relationships may apply to heterosexual relationships, but as yet, little direct information exists on the similarities and differences of heterosexual and same-sex relationships. Russell, Watson, and Muraco (2011 [also Chapter 10 of this volume]), however, provide a review of the existing literature on same-sex relationships.

We are also primarily referring to heterosexual romantic relationships in Western cultures in the late 20th or 21st century. The majority of the research has been done in the United States with some other work done in Canada, Europe, Israel, and Australia, yet striking cultural differences can be expected (see Brown, Larson, & Saraswathi, 2000; Schneider, Lee, & Alvarez-Valdivia, 2011 [also Chapter 6 of this volume]). In fact, it is likely that differences exist among the Western cultures that have been studied, but we have little firm bases for knowing exactly what these differences are.

The review focuses on transitions and changes from adolescence to early adulthood. As the research has primarily been conducted with samples drawn from schools in Western cultures, we examine differences between the relationships of adolescents in high school (approximately 15 to 18 years old) and the relationships of young adults who have completed high school (18 to 25 years old). Although we show that romantic relationships in adolescence and early adulthood tend to differ in certain ways, such differences do not apply to all romantic relationships, even within a particular culture. Marked diversity exists. The relationships of young adults are typically more interdependent than adolescents, but some adolescent romantic relationships entail high levels of interdependence and commitment; conversely, many young adults' relationships are brief and superficial in nature. Thus, the changes from adolescence to early adulthood are noteworthy, but we are reluctant to characterize them as normative or to suggest that most youth are on the same pathway of romantic development.

In the sections that follow, we first describe relevant theories of the changes in romantic relationships. We then review the existing empirical literature. Finally, we delineate a series of directions for future research.

THEORIES OF DEVELOPMENT IN ROMANTIC RELATIONSHIPS

Many of the classic theorists in psychology focused on developmental changes from infancy to adolescence, but some theorists have also incorporated changes later in the life span. One of the earliest of such formulations was Erikson's (1950) theory of eight psychosocial stages of development. In each stage, a "crisis" or developmental task needs to be resolved. In adolescence, the task is the development of an identity, and peer relationships play a key role in the resolution of this task. In early adulthood, the task is the development of intimacy, and romantic relationships play a key role. Thus, romantic relationships move to the forefront and become more intimate. Erikson did not provide detailed descriptions of the expected changes in romantic experience as his emphasis was on the individual's personality development. Nevertheless, his conceptualization of such stages was built on the changing nature of relationships over the course of development.

Attachment theorists also describe changes in romantic relationships. Bowlby (1979) proposed that a long-term romantic partner eventually replaces a parent as the primary attachment figure. The shift from parent to partner is hypothesized to begin in adolescence because of the hormonal changes that occur with puberty (Ainsworth, 1989). Such changes lead adolescents to search for a peer with whom to establish a relationship. Most adolescent romantic relationships, however, do not meet all the criteria for an attachment bond—that is, a persistent affectional bond that entails proximity seeking, distress over inexplicable separation, pleasure at reunion, grief at loss, and importantly, the use of the partner as a safe haven (a source of comfort and safety) and secure base (a source of support for exploration; Ainsworth, 1989). Instead, such romantic relationships began to gradually acquire such characteristics, both over the course of a particular relationship and with age. Accordingly, Hazan and Zeifman (1994) proposed that attachments are transferred from parent to peer function by function. In particular, proximity seeking first occurs, then safe haven behavior, and finally separation protest and secure base behavior.

In an effort to integrate the insights of attachment and Sullivanian theorists, Furman and Wehner (1994, 1997) proposed a behavioral systems theory in which romantic partners are hypothesized to become major figures in the functioning of the attachment, caregiving, affiliative, and sexual/reproductive behavioral systems. Affiliation and sexuality are expected to be the central systems in romantic relationships initially, but eventually the attachment and caregiving systems become salient as well. The emergence of these systems is reflected in four developmental stages in the nature of their romantic relationships. Initially, their interactions could be characterized as *simple interchanges* as they develop a sense of comfort interacting with potential sexual or romantic partners. As they become comfortable, they may move to *casual dating* in which affiliative behavior and sexual experimentation occur in a number of short-term relationships. Romantic partners are not expected to emerge as attachment figures or recipients of caretaking until they begin to develop *stable relationships*—exclusive, longer-term relationships. In fact, these systems may not fully emerge in romantic relationships until the appearance of *committed relationships*—that is, relationships that may become a marriage or lifetime partnership; such relationships typically do not appear until early adulthood or later.

Individuals also develop representations, or *views*, of romantic relationships (Furman & Wehner, 1994, 1997). Such views are cognitive expectations regarding romantic relationships, the self in romantic relationships and the romantic partner. Views are expected to guide a person's behavior and serve as a basis for predicting and interpreting the partner's behavior. They are hypothesized to affect and be affected by romantic experiences. With regard to developmental changes in representations, Furman and Wehner did not think that views followed any one particular developmental trajectory. Instead, they become more secure, less secure, or remain relatively consistent depending on the nature of the romantic experiences a person has.

Several other theorists have described developmental changes in romantic relationships in adolescence and adulthood. Connolly and Goldberg (1999) described four phases of romantic relationships: (1) an initial infatuation stage in which passion and physical attraction are most salient; (2) an affiliative stage in which romantic relationships emerge in the context of the peer group; (3) an intimate stage in which emotional intimacy emerges; and (4) a committed romantic relationship stage in which commitment joins passion, affiliation, and intimacy as motivating and defining features of romantic relationships.

Similarly, Brown (1999) proposed a four-stage sequence: (1) an initiation phase in early adolescence during which heterosexual youths' interest in the other sex increases and short-term relationships are established, (2) a status phase in early and middle adolescence in which the focus is on establishing relationships that are approved of by one's peers, (3) an affection phase in which the emphasis is placed on the relationship itself, and (4) a bonding phase in which the possibility of a long-term commitment is considered. Brown thought this phase typically emerged in late adolescence and early adulthood in the United States. An important implication of the emergence of this phase is that pragmatic and personal concerns about whether to make a long-term commitment to a particular person become salient, as well as the feelings of intimacy and affection that emerge in the prior stage. In effect, Brown and Connolly and Goldberg's theories identify commitment and the pragmatic concerns that accompany it as the key difference between relationships in adolescence and adulthood.

Finally, social exchange theory and evolutionary theory have been frequently used in the study of adult romantic relationships but have received little attention in the adolescent literature. In a noteworthy exception, Laursen and Jensen-Campbell (1999) proposed that a shift occurs over the course of adolescence and early adulthood in the resources associated with romantic relationships. In early adolescence, status and physical attractiveness are highly salient, but kindness and reciprocity increase in saliency with age. Consequently, the social exchanges in early adolescence are predominately selfish in nature, with personal gain and reproductive success being maximized. In late adolescence and early adulthood, the exchanges provide mutual gains, such that relationship stability and interdependence are promoted.

As can be seen in this review, the different theories all describe some fundamental changes in romantic relationships from adolescence to early adulthood. Although the terminology and details may differ, the central description of the transformation is similar in the different conceptualizations. This shared description is encouraging, but our theories of such romantic relationships and their changes remain underdeveloped. Many theories are primarily descriptions, rather than explanations of change. Formulations of underlying mechanisms and processes have been brief and rarely have guided empirical studies. Additional theoretical development is required for further progress in the field.

∭ RECENT EMPIRICAL ADVANCEƒ

In the sections that follow, we first review the literature on developmental changes in the involvement of youth in romantic relationships. We then discuss changes in the qualities of the romantic relationships that occur.

Romantic Involvement

Being involved in a romantic relationship is quite common in adolescence and early adulthood. In a retrospective study from age 17 to 27, participants reported having 1 to 10 partners, with an average of 2.6 partners. They had a steady partner about two thirds of time, with the average relationship lasting 37 months (Chen et al., 2006). However, developmental changes in both romantic status and relationship duration also occur during the transition from adolescence to early adulthood.

Status

Findings from multiple studies demonstrate increases in the proportion of dating individuals during the transition to young adulthood. During an 18-month period, in a study of American youth, approximately 25% of 12-year-olds, 50% of 15-year-olds, and 69% of 18-year-olds are in "special" romantic relationships (Carver, Joyner, & Udry, 2003). In a longitudinal study of German youth, 40% of participants were in a romantic relationship at age 13, 43% were in a relationship at age 15, 47% had a relationship at age 17, and 65% were in a romantic relationship at age 21 (Seiffge-Krenke, 2003).

Changes in the frequency of cohabitation and marriage occur as well. In 2002, 5.6% of 15- to 19-year-old American women cohabited with their partners, whereas 15.7% of 20- to 24- year-old women were cohabiting. Similarly, 1.9% of adolescent men and 13.4% of young adult men lived with their partners (Goodwin, Mosher, & Chandra, 2010). Only 1.5% of 15- to 17-year-old adolescents are married. Among 18- and 19-year-olds, 2.2% are married, whereas 14.9% of 20- to 24-year-olds are married. The estimated median age at marriage in 2009 in the United States was 28.1 for men and 25.9 for women (U.S. Census Bureau, 2009), and these ages have been increasing in recent years.

Involvement in early adulthood is also predicted by involvement in adolescence. Romantic involvement in 11th and 12th grade is associated with increased rates of both cohabitation and marriage in early adulthood (ages 23–25) (Raley, Crissy, & Muller, 2007).

Duration

Relationship duration tends to increase throughout adolescence and into adulthood. Among adolescents 16 or older, 55% report having "special" romantic relationships of more than 11 months, whereas only 35% of 14- and 15-year-olds report having relationships of such a long duration (Carver et al., 2003). Although the duration of such "special" romantic relationships is longer than romantic relationships in general (Furman & Hand, 2006), the trend of increasing duration appears to apply to romantic relationships in general and, in fact, continues into early adulthood. In a German sample, mean romantic relationship duration is 5.1 months at age 15, 11.8 months at age 17, and 21.3 months at age 21 (Seiffge-Krenke, 2003). In a longitudinal study of Ohio youth, the average relationship duration among adolescents ages 12 to 17 is 4.8 months, whereas the average for young adults ages 18 to 23 is 10.5 months (Giordano, Flannigan, Manning, & Longmore, 2009). The average relationship length for young adults living with their partners is 15.8 months, three times as long as adolescents'.

Relationship Qualities

Support

Support increases in romantic relationships from adolescence to early adulthood (Furman & Buhrmester, 1992; Giordano et al., 2009; Seiffge-Krenke, 2003). These changes are also evident in young adults' characterizations of their current relationships and the relationships they had in adolescence (Shulman & Kipnis, 2001). Young adult relationships were primarily described as trusting and supportive, whereas adolescent romantic relationships were mainly portrayed in terms of companionship.When asked to describe differences in their current and adolescent relationships, they characterized their adolescent relationships in terms of social activities, whereas current relationships were often portrayed as mature and emotionally close.

The developmental changes not only occur in terms of the rates of support, but also in terms of the rates of support relative to that provided by other individuals. For example, the romantic partner's place in the hierarchy of perceived support figures goes from fourth in the 7th grade, to third in the 10th grade, and then to the most supportive in college for men and tied for first for women (Furman & Buhrmester, 1992). Similarly, from high school to college, romantic partners move up in the hierarchy of attachment figures and are increasingly preferred in both support-seeking and affiliative contexts (Rosenthal & Kobak, 2010). Hazan and Zeifman's (1994) theory of the sequence of the transfer of attachment functions also has received support. Middle adolescents seek proximity to romantic partners more than other important individuals, whereas others are turned to more often for a safe haven or secure base (Markiewicz, Lawford, Doyle, & Haggart, 2006). Early adults also seek proximity to romantic partners most often, but they also turn to romantic partners and friends most often for a secure base. Mothers, however, remain the most commonly sought secure base.

Love

The likelihood of *currently* being in love remains stable (at about 50%) from early adolescence to young adulthood. Differences arise, however, when individuals are asked about the *number of times* they have been in love. Early adolescent males report having been in love more times than young adult males and more times than females at all ages. Females report having been in love a similar number of times across ages (Montgomery, 2005).

Although the likelihood of currently being in love is generally stable during the transition from adolescence to adulthood, the intensity of passionate love (intense longing to be with another) increases. Passionate love scores are also higher for young adults living with their partners than young adults who are just dating (Giordano et al., 2009). Conversely, feelings of infatuation are more common in adolescent relationships (Shulman & Kipnis, 2001).

In addition to the frequency and intensity of feelings of love, perceptions regarding the nature of love change over time. Fourteen- and 16-year-olds are more likely to perceive romantic love as friendship (Storge love style) than 19-year-olds are (Shulman & Scharf, 2000).

Sexual Behavior

The proportion of individuals who have engaged in different sexual behaviors increases through adolescence and early adulthood. In the 2002 National Survey of Family Growth, 26% of 15-year-old women, 70% of 18-year-olds, and 92% of 22- to 24-year-olds have had vaginal intercourse with a male. Frequencies for males were similar: 24.9% of 15-year-olds, 62.3% of 18-year-olds, and 89% of 22- to 24-year-olds have had vaginal intercourse with a female (Mosher, Chandra, & Jones, 2005). The number of partners per year also increases from late adolescence to early adulthood (Lansford et al., 2010). Finally, the frequency of sexual intercourse is negatively associated with relationship satisfaction in adolescence, but it tends to be positively related to relationship commitment in early adulthood (Welsh, Haugen, Widman, Darling, & Grello, 2005). Thus, the meaning or significance of sexual intercourse changes developmentally.

Other Positive Features

Young adults describe their current relationships as more enjoyable and closer than their recollections of their adolescent romantic relationships (Shulman & Kipnis, 2001). Similarly, relationship satisfaction increases from adolescence to early adulthood (Young, Furman, & Laursen, 2011).

Conflict

Several investigators have examined changes from adolescence to adulthood in the frequency and intensity of conflict in romantic relationships, but the results across studies are not consistent. Two studies reported decreases between 15 and 20 years of age (Chen et al., 2006; Vujeva & Furman, 2011), but another study found increases (Furman & Buhrmester, 1992). Similarly, decreases from 21 to 25 are found in one study (Robins, Caspi, & Moffitt, 2006), and increases are found in another (Chen et al., 2006). The mean level of conflict is also higher for married and cohabiting couples compared to others (Chen et al., 2006), which would suggest that increases may occur as more individuals cohabit and marry.

The developmental picture is clearer regarding changes in conflict resolution. Compromise is used in conflict resolution more often by older high school students than by younger ones (Feldman & Gowen, 1998), and skills such as problem solving tend to increase from age 15 to 20 (Vujeva & Furman, 2011). In adolescence, resolution most often includes negotiation, followed by coercion and then disengagement, but compromise is relatively superficial (Laursen, Finkelstein, & Betts, 2001). Late adolescent couples (17–18 years old) tend to avoid or minimize their differences by seeking a quick and easy compromise or rescinding previous statements of disagreement (Tuval-Maschiach & Shulman, 2006). When asked to discuss a disagreement, conversations among adolescent couples are concise; couples do not solicit the partner's perspective and rarely refer to the relationship itself. Even adolescents in longer relationships tend to minimize and downplay disagreements. In early adulthood, negotiation becomes more common as young adult couples are able to examine their relationships in the context of differences (Laursen et al., 2001). Their conversations are characterized by humor and emotional expression, even if such expressions lead to painful realizations (Tuval-Maschiach & Shulman, 2006).

Other Negative Features

Although conflict has received the most attention, some research indicates that romantic stress decreases from adolescence to adulthood (Seiffge-Krenke, 2006). Young adults also recollect their adolescent romantic relationships as having more frequent relationship problems than their current relationships (Shulman & Kipnis, 2001). On the other hand, intimate partner violence victimization (sexual or physical) increases from adolescence to early adulthood (Halpern, Spriggs, Martin, & Kupper, 2009).

Cognitive Representations of Relationships

Developmental changes also occur in the security of representations of romantic relationships. Representations are commonly conceptualized along anxious and avoidant dimensions. Anxious individuals worry about having their needs met in romantic relationships, whereas avoidant individuals tend to dismiss the value of close romantic relationships (Brennan, Clark, & Shaver, 1998). In an early cross-sectional comparison (Furman & Wehner, 1997), college students had less avoidant and anxious romantic styles than high school students. In two longitudinal studies of community samples, similar decreases in avoidant representations occurred from adolescence to early adulthood on both a self-report measure of styles (Collins, Cooper, Albino, & Allard, 2002; Furman & Stephenson, 2010) and an interview measure of working models (Furman & Stephenson, 2010). Changes in anxious representations are less clear, as increases, decreases, and no changes have been reported (Collins et al., 2002; Furman & Stephenson, 2010).

Developmental changes also occur in other cognitions about romantic relationships. Perceptions of romantic competence and confidence increase, whereas feelings of awkwardness in communication decrease (Giordano et al., 2009; Young et al., 2011).

Dating Goals and Partner Characteristics

What individuals seek in romantic relationships changes during the transition from adolescence to early adulthood. College students are more likely to report companionship, sexual activity, and mate selection as reasons for dating, whereas adolescents are more likely to report recreation and status as reasons (Roscoe, Diana, & Brooks, 1987). College students report that shared interests is an important characteristic of a partner, whereas adolescents are concerned about the relative age of the partner. Young adult males also place importance on their partner being sexually active, and young adult females valued partners that would some day have a good job and have set goals for the future. Roscoe and colleagues suggested that these differences reflect a change from an emphasis on immediate gratification and social activity to an emphasis on personal fulfillment. Consistent with this idea, looks and appearance become less important reasons for establishing a romantic commitment over the course of adolescence and into early adulthood, whereas mutual feelings and compatibility become more important reasons (Galotti, Kozberg, & Appleman, 1990).

Other Developmental Changes

Up to this point, we have reviewed research that has examined changes in the mean level of a characteristic of a romantic relationship. For example, we have reported evidence that the average level of support increases. Conceptually, other types of change are possible, including changes in stability and centrality (see Connell & Furman, 1984).

Changes in stability refer to changes in consistency over time. The literature showing developmental increases in the average length of romantic relationships (e.g., Giordano et al., 2009; Seiffge-Krenke, 2003) indicates that romantic relationships themselves become more stable. A change in stability would also be indicated if the correlation between scores at Time 1 and 2 differed from that between Time 2 and 3. Using this criterion, relationship satisfaction has been shown to become more stable (Young et al., 2011). It seems possible that other romantic relationship qualities would also become more stable with development as individuals acquire romantic experience and develop patterns of interaction.

Changes in centrality refer to changes in the pattern of relations of variables. For example, Roisman, Masten, Coatsworth, and Tellegen (2004) proposed that romantic relationships are an emerging developmental task in adolescence and early adulthood and become a salient developmental task later in adulthood. As an emerging developmental task, romantic relationships would not be expected to have long-term stability and predictiveness, but they would as a salient developmental task. This developmental change in centrality has not been fully tested yet, but romantic relationship quality appears more related to adjustment in early adulthood than adolescence. For example, the associations between depression and conflict frequency and resolution seem to increase from adolescence to early adulthood (Vujeva & Furman, 2011). Similarly, commitment to a romantic partner is associated with fewer emotional problems in early adulthood, but not in adolescence (Meeus, Branje, van der Valk, & de Wied, 2007). As yet, however, we know relatively little about other changes in centrality.

Accounting for the Changes

Although the empirical literature is not very extensive, it provides a relatively consistent picture of changes from adolescence to early adulthood. Consistent with the theoretical formulations reviewed previously, relationships become more serious, committed, and interdependent. For example, changes occur in relationship duration, support, feelings of love, sexual activity, and centrality of romantic relationships. Similarly, interdependence, daily social interaction, and weekly activity diversity increase (Adams, Laursen, & Wilder, 2001). Why such changes occur has received less attention.

In their research on age changes described in the prior sections, Giordano et al. (2009) included relationship duration, having had sexual intercourse in the relationship, and cohabiting, as well as age as predictors of growth from adolescence to early adulthood. Each of the four variables was a significant predictor for most of the characteristics. Thus, part of the reason for the observed age changes could be because relationships become longer, are more likely to include sexual intercourse, or include a higher proportion of cohabiting couples. Alternatively, duration, sexual intercourse, or cohabitation could themselves be reflections of some other processes. For example, the greater likelihood of intercourse could reflect societal norms, developmental changes in biological processes, or increases in emotional intimacy. Importantly, age remained a significant predictor of growth in almost all instances, even when these other variables were included in the equation. It is possible that the addition of still other variables could eliminate the predictive power of age. For example, cohabitation is not the only noteworthy indicator of a change in the nature of a romantic relationship. Being in love or decisions to get married could also account for some of the seeming age changes. Alternatively, the changes could reflect processes more closely linked to age. For example, as they grow older, individuals acquire more experience, become more skilled, and develop socially and cognitively. Their ability to select a compatible partner may also improve.

Thus, multiple factors could account for the observed changes. For example, consider the changes in conflict resolution that occur during the transition to adulthood. First, they gain more experience in resolving conflicts and as a consequence may become more skillful in doing so. Second, adolescents have idealistic views of romantic relationships and feelings of infatuation and acting "crazy" when in love (Shulman & Kipnis, 2001). Worries about losing the excitement in a relationship may motivate adolescents to focus on agreement rather than acknowledging problems and discussing them honestly. Third, young adults are more cognitively developed than adolescents. Effective negotiation may become more frequent as individuals develop cognitive capacities for viewing the perspectives of others and integrating multiple wants and needs. Fourth, they may also be more likely to initiate or maintain relationships with partners with whom they can effectively resolve conflicts. Finally, factors like increased relationship duration or the increased intimacy and interdependence that comes with sexual intercourse or cohabitation could partially account for some of the changes. As relationships become longer, one may learn how to effectively resolve conflicts with that particular partner. Increases in intimacy and interdependence may motivate individuals to work through problems, whereas feelings of intimacy allow them to talk openly and express their own needs. Unfortunately, we still know relatively little about what factors could be responsible for the age changes that have been observed.

⫸ FUTURE DIRECTIONS

Although it is rather hackneyed to say that additional research is needed, such a statement is particularly true for this topic. Unfortunately, the literatures on adolescent romantic relationships and early adult romantic relationships have been quite separate. Most studies of developmental changes and transitions in romantic relationships have examined changes *within* the adolescent years (i.e., the middle school and high school years), rather than changes from adolescence into early adulthood. Moreover, the majority of studies of romantic relationships in early adulthood consist of cross-sectional studies of college students, which are often retrospective in nature. In some cases, investigators compare cross-sectional samples of high school students and college students, but such comparisons confound selection and developmental effects. Longitudinal studies with representative samples are essential to understand the developmental changes, and unfortunately, many of the well-known longitudinal studies in the developmental field did not examine romantic relationships extensively until the participants were adults. Until recently, social scientists failed to appreciate the significance of adolescent romantic relationships (Brown, Feiring, & Furman, 1999; Collins, 2003).

As we can see from the present review, some facets of romantic experiences have received surprisingly little attention. For example, little work exists on changes in power and influence, and the work that does exist is inconsistent (cf. Adams, Laursen, & Wilder, 2001; Furman & Buhrmester, 1992; Giordano et al., 2009). Similarly, the subtitle of this chapter ("Meet Me at the Bleachers . . . I Mean the Bar") refers to expected changes in the nature of the activities in romantic interactions, but as yet, such changes have not been documented. Even the topics that have received more attention, such as support and conflict, have been examined in only a handful of studies. Clearly, more work is needed.

Variations in Transitions

Up to this point, we have focused on the changes from adolescence to early adulthood in the typical characteristics of romantic experiences. Equally noteworthy is the variability in romantic experiences. Not only do individuals of a particular age vary in their romantic experiences, but differences also exist in the developmental course of romantic experiences in adolescence and early adulthood—both across and within cultures.

One important kind of difference across cultures is in the timing of particular romantic experiences or events. For example, the average age of first marriage for women is 17.6 in the Republic of Niger but 32.9 in Spain ("Age at First Marriage," n.d.). Within cultures, variation in timing has been studied more extensively. For instance, investigators have examined the predictors and consequences of the age of marriage in the United States (Glenn, Uecker, & Love, 2010; Lehrer, 2008; Ryan, Franzetta, Schelar, & Manlove, 2009; Uecker & Stokes, 2008). Relatedly, those young adults who desire to get married in their early 20s differ in substance use, sexual permissiveness, and family formation values from those who desire to get married in their mid-20s or later (Carroll et al., 2007).

Work also exists on the consequences of romantic involvement at an early age (see Connolly & McIsaac, 2009). Less is known about the timing of experiences later in adolescence or in early adulthood. We hypothesized that variation in timing and degree of romantic involvement would be strongly influenced by biological maturity, cultural and local norms, and peer prestige variables (Furman & Wehner, 1994). Consistent with these ideas, casual and serious romantic involvement in late adolescence are related to physical appearance and friends' normative romantic involvement in late adolescence (Furman & Winkles, 2010). Serious involvement also predicted decreases in avoidant representations and increases in anxious representations and in satisfaction (Winkles & Furman, 2010). Casual dating involvement predicted increases in romantic appeal. Otherwise, little is known about romantic involvement in late adolescence or early adulthood.

The variation in the timing of marriage or other transitions in romantic experiences not only illustrates the variability in the developmental course but also means that the significance or effect of such a transition may vary as a function of timing as well. For example, getting married at an early age has different consequences than getting married at a later age (Glenn et al., 2010; Lehrer, 2008). Moreover, the difference between those who are married at an early age and those who are not may be unlike the difference between those who have married by a later age and those who have not. In other words, the meaning or significance of getting married changes developmentally. Much of the literature has focused on the former comparisons (predictors/effects of timing), but the latter comparisons (developmental changes in the effects of romantic status) warrant attention as well (see Meeus et al., 2007).

Individuals not only vary in the timing of their romantic experiences but in the experiences they have. Not everyone is on the path to marriage or wants to be. Not everyone will have the same amount or kind of romantic experience. Research on the predictors and consequences of such variation is being conducted (see Connolly & McIsaac, 2009; Furman & Collins, 2008). Studying such variation can shed light on the nature of the developmental changes that occur. For example, if we can determine what is characteristic of individuals who do and do not have certain romantic experiences, we may get some clues about what is required or underlying such experiences or developmental changes.

The Nature of Change

In the present review, we have focused on changes that occur in the transition from adolescence to early adulthood. In some cases, the changes may be specific or more marked during the transitional period, but often these developmental changes have begun earlier in adolescence or continue further into adulthood. For example, support increases throughout adolescence (Furman & Buhrmester, 1992) and seems likely to continue to increase through early adulthood as relationships become more interdependent and committed. Reviews of the developmental changes during adolescence or during early adulthood are beyond the scope of this paper (see Collins & van Dulmen, 2006; Connolly & McIsaac, 2009; Furman & Collins, 2008). Identifying the developmental patterns over a wide age span remains challenging, as most of the research to date has simply compared scores at two or perhaps three different ages, which are usually relatively close together. Thus, inferences about the developmental changes from the onset of adolescence into adulthood would require piecing together different studies, which are likely to have used somewhat different samples and measures. Clearly, more long-term developmental research is needed.

It is also important to realize that change can take different forms (Young et al., 2011). *Stochastic* processes of change are those in which there is a variable or even random element of change over time. Stochastic change arises when a variable is influenced by proximal factors that are themselves in the midst of change. For example, relationship satisfaction may fluctuate as a function of changes in a relationship. In contrast, *deterministic* processes of change are those in which change is a steady unfolding continuous process; the processes unfold in a consistent, developmentally driven model. For example, the development of romantic competence may follow a continuous trajectory.

Importantly, the hypothesized nature of change should be considered in selecting an analytic tool. Autoregressive cross-lagged models are appropriate when changes are stochastic in nature, whereas growth curve models are appropriate for deterministic processes. Both of these approaches assume that there is one form of change; if multiple types of trajectories exist, growth mixture modeling may be appropriate. As yet, we know little about how to characterize the type of change that different aspects of romantic relationships undergo. And if we analyze the type of change using the wrong model, we may not capture it.

It is also important to consider whether changes occur as a function of a series of ongoing experiences or if highly salient events may lead to marked, discontinuous changes in romantic experiences. For example, decreases in security of representations may occur as a consequence of a series of unsupportive experiences. On the other hand, a particularly marked experience may lead to a quick change in security. For example, after experiencing sexual coercion, adolescents display a marked increase in anxious representations of romantic relationships; they also engage in sexual intercourse with more casual sex partners, and this behavior continues to increase at a faster rate over time (Young, Furman, & Jones, in press). Whether such discontinuous changes occur after other events, such as declaring love, engaging in intercourse, or cohabiting, remains to be determined.

Additionally, the degree to which individuals are affected by events is also important in its own right. Those partners whose commitment is substantially affected by particular events experience more negative events and are less compatible with their partner than those in which commitment increases more smoothly (Surra & Hughes, 1997).

The Broader Context

Transitions in romantic experiences, such as the establishment of a committed relationship, are not the only developmental milestones that commonly occur in early adulthood. Completing one's education, beginning to work full-time, establishing independent residence, and having a child are all significant milestones that commonly occur in early adulthood as well. These different milestones are not independent of one another; thus, if we are to understand the impact of romantic milestones, such as the establishment of a committed relationship, we need to consider how these other milestones may be related or even responsible for any seeming effect.

Moreover, no single normative sequence of these events exists in contemporary Western society. For example, Osgood, Ruth, Eccles, Jacobs, & Barber (2005) identified six different patterns that characterized individuals in their mid-20s: (1) fast starters (married and employed full-time with less education and half with children); (2) parents without careers (married/cohabiting with children, less education, and only a short-term job or no job); (3) educated partners (married/cohabiting, high levels of education, and no children); (4) educated singles (high levels of education but not married/cohabiting); (5) working singles (employed full-time and often living with parents); and (6) slow starters (living at home, limited education and employment). The pattern of milestones a person has experienced or not experienced may play a role, as well as the particular ones (but see Mouw, 2005).

Investigators have considered how demographic variables and cultural context affect the changes that occur in the romantic milestones, such as cohabitation and marriage. For example, African Americans are less likely to marry by early adulthood, even when income status is controlled for (Meier & Allen, 2009). Not only are such demographic characteristics predictive of different experiences but in some cases the romantic experiences in adolescence interact with such demographic characteristics in predicting experiences in early adulthood. For example, overall African Americans are less likely to cohabit in early adulthood; however, if they were involved in a steady relationship in adolescence, they are more likely to cohabit (Meier & Allen, 2009). Thus, our developmental models are not only going to need to consider contextual factors, but also take into account the experiences a person has had during various developmental periods.

◆ SUMMARY

Although only a limited amount of research has examined the transition in heterosexual romantic relationships from adolescence to early adulthood, a relatively coherent picture is emerging—both theoretically and empirically. Relationships become more serious, committed, and interdependent. Such change reflects both transformations in the kind of romantic relationships that emerge and changes in other age or experience-related processes. Further work is needed, however, both to describe the changes and identify the underlying processes. Attention to the variability in the nature and timing of the changes and the larger context in which romantic relationships occur should provide us further understanding of the nature of these transitions.

⧓ SUGGESTED READINGS

Collins, W. A., & van Dulmen, M. (2006). "The course of true love(s) . . .": Origins and pathways in the development of romantic relationships. In A. Booth & A. Crouter (Eds.), *Romance and sex in adolescence and emerging adulthood: Risks and opportunities* (pp. 63–86). Mahwah, NJ: Lawrence Erlbaum.

Furman, W., & Buhrmester, D. (1992). Age and sex differences in perceptions of networks of personal relationships. *Child Development, 63,* 103–115.

Furman, W., & Collins, W. A. (2008). Adolescent romantic relationships and experiences. In K. H. Rubin, W. Bukowski, & B. Laursen (Eds.). *Peer interactions, relationships, and groups* (pp. 341–360). New York: Guilford Press.

Seiffge-Krenke, I. (2003). Testing theories of romantic development from adolescence to young adulthood: Evidence of a developmental sequence. *International Journal of Behavioral Development, 27,* 519–531.

Shulman, S., & Kipnis, O. (2001). Adolescent romantic relationships: A look from the future. *Journal of Adolescence, 24,* 337–351.

⧓ REFERENCES

Adams, R., Laursen, B., & Wilder, D. (2001). Characteristics of closeness in adolescent romantic relationships. *Journal of Adolescence, 24,* 353–363.

Age at First Marriage. (n.d.). *Wikipedia.* Retrieved from http://en.wikipedia.org/wiki/Age_at _first_marriage.

Ainsworth, M. S. (1989). Attachments beyond infancy. *American Psychologist, 44,* 709–716.

Bowlby, J. (1979). *Attachment and Loss: Vol 1. Attachment.* New York: Basic Books.

Brennan, K. A., Clark, C. L., & Shaver, P. R. (1998). Self-report measurement of adult romantic attachment: An integrative overview. In J. A. Simpson & W. S. Rholes (Eds.), *Attachment theory and close relationships* (pp. 46–76). New York: Guilford Press.

Brown, B. (1999). "You're going out with who?": Peer group influences on adolescent romantic relationships. In B. B. Brown, C. Feiring, & W. Furman (Eds.), *The development of romantic relationships in adolescence* (pp. 1–16). New York: Cambridge University Press.

Brown, B. B., Feiring, C., & Furman, W. (1999). Missing the love boat: Why researchers have shied away from adolescent romance. In W. Furman, B. B. Brown, & C. Feiring (Eds.), *The development of romantic relationships in adolescence* (pp. 1–16). New York: Cambridge University Press.

Brown, B. B., Larson, R. W., & Saraswathi, T. S. (Eds). (2000). *The world's youth: Adolescence in eight regions of the globe.* Cambridge, UK: Cambridge University Press.

Carroll, J., Willoughby, B., Badger, S., Nelson, L., Barry, C., & Madsen, S. (2007). So close, yet so far away: The impact of varying marital horizons on emerging adulthood. *Journal of Adolescent Research, 22,* 219–247.

Carver, K., Joyner, K., & Udry, J. R. (2003). National estimates of adolescent romantic relationships. In P. Florsheim (Ed.), *Adolescent romantic relationships and sexual behavior: Theory, research, and practical implications* (pp. 291–329). New York: Cambridge University Press.

Chen, H., Cohen, P., Kasen, S., Johnson, J. G., Ehrensaft, M., & Gordon, K. (2006). Predicting conflict with romantic relationships during the transition to adulthood. *Personal Relationships, 13,* 411–427.

Collins, N., Cooper, M., Albino, A., & Allard, L. (2002). Psychosocial vulnerability from adolescence to adulthood: A prospective study of attachment style differences in relationship functioning and partner choice. *Journal of Personality, 70,* 965–1008.

Collins, W. A. (2003). More than myth: The developmental significance of romantic relationships during adolescence. *Journal of Research on Adolescence, 13,* 1–25.

Collins, W. A., & van Dulmen, M. (2006). "The course of true love(s) . . .": Origins and pathways in the development of romantic relationships. In A. Booth & A. Crouter (Eds.), *Romance and sex in adolescence and emerging adulthood: Risks and opportunities* (pp. 63–86). Mahwah, NJ: Lawrence Erlbaum.

Connell, J. C., & Furman, W. (1984). Conceptual and methodological issues in the study of transitions. In R. Harmon & R. Emde (Eds.), *Continuity and discontinuity in development* (pp. 153–173). New York: Plenum.

Connolly, J. A., & Goldberg, A. (1999). Romantic relationships in adolescence: The role of friends and peers in their emergence and development. In W. Furman, B. B. Brown, & C. Feiring (Eds.), *The development of romantic relationships in adolescence* (pp. 266–290). New York: Cambridge University Press.

Connolly, J., & McIsaac, C. (2009). Romantic relationships in adolescence. In R. M. Lerner & L. Steinberg (Eds.), *Handbook of adolescent psychology, Vol. 2: Contextual influences on adolescent development* (3rd ed., pp. 104–151). Hoboken, NJ: Wiley.

Erikson, E. H. (1950). *Childhood and society.* New York: Norton.

Feldman, S. S., & Gowen, L. K. (1998). Conflict negotiation tactics in romantic relationships in high school students. *Journal of Youth and Adolescence, 27,* 691–717.

Furman, W., & Buhrmester, D. (1992). Age and sex differences in perceptions of networks of personal relationships. *Child Development, 63,* 103–115.

Furman, W., & Collins, W. A. (2008). Adolescent romantic relationships and experiences. In K. H. Rubin, W. Bukowski, & B. Laursen (Eds.). *Peer interactions, relationships, and groups* (pp. 341–360). New York: Guilford Press.

Furman, W., & Hand, L. S. (2006). The slippery nature of romantic relationships: Issues in definition and differentiation. In A. Booth & A. C. Crouter (Eds.), *Romance and sex in adolescence and emerging adulthood: Risks and opportunities* (pp. 171–178). Mahwah, NJ: Lawrence Erlbaum.

Furman, W., & Stephenson, C. (2010). *Changes in representations and interactions in romantic relationships.* Manuscript in preparation.

Furman, W., & Wehner, E. A. (1994). Romantic views: Toward a theory of adolescent romantic relationships. In R. Montemayor, G. R. Adams, & G. P. Gullota (Eds.), *Advances in adolescent development: Vol. 6, Relationships during adolescence* (pp. 168–175). Thousand Oaks, CA: Sage.

Furman, W., & Wehner, E. A. (1997). Adolescent romantic relationships: A developmental perspective. In S. Shulman & W. A. Collins (Eds.), *New directions for child development (No. 78). Romantic relationships in adolescence: Developmental perspectives* (pp. 21–36). San Francisco: Jossey-Bass.

Furman, W., & Winkles, J. K. (2010). Predicting romantic involvement, relationship cognitions, and relationship qualities from physical appearance, perceived norms, and relational styles regarding friends and parents. *Journal of Adolescence, 33,* 827–836.

Galotti, K. M., Kozberg, S. P., & Appleman, D. (1990). Younger and older adolescents' thinking about commitments. *Journal of Experimental Child Psychology, 50,* 324–339.

Giordano, P. C., Flannigan, C. M., Manning, W. D., & Longmore, M. A. (2009). Developmental shifts in the character of romantic relationships from adolescence to early adulthood. *National Center for Family & Marriage Research Working Paper Series.*

Glenn, N. D., Uecker, J. E., & Love, R. W. B., Jr. (2010). Later first marriage and marital success. *Social Science Research, 39,* 787–800.

Goodwin, P. Y., Mosher, W. D., & Chandra, A. (2010). Marriage and cohabitation in the United States: A statistical portrait based on Cycle 6 (2002) of the National Survey of Family Growth. *National Center for Health Statistics. Vital Health Statistics, 23,* 1–55.

Halpern, C. T., Spriggs, A. L., Martin, S. L., & Kupper, L. L. (2009). Patterns of intimate partner violence victimization from adolescence to young adulthood in a nationally representative sample. *Journal of Adolescent Health, 45,* 508–516.

Hazan, C., & Zeifman, D. (1994). Sex and the psychological tether. In K. Bartholomew & D. Perlman (Eds.), *Advances in personal relationships: Vol. 1. Attachment processes in adulthood* (pp. 151–180). London: Jessica Kingsley.

Lansford, J. E., Yu, T., Erath, S. A., Pettit, G. S., Bates, J. E. & Dodge, K. A. (2010). Developmental precursors of number of sexual partners from ages 16 to 22. *Journal of Research in Adolescence, 20,* 678–705.

Laursen, B., Finkelstein, B. D., & Betts, N. T. (2001). A developmental meta-analysis of peer conflict resolution. *Developmental Review, 21,* 423–449.

Laursen, B., & Jensen-Campbell, L. A. (1999). The nature and functions of social exchange in adolescent romantic relationships. In W. Furman, B. B. Brown, & C. Feiring (Eds.), *The development of romantic relationships in adolescence* (pp. 50–74). Cambridge, UK: Cambridge University Press.

Lehrer, E. L. (2008). Age at marriage and marital instability: Revisiting the Becker–Landes–Michael hypothesis. *Journal of Population Economics, 31,* 463–484.

Markiewicz, D., Lawford, H., Doyle, A., & Haggart, N. (2006). Developmental differences in adolescents' and young adults' use of mothers, fathers, best friends, and romantic partners to fulfill attachment needs. *Journal of Youth and Adolescence, 35,* 127–140.

Meeus, W., Branje, S., van der Valk, I., & de Wied, M. (2007). Relationships with intimate partner, best friend, and parents in adolescence and early adulthood: A study of the saliency of the intimate partnership. *International Journal of Behavioral Development, 31,* 569–580.

Meier, A., & Allen, G. (2009). Romantic relationships from adolescence to young adulthood: Evidence from the National Longitudinal Study of Adolescent Health. *The Sociological Quarterly, 50,* 308–335.

Montgomery, M. J. (2005). Psychosocial intimacy and identity: From early adolescence to emerging adulthood. *Journal of Adolescent Research, 20,* 346–374.

Mosher, W. D., Chandra, A., & Jones, J. (2005). Sexual behavior and selected health measures: Men and women 15–44 years of age, United States, 2002. *Advance Data from Vital Health and Statistics (No. 132).* Hyattsville, MD: National Center for Health Statistics.

Mouw, T. (2005). Sequences of early adult transitions: A look at variability and consequences. In R. A. Settersten, F. F. Furstenberg, & R. G. Rumbaut (Eds.), *On the frontier of adulthood: Theory, research, and public policy* (pp. 256–291). Chicago: University of Chicago Press.

Osgood, D., Ruth, G., Eccles, J., Jacobs, J., & Barber, B. (2005). Six paths to adulthood: Fast starters, parents without careers, educated partners, educated singles, working singles, and slow starters. In R. A. Settersten, F. F. Furstenberg, & R. G. Rumbaut (Eds.), *On the frontier of adulthood: Theory, research, and public policy* (pp. 320–355). Chicago: University of Chicago Press.

Raley, R. K., Crissy, S., & Muller, C. (2007). Of sex and romance: Late adolescent relationships and young adult union formation. *Journal of Marriage and Family, 69,* 1210–1226.

Robins, R. W., Caspi, A., & Moffitt, T. E. (2006). It's not just who you're with, it's who you are: Personality and relationship experiences across multiple relationships. *Journal of Personality, 70,* 925–963.

Roisman, G., Masten, A., Coatsworth, J., & Tellegen, A. (2004). Salient and emerging developmental tasks in the transition to adulthood. *Child Development, 75,* 123–133.

Roscoe, B., Diana, M. S., & Brooks, R. H. (1987). Early, middle, and late adolescents' views on dating and factors influencing partner selection. *Adolescence, 22,* 59–68.

Rosenthal, N. L. & Kobak, R. (2010). Assessing adolescents' attachment hierarchies: Differences across developmental periods and associations with individual adaptation. *Journal of Research in Adolescence, 20,* 678–706.

Russell, S. T., Watson, R., & Muraco, J. A. (2011). The development of same-sex intimate relationships during adolescence. In B. Laursen & W. A. Collins (Eds.), *Relationship pathways: From adolescence to young adulthood.* Thousand Oaks, CA: Sage.

Ryan, S., Franzetta, K., Schelar, E., & Manlove, J. (2009). Family structure history: Links to relationship formation behaviors in young adulthood. *Journal of Marriage and Family, 71,* 935–953.

Schneider, B. H., Lee, M. D., & Alvarez-Valdivia, I. (2011). Adult friendship bonds in cultures of connectedness. In B. Laursen & W. A. Collins (Eds.), *Relationship pathways: From adolescence to young adulthood.* Thousand Oaks, CA: Sage.

Seiffge-Krenke, I. (2003). Testing theories of romantic development from adolescence to young adulthood: Evidence of a developmental sequence. *International Journal of Behavioral Development, 27,* 519–531.

Seiffge-Krenke, I. (2006). Coping with relationship stressors: The impact of different working models of attachment and links to adaptation. *Journal of Youth and Adolescence, 35,* 25–39.

Shulman, S., & Kipnis, O. (2001). Adolescent romantic relationships: A look from the future. *Journal of Adolescence, 24,* 337–351.

Shulman, S., & Scharf, M. (2000). Adolescent romantic behaviors and perceptions: Age- and gender-related differences, and links with family and peer relationships. *Journal of Research in Adolescence, 10,* 91–118.

Surra, C. A., & Hughes, D. K. (1997). Commitment processes in accounts of the development of premarital relationships. *Journal of Marriage and the Family, 59,* 5–21.

Tuval-Maschiach, R., & Shulman, S. (2006). Resolution of disagreements between romantic partners, among adolescents, and young adults: Qualitative analysis of interaction discourses. *Journal of Research on Adolescence, 16,* 561–588.

U.S. Census Bureau. (2009). Table MS-2: Estimated median age at first marriage, by sex: 1980 to the present. Retrieved from http://www.census.gov/population/socdemo/hh-fam/ms2.csv

Uecker, J., & Stokes, C. (2008). Early marriage in the United States. *Journal of Marriage and Family, 70*(4), 835–846.

Vujeva, H. M., & Furman, W. (2011). Depressive symptoms and romantic relationship qualities from adolescence through emerging adulthood: A longitudinal examination influences. *Journal of Clinical Child & Adolescent Psychology, 40*(11), 123–135.

Welsh, D. P., Haugen, P. T., Widman, L., Darling, N., & Grello, C. M. (2005). Kissing is good: A developmental investigation of sexuality in adolescent romantic couples. *Sexuality Research and Social Policy, 2,* 32–41.

Winkles, J. K., & Furman, W. (2010). *Adolescent serious and casual dating involvement predict changes in romantic cognitions and emotions.* Manuscript under review.

Young, B. J., Furman, W., & Jones, M. C. (in press). Changes in adolescents' risk factors following peer sexual coercion: Evidence for a feedback loop. *Development and Psychopathology.*

Young, B. J., Furman, W., & Laursen, B. (2011). Models of change and continuity in romantic experiences. In F. D. Fincham (Ed.), *Romantic relationships in emerging adulthood.* Cambridge, UK: Cambridge University Press.

10

The Development of Same-Sex Intimate Relationships During Adolescence

Stephen T. Russell

Ryan J. Watson

Joel A. Muraco

Same-sex intimate relationships are more visible and part of public discourse than perhaps at any other period in history. Only a generation ago, same-sex intimacy was stigmatized to the point of invisibility; today, same-sex marriage is possible in several countries and is the topic of prominent social and political debate. The discourse of these debates largely assumes a focus on adults, even though access to marriage is perhaps most relevant for adolescents and young adults who are at the threshold of the years at which most people develop long-term couple relationships and marriage. For young people, these debates play

Acknowledgments: The authors acknowledge support for this research from the Fitch Nesbitt Endowment of the Norton School of Family and Consumer Sciences; the Frances McClelland Institute for Children, Youth, and Families; and a University of Arizona Graduate Diversity Fellowship to Ryan J. Watson.

out in community anxieties regarding the high school prom or same-sex couples on the homecoming court. The implication is that same-sex intimate relationships are more visible than ever, and contemporary (Western) youth are among the first cohorts to have the opportunities to come out as lesbian, gay, or bisexual (LGB) during adolescence and to engage in same-sex relationships; however, these identities and relationships remain stigmatized.

The study of intimate relationships during adolescence has typically been framed from a normative perspective. Although there has been attention to the ways that adolescent romance and relationships may be associated with, for example, emotional vulnerability (see Joyner & Udry, 2000), scholars typically conceptualize intimate relationships as a dimension of the typical and normative progression of interpersonal relationship development and the shift from the primacy of parental and family relationships in childhood to the development of social relationships during the transitions into adolescence. Romantic relationships are understood as essential to the exploration of adolescents' identities; they serve as tools to help navigate environments that may seem lonely and confusing. These relationships help adolescents discover more about themselves and inform self-perceptions (Furman & Schaffer, 2003). Healthy relationships in adolescence build essential skills that are needed for a lifetime of successful development (Diamond, 2003). Thus, romantic relationships are understood as key rites of passage for (heterosexual) adolescents.

In contrast to the study of adolescent relationships, the study of sexual minority or LGB adolescents[1] has typically been framed from a risk perspective (Russell, 2005). LGB youth report disproportionate health and behavior risk (in many studies the risks are dramatically higher than for heterosexual counterparts); contemporary explanations for these risks focus on stigma, victimization, and minority stress (Meyer, 2003). Although there are recent exceptions, by and large the research on LGB adolescents has paid much less attention to dimensions of normative or typical development. Consistent with the focus on risk for LGB youth, there is a modest body of research on same-sex sexual behavior among adolescence; however, there has been little research on same-sex adolescent intimate relationships in the past three decades (although there is a body of literature on adult same-sex relationships) (Allen & Demo, 1995).

---

[1]We use *LGB* when referring specifically to same-sex sexual identities and in reference to prior studies of LGB adolescents. *Sexual minority* is an umbrella term that we use to be inclusive of same-sex attractions and behaviors, as well as identities.

Aside from the emphasis on risk, challenges for research on adolescent same-sex intimate relationships are compounded by multiple factors. Because of social stigma and resulting internalized homophobia (i.e., negative feelings toward oneself because of same-sex attractions), many sexual minority youth do not "come out" (i.e., identify their same-sex attractions to others) as adolescents or choose to conceal their same-sex sexualities. Further, being in a same-sex relationship actually does place young people "at risk" to some degree because being a member of a same-sex couple makes one visible and potentially vulnerable to discrimination and harassment. For this reason, many sexual minority youth do not date or—more to the point—do not date members of the same sex.

In light of the tension between normative and "risky" development, there are a number of conceptual frameworks or perspectives that we suggest can provide a foundation for understanding same-sex intimate relationships among youth: heteronormativity, models of sexual identity development, and minority stress. We begin the chapter with a discussion of these frameworks. We then review the existing empirical research on adolescent same-sex intimate relationships. This work includes studies that provide basic descriptive information as well as patterns of relationship development and progression for same-sex couples. A number of studies have considered the role of gender in same-sex relationships. Finally, we discuss the research on "outcomes" or correlates of same-sex intimacy: relationship violence, emotional and behavior health risks, and positive development. The chapter ends with future directions for the study of same-sex adolescent romantic relationships.

⟩⟩⟩ THEORETICAL OVERVIEW

Heteronormativity, Coming Out, and Minority Stress

Heteronormativity refers to the taken-for-granted system of privilege based on binary attitudes or beliefs about gender and sexuality that define what is considered "normal" or the moral standard (Oswald, Blume, & Marks, 2005). These normative values and moral standards are central to the development of gender and sexuality for children who are reared in a world that presumes there are only two sexes, that heterosexual coupling is "normal" or "natural," that "normal" relationships should be publicly displayed and celebrated, and that any deviation from what is "normal" is considered deviant or "unnatural" (Kitzinger, 2005). Understanding heteronormativity provides a basis for thinking about the ways that LGB youth must navigate institutions and interpersonal interactions that presume heterosexuality.

Adolescence is a time when conformity to social norms is particularly salient in general. In particular, it is a time when norms regarding gender and sexuality are intensified (Galambos, Almeida, & Petersen, 1990; Hill & Lynch, 1983); it is the time when heteronormativity is learned and practiced. Heterosexual youth begin to spend less time in same-sex friendships as they show increasing romantic and sexual interest in the opposite sex (Collins & Sroufe, 1999). These patterns are understood as "normal," and become salient to sexual minority youth as they come to realize that because of their same-sex attractions they may be "abnormal" (Savin-Williams & Diamond, 2004). The pressure to maintain distance from same-sex peers and appear to harbor attractions and desires for opposite sex peers can and does result in increased stress for LGB youth; they may begin to monitor their interpersonal interactions and may even terminate friendships rather than risk that their true attraction may be discovered (Savin-Williams, 1994).

Despite this context of heteronormativity, more youth are coming out and doing so at younger ages (Grov, Bimib, Nanin, & Parsons, 2006). These changes are interpreted in relation to the dramatic social changes in visibility of LGB people and issues; the younger age for same-sex identity development has clear implications for possibilities for intimate relationships for youth. Several decades ago, a body of research began to conceptualize same-sex identity development, a process that is a relevant precursor for understanding same-sex intimate relationships. Early models postulated linear stages of identity development (e.g., Cass, 1984; Troiden, 1989) and the coming out process (Rust, 2004) that unfolded over time. Notably, these models were initially conceptualized when coming out was primarily relevant for adults. Briefly, these models conceptualized progression from stages that included initial awareness and confusion about same-sex sexuality; recognition that same-sex identities might apply to oneself; self-acceptance and labeling; disclosure to others; and ultimate identity integration, "coming out," and pride. While the identity development models focus on psychological processes and self-awareness, the coming out models explicitly integrate LGB community participation and same-sex relationships as stages in the progression toward coming out. For the most part, these models have been rejected because they fail to capture complexities of these processes: For many people, these dimensions do not progress in neat, linear patterns, and scholars have pointed out that the presumed end state or goal of identity integration and pride (or being "out") may hold different meaning for different people or in different cultural groups and thus is not universal. Others argue that the process of coming out is not simply a singular process but is ongoing across time and context (Rust, 2004) or as individual sexual preferences and behaviors change (Diamond, 2003; Udry & Chantala, 2002).

Although these models have been critiqued in light of their original purpose for theorizing same-sex identity development or coming out, the dimensions they identify continue to be relevant for understanding same-sex identity and intimacy for youth. For contemporary youth, the issues of confusion and recognition of same-sex attractions, self-acceptance and labeling, and disclosure to others are all relevant aspects of emerging same-sex sexuality (D'Augelli, 2005). Yet given younger ages at coming out, the timing and sequencing of these dimensions for individual youth is compressed, or they may co-occur. For young couples in intimate relationships, it is likely that partners have different perspectives or experiences regarding each dimension (Diamond, Savin-Williams, & Dubé, 1999). For same-sex daters, one partner may be only just beginning to explore a same-sex identity while the other may have been "out" for several years. For two youth who are beginning to understand their personal identity at the same time as they begin a relationship, the relationship may become a primary venue for exploring personal identity. This could be a comfort. On the other hand, it is well-known that endings to adolescent romantic relationships are often experienced as particularly difficult or traumatic (Joyner & Udry, 2000); if the typical angst associated with a teenage breakup is intertwined with vulnerabilities related to an emerging sexual identity, the experience could be particularly difficult. Yet in other cases, a partner who has experience in prior same-sex relationships or has a more consolidated or integrated same-sex sexual identity may become a guide as well as companion. The point is that dynamics in adolescent romantic relationships typically due to age and experience may be expressed in same-sex couples through differences in sexual identity expression and integration. Although others have discussed similar questions (Diamond et al., 1999), we are not aware of studies that directly examine these questions within same-sex relationships.

Finally, once youth come out, they are more likely to directly confront heteronormative expectations and to experience the stigma of same-sex sexuality; for example, coming out is a period when youth are more likely to be harassed or victimized (D'Augelli, Pilkington, & Hershberger, 2002; Pilkington & D'Augelli, 1995). The minority stress model proposes that sexual minorities are subjected to chronic stress related to the stigmatization associated with being a sexual minority in a heteronormative society (Meyer, 2003). This model is important because it integrates the role of stigma into an understanding of the stress process for sexual minorities. The model was developed to explain elevated mental and behavioral health risks for sexual minorities. Specifically, Meyer (2003) argued that the link between sexual minority status and negative outcomes is largely explained by minority stress—both experiences of discrimination and possible violence but also internalized processes that include expectations of rejection, concealment, and internalized homophobia. A key aspect of this model that is relevant for understanding intimate relationships is that the link between minority stress and negative adjustment is dependent to some extent upon coping and available social support. Supportive relationships, including and especially intimate relationships, may be a key for buffering the negative impact of minority stressors.

Thus, heteronormativity provides a vantage point for understanding the broader contexts of adolescence for sexual minority youth: the stigma and potential discrimination that they may face at home, in schools, and in the community. The dimensions of coming out or identity development, which are shaped by heteronormativity, are relevant for youth as they begin intimate relationships; indeed, for many young people, intimacy is a key dimension in their coming out process. Finally, the minority stress model suggests a potentially distinctive role of same-sex intimate relationships for sexual minorities. On one hand, being in a same-sex relationship in adolescence may increase stress due to harassment or victimization that may accompany the visibility of being out; on the other hand, intimate relationships may be particularly important sources of personal and social support that may buffer against the well-known negative outcomes among sexual minority young people. Altogether, these three perspectives provide a backdrop for interpreting the research on same-sex intimate relationships in adolescence.

☗ RECENT EMPIRICAL ADVANCES

We have argued that there is little existing empirical research on same-sex intimate relationships in adolescence and young adulthood. Indeed, it is possible to review nearly all that has been done within this chapter. We begin by reviewing the most basic information: What are the patterns and progressions of same-sex intimate relationships? Much of the literature on intimate relationships has focused on gender—specifically, the differences between males and females in heterosexual relationships. Given the rich literature on gender differences in relationships, some scholars have considered the implications for relationships when they are made up of two young men or two young women; we review the research pertaining to adolescence. Finally, given the role of heterosexual relationships in adolescents' well-being, a body of research considers relationship violence, risk outcomes, and positive development associated with same-sex intimate relationships.

Before we begin the review, we acknowledge methodological challenges in the study of same-sex sexuality and relationships in adolescence. A complete review is beyond the scope of this chapter (see Russell, 2003; Savin-Williams, 2001), but two issues are particularly relevant. First, for years, scholars struggled with naming and measuring the population of interest: Should we study self-labeled LGB youth, those who engage in sexual behavior with the same sex, or those who are in same-sex relationships? As a result, questionnaire studies have used different measures with different populations, making comparisons across studies difficult if not impossible. In the past decade, general consensus has emerged, as reflected in work by Saewyc and colleagues (2004), who recommend the inclusion of three related but distinct indictors: (1) same-sex attractions, (2) behaviors, and (3) self-labels (the authors review the advantages and drawbacks of each, particularly in regard to the study of adolescent health). However, few of the studies we will review include more than one measure, and none include each of these recommended three. Other scholars argue that fullest understanding of the lives of sexual minority youth can come through using narrative methods that give voice to the complex stories and pathways through which young people come to understand their same-sex sexualities (Hammack, Thompson, & Pilecki, 2009).

Second, sexual minorities are a (potentially) hidden population, one that is difficult to identify through traditional research sampling strategies due in part to the issues previously described (who should be included as a sexual minority and how should that be measured?). These matters are compounded by the fact that, due to the pressures of heteronormativity, even if they are self-labeled as LGB they may not choose to disclose their sexual minority status to researchers. Thus, historically, studies of LGB youth have been based on small samples of self-labeled youth, typically from community-based organizations or programs; more recent scholars have made use of the Internet to reach LGB youth through e-mail lists, websites, or through targeted social networking sites (e.g., Kosciw, Greytak, Diaz, & Bartkiewicz, 2010). These methods are useful for within-group studies of LGB-identified youth, but the degree to which they are representative of the true population of sexual minority youth remains unclear. Large-scale, population-based studies have begun to include measures suggested by Saewyc and colleagues (2004) but are costly and must have very large samples in order to include enough youth who represent this small subgroup of the larger adolescent population.

Patterns and Progressions of Intimate Relationships

Data from the National Longitudinal Study of Adolescent Health (the Add Health study) has been used to examine same-sex romantic attractions as well as reports of same-sex relationships in a national cohort; the study began in the United States in the mid-1990s when participants were 7th to 12th graders and is one of the largest and most comprehensive prospective study of U.S. adolescents. Using Add Health, Russell & Consolacion (2003) found that just less than 10% of same-sex attracted adolescents reported having ever had a same-sex romantic relationship (same-sex attracted boys and girls were equally likely to report same-sex relationships at 8.2% and 9.2%, respectively). Yet dramatically, more same-sex attracted youth reported heterosexual relationships, although less in comparison to heterosexual youth. Same-sex attracted youth girls reported more heterosexual relationships than boys (60.6% of same-sex attracted boys and 67.9% of same-sex attracted girls reported other-sex relationships; for heterosexual youth, by comparison, 70.9% of boys and 73.8% of girls reported heterosexual relationships). According to these results, it is not as though sexual minority youth do not or cannot date: Rather, their primary dating experiences are heterosexual (Savin-Williams, 1994). Sexual minority youth must weigh the consequences to decide whether the risk of pursuing a romantic relationship is worth the negative peer and social reactions they may receive (Diamond et al., 1999).

Another large national study was conducted in Norway during the same period (Pedersen & Kristiansen, 2008); it asked an older age group (young adults ages 19 to 26) about steady relationships and cohabitation or marriage. That study found that gay and bisexual men were far more likely to be living alone (85.7% compared to 56.7% for heterosexual men) and less likely to report steady relationships (3.6% compared to 26.4%). Although lesbian and bisexual women were somewhat more likely to be single (47.9%) than heterosexual women (34.9%), the sexual orientation differences were much less pronounced for young women. Together these results pose the possibility that in the 1990s, school-aged LGB youth had many fewer opportunities for same-sex relationships than heterosexual ones and that the patterns were similar for boys and girls; by young adulthood, when intimate relationships begin to become more serious and lasting, lesbian and bisexual females begin to move into these young adult relationships—but such relationships remain remarkably unlikely for gay and bisexual men.

More recent studies suggest that relationship pathways for LGB youth may have changed in the past decades. Contrary to the assumption that LGB adolescents have few opportunities for dating and relationships, one study conducted 10 years after the Add Health and Norwegian studies (in 2005) showed that the majority of LGB youth from a primarily community-based sample (ages 14 to 21) were currently or had been recently involved in romantic or sexual relationships (Glover, Galliher, & Lamere, 2009). It is worth noting that this was not a sample from a major metropolitan area known to be LGB-friendly; the sample was collected in communities in Utah, and nearly half of the participants (48%) reported that they were Mormon—a religious group that historically has not been affirming of LGB relationships. It is likely that youth contacted through LGB community organizations would be much more likely than LGB youth from a nationwide sample to have access to same-sex relationships; in a very early study, for example, three fourths of the young gay men in the study reported current or recent same-sex relationships (Remafedi, 1987). Similarly, a recent longitudinal study of over 500 New York City area LGB youth (ages 15–19) found that over a third of the study participants reported current same-sex relationships. This study, however, also found important gender differences: Lesbian and bisexual girls were more likely to have been in a relationship for longer periods of time and reported having had more serious relationships (lasting 3 months or more) compared to gay and bisexual boys (Bauermeister et al., 2010). The recent studies point out that dating may be increasingly possible for LGB adolescents but that the differences found for young adult gay and bisexual men (Pedersen & Kristiansen, 2008) may begin during the adolescent years through the experience of shorter-term, less serious intimate relationships.

Beyond whether, who, and how long LGB youth and young adults date, other questions pertain to the patterns and character of intimacy in adolescence. Studies of heterosexual adolescent relationships have identified patterns in the typical progression of intimate relationships.

Data from the Add Health study points out a progression of relationships that is similar for girls and boys in the general popluation: Spending time with a partner as part of a group typically precedes holding hands, which is followed by thinking of themselves as a couple and ultimately telling others that they were a couple (O'Sullivan, Cheng, Harris, & Brooks-Gunn, 2007). What is notable here is that each of these typical and public aspects of heterosexual relationship initiation may be less likely for same-sex relationships. It is also the case that adolescents (and adults) are more likely to date those who are similar to them in terms of personal characteristics and interests (Furman & Simon, 2008), but because the pool of available partners is smaller, it may be harder for LGB adolescents to find partners who share their similarities. In fact, studies of adults indicate that heterosexual couples report more similarities in age, education, and interests than do lesbian and gay male couples (Peplau & Spalding, 2003).

These studies point out the potential barriers to same-sex intimacy for adolescents. Simply finding a compatible partner may be more difficult for sexual minority youth, particularly those in small or rural communities. Despite the fact that most LGB adolescents report wanting to feel close and connected to a partner (Diamond & Dubé, 2002), many may feel too personally or socially vulnerable to date someone of the same sex. Others may choose heterosexual dating because of legitimate interest in their partner and other-sex intimacy, to assuage concerns that they may be lesbian or gay, or simply due to pressures by family and friends (Diamond et al., 1999; Russell & Consolacion, 2003; Savin-Williams, 1994). And yet at least some youth engage in same-sex intimate relationships; we consider characteristics of their relationships in the following sections.

Gender and Same-Sex Relationships

Gender is a fundamental dimension of relationship dynamics. Research on heterosexual adolescent relationships reveals complex patterns that are both consistent with the long-standing stereotype that "girls want love and boys want sex" yet challenge a simplistic interpretation of the implications for youth (Ott, 2010). Adolescent girls may be more attuned to emotional intimacy and closeness in romantic relationships, and adolescent boys may need to maintain emotional distance consistent with codes of masculinity (Tolman, Spencer, Harmon, Rosen-Reynoso, & Striepe, 2004). Yet one study points out that the implications for relationships is that girls have more power in relationships (Giordano, Longmore, & Manning, 2006); in a study of over 900 7th to 11th graders, boys were perceived to have less power and be less confident in relationships, even though levels of love and attachment were similar. In essence, boys may desire more intimacy than they can accommodate in maintaining masculinity (Tolman et al., 2004). Given that gender norms and roles are defining for all young people, how do these dynamics play out when a relationship is made up of two girls or two boys? In a rare study of relationships of both same- and opposite-sex college-aged couples, Darling and Clarke (2009) found that male–male partners reported lower connections to their partners than their heterosexual counterparts, including more negative behaviors (e.g., conflict, frustration, sarcasm, discomfort). One can see that the navigation of codes of masculinity while exploring same-sex intimacy may seem impossible for some gay and bisexual boys. In the national study from Norway, which was previously cited, the authors conclude that norms of masculinity may lead to loneliness for men, particularly those who are gay or bisexual (Pedersen & Kristiansen, 2008).

In one study (Diamond & Dubé, 2002), gay male youth described intimate relationships as typically beginning with a sexual experience and progressing to intimacy, romance, or dating. Lesbian youth, however, described relationships that began as close friendships and that progressed to sexual behavior only after becoming romantic. Lesbian youths' relationships were characterized as emotionally closer and more supportive than young gay males' (Diamond, 2003). In another study (73 LGB youth recruited through community organizations or LGB youth conferences and 95 heterosexual youth recruited from a northeastern university), gay and bisexual males reported less attachment to romantic partners compared to heterosexual males (Diamond & Dubé, 2002). These studies indicate that gender may play a key role in the character of the beginning and progression of the intimate relationships of LGB youth.

Harmful and Healthy Outcomes

Relationship Violence

Sexual minority adolescents may experience abuse like any other youth in dating relationships; however, there may be distinct forms of abuse, for example, threats of disclosure of same-sex identity or relationship to others. In one study (a community sample of over 500 LGB adolescents),

LGB adolescents experienced abuse in dating relationships at levels equivalent to heterosexual peers, and the prevalence was similar for male and female LGB adolescents (Freedner, Freed, Yang, & Austin, 2002). Data from the Add Health study has shown that almost a quarter of adolescents in same-sex romantic relationships are victims of partner violence (Halpern, Young, Waller, Martin, & Kupper, 2004). That study examined multiple forms of relationship victimization and violence and showed that girls in same-sex relationships were more likely to report relationship violence overall and were more likely specifically to report insults or being sworn at, while males were more likely to report having received threats (Halpern et al., 2004). Thus there appear to be some differences in the forms of relationship violence for female and male sexual minorities.

There are also differences in relationship violence among sexual minorities: Bisexual youth may be particularly vulnerable. Bisexual males were much more likely than bisexual females and even gay males or lesbians to report being threatened with being "outed" by a partner (Freedner et al., 2002). The authors suggest that bisexuals may be less accepted among both lesbian/gay and heterosexual peers and may be more vulnerable or isolated. Further, the threat of same-sex disclosure may be particularly salient for males, for whom boundaries of gender and sexuality are most rigid. Bisexual females in that study, on the other hand, were more likely than heterosexual females to report sexual abuse. Further, bisexual youth (both male and female) were less likely than gay/lesbian youth to have disclosed the abuse to a friend or family member (Freedner et al., 2002). These findings point out differences based on gender as well as LG compared to bisexual identities and suggest that more careful attention is needed in order to understand the implications of dynamics of gender and sexual relational power in the intimate relationships of sexual minority adolescents and young adults.

Emotional and Behavioral Health

Several studies have examined health and behavioral risk for same-sex relationships using data from Add Health. In one study, same-sex daters were more likely than singles or youth in other-sex relationships to report suicidal thoughts (Russell & Consolacion, 2003). There were complex results for anxiety; independently, same-sex attraction and same-sex relationships were associated with higher anxiety, but the exception was for youth who reported same-sex attraction and also same-sex relationships: They were actually less anxious. It appears then that youth with same-sex attractions who had found romantic partners fared better—at least in terms of anxiety (Russell & Consolacion, 2003). A closer look at boys in the Add Health study shows that those in same-sex only relationships appear at risk for emotional but not behavioral health problems. Adolescent boys with same-sex only partners were more likely than boys with other-sex partners to report suicidal thoughts and depression, but were no more likely to report delinquency (Udry & Chantala, 2002).

In terms of substance use and abuse and problem behavior, it appears that, like for relationship violence, bisexual youth are most vulnerable. Boys with both-sex partners were more likely to use illegal drugs or to sell sex for drugs or money (Udry & Chantala, 2002). That study also showed that girls with both-sex partners were at high risk for nearly all of the health and behavior risk indicators included in the study. Another study showed that youth who report having had relationships with both sexes report more cigarette use, more drinking alone and more times having been drunk, a higher number of problems related to alcohol use, and more marijuana and drug use (Russell, Driscoll, & Truong, 2002). Taken altogether, these studies suggest that youth who report relationships with both males and females are most at risk across multiple domains. For sexual minority girls, same-sex relationships do not appear to be a marker for elevated (or lower) risk outcomes. And boys in same-sex relationships may be more emotionally vulnerable but appear to actually be at lower risk for anxiety and for some indicators of substance use.

Positive Outcomes

The minority stress model would suggest that intimate relationships might be an important buffer to minority stress for sexual minorities, yet few studies have considered positive outcomes of same-sex relationships for LGB youth. One report from the Add Health study showed no differences based on same-sex relationships in adolescents' self-esteem (Russell & Consolacion, 2003), leading the authors to conclude that same-sex relationships may have implications for negative but not positive adjustment. Another study showed that boys in same-sex relationships were less likely to smoke and reported fewer drinking-related problems (Russell et al., 2002). Further, in the New York City study of LGB youth, gay and bisexual males who reported same-sex relationships reported greater self-esteem over time, and lesbian and bisexual females in same-sex relationships reported less internalized homophobia (Bauermeister et al., 2010). One noteworthy finding from that study is that some of the LGB youth reported heterosexual dating: Those who did subsequently reported higher internalized homophobia. Some LGB youth may use heterosexual dating as a hiding strategy, yet it appears to undermine their mental health (Martin, 1982). Finally, the study conducted in Utah included attention to the feelings that LGB adolescents have about their relationships. It showed that LGB adolescents who were not in relationships reported higher rates of relational depression (feeling disappointed about your relationship status) and lower rates of relational esteem (positive evaluation of your capacity for intimacy) compared to those who reported same-sex relationships (Glover et al., 2009).

\\\ FUTURE DIRECTIONƒ

The study of same-sex intimate relationships for adolescents and young adults must be understood within the context of dramatic, fast-paced social change. In many ways, the body of research is barely catching up with the experiences of contemporary young people. Published empirical studies are largely based on earlier cohorts (for example, the cohort of participants in the Add Health Study were teenagers in the mid-1990s) and thus included youth who were growing up at times when the stigma of same-sex relations may have been greater, but the visibility was not. Thus, contemporary young people have access to opportunities that were unimaginable just a decade ago. Not only is this social change affecting possibilities for youth but it is offering new areas of inquiry for our understanding of intimacy and romance in adolescence and young adulthood.

Prior studies indicate that despite the barriers sexual minority youth may face, they are like all adolescents in their desire for intimacy and in fact they are quite engaged in romantic and dating relationships. Gender norms and expectations play out in these relationships as we might expect at the personal level: Boys' and girls' expectations appear to be guided or shaped by the codes of masculinity and femininity (i.e., heteronormativity). Important differences appear at the level of the couple as couples navigate these gendered feelings, attitudes, and behaviors. There has been very little research that explicitly has studied same-sex couples (see Darling & Clarke, 2009); such studies could inform research on sexual minority adolescent development and well-being as well as the complexities of gender in intimate relationships. A unique factor for understanding same-sex intimacy in adolescence is that for many young people who desire same-sex intimacy, relationships may not be congruent with same-sex desires. And just as dating has implications for heterosexual adolescents' well-being, both heterosexual dating and not dating at all appear to have real implications for sexual minority youth. In fact, heterosexual dating by sexual minority youth may be a symptom of minority stress; this is a topic worthy of future research attention.

Another area that has been notably understudied is the contexts for same-sex intimate relationships in adolescence. There are growing bodies of research on the settings that shape the lives of sexual minority youth (Horn, Kosciw, & Russell, 2009), but little of that work considers intimate relationships. Yet it is clear that there are unique issues related to how and where same-sex attracted youth find one another. Some same-sex attracted adolescents may have typical opportunities for intimate relationships at school, in their faith communities, or in their larger social or community networks. However, for most sexual minority youth, much may depend on circumstance (Diamond, 2003) because the typical contexts (e.g., school, faith group) remain circumscribed: For example, even if there are visible and "out" LGB students in school, same-sex dating may remain too transgressive. LGB-focused youth groups or online social network spaces continue to be more conducive to intimate relationship exploration and formation for LGB adolescents. Several scholars have written about the possibilities that the Internet affords for youth, not only in exploring identity but in finding same-sex relationships (Diamond, 2003; Russell, 2002). Of course, online spaces are used for intimacy by all youth; the point is that if typical spaces are unsafe for same-sex intimacy, these alternate spaces may be all the more important for LGB adolescents. As research on youth and media continues to grow, studies should compare the online relationships experiences of sexual minority and heterosexual adolescents.

LGB-focused, community-based youth programs are another important venue for youth to explore and develop same-sex intimate relationships. Many communities now host LGB youth groups. Originally envisioned as spaces for social or crisis support, such organizations have increasingly taken on the role that typical youth programs play in the lives of teens by offering recreational and social activities. For many young people, these are especially important spaces for developing friendships and finding romantic partners. Yet it is important to note that support for many of these programs or organizations comes through funding designed to prevent the host of health and behavioral risks so prevalent among LGB youth and adults, including victimization, depression, substance use and abuse, and high-risk sexual behavior. Thus, while these programs exist to provide safe space for LGB youth to socialize with one another, many remain at least partly if not predominantly focused on prevention. Such a focus raises important questions about the context for intimacy development: What does it mean for youth to first explore intimacy in a setting where at least part of the explicit message is about risk? Although such spaces are lifelines for some LGB youth, might they unintentionally instill and perpetuate stereotypes that LGB relationships are "risky"?

Finally, research is beginning to catch up to the realities of sexuality in the lives of contemporary youth, including new relationship forms and the dramatic influence of new media. For example, studies of "hookups" and "friends with benefits" suggest that the world of youthful sexuality is changing (e.g., Bisson & Levine, 2009); the degree to which same-sex sexuality has been influenced—or influential—remains understudied. Also, while the Internet has provided youth with opportunities to explore or test out same-sex identities (Russell, 2002), recent research illustrates the ways that these opportunities create new possibilities for heterosexuals as well. "Dude sex," for example, is argued to be an authentic heterosexuality for young men who go online to seek sex with other men (Ward, 2007). These new possibilities for intimacy made possible by technology and media largely blur the boundaries of "relationships" and the borders of sexual identities. These are rich sites for further research on adolescent and young adult same-sex intimacy.

☑ *SUGGESTED READINGS*

Diamond, L. M., Savin-Williams, R. C., & Dubé , E. M. (1999). Sex, dating, passionate friendships, and romance: Intimate peer relations among lesbian, gay, and bisexual adolescents. In W. Furman, B. B. Brown, & C. Feiring (Eds.), *The development of romantic relationships in adolescence* (pp. 175–210). New York: Cambridge University Press.

Meyer, I. H. (2003). Prejudice, social stress, and mental health in lesbian, gay, and bisexual populations. *Psychological Bulletin, 129*(5), 674–697.

Russell, S. T., Franz, B., & Driscoll, A. (2001). Same-sex romantic attraction and experiences of violence in adolescence. *American Journal of Public Health, 91*(6), 903–906.

Savin-Williams, R. C. (1996). Dating and romantic relationships among gay, lesbian, and bisexual youths. In R. C. Savin-Williams & K. M. Cohen (Eds.), *The lives of lesbians, gays, and bisexuals: Children to adults*. Fort Worth, TX: Harcourt Brace.

⁂ REFERENCEʃ

Allen, K. R., & Demo, D. H. (1995). The families of lesbians and gay men: A new frontier in family research. *Journal of Marriage and the Family, 57,* 111–127.

Bauermeister, J. A., Johns, M. M., Sandfort, T. G. M., Eisenberg, A., Grossman, A. H., & D'Augelli, A. R. (2010). Relationship trajectories and psychological well-being among sexual minority youth. *Journal of Youth and Adolescence, 39*(10), 1148–1163.

Bisson, M., & Levine, T. (2009). Negotiating a friends with benefits relationship. *Archives of Sexual Behavior, 38*(1), 66–73.

Cass, V. C. (1984). Homosexual identity formation: Testing a theoretical model. *The Journal of Sex Research, 20*(2), 143–167.

Collins, W. A., & Sroufe, L. A. (1999). Capacity for intimate relationships: A developmental construction. In W. Furman, B. B. Brown, & C. Feiring (Eds.), *The development of romantic relationships in adolescence* (pp. 125–147). New York: Cambridge University Press.

D'Augelli, A. R. (2005). Developmental and contextual factors and mental health among lesbian, gay, and bisexual youths. In A. M. Omoto & H. S. Kurtzman (Eds.), *Sexual orientation and mental health: Examining identity and development in lesbian, gay, and bisexual people* (pp. 37–53). Washington, DC: American Psychological Association.

D'Augelli, A. R., Pilkington, N. W., & Hershberger, S. L. (2002). Incidence and mental health impact of sexual orientation victimization of lesbian, gay, and bisexual youths in high school. *School Psychology Quarterly, 17*(2), 148–167.

Darling, N., & Clarke, S. (2009). Seeing the partner: A video recall study of emotional behavior in same- and mixed-sex late adolescent romantic couples. *Journal of Adolescence, 38*(7), 1015–1026.

Diamond, L. M. (2003). Love matters: Romantic relationships among sexual-minority adolescents. In P. Florsheim (Ed.), *Adolescent romantic relations and sexual behavior: theory, research, and practical implications.* Mahwah, NJ: Lawrence Erlbaum.

Diamond, L. M., & Dubé, E. M. (2002). Friendship and attachment among heterosexual and sexual-minority youths: Does the gender of your friend matter? *Journal of Youth and Adolescence, 31*(2), 155–166.

Diamond, L. M., Savin-Williams, R. C., & Dubé, E. M. (1999). Sex, dating, passionate friendships, and romance: Intimate peer relations among lesbian, gay, and bisexual adolescents. In W. Furman, B. B. Brown, & C. Feiring (Eds.), *The development of romantic relationships in adolescence* (pp. 175–210). New York: Cambridge University Press.

Freedner, N., Freed, L. H., Yang, Y. W., & Austin, S. B. (2002). Dating violence among gay, lesbian, and bisexual adolescents: Results from a community survey. *Journal of Adolescent Health, 31*(6), 469–474.

Furman, W., & Schaffer, L. (2003). The role of romantic relationships in adolescent development. In P. Florsheim (Ed.), *Adolescent romantic relations and sexual behavior: Theory, research, and practical implications.* Mahwah, NJ: Lawrence Erlbaum.

Furman, W., & Simon, V. (2008). Homophily in adolescent romantic relationships. In M. J. Prinstein & K. A. Dodge (Eds.), *Understanding peer influence in children and adolescents* (pp. 203–224). New York: Guilford Press.

Galambos, N. L., Almeida, D. M., & Petersen, A. C. (1990). Masculinity, femininity, and sex-role attitudes in early adolescence—exploring gender intensification. *Child Development, 61*(6), 1905–1914.

Giordano, P. C., Longmore, M. A., & Manning, W. D. (2006). Gender and the meanings of adolescent romantic relationships: A focus on boys. *American Sociological Review, 71,* 260–287.

Glover, J., Galliher, R., & Lamere, T. (2009). Identity development and exploration among sexual minority adolescents: Examination of a multidimensional model. *Journal of Homosexuality, 56*(1), 77–101.

Grov, C., Bimib, D. S., Nanin, J. E., & Parsons, J. T. (2006). Race, ethnicity, gender, and generational factors associated with the coming-out process among gay, lesbian, and bisexual individuals. *The Journal of Sex Research, 43*(2), 115–121.

Halpern, C. T., Young, M. L., Waller, M. W., Martin, S. L., & Kupper, L. L. (2004). Prevalence of partner violence in same-sex romantic and sexual relationships in a national sample of adolescents. *Journal of Adolescent Health, 35*(2), 124–131.

Hammack, P. L., Thompson, E. M., & Pilecki, A. (2009). Configurations of identity among sexual minority youth: Context, desire, and narrative. *Journal of Youth and Adolescence, 38*(7), 867–883.

Hill, J. P., & Lynch, M. E. (1983). The intensification of gender-related role expectations during early adolescence. In J. Brooks-Gunn & A. C. Petersen (Eds.), *Girls at puberty: Biological and psychosocial perspectives* (pp. 201–228). New York: Plenum.

Horn, S. S., Kosciw, J. G., & Russell, S. T. (2009). Special issue introduction: New research on lesbian, gay, bisexual, and transgender youth: Studying lives in context. *Journal of Youth and Adolescence, 38*(7), 863–866.

Joyner, K., & Udry, J. R. (2000). You don't bring me anything but down: Adolescent romance and depression. *Journal of Health and Social Behavior, 41,* 369–391.

Kitzinger, C. (2005). Heteronormativity in action: Reproducing the heterosexual nuclear family in after-hours medical calls. *Social Problems, 52*(4), 477–498.

Kosciw, J. G., Greytak, E. A., Diaz, E. M., & Bartkiewicz, M. J. (2010). *The 2009 National School Climate Survey: The experiences of lesbian, gay, bisexual, and transgender youth in our nation's schools.* New York: GLSEN.

Martin, A. D. (1982). Learning to hide: The socialization of the gay adolescent. In S. C. Feinstein, J. G. Looney, A. Schwartzberg, & J. Sorosky (Eds.), *Adolescent psychiatry: Developmental and clinical studies* (pp. 52–65). Chicago: University of Chicago Press.

Meyer, I. H. (2003). Prejudice, social stress, and mental health in lesbian, gay, and bisexual populations. *Psychological Bulletin, 129*(5), 674–697.

O'Sullivan, L. F., Cheng, M. M., Harris, K. M., & Brooks-Gunn, J. (2007). I wanna hold your hand: The progression of social romantic and sexual events in adolescent relationships. *Perspectives on Sexual and Reproductive Health, 39*(2), 100–107.

Oswald, R. F., Blume, L. B., & Marks, S. R. (2005). Decentering heteronormativity: A model for family studies. In V. L. Bengston, A. C. Acock, K. R. Allen, P. Dilworth-Anderson, & D. M. Klein (Eds.), *Sourcebook of family theory and research* (pp. 143–165). Thousand Oaks, CA: Sage.

Ott, M. A. (2010). Examining the development and sexual behavior of adolescent males. *The Journal of Adolescent Health: Official Publication of the Society for Adolescent Medicine, 46*(4), S3–S11.

Pedersen, W., & Kristiansen, H. W. (2008). Homosexual experience, desire and identity among young adults. *Journal of Homosexuality, 54*(1), 62–102.

Peplau, L., & Spalding, L. (2003). The close relationships of lesbians, gay men, and bisexuals. In L. Garnets & D. Kimmel (Eds.), *Psychological perspectives on lesbian, gay, and bisexual experiences* (2nd ed.). New York: Columbia University Press.

Pilkington, N. W., & D'Augelli, A. R. (1995). Victimization of lesbian, gay, and bisexual youth in community settings. *Journal of Community Psychology, 23*, 34–56.

Remafedi, G. (1987). Adolescent homosexuality: Psychosocial and medical implications. *Pediatrics, 79*(3), 331–337.

Russell, S. T. (2002). Queer in America: Sexual minority youth and citizenship. *Applied Developmental Science, 6*, 258–263.

Russell, S. T. (2003). Sexual minority youth and suicide risk. *American Behavioral Scientist, 46*(9), 1241–1257.

Russell, S. T. (2005). Beyond risk: Resilience in the lives of sexual minority youth. *Journal of Gay and Lesbian Issues in Education, 2*(3), 5–18.

Russell, S. T., & Consolacion, T. B. (2003). Adolescent romance and emotional health in the United States: Beyond binaries. *Journal of Clinical Child and Adolescent Psychology, 32*(4), 499–508.

Russell, S. T., Driscoll, A. K., & Truong, N. L. (2002). Adolescent same-sex romantic attractions and relationships: Implications for substance use and abuse. *American Journal of Public Health, 92*, 198–202.

Rust, P. (2004). Finding a sexual identity and community: Therapeutic implications and cultural assumptions in scientific models of coming out. In L. Garnets & D. C. Kimme (Eds.), *Psychological perspectives on lesbian, gay, and bisexual experiences* (pp. 227–269). New York: Columbia University Press.

Saewyc, E., Bauer, G., Skay, C., Bearinger, L., Resnick, M., Reis, E., et al. (2004). Measuring sexual orientation in adolescent health surveys: Evaluation of eight school-based surveys. *Journal of Adolescent Health, 35*(4), 345.e1–15.

Savin-Williams, R. C. (1994). Dating those you can't love and loving those you can't date. In R. Montemayor, G. Adams, & T. Gullotta (Eds.), *Personal relationships during adolescence* (pp. 163–175). Thousand Oaks, CA: Sage.

Savin-Williams, R. C. (2001). A critique of research on sexual-minority youths. *Journal of Adolescence. Special Issue: Gay, Lesbian, and Bisexual Youth, 24*(1), 5–13.

Savin-Williams, R. C., & Diamond, L. (2004). Sex. In R. M. Lerner & L. D. Steinberg (Eds.), *Handbook of adolescent psychology*. Hoboken, NJ: Wiley.

Tolman, D. L., Spencer, R., Harmon, T., Rosen-Reynoso, M., & Striepe, M. (2004). Getting close, staying cool: Early adolescent boys' experiences with romantic relationships. In N. Way & J. Chu (Eds.), *Adolescent boys: Exploring diverse cultures of boyhood* (pp. 235–255). New York: New York University Press.

Troiden, R. R. (1989). The formation of homosexual identities. *Journal of Homosexuality, 17*, 43–73.

Udry, J. R., & Chantala, K. (2002). Risk assessment of adolescents with same-sex relationships. *Journal of Adolescent Health, 31*, 84–92.

Ward, J. (2007). Straight dude seeks same: Mapping the relationship between sexual identities, practices, and cultures. In M. Stombler, D. M. Baunauch, E. O. Burgess, & D. Donnelly (Eds.), *Sex matters: The sexuality and society reader* (2nd ed., pp. 3–17). New York: Allyn & Bacon.

PART IV

Developmental Pathways and Processes

11

Gene-Environment Interplay in Adolescent Relationships

Kirby Deater-Deckard

Zhe Wang

Humans and their many cultures have coevolved for hundreds of thousands of years. The establishment of social relationships as a basic and essential element in reproductive success and survival is one of the fundamental human features to emerge in this coevolution. Contemporary theories of social relationships in adolescence and young adulthood readily incorporate this perspective by generating hypotheses about the interplay of genetic and nongenetic (or "environmental") influences on relationships. Empirical studies then test the hypotheses, typically using quasiexperimental behavioral genetic (e.g., twin and adoption studies) and molecular genetic designs (e.g., examination of specific genes).

Acknowledgments: The authors are grateful to Anarkali Morrill for assistance with library research. The authors were supported by National Institute of Child Health & Human Development (NICHD) grants HD60110, HD54481, and HD38075. The content is solely the responsibility of the authors and does not necessarily represent the official views of the National Institutes of Health (NIH) or NICHD.

Adolescence and young adulthood is a particularly interesting developmental period for examining gene-environment interplay in social relationships. It is during this phase of life that the biological mechanisms of puberty operate on the body and nervous system to ensure sexual maturation. Over adolescence, developmental changes in neurological systems support rapid growth in risk taking and sensation seeking, with comparatively slow but continuing enhancement of self-regulation of thoughts, emotions, and behaviors. There also is a dramatic shift (rapid or prolonged, depending on the context and culture) in the structure and function of social relationships. This includes changes in parent–adolescent relationships as well as platonic and romantic peer relationships, as the individual moves from sexual maturity to cultural/social maturity (Steinberg, 2003, 2004). This provides a fascinating context in which to explore and test hypotheses about gene-environment interplay in developmental processes.

In the coming decades, the behavioral sciences will see an explosion of empirical findings and new theories about specific genetic and environmental mechanisms and their transactions as they operate in family, peer, and partner relationships. Increasingly, behavioral scientists who study development and social relationships will need to be well versed in methods and theories that span traditional boundaries between socialization and biological frameworks of inquiry. To this end, in the current chapter, we review the literature on behavioral genetic (e.g., twin and adoption) and molecular genetic studies (e.g., estimating associations between social behaviors and specific genes), highlight some key findings in regard to gene-environment interplay in social relationship processes, provide broad conclusions about what we know, and offer some ideas for future research to address the many questions that remain unanswered. Furthermore, as the title of this volume attests, the leading edge of the science of social relationships is on pathways and development. Therefore, whenever possible we take into consideration a view of processes that involve relationship partners as well as the individual and an emphasis on the biology–environment interface as dynamic rather than static.

☙ THEORETICAL OVERVIEW

Relationships comprise individuals, yet researchers cannot reduce relationships to the sum of each individual's attributes or behaviors. In the same way, gene-environment interplay and its influences on the formation, maintenance, and dissolution of social relationships cannot be broken down into the sum of all of the additive and interactive effects arising from variability in experience and DNA structure and function. However, it is plausible to use quasiexperimental and correlational methods to develop mathematical models that test competing theories about gene-environment interplay, resulting in findings that have implications for basic and applied research.

Behavioral genetics research with humans relies on quasiexperimental "experiments of nature" to explore and explain the genetic and environmental similarity among family members, using parsimonious mathematical representations of genetic and environmental influences. The three basic designs include family, adoption, and twin studies (Plomin, DeFries, McClearn, & McGuffin, 2008). The family design is useful for comparing sibling or parent–child pairs who live together and share 50% on average of their genetic variants (i.e., alleles) identical by descent. This design permits initial examination of potential genetic and environmental influences, whereby the researcher can derive baseline estimates of family member resemblance to determine whether there is any evidence of effects of shared genes or co-residence on variables of interest. If there is no family member resemblance for a particular variable (as it turns out, an extremely rare situation), it suggests that there are no systematic genetic and environmental influences on that variable that operate within families. In contrast, if family member resemblance for the variable is found (a common situation), it implicates genetic and environmental influences that operate within families. However, examining family members alone does not permit distinguishing the potential genetic and environmental influences from each other.

When familial resemblance is found, a more specific quasiexperimental design is required to statistically differentiate genetic and nongenetic influences that are defined as sources of variance. There are a variety of designs that scientists can use that are based on the comparison of different types of family member pairs who differ in their average level of genetic similarity. This can range from genetically unrelated adoptive or stepsibling and parent–child pairs, to cousins (12.5% average genetic similarity), to half-siblings (25% average genetic similarity), to full siblings and fraternal (i.e., dizygotic) twins or biological parent–child pairs (50% average genetic similarity), to identical (i.e., monozygotic) twins (100% similarity). The most common designs rely on adoptive siblings and twins. The adoption design involves comparison of biological parents or adoptive parents with adopted children as well as adopted siblings, to estimate proportions of variance that represent the aggregated effects of child rearing experiences and inherited genetic factors. In the twin design, monozygotic and dizygotic twins who reside with their biological parents are compared to estimate the genetic and nongenetic sources of variance.

The estimation of genetic and nongenetic influences is based on a multiple regression model from which independent statistical parameters are derived (Neale & Cardon, 1992). These parameters are used to estimate proportions of variance in the individual differences in the variable of interest, including genetic variance referred to as "heritability," which accounts for family member similarity; nongenetic variance called "shared environment," which accounts for family member similarity; and residual variance called "nonshared environment," which includes the remaining nongenetic variance that does not contribute to family member similarity. Nonshared environment variance also includes all of the random error variance in the variable (Plomin et al., 2008).

Estimation of the "main effects" of genetic and nongenetic variance includes a number of assumptions, and it is important to note that the methodology and findings in the behavioral genetic literature are controversial. Critics of behavioral genetics raise a number of concerns about conceptual and methodological features (Partridge, 2005). These include violations of some of the method's assumptions (e.g., environments are functionally equivalent for the different family pair types), limited or questionable construct validity of the genetic and nongenetic parameters, and emphasis on additive rather than interactive genetic and environmental effects. More recently, molecular genetics research is raising new concerns such as the "missing heritability" problem—that studies testing potential effects of specific genes are not finding the often substantial genetic effect sizes that are detected in behavioral genetic studies (McClellan & King, 2010).

Some of these critiques and concerns are addressed by the behavioral genetic research on social relationships. Of particular interest to many scientists who study relationships is the assumption in basic behavioral genetic designs that genetic and nongenetic influences are independent (rather than correlated) and additive (rather than interactive) in their effects. There are two known types of gene-environment interplay that violate this assumption: (1) gene-environment correlation and (2) gene-environment interaction (for a review, see Jaffee & Price, 2007). The first class of gene-environment interplay is gene-environment correlation. It is present when individual differences in genetically-influenced attributes are correlated with exposure to particular environmental factors or experiences. There are three types of gene-environment correlation

(Plomin, DeFries, & Loehlin, 1977). *Passive* gene-environment correlation occurs when offspring inherit from their parents both a family environment factor and a correlated genetic factor. *Active* gene-environment correlation occurs when individuals' genetically-influenced attributes lead to selection or alteration of the environment. *Evocative or reactive* gene-environment correlation arises when individuals' genetically-influenced attributes evoke particular behaviors from other people.

A second class of gene-environment interplay is referred to as gene-environment interaction—the interactive effect of genes and environments above and beyond any main effects of those genes and environments. It can arise when the effect of a particular set of genes differs depending on the environment or context. Because gene-environment correlation and interaction are known to occur, researchers should consider with caution the findings from basic behavioral genetic models that do not include these more complex effects (Jaffee & Price, 2007).

Both types of interplay are necessary for understanding transactions between biology and experience in the social worlds of adolescents and young adults. Most of the genetically informative research on social relationships has reported main effects and gene-environment correlation effects but not gene-environment interaction effects. There is a great deal of interest in gene-environment interaction in the behavioral sciences, but traditional behavioral genetic designs are underpowered statistically for detecting interaction effects and so they are difficult to find and even more difficult to replicate. In contrast, in most of the behavioral genetic literature, the studies have had adequate statistical power for detecting main effects and gene-environment correlation effects—in part because these effect sizes are moderate to substantial (Kendler & Baker, 2007). Molecular genetic approaches that examine DNA and permit more direct tests of both gene-environment interaction and correlation will become more common in the future and eventually will lead to a more balanced consideration of both types of gene-environment interplay.

☖ RECENT EMPIRICAL ADVANCES

Genotype-Environment Correlation

Behavioral scientists believe that individuals are not merely passive recipients of experience but often are the critical active agents in selecting and changing their own environments (Caspi, Roberts, & Shiner, 2005).

The individual and interpersonal processes involved in the initiation, maintenance, and dissolution of close personal relationships exemplify these kinds of processes. To the extent that genetically influenced attributes of individuals are involved, gene-environment interplay operates on social relationships through gene-environment correlation. Empirical findings are consistent with this notion; the data show that various aspects of parent–child, sibling, and peer relationships include heritable as well as nonshared environment influences (O'Connor, Jenkins, Hewitt, DeFries, & Plomin, 2003; Reiss, Neiderhiser, Hetherington, & Plomin, 2000).

Gene-environment correlations may change as a function of development. Based on the three types of gene-environment correlation defined by Plomin et al. (1977) and just described, Scarr and McCartney (1983) proposed a developmental shift in genotype → environment correlation. Shared environmental influences are most prominent in early childhood, but as development proceeds, youth gain skills and are exposed to more frequent and varied opportunities for selecting the people they spend time with and the experiences they encounter (i.e., *active* gene-environment correlation). Also over time and with experience, youth encounter more experiences in which they elicit behavior from other people (i.e., *evocative* or *reactive* gene-environment correlation). Accordingly, while shared environmental influences decrease in their influence on individual differences over childhood, heritable influences increase in their influence. This is due in part to the effects of active and evocative person-environment correlation processes that are operating within personal relationships. Thus, over adolescence and into young adulthood, genetic influences on the qualities (e.g., warmth, conflict) of close family and peer relationships may increase in magnitude—a pattern that has been seen in some but not all studies (McGue, Elkins, Walden, & Iacono, 2005).

Family Relationships

Most of the relevant behavioral genetic research has focused on the emotional qualities of family relationships. This is not surprising, given that adolescents' and young adults' close relationships begin in a family context that provides the developmental foundations for many aspects of social behavior and adjustment. One of the important observations about family relationships is that emotional warmth, closeness, negativity, and conflict all vary markedly across relationship pairs within the same family. A parent typically has distinct relationships with each of her or his multiple children, and an adolescent typically has distinct relationships with each parent and each sibling (Deater-Deckard, 2009; Reiss, 2005). Thus, adolescents who are born to the same parents and raised together typically have distinct experiences from their siblings, because each parent–adolescent and sibling relationship is different. This is because each adolescent in the family brings a unique combination of individual attributes to that relationship—attributes that are heritable, as well as influenced by nongenetic factors that do not contribute to sibling similarity (i.e., nonshared environment; see Dunn & Plomin, 1990; Plomin, 1994). Thus, within-family variation in positivity and negativity in relationships arises from genetic and nongenetic influences that may operate in part through gene-environment correlation mechanisms.

Most of the family studies examining parent–adolescent relationship processes have not addressed whether and how gene-environment correlation mechanisms contribute to the qualities of each parent–adolescent relationship within the family. To do so, behavioral genetic designs are needed because they permit statistical decomposition of genetic and nongenetic influences (Neale & Cardon, 1992). Researchers have developed the theories and empirical methods for investigating gene-environment correlation processes over the past several decades (Dunn, 1993; Lytton, 1977; Plomin, 1994; Rowe, 1981, 1983), as seen in the large longitudinal studies conducted in that era such as the Colorado Adoption Project (Petrill, Plomin, DeFries, & Hewitt, 2003) and the Nonshared Environment in Adolescent Development Project (Reiss et al., 2000).

These and other behavioral genetic studies have shown that genetic influences on children's and adolescents' behaviors account for a substantial portion of the variance in adolescent–parent warmth and negativity—effects that probably reflect evocative or reactive gene-environment correlation mechanisms (Reiss, 2005). For instance, data from the Colorado Adoption Project showed that in middle childhood and early adolescence, adopted youth who were genetically at risk for conduct problems (based on the levels of conduct problems of their biological parents) had more hostile relationships with their adoptive mothers—an effect that might be explained by evocative or reactive gene-environment correlation mechanisms (O'Connor, Deater-Deckard, Fulker, Rutter, & Plomin, 1998). Another adoption study of adolescents revealed a similar pattern (Ge et al., 1996), as did data from the Nonshared Environment in Adolescent Development study of twins and stepsiblings (O'Connor, Hetherington, Reiss, & Plomin, 1995). In subsequent work, researchers combined existing data from the Nonshared Environment in Adolescent Development study with new data from a study of twin parents. The results pointed to evocative or reactive gene-environment correlation effects for multiple aspects of adolescent problem behavior and maternal and paternal negativity and control (Neiderhiser, Reiss, Lichtenstein, Spotts, & Ganiban, 2007; Neiderhiser, Reiss, Pedersen, Lichtenstein, & Spotts, 2004). Yet another study found that genetic variance in adolescent–parent warmth and negativity increased over time in adolescence (Herndon, McGue, Krueger, & Iacono, 2005; McGue et al., 2005)—a pattern that probably reflects increasing strength of reactive or evocative gene-environment correlation mechanisms over development (Scarr & McCartney, 1983). It also is worth noting that there is a small body of research that implicates gene-environment interactions between parent–adolescent relationship factors and genetic influences on antisocial behavior outcomes in adolescence and young adulthood (Riggins-Caspers & Cadoret, 2001).

The behavioral genetic literature on parent–adolescent relationships points to the link between adolescent conduct problems and adolescent–parent hostility as being one of the strongest genetically-influenced evocative relationship mechanisms yet identified. However, the mechanisms are not limited to adolescent–parent negativity and conflict. Observational and questionnaire data on youth behavior and parent–child relationships from two twin studies (spanning preschool to early adolescence), an adoption study (spanning middle childhood and early adolescence), and a family study of mother–father–child triads (middle childhood) point to evocative gene-environment correlation mechanisms involving parent–child mutually positive affect and reciprocity (Deater-Deckard, 2009; Deater-Deckard, Atzaba-Poria, & Pike, 2004; Deater-Deckard & Petrill, 2004). This is consistent with a review of behavioral genetic studies of youth adjustment and parenting, in which the authors concluded that the effect sizes for gene-environment correlations were comparable for warm and hostile parent–child relationship dimensions (Kendler & Baker, 2007).

Although gene-environment correlation mechanisms are important to consider, the distinct features of each parent–adolescent relationship within a family also arise from *nonshared environment* mechanisms (Carbonneau, Rutter, Silberg, Simonoff, & Eaves, 2002; Plomin, 1994; Reiss et al., 2000). Nonshared environment influences are specific to each parent–adolescent dyad in the family and do not contribute to sibling similarity in their family relationships (Plomin & Daniels, 1987). Researchers have not identified and replicated the specific environmental factors that account for these nonshared environment effects. However, likely candidates include peer relationship factors and other social experiences outside of the home that siblings are less likely to experience in the same way. It is important to note that the effects of gene-environment correlation and nonshared environment mechanisms on dyadic relationships may also have influences beyond the level of each dyad, with effects on the overall family climate of warmth and hostility (Horwitz et al., 2010).

Peers and Partners: Selection and Socialization

Adolescents' and young adults' social relationships in families are linked with peer, friend, and romantic relationship processes. Gene-environment correlation and nonshared environmental mechanisms in family relationship qualities overlap with the mechanisms that are operating in relationships outside of the family (O'Connor et al., 2003). But how do gene-environment correlation and nonshared environment mechanisms work when it comes to social relationships with peers, friends, and partners? The answer to this question is complex and requires consideration of several categories of interpersonal processes.

The two most commonly studied categories of processes are social selection and social influence (Gilson, Hunt, & Rowe, 2001). "Selection" is said to occur when the attributes of the friend or romantic partner are used by an individual (consciously or unconsciously) to form and maintain a relationship—that is, becoming friends or partners is not a random process. "Social influence" is a learning process through which the behavior of each individual causes behavior change in the other individual in the pair, typically causing the two to become more alike as they come to know each other, if the relationship lasts. Selection and social influence operate in tandem with each other in the formation and maintenance of close and lasting peer relationships and friendships in adolescence and adulthood (Deater-Deckard, 2001).

In most settings, adolescents have ample opportunity to select friends and partners within their peer groups. Physical and temporal proximity are major factors in social selection (e.g., being in the same neighborhood and same school and class grade; Epstein, 1983), but other factors matter as well. Adolescents and young adults tend to form relationships with peers who have similar interests and activities that they enjoy. These shared interests can be prosocial (e.g., clubs, teams) or antisocial (e.g., substance use, bullying) in nature, and they provide a foundation for social influence to occur as well. Many antisocial activities are inherently social in nature, typically involving small groups of youth or young adults (Simons, Stewart, Gordon, Conger, & Elder, 2002; for a review, see Rhule-Louie & McMahon, 2007). Some adolescents increase their antisocial behavior and substance use over time, and the scientists who study this developmental pattern are particularly interested in friend and partner selection and social influence processes. Data from those studies suggest the presence of powerful effects of both deviant peer selection and peer socialization effects on growth in antisocial behaviors (Dishion, 2000; Elliott, Huizinga, & Ageton, 1985).

Scientists can use behavioral genetic designs to identify potential social selection and social influence effects. These processes are evident in sibling differences in the attributes of their peers and friends—and more specifically, in gene-environment correlation and nonshared environment effects. There is clear evidence from a number of twin and adoption studies showing gene-environment correlation and nonshared environment effects with respect to friends' antisocial and prosocial behavior (for a review, see Brendgen & Boivin, 2008). For example, in one twin study of young adolescents, there was very little sibling similarity in their friends' levels of delinquency or relationship conflict (Bullock, Deater-Deckard, & Leve, 2006; Leve, 2001). The average sibling correlation was about .20, regardless of informant or degree of twin genetic similarity. Nonshared environment processes accounted for up to three-quarters of the variance in deviant peer affiliation. The Colorado Adoption Project and Nonshared Environment in Adolescent Development studies showed a similar pattern of moderate to large nonshared environment effects for friends' antisocial and prosocial functioning (Iervolino et al., 2002). A recent prospective longitudinal behavioral genetic study showed moderate to large nonshared environment effects, indicating that siblings are quite different in the friends that they select and are influenced by in adolescence (Burt, McGue, & Iacono, 2009).

As different as siblings' friends typically can be, peer selection and social influence effects are by no means random within families—there is some sibling similarity in friends' attributes and friendship qualities. A number of studies suggest that the sibling similarity that is found is attributable to the degree of genetic similarity of the siblings. These genetic influences are thought to operate through active and evocative gene-environment correlation mechanisms, whereby genetic influences on adolescents' behaviors dispose them toward forming relationships with similarly antisocial or prosocial youth (Cleveland, Wiebe, & Rowe,

2005; Kendler & Baker, 2007; Manke, McGuire, Reiss, Hetherington, & Plomin, 1995; Rose, 2002; Walden, McGue, Iacono, Burt, & Elkins, 2004). In this group of studies, the genetic and nongenetic effect sizes differ to some degree depending on informant and method. The strongest evidence for gene-environment correlation mechanisms is found with broad measures based on parents' reports, whereas the strongest evidence for non-genetic influences is found with fine-grained measures based on self-reports and observations (Brendgen & Boivin, 2008; Bullock et al., 2006; Kendler & Baker, 2007).

Turning to romantic relationships, several decades of behavioral genetic research implicates genetic and environmental influences on partnership selection (i.e., assortative or selective "mating") and duration, with most studies focusing on married couples (for reviews, see Mathews & Reus, 2001; Hammen, 2003; Rhule-Louie & McMahon, 2007). These influences appear to operate through the attributes of each individual (e.g., interests, personalities) in their effects on relationship quality and likelihood of relationship dissolution (Jockin & McGue, 1996; Spotts et al., 2004). As with peer and friendship selection and social influence processes, the genetic influences that are evident in romantic relationships' qualities probably reflect underlying active and evocative gene-environment correlation mechanisms (Kendler & Baker, 2007).

The participants in studies of romantic partner selection and relationship quality tend to be adults. However, the interpersonal selection and social influence processes in romantic relationships in adulthood probably are like those that occur in adolescence and young adulthood. There is a large amount of literature documenting modest to moderate effect sizes for assortative mating in romantic relationships—partner selection that reflects the motivation of each partner to be with someone who has similar interests, attitudes, and behaviors. Like the findings for adolescent friendship formation previously described, romantic partner selection and social influences are most prominent for antisocial behaviors spanning minor to serious criminal activity and substance use, with broader personality attributes playing a comparatively modest role in partner selection (Krueger, Moffitt, Caspi, Bleske, & Silva, 1998). Researchers also have found evidence of selection for each partner's level of mood disturbance or presence of a mood disorder such as depression (Hammen, 2003; Mathews & Reus, 2001). But partner similarity likely reflects social influence effects as well. For example, a stable and supportive relationship with a well-functioning and prosocial romantic partner can ameliorate behavioral and emotional problems. In short, peers and partners select each other and also socialize each other (Deater-Deckard, 2001; Rhule-Louie & McMahon, 2007).

If gene-environment correlation mechanisms are important to the formation and maintenance of platonic and romantic relationships in adolescence and young adulthood, what is the broad theoretical basis for the role of genes in these interpersonal processes? One potential explanation comes from evolutionary theory. Social partners' behavioral and genetic similarity may be critically important to forming and maintaining interpersonal positivity and closeness in all of our social relationships. According to sociobiological theories that emphasize inclusive fitness through genetic recognition in kin and non-kin, the "fitness" of a genotype is enhanced through altruistic behaviors directed at individuals (be they family or friends) who are more genetically similar to ourselves (Hamilton, 1964; Rushton, 1989). Evidence supports this view. Emotional warmth and closeness within a family dyad is related to one individual's willingness to assist the other family member in a time of need. Willingness to assist—and perceived warmth and closeness—are more substantial if the family member in question is genetically similar to the individual (Korchmaros & Kenny, 2001). More recently, investigators tested the influence of genetic similarity in a study of adult identical and fraternal twins who were parents. They assessed participants' relationships with their own children and their co-twins' children (i.e., their nieces and nephews). Even with physical proximity controlled statistically, adults reported greater emotional closeness toward those nieces and nephews who were more genetically similar to themselves (Segal, Seghers, Marelich, Mechanic, & Castillo, 2007). Furthermore, the effect of genetic similarity was strongest if the co-twin was female—further evidence for the theory, given that genetic relatedness of aunts and uncles to their nieces and nephews is certain in maternal but not paternal parent–child relationships.

In sum, dyadic family and peer relationships are distinct across siblings within the same family. These distinct relationships arise from genetic influences (through gene-environment correlation mechanisms) and nongenetic influences (through nonshared environment mechanisms) that are operating through social selection and social influence processes. However, there are some caveats to bear in mind. First, some of the research also has pointed to shared environment mechanisms— nongenetic mechanisms that contribute to family member similarity in social relationships. This might be due to social "homogamy," another social process that is rarely considered in developmental and family science but that may be just as important as social selection and social influence

(Gilson et al., 2001). Homogamy is defined as similarity between two individuals arising from sharing the same broad social contexts (e.g., homes, neighborhoods, schools). When shared environment variance is found in behavioral genetic studies of peer and partner relationships, social homogamy may be implicated. For example, using data from the National Longitudinal Study of Adolescent Health (Add Health study), Gilson and colleagues (2001) reported evidence of social homogamy for delinquent behaviors based on their analysis of full siblings' similarities in friends. Other behavioral genetic studies of adolescent deviant behavior and substance use have indicated some shared environmental effects in peers' and friends' behaviors (Gillespie, Neale, Jacobson, & Kendler, 2009; Walden et al., 2004)—again, effects that may be due to social homogamy. It is likely that homogamy, selection, and socialization all are occurring as part of the complex gene-environment interplay within relationship processes.

A second caveat is that a traditional behavioral genetic approach may not be sufficient because it does not distinguish the attributes of each person in the dyad from the emergent properties of the dyad itself. In an attempt to address this limitation, Manke and Pike (2001) extended the social relations model (Kenny & LaVoie, 1984) to incorporate estimates of gene-environment variance components in family relationships in adolescence. The social relations model is a measurement and statistical method that distinguishes influences on social relationship qualities that arise from each individual within a given family dyad (actor and partner effects) and from the dyad itself (dyadic relationship effects). Examining data from three behavioral genetic studies of children and adolescents, Manke and Pike found that most of the variance in sibling and parent–adolescent relationship qualities—ranging from warmth to conflict to self-disclosure to humor—reflected dyad-level effects that could not be reduced to individual influences of one or another partner in the dyad. Furthermore, although genetic influences on dyad-level effects (operating through gene-environment correlation mechanisms) was evident, nonshared environment accounted for most of the variance in dyad, actor, and partner effects. The findings make clear that the qualities of social relationships (e.g., conflict, closeness, warmth) may not be reduced to the sum of the behaviors of each individual, nor construed as simply the consequence of genetic influences on each individual's behavior.

A third caveat is that the theories that form the basis for behavioral genetic research on social relationships are inherently developmental, but little of the extant empirical literature actually addresses development. Although there are some exceptions (as noted for some of the studies previously reviewed), nearly all of the genetically informative studies of social relationship processes are based on cross-sectional or short-term longitudinal designs. Long-term longitudinal behavioral genetic studies exist, but most of them have few measures of social relationships inside and outside of the family—and if they do, the tests of long-term longitudinal stability and change in gene-environment interplay have not been published. At least with respect to measures of social relationships, Scarr and McCartney's (1983) hypotheses about developmental changes in gene-environment interplay still need to be rigorously and systematically tested.

⟨⟨ FUTURE DIRECTIONſ

Molecular Genetics

The challenge for behavioral scientists today is to figure out how to use behavioral genetic and other quasiexperimental and experimental methods to test competing hypotheses that will refine our understanding of adolescents' and young adults' important social relationships. In the future, scientists studying gene-environment interplay in social relationships will use molecular genetics methods, in which variability in gene structure is measured directly and is examined for correlations with behavioral outcomes of interest. In molecular genetics methods, scientists extract DNA molecules from cell nuclei and then genotype each individual to measure the form or "allele" of a particular gene. The genotyping process can target a specific "candidate" gene or location on a chromosome that is thought to play a role in the biological processes underlying the behavior. In addition, genotyping can be use to scan large swaths of the DNA molecule using a genome-wide association or "GWAS" method (McClellan & King, 2010).

Although the literature will change rapidly as molecular genetics methods become more mainstream and affordable, to date nearly all of the molecular genetics research in human behavioral science has focused on neurophysiology and neural activation, personality, cognitive performance, and psychopathology (for a recent review, see McClellan & King, 2010). There are few published investigations of human gene variants and social relationship processes, let alone investigations of relationship processes in adolescence or young adulthood. Of the most relevant studies done so far, most have focused on parent–child (typically mother) relationship quality or dyadic interaction processes with particular emphasis on parent behavior and have not focused on the dyadic relationship process per se. It also is noteworthy that tests of gene-environment interaction (i.e., the effect of a gene variant being moderated by some environmental factor or vice versa) figure prominently in this small but rapidly growing literature, in contrast to a behavioral genetic literature that has tended to focus on gene-environment correlation mechanisms.

It is early days for the exciting emergence of studies that integrate molecular genetics and social relationship science, but consider the following recent examples as illustrations of what the future holds. In one study of adults' retrospective reports of their childhood family relationships, researchers found evidence for gene-environment correlation between variation in the DRD2 and GABA (A) Alpha 6 receptor genes and several aspects of fathers' negativity and rejection (Lucht et al., 2006). In another study, Koonce et al. (2007) reported that variation in infants' dopamine DRD2 gene was associated with variance in maternal sensitive responsive behavior. In turn, maternal sensitivity moderated the link between maternal behavior and the infant's subsequent emotional problems. These data implicated a combined evocative gene-environment correlation and interaction process. In yet another study of maternal genetic variation in two dopamine genes (DRD4 and COMT), maternal nonresponsive and insensitive behavior was associated with parenting stress for a subgroup of mothers with a particular combination of alleles—again implicating gene-environment interaction in a parent–child relationship process (Van IJzendoorn, Bakermans-Kranenburg, & Mesman, 2008). More recently, Lee et al. (2010) extended the nascent molecular genetics research on dopamine genes and child–parent relationship processes. They found an association between another dopamine system gene (DAT1) and maternal negativity but only for families in which child conduct problems were evident. This suggested gene-environment interaction between parent genetic factors and child behavior, in the prediction of parenting behavior during social interaction with the child.

In molecular genetic studies like those just described, researchers tend to use correlational or quasiexperimental designs, but experiments also are an option. Individuals with known versions of particular genes can be randomly assigned to social experiences, and the resulting behaviors can be examined. In one example of such a study, researchers had young adult males meet and interact in small groups as part of an experiment.

The results showed that the effect of a common variant of a serotonin neurotransmitter gene (5HT2A) operated through a gene-environment correlation between rule-breaking behavior and the "likability" of the rule breaker, as rated by other group members (Burt, 2006, as cited by Jaffee & Price, 2007). Another example comes from a long-standing line of correlational and experimental research examining variation in arginine vasopressin genes and associations with pair bonding behaviors in voles. Scientists now are extending those findings to human adult romantic pair bonding (Walum et al., 2008). This line of research eventually may lead to genetically informative experimental studies that investigate the processes of friendship and romantic partnership formation and maintenance.

Findings such as these are useful for generating hypotheses regarding adolescents' and young adults' relationships with peers and partners, siblings, and parents. However, gene-environment interplay may change across development, and results may vary depending on the specific developmental periods in question. Furthermore, it is critical for researchers to regard as preliminary the molecular genetics methods used for examining gene-environment interplay. In this literature, effect sizes are small, and nonreplications are common. Nevertheless, researchers are making progress, and as previously noted there are some promising preliminary findings with respect to social relationship processes (Jaffee & Price, 2007). In conclusion, there remains little doubt that behavioral and molecular genetics methods are useful additions to the toolbox for studying social relationship processes. The challenge will be figuring out how to use these methods in a way that best integrates the strengths of molecular biology and behavioral science, as researchers work together to answer the many tough questions about gene-environment interplay that remain to be answered.

※ SUGGESTED READINGS

Brendgen, M., & Boivin, M. (2008). Genetic factors in children's peer relations. In K. H. Rubin, W. M. Bukowski, & B. Laursen (Eds.), Handbook of peer interactions, relationships, and groups (pp. 455–472). New York: Guilford Press.

Deater-Deckard, K. (2009). Parenting the genotype. In K. McCartney & R. Weinberg (Eds.), Experience and development: A festschrift in honor of Sandra Wood Scarr (pp. 141–161). New York: Taylor and Francis.

Reiss, D. (2005). The interplay between genotypes and family relationships. Current Directions in Psychological Science, 14(3), 139–143.

Spotts, E. L., Neiderhiser, J. M., Towers, H., Hansson, K., Lichtenstein, P., Cederblad, M., et al. (2004). Genetic and environmental influences on marital relationships. *Journal of Family Psychology, 18,* 107–119.

REFERENCES

Brendgen, M., & Boivin, M. (2008). Genetic factors in children's peer relations. In K. H. Rubin, W. M. Bukowski, & B. Laursen (Eds.), *Handbook of peer interactions, relationships, and groups* (pp. 455–472). New York: Guilford Press.

Bullock, B. M., Deater-Deckard, K., & Leve, L. D. (2006). Deviant peer association and problem behavior: A test of genetic and environmental influences. *Journal of Abnormal Child Psychology, 34,* 29–41.

Burt, A. (2006, July). *Genes, rule-breaking, and popularity: Identification of an evocative rGE.* Paper presented at the Annual Meeting of the Behavioral Genetics Association, Storrs, CT.

Burt, A. S., McGue, M., & Iacono, W. G. (2009). Nonshared environmental mediation of the association between deviant peer affiliation and adolescent externalizing behaviors over time: Results from a cross-lagged monozygotic twin differences design. *Developmental Psychology, 45,* 1752–1760.

Caspi, A., Roberts, B. W., Shiner, R. L. (2005). Personality development: stability and change. *Annual Review of Psychology, 56,* 453–484.

Carbonneau, R., Rutter, M., Silberg, J. L., Simonoff, E., & Eaves, L. J. (2002). Assessment of genetic and environmental influences on differential ratings of within-family experiences and relationships in twins. *Psychological Medicine, 32,* 729–741.

Cleveland, H. H., Wiebe, R. P., & Rowe, D. C. (2005). Sources of exposure to smoking and drinking friends among adolescents: A behavioral genetic evaluation. *Journal of Genetic Psychology, 166,* 153–169.

Deater-Deckard, K. (2001). Recent research examining the role of peer relationships in the development of psychopathology. *Journal of Child Psychology and Psychiatry, 42,* 565–579.

Deater-Deckard, K. (2009). Parenting the genotype. In K. McCartney & R. Weinberg (Eds.), *Experience and development: A festschrift in honor of Sandra Wood Scarr* (pp. 141–161). New York: Taylor and Francis.

Deater-Deckard, K., Atzaba-Poria, N., & Pike, A. (2004). Mother-child and father-child mutuality in Anglo and Indian British families: A link with lower externalizing problems in middle childhood. *Journal of Abnormal Child Psychology, 32,* 609–620.

Deater-Deckard, K., & Petrill, S. A. (2004). Parent-child dyadic mutuality and child behavior problems: Gene-environment processes. *Journal of Child Psychology and Psychiatry, 45,* 1171–1179.

Dishion, T. J. (2000). Cross-setting consistency in early adolescent psychopathology: Deviant friendships and problem behavior sequelae. *Journal of Personality, 68,* 1109–1126.

Dunn, J. (1993). *Young children's close relationships: Beyond attachment.* Newbury Park, CA: Sage.

Dunn, J., & Plomin, R. (1990). *Separate lives: Why siblings are so different.* New York: Basic Books.

Elliott, D. S., Huizinga, D., & Ageton, S. S. (1985). *Explaining delinquency and drug use.* Beverly Hills, CA: Sage.

Epstein, J. (1983). Examining theories of adolescent friendships. In J. Epstein & N. Karweit (Eds.), *Friends in school: Patterns of selection and influence in secondary schools.* New York: Academic Press.

Ge, X., Conger, R. D., Cadoret, R. J., Neiderhiser, J. M., Yates, W., Troughton, E., et al. (1996). The developmental interface between nature and nurture: A mutual influence model of child antisocial behavior and parent behaviors. *Developmental Psychology, 32,* 574–589.

Gillespie, N. A., Neale, M. C., Jacobson, K., & Kendler, K. S. (2009). Modeling the genetic and environmental association between peer group deviance and cannabis use in male twins. *Addiction, 104,* 420–429.

Gilson, M. S., Hunt, C. B., & Rowe, D. C. (2001). The friends of siblings: A test of social homogamy vs. peer selection and influence. *Marriage & Family Review, 33,* 205–223.

Hamilton, W. D. (1964). The genetical evolution of social behaviour: I. *Journal of Theoretical Biology, 7,* 1–16.

Hammen, C. (2003). Interpersonal stress and depression in women. *Journal of Affective Disorders, 74,* 49–57.

Herndon, R. W., McGue, M., Krueger, R. F., & Iacono, W. G. (2005). Genetic and environmental influences on adolescents' perceptions of current family environment. *Behavior Genetics, 35,* 373–380.

Horwitz, B. N., Neiderhiser, J. M., Ganiban, J. M., Spotts, E. L., Lichtenstein, P., & Reiss, D. (2010). Genetic and environmental influences on global family conflict. *Journal of Family Psychology, 24,* 217–220.

Iervolino, A. C., Pike, A., Manke, B., Reiss, D., Hetherington, M., & Plomin, R. (2002). Genetic and environmental influences in adolescent peer socialization: Evidence from two genetically sensitive designs. *Child Development, 73,* 162–174.

Jaffee, S., & Price, T. (2007). Gene-environment correlations: A review of the evidence and implications for prevention of mental illness. *Molecular Psychiatry, 12,* 432–442.

Jockin, V., & McGue, D. T. (1996). Personality and divorce: A genetic analysis. *Journal of Personality and Social Psychology, 71,* 288–299.

Kendler, K. S., & Baker, J. S. (2007). Genetic influences on measures of the environment: A systematic review. *Psychological Medicine, 37,* 615–626.

Kenny, D. A., & LaVoie, L. (1984). The social relations model. *Advances in Experimental Social Psychology, 18,* 141–182.

Koonce, W. R., Propper, C. B., Gariepy, J. L., Blair, C. B., Peters, P. G., & Cox, M. J. (2007). Bidirectional genetic and environmental influences on mother and child behavior: The family system as the unit of analyses. *Development and Psychopathology, 19,* 1073–1087.

Korchmaros, J. D., & Kenny, D. A. (2001). Emotional closeness as a mediator of the effect of genetic relatedness on altruism. *Psychological Science, 12,* 262–265.

Krueger, R. F., Moffitt, T. E., Caspi, A., Bleske, A., & Silva, P. A. (1998). Assortative mating for antisocial behavior: Developmental and methodological implications. *Behavior Genetics, 28,* 173–186.

Lee, S. S., Chronis-Tuscano, A., Keenan, K., Pelham, W. E., Lney, J., Van Hulle, C. A., et al. (2010). Association of maternal dopamine transporter genotype with negative parenting: Evidence for gene x environment interaction with child disruptive behavior. *Molecular Psychiatry, 15,* 548–558.

Leve, L. (2001). Observation of externalizing behavior during a twin-friend discussion task. *Marriage & Family Review, 33,* 225–250.

Lucht, M., Barnow, S., Schroeder, W., Grabe, H., Finckh, U., John, U., et al. (2006). Negative perceived paternal parenting is associated with dopamine D2 receptor exon 8 and GABA(A) Alpha 6 receptor variants. *American Journal of Medical Genetics: Part B, 141B,* 167–172.

Lytton, H. (1977). Do parents create, or respond to, differences in twins? *Developmental Psychology, 13*(5), 456–459.

Manke, B., McGuire, S., Reiss, D., Hetherington, E. M., & Plomin, R. (1995). Genetic contributions to adolescents' extrafamilial social interactions: Teachers, best friends, and peers. *Social Development, 4,* 238–256.

Manke, B., & Pike, A. (2001). Combining the social relations model and behavioral genetics to explore the etiology of familial interactions. *Marriage and Family Review, 33,* 179–204.

Mathews, C. A., & Reus, V. I. (2001). Assorative mating in the affective disorders: A systematic review and meta-analysis. *Comprehensive Psychiatry, 42,* 257–262.

McClellan, J., & King, M. C. (2010). Genetic heterogeneity in human disease. *Cell, 141,* 210–217.

McGue, M., Elkins, I., Walden, B., & Iacono, W. G. (2005). Perceptions of the parent-adolescent relationship: A longitudinal investigation. *Developmental Psychology, 41,* 971–984.

Neale, M. C. & Cardon, L. R. (Eds.). (1992). *Methodology for genetic studies of twins and families.* Dordrecht, The Netherlands: Kluwer Academic Publishers B.V.

Neiderhiser, J. M., Reiss, D., Lichtenstein, P., Spotts, E. L., & Ganiban, J. (2007). Father-adolescent relationships and the role of genotype-environment correlation. *Journal of Family Psychology, 21,* 560–571.

Neiderhiser, J. M., Reiss, D., Pedersen, N. L., Lichtenstein, P., & Spotts, E. L. (2004). Genetic and environmental influences on mothering of adolescents: A comparison of two samples. *Developmental Psychology, 40,* 335–351.

O'Connor, T. G., Deater-Deckard, K., Fulker, D. W., Rutter, M., & Plomin, R. (1998). Gene-environment correlations in late childhood and early adolescence. *Developmental Psychology, 34,* 970–981.

O'Connor, T. G., Hetherington, E. M., Reiss, D., & Plomin, R. (1995). A twin-sibling study of observed parent-adolescent interactions. *Child Development, 66,* 812–824.

O'Connor, T. G., Jenkins, J. M., Hewitt, J., DeFries, J. C., & Plomin, R. (2003). Longitudinal connections between parenting and peer relationships in adoptive and biological families. *Marriage & Family Review, 33,* 251–271.

Partridge, T. (2005). Are genetically informed designs genetically informative? Comment on McGue, Elkins, Walden, and Iacono (2005) and quantitative behavioral genetics. *Developmental Psychology, 41,* 985–988.

Petrill, S., Plomin, R., DeFries, J. C., & Hewitt, J. K. (2003). *Nature, nurture, and the transition to adolescence.* New York: Oxford University Press.

Plomin, R. (1994). *Genetic and experience: The interplay between nature and nurture.* Thousand Oaks, CA: Sage.

Plomin, R., & Daniels, D. (1987). Why are children in the same family so different from each other? *Behavioral and Brain Sciences, 10,* 1–16.

Plomin, R., DeFries, J. C., & Loehlin, J. C. (1977). Genotype-environment interaction and correlation in the analysis of human behavior. *Psychological Bulletin, 84*(2), 309–322.

Plomin, R., DeFries, J. C., McClearn, G. E., & McGuffin, P. (2008). *Behavioral genetics* (5th ed.). New York: Worth Publishers.

Reiss, D. (2005). The interplay between genotypes and family relationships. *Current Directions in Psychological Science, 14*(3), 139–143.

Reiss, D., Neiderhiser, J. M., Hetherington, E. M., & Plomin, R. (Eds.). (2000). *The relationship code: Deciphering genetic and social influences on adolescent development.* Cambridge, MA: Harvard University Press.

Rhule-Louie, D. M., & McMahon, R. J. (2007). Problem behavior and romantic relationships: Assortative mating, behavior contagion, and desistance. *Clinical Child and Family Psychology Review, 10,* 53–100.

Riggins-Caspers, K., & Cadoret, R. J. (2001). Family process as mediator of biology X environment interaction. *Marriage & Family Review, 33,* 101–130.

Rose, R. J. (2002). How do adolescents select their friends? A behavior–genetic perspective. In L. Pulkkinen & A. Caspi (Eds.), *Paths to successful development: Personality in the life course* (pp. 106–125). Cambridge, UK: Cambridge University Press.

Rowe, D. C. (1981). Environmental and genetic influences on dimensions of perceived parenting: A twin study. *Developmental Psychology, 17,* 203–208.

Rowe, D. C. (1983). A biometrical analysis of perceptions of family environment: A study of twin and singleton sibling kinships. *Child Development, 54,* 416–423.

Rushton, J. P. (1989). Genetic similarity, human altruism, and group selection. *Behavioral and Brain Sciences, 12,* 503–559.

Scarr, S., & McCartney, K. (1983). How people make their own environments: A theory of genotype → environment effects. *Child Development, 54,* 424–435.

Segal, N. L., Seghers, J. P., Marelich, W. D., Mechanic, M. B., & Castillo, R. R. (2007). Social closeness of MZ and DZ twin parents towards nieces and nephews. *European Journal of Personality, 21,* 487–506.

Simons, R. L., Stewart, E., Gordon, L. C., Conger, R. D., & Elder, G. H. (2002). A test of lifecourse explanations for stability and change in antisocial behavior from adolescence to young adulthood. *Criminology, 40,* 401–434.

Spotts, E. L., Neiderhiser, J. M., Towers, H., Hansson, K., Lichtenstein, P., Cederblad, M., et al. (2004). Genetic and environmental influences on marital relationships. *Journal of Family Psychology, 18,* 107–119.

Steinberg, L. (2003). We know some things: Parent-adolescent relationships in retrospect and prospect. *Journal of Research on Adolescence, 11,* 1–19.

Steinberg, L. (2004). Cognitive and affective development in adolescence. *Trends in Cognitive Sciences, 9,* 69–74.

Van IJzendoorn, M. H., Bakermans-Kranenburg, M. J., & Mesman, J. (2008). Dopamine system genes associated with parenting in the context of daily hassles. *Genes, Brain and Behavior, 7,* 403–410.

Walden, B., McGue, M., Iacono, W. G., Burt, S., & Elkins, I. (2004). Identifying shared environment contributions to early substance use: The importance of peers versus parents. *Journal of Abnormal Psychology, 113,* 440–450.

Walum, H., Westberg, L., Henningsson, S., Neiderhiser, J. M., Reiss, D., Igl, W., et al. (2008). Genetic variation in the vasopressin receptor 1a gene (AVPR1A) associates with pair-bonding behavior in humans. *Proceedings of the National Academy of Sciences, 105,* 14153–14156.

12

Interpersonal and Intrapersonal Processes in the Development of Adolescent Relationships

Susan Branje

Loes Keijsers

Muriel van Doorn

Wim Meeus

F amily relationships and friendships are among the most important and central of adolescent relationships and provide a context for adolescent development. These relationships are not only thought to influence adolescents' behavior and development (Reis, Collins, & Berscheid, 2000); they also undergo important developmental changes themselves. During adolescence, both parent–child relationships and friendships are thought to develop toward increasing equality, interdependence, and reciprocity (Laursen & Bukowski, 1997; Laursen, Coy, & Collins, 1998; Youniss & Smollar, 1985). Adolescents report the quality of their relationship with their parents to decline from early to middle adolescence and to improve from middle to late adolescence, and youths gradually perceive their parents as less powerful and controlling over the course of adolescence (De Goede, Branje, & Meeus, 2009a; Keijsers, Frijns, Branje, & Meeus, 2009). Adolescents' friends are perceived as increasingly supportive and decreasingly dominant over time (De Goede, Branje, & Meeus, 2009b). Whereas much research has been done to identify what is being reorganized in relationships through adolescence, we have much less understanding of how these reorganizations occur. In this chapter, we will discuss three features of relationships that need to be considered in research aimed at capturing the underlying processes and mechanisms in the development of adolescents' relationships: (1) the role of interdependence, (2) the role of interpersonal and intrapersonal processes, and (3) the role of variability.

First, we will describe the role of interdependence in the development of adolescents' relationships. Interdependence characterizes close relationships and refers to the causal connections between the actions, reactions, thoughts, and emotions of relational partners within their interactions (Kelley et al., 1983). Interdependence is apparent not only between dyad members within adolescents' relationships but also between relationships and the context in which they operate, such as the family. Moreover, interdependence results in statistical nonindependence of observations that needs to be controlled for in analyses (Cook & Kenny, 2005)—that is, the behaviors, thoughts, and emotions of two relational partners are more likely to be similar than the behaviors, thoughts, and emotions of two random individuals. We will discuss theoretical models emphasizing interdependence and empirical studies that have taken into account issues of interdependence in the development of adolescent relationships.

Second, we will focus on the role of interindividual (i.e., between-person) and intraindividual (i.e., within-person) processes that underlie developmental changes and transitions in relationships during adolescence. Research into the development of youths' relationships has mostly investigated changes at the group level such as mean level development or changes in interindividual differences. That is, most research has examined average processes across individuals. However, a mean level change or correlation on the level of the group does not necessarily inform us about the specific changes or processes of the individuals within that group. Thus, despite the fact that these studies have led to important theoretical advances, they teach us little about the underlying intraindividual developmental mechanisms, such as whether and how relationship changes occur and what the implications of these developmental changes are for specific individuals.

Third, we will focus on the role of variability as a phenomenon in itself. Variability reflects the day-to-day or moment-to-moment fluctuations in perceived relationship aspects or in interaction behavior. Usually relationship aspects are assessed as relatively static characteristics, and changes are examined only over an extended period of time. Short-term fluctuations in perceived relationship aspects or interaction behavior are typically attributed to lower reliability or measurement error; however, these fluctuations may in fact be a key feature of relationships and relationship development. Thus, investigating variability may expose fundamental relational processes.

This chapter is divided into three main sections. The first section delineates some theoretical views that stress the importance of considering interdependence, intraindividual versus interpersonal processes, and variability when examining relationship development. The second section demonstrates the use and relevance of these perspectives by presenting recent empirical work focusing on processes of relationship change in adolescence. The third section sketches a number of future directions in this line of research. We will describe how these innovative paradigms may expand the range of ideas that can be examined empirically. In our view, these issues can advance our knowledge of the underlying mechanisms of relationship change.

≫ CONCEPTUAL/THEORETICAL OVERVIEW

The Interdependent Nature of Relationships and Their Development

Adolescents' relationships with parents and friends are generally characterized as close relationships in the sense that the relationship partners are highly interdependent and exert a frequent and strong influence on each others' behavior for an extended period of time (Kelley et al., 1983). Different theories emphasize a transactional model in which dyad members reciprocally affect each other over time (Bell, 1968; Lerner & Kauffman, 1985; Lollis & Kuczynski, 1997; Sameroff, 1983). Although adolescents develop increasing autonomy and individuation in relationships with parents and friends, these relationships are characterized by interdependence throughout adolescence. In fact, adolescent individuation develops most optimally when adolescents maintain intimate and interdependent relationships with parents and friends (Grotevant & Cooper, 1986; Shulman & Knafo, 1997).

Even though the interdependence of relationship partners and the dyadic nature of relationships are widely recognized, relational pathways in adolescence are studied predominantly by focusing on the perception of one individual in the relationship. Nevertheless, it is important to consider both dyad members in the study of relationship change, as well as the context in which they are embedded. Adolescents' dyadic relationships with parents and friends are part of a system, consisting of multiple levels of social complexity: the level of the individuals, the level of the relationships, and the level of the group (Hinde, 1997). At the level of the individual, relationships are composed of two individuals that bring their personal attributes with them in all situations. A dyadic relationship is determined not only by the personal characteristics of both individuals in the relationship but also by the content and qualities of their dyadic interactions and the frequency and patterning of these interactions at the level of the relationship. These characteristics cannot be explained completely by the characteristics of the individuals within the dyad but emerge within the dyadic interaction. The group level forms a relational network that consists of multiple dyadic relationships. An example of these three levels is that parents and adolescents form dyadic relationships that are embedded within the family at the group level. Comparably, adolescents and their friends form dyadic friendships that are embedded in the larger peer group.

These different levels of a relationship system are reciprocally related and influence each other within the system (Hinde, 1997). For instance, individuals may be affected by their relationships and vice versa. Including both members of the dyadic relationship in the analysis of change allows us to examine the relational character of change and to understand the interactive processes between both dyad members' characteristics and perceptions that constitute the relationship and relationship change (Cook & Kenny, 2005). The relationships and the relationship partners may also be affected by the group in which they are embedded (Reis et al., 2000). This interdependence of the levels of individuals, relationships, and groups is apparent in the nature and development of adolescents' relationships with their parents and friends (Cook, 1994). For example, family systems theory emphasizes that bidirectional effects can be found not only within dyadic family relationships but also between dyadic family relationships: One dyad may influence the other dyads within the family

(O'Connor, Hetherington, & Clingempeel, 1997). Because each individual member of a relationship develops over time, dyad members have to constantly accommodate and coordinate their dyadic relationships according to their own and the dyadic partner's developmental changes within the larger group context. Thus, in family relationships and friendships, development arises from the interactive fit between the individual characteristics of the relationship partners, their dyadic relationship, and the family or peer context in which they are embedded.

Interindividual Versus Intraindividual Processes

An important theoretical distinction in relationship development is the difference between interindividual and intraindividual processes. A common approach to the study of adolescents' relationships is to examine interindividual (between-person) differences in these relationships. The increased application of latent growth models has resulted in an increased appreciation of the notion that development needs to be studied by examining intraindividual (within-person) changes. That is, all individuals have their unique developmental trajectory over time, and individuals may differ from each other in this respect. Indeed, many studies concentrate on the average mean level development of relationship characteristics and interindividual differences in this development. Nevertheless, the average mean level development typically does not apply to intraindividual developmental pattern, or in other words: Virtually no individual adolescent follows the average relationship pathway. The examination of intraindividual processes may offer important theoretical insights in relationship pathways, specifically about why and how relationship pathways evolve (Bolger, Davis, & Rafaeli, 2003; Papp, 2004).

Whereas interindividual processes offer knowledge on why adolescents differ from other adolescents in their relationship quality and development, intraindividual processes are informative on the extent to which relationship partners influence each other within the relationship, thereby addressing the sources of intraindividual day-to-day fluctuations in relationship characteristics. Instead of asking, for instance, whether parents who experience high marital conflict perceive more conflict with their adolescent child than parents who experience low marital conflict, we can ask whether parental conflict is correlated with parent–child conflict within a family over time. Stated otherwise, are parents more likely to perceive conflicts with their children on days when parents have a conflict with their spouse than on days on which they do not experience a conflict with their spouse? The examination of intraindividual processes has the advantage that it controls for unmeasured third variables that may explain interindividual associations (Almeida, Wethington, & McDonald, 2001). Interindividual associations and intraindividual associations are independent from each other (Nezlek, 2001), and they do not necessarily have the same direction. For example, adolescents who report on average more intimacy in their friendships perceive their friendships as more satisfactory, more intimate interactions within a friendship do not necessarily have to be more satisfactory (Nezlek, 2003). Although not all interactions may have an impact on the relationship, salient interactions such as conflicts may temporarily or permanently affect the relationship (Kelley et al., 1983). Thus, to acquire a better understanding of the underlying processes of relationship change, examining intraindividual (intradyadic or within-dyad when the unit is the dyad; Lyons & Sayer, 2005) processes may reveal other things than examining interindividual processes.

Short-Term Fluctuations as Intrinsic Processes

Theoretically, short-term processes may offer interesting insights into relationships and their development. The dynamic nature of relationships is widely recognized, but most of the time relationship aspects are assessed as relatively static characteristics in which individuals may differ, and changes are examined only over an extended period of time. Consequently, short-term (daily or moment-to-moment) intraindividual fluctuations in these relationship aspects are often ignored or considered measurement error. However, investigating this intraindividual variability may not only divulge information about the precursors, correlates, and consequences of intraindividual relationship experiences (Bolger et al., 2003) but it may also reflect fundamental intraindividual processes by itself. A dynamic systems approach regards relationships as self-organizing developing systems that organize behavior around coherent and stable patterns or attractors (Fogel, 2000; Ford & Lerner, 1992; Thelen, 1989; Weigel & Murray, 2000). There is multistability in the system in that multiple attractors or preferred interaction patterns might coexist. Systems tend to stabilize and settle into regularly occurring patterns of interaction or attractor states, but at the same time the system is also characterized by a certain degree of variability. A dynamic systems approach suggests that this variability reflects intrinsic processes in which relationship characteristics fluctuate around an equilibrium to which they are attracted (Boker & Laurenceau, 2007). From this perspective, variability in relationships is examined as a phenomenon in itself. This variability can be adaptive in some contexts but nonadaptive in other contexts.

Generally, variability in interaction behavior is thought to be adaptive, with higher variability reflecting behavioral flexibility or the ability to effectively adapt and reorganize behavior in response to varying interpersonal and contextual demands (Moskowitz & Zuroff, 2004). Adaptive relationships are able to flexibly reorganize when changes occur (Thelen & Smith, 1998). In these relationships, dyad members can easily adjust to environmental changes and will make fluent adjustments to these changes. For instance, mothers and daughters might show negative emotions when having a disagreement or conflict regarding the daughter's curfew but go to a state of support and mutual trust when they talk about fun activities. Lack of variability can be conceptualized as a limited capacity to switch among behaviors in response to changes in the environment and has also been labeled rigidity (e.g., Hollenstein, Granic, Stoolmiller, & Snyder, 2004). This is evident, for example, when the mother and daughter are not able to get out of their negative state when they switch from their conflict about curfews to talking about fun activities.

Variability does not necessary have to be favorable under all circumstances and for all personal and relationship characteristics. In some contexts, higher levels of variability might indicate behavioral lability or variability in interpersonal behavior that is not well-controlled and not very adaptive (Charles & Pasupathi, 2003). Higher levels of variability have been associated with poorer outcomes in several domains. For example, higher intraindividual variability in personality was found to be related to poor subjective well-being and behavioral maladaptiveness (Moskowitz & Zuroff, 2004), higher variability in self-descriptions was related to negative affect (Charles & Pasupathi, 2003), and higher emotional variability was associated with a lack of willingness to deal with challenges or difficult situations (Eaton & Funder, 2001). Hence, although variability in relationships is often considered to be adaptive, variability in personal characteristics may be indicative of maladjustment.

Intraindividual (or intradyadic when the unit of analysis is the dyad) variability also has a role in developmental change. From a dynamic systems perspective, variability is a necessary presumption for developmental changes. Developmental changes emerge from within the system as the result of an increasing destabilization of previously stable patterns of behavior (Lewis, 2000; Thelen, 1989) when key elements of the system change. Relationship change is thought to occur when the components of the parent–adolescent or adolescent–friend relational system change in such a way that the system cannot adjust to it while maintaining existing stable attractor states and the relationship has to be reorganized. These changes are marked by a temporary increase in intradyadic behavioral variability (i.e., moment-to-moment fluctuations in behavior; Van Geert & Van Dijk, 2002; see Figure 12.1), after which the relationship restabilizes and settles into new regularly occurring and often more age-appropriate interaction patterns. Thus, a relatively brief phase transition characterized by increased variability marks the nonlinear change from one or a few stable attractors to other stable attractors. From this perspective, real-time (moment-to-moment) intradyadic processes in parent–adolescent or friendship interactions are considered the proximal engines of development or the processes that drive development (Bronfenbrenner & Morris, 1998). So, examining intraindividual or intradyadic variability as a key feature of developmental change may offer essential insights in the nature of this change. It is important to examine how adolescent interaction behavior is related to relationship pathways, thereby shedding light on the processes underlying intraindividual or intradyadic developmental changes in adolescents' relationships with parents and friends.

Figure 12.1 Developmental-Time Variability: Monthly Changes in Real-Time Behavior Patterns

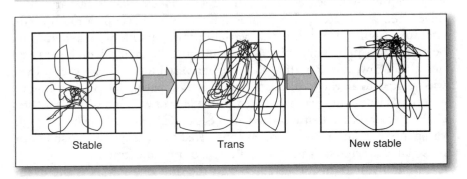

Stable   Trans   New stable

In sum, research on developmental pathways in adolescent relationships needs to consider three features of relationship development. First, relationships include the characteristics of both dyadic partners and are embedded in a larger context. Second, the examination of intraindividual processes is particularly useful for understanding the mechanisms underlying relational pathways. Third, variability in interaction behavior or relationship perceptions may offer important information on relationships and their development. In the next section, we will address recent empirical work that illustrates these issues.

RECENT EMPIRICAL ADVANCES

The Interdependent Nature of Relationships and Their Development

In this section, we will present some empirical studies that explicitly take the family or peer context of relationships into account. The role of broader family relationships in the development of the parent–child relationship has long been recognized, in particular by examining the effect of the marital relationship on parent–child relationships (O'Connor et al., 1997). According to family systems theory, the marital relationship has a strong influence on other relationships in the family, such as the parent–child relationships. For example, marital conflict and divorce is associated with lower parent–child relationship quality (Erel & Burman, 1995). Another way in which the marital relationship may affect the parent–child relationship is through intergenerational transmission, or the process of transfer of mood, affect, or behavior from one person to another person (Larson & Almeida, 1999). Adolescents may observe the behavior that parents display in their marital relationship and use this behavior in their relationship with their parents or peers. For example, when parents use more negative conflict resolution in their marital relationship, adolescents increasingly use more negative conflict resolution over time in their relationship with their parents (van Doorn, Branje, & Meeus, 2007). Thus, the marital relationship tends to affect the development of the parent–child relationship.

Moreover, relationship development may be affected by experiences with other, comparable, relationships. Pertaining to the parent–adolescent relationship, parents and adolescents may adjust their behavior to each other based on experiences with an older sibling. Parents may learn from their experiences with an older sibling in dealing with the challenges of the transitional period of adolescence for the parent–child relationship, or behavior from the older sibling may spill over to the adolescent (Shanahan, McHale, Crouter, & Osgood, 2007; Shanahan, McHale, Crouter,

& Osgood, 2007). Thus, developmental changes in parent–child relationships may depend on birth order and the context of the other siblings in the family. Within-family comparisons revealed that parental warmth declined for both firstborn and second-born adolescents from early to middle adolescence, yet these declines were less pronounced for second-borns than for firstborns (Shanahan et al., 2007a). This finding supports a learning-from-experience perspective in which parents learn from their experience with an older child. Comparably, although conflict with parents peaked in early adolescence for both firstborn and second-born adolescents, conflict with the firstborn adolescent spilled over to conflict with the second-born adolescent, so that second-born adolescents experienced a peak in conflict at an earlier age during early adolescence than firstborn adolescents (Shanahan et al., 2007b). Specific transitions in the larger family system can also affect development of the parent–adolescent relationship. For instance, when the firstborn adolescent leaves home, the second-born's perceived conflict with parents increases (Whiteman, McHale, & Crouter, in press). Moreover, after leaving home, firstborn's conflict with parents decreased and parental intimacy and acceptance increased, showing the relevance of examining relationship change during transitional periods. These findings show that developmental processes in parent–adolescent relationships operate differentially depending on the adolescent's position in the family and the development of other relationships within the family.

Comparable to the development of parent–adolescent relationships in the larger context of the family, development of friendships takes place in and is affected by the larger peer group. In the past decade, techniques such as social network analyses (Snijders, Steglich, & van de Bunt, 2010) have shown the role of the peer group in friendship formation and development. Friendships are embedded in a larger network of peers, and friendships are often formed based on connections in the larger peer network—that is, adolescents often befriend the friends of their friends (Selfhout et al., 2010). Moreover, the peer group tends to affect who adolescents befriend. Not only has adolescents' perceived similarity in their own personality and the personality of their just-acquainted peers predicted friendship intensity over 4 months but similarity in personality as perceived by the peer group also predicted higher friendship intensity (Selfhout, Denissen, Branje, & Meeus, 2009). The effect of perceived similarity by the peer group on friendship intensity was mediated by frequency of communication between adolescent and their just-acquainted peers, suggesting that the perceptions of the peer group push individuals together to interact more and form friendships. These findings show that develop-ment of friendships does not occur in isolation but is nested within and affected by the peer group.

The development of parent–adolescent relationships and friendships is furthermore bidirectionally related. Adolescents may use the mental representations they have formed based on experiences in the relation-ships with their parents to understand and construct their relationships with friends (Furman, Simon, Shaffer, & Bouchey, 2002). Simultaneously, the more egalitarian and symmetrical interactions with friends may be generalized to the relationship with parents (Laursen & Bukowski, 1997). Indeed, parent–adolescent relationships and friendships tend to bidirec-tionally affect each other, with generally stronger effects from parent–adolescent relationships to friendships in early adolescence and equal bidirectional effects in middle and late adolescence for perceived support and negative interaction (De Goede, Branje, Delsing, & Meeus, 2009) and conflict resolution styles (van Doorn, Branje, Van der Valk, De Goede, & Meeus, 2011). Thus, the different pathways of adolescents' relationships are linked and affect each other throughout adolescence.

Interindividual Versus Intraindividual Processes

Examining intraindividual processes in adolescents' relationships may enlighten the mechanisms underlying relationship pathways. Despite the increasing number of studies that examine mean level development of adolescent relationships with longitudinal data and advanced methods such as latent growth curve models (e.g., De Goede et al., 2009a, 2009b; Keijsers et al., 2009), only a few studies addressed intraindividual pro-cesses in adolescents' relationships with parents from a short-term per-spective. Results of a daily diary study showed that fathers were more likely to have supportive interactions with their children on days when they were more involved in child care activities. On these days, they were also more likely to have conflictual interactions with their children, espe-cially when they were in a negative mood (Almeida et al., 2001). Van Doorn, Branje, Hox, and Meeus (2009) investigated whether daily con-flict was related to daily fluctuations in perceived relationship satisfaction in adolescents' relationships with parents and friends and how conflict resolution moderated these associations. Consistent with evidence that adolescents who have more conflict with their parents perceive the parent–adolescent relationship quality to be lower than adolescents who have less conflicts with their parents (e.g., De Goede et al., 2009a), conflict and perceived relationship satisfaction were found to be negatively related to each other on the same day within adolescents' relationships with their mothers, fathers, and best friends, and this association was stronger when adolescents unconstructively handled these conflicts than when adolescents constructively handled these conflicts. In addition, however, conflict was positively related to perceived relationship satisfaction with best friends 1 day later, in particular when these conflicts were unconstructively handled, suggesting it may be beneficial for adolescents' friendships to express differences of opinions now and then. These findings shed light on the within-dyad mechanisms of relationship maintenance.

Similarly, although intergenerational transmission has been shown with interindividual (between-person) associations, these findings do not support transmission or spillover between relationships within specific families. Investigating intraindividual (within-person) effects of other family relationships on parent–adolescent relationships allows conclusions about spillover within families. For example, parent–child conflict mediated the association between interparental conflict and adolescent emotional distress not only at the individual level but also at the daily intraindividual level (Chung, Flook, & Fuligni, 2009). These findings show that spillover from the marital relationship to the parent–adolescent relationship not only occurs at the interindividual level but also in interactions on a daily basis within specific relationships. Thus, examining intraindividual processes complements the examination of interindividual associations and increases our understanding of relationship processes.

Short-Term Fluctuations as Intrinsic Processes

Although variability may offer valuable information about relationship processes and development of relationships, only a limited number of studies have examined the role of variability in adolescent relationships. These studies demonstrate that the role of variability for adolescent relationships depends on the context and measurement of variability. In some contexts, variability is considered to be a beneficial feature, indicating behavioral flexibility. Low variability is then a sign of rigidity. In other contexts, variability is indicative of lability and has more detrimental outcomes. Moreover, variability may play a role in development in that it marks developmental transitions. We will discuss evidence for these possible roles of variability in adolescent relationships next.

That intraindividual fluctuations may reflect disadvantageous relational processes was shown in a study of Arriaga, Reed, Goodfriend, and Agnew (2006). In a sample of late adolescents, they showed that individuals who fluctuate in perceived partner commitment over time were more likely to be in a romantic relationship that sooner or later ended than were individuals with relatively stable perceptions of partner commitment. These associations were significant while controlling for the initial level and the trend of perceived partner commitment and suggest that the extent of fluctuation in perceived partner commitment reflects the certainty or doubt about where the partner stands with respect to the relationship. Thus, in some contexts, relationship fluctuations may reflect detrimental processes.

In contrast, results of a number of studies suggest that rigid response patterns in parent–adolescent relationships, in which parents and adolescents use a limited number of interaction behaviors and are unable to adapt their interaction behavior to the demands of the situation, are associated with more problematic behaviors and relationships. For example, families of aggressive children engage in perseverative cycles of coercive behavior (Granic & Patterson, 2006), and rigidity of the interactions between parents and children was found to predict antisocial behavior in children beyond the content of the interaction (Hollenstein et al., 2004). Among adolescent girls, intraindividual variability in emotional responses to conflict with mother was curvilinearly related to the number of conflicts, with both a high and limited variability being related to high conflict frequency (Lichtwarck-Aschoff, Kunnen, & van Geert, 2009). Also, improvements in aggressive early adolescents' externalizing behavior after a combined parent management training and a cognitive-behavioral program were associated with increases in parent–child emotional flexibility during problem solving interactions (Granic, O'Hara, Pepler, & Lewis, 2007). These findings indicate that higher variability in dyadic emotion regulation is related to higher quality parent–adolescent relationships and adolescent adjustment, whereas rigidity indicates problematic relationships and adjustment problems.

The role of increased variability as an indicator of developmental transitions has received less attention. One study showed that when mothers and daughters revealed greater intradyadic variability in their conflict management behavior, mothers and daughters perceived each other as more dominant, mothers perceived more criticism from daughters, and daughters perceived mothers' communication as less effective

(Branje, 2008). These findings may indicate that mother–daughter dyads characterized by more intradyadic variability might be in the midst of a transition to a more egalitarian and reciprocal relationship (Collins, 1997; Russell, Pettit, & Mize, 1998). Higher levels of variability might reflect the dyad's change toward a more horizontal relationship and a search for new behavioral patterns when old patterns do not work anymore (Cox & Paley, 1997). Only one study has longitudinally examined behavioral variability in development of parent–adolescent relationships and found that intraindividual variability in parent–son relationships was at its peak when boys were 13 to 14 years old (Granic, Hollenstein, Dishion, & Patterson, 2003). As boys generally develop a bit later than girls during early adolescence, these findings are consistent with the suggestion that there is a transition in the parent–child relationship during early adolescence toward a more egalitarian relationship (Collins, Laursen, Mortensen, Luebker, & Ferreira, 1997).

In sum, variability may reflect both positive and negative relationship processes and may play a role in development of relationships as well. It should be noted that the different studies that showed the detrimental versus beneficial role of variability measured variability with different methods (i.e., observations vs. self-reports) and over different time intervals (i.e., in real-time vs. across days), and future studies should address under which conditions and in which contexts relationship fluctuations reflect positive versus negative features of relationships. Moreover, more research is needed to integrate the positive versus negative function of variability for relationships with the role of variability in developmental processes.

※ FUTURE DIRECTIONS

In this selective chapter, we discussed several principles of development in relationships during adolescence. Although it has been well-documented what is changing in relationships over the course of adolescence, the underlying mechanisms of relationship change have yet to be unraveled. Therefore, the goal of this chapter was to discuss a number of principles and issues that may help to elaborate the interpersonal and intrapersonal processes of relationship change. In this section, we will delineate some of the directions for future research that follow from these principles and issues.

A first recommendation is the importance of the correspondence of theory, study design, and analytical techniques (Lerner, Schwartz, & Phelps, 2009; Ram & Grimm, 2007). Specifically, it is essential to distinguish different time scales of development and select the appropriate time scale for the research questions under study. The past decades have shown an increase in studies that examine development of adolescents' relationships with longitudinal designs. Yet, most studies arbitrarily choose equally spaced time intervals for the assessments—for example, by using annual or biannual measurement intervals—and thereby fail to consider the frequency and rate of change as specified by theory (Collins, 2006; Lerner et al., 2009). Relationships may be stable for some periods during adolescence and show fast changes during other periods. When the rate of change of adolescents' relationships is discontinuous, different time intervals of measurement with more frequent measurements during the transitional period than during the stable periods are needed to be able to accurately interpret developmental pathways. Moreover, growth curve models with linear and curvilinear developmental patterns are widely considered, but the linear and quadratic components of these models often do not correspond to theoretical ideas regarding relationship development (Lerner et al., 2009; Ram & Grimm, 2007). Other nonlinear models, such as exponential and multiphase development, may be considered that better fit the theoretical ideas regarding development. Thus, identifying theoretically meaningful periods of development, adapting the time intervals between assessments to the pace of development, and considering different developmental models enables to examine the underlying mechanisms of adolescent relationship development in greater detail.

A second important next step for future research would be to include contextual influences such as the family or peer context when examining relationship change. The studies reviewed in this chapter clearly demonstrated that developmental pathways of adolescents' relationships with parents and friends may differ depending on the setting of the family or peer group and the other relationships within the larger context, such as the role of other siblings in the family. Relationships in adolescence are most likely to go through significant changes during transitions and turning points, and therefore, considering intraindividual processes during transitional periods in the family and peer context can increase our understanding of reorganizations in relationships. For example, changes in parent–child relationships may occur when an older sibling is entering puberty or leaving the parental home (Shanahan et al., 2007a, 2007b).

Increasing consideration of the role of context in relational changes enables to distinguish disparate normative developmental pathways and developmental transitions in relationships during adolescence under different contextual circumstances.

A third point of interest in unraveling the dynamical change processes is to focus on intraindividual and intradyadic processes rather than on interindividual processes. Although interindividual processes tell us important issues about interindividual differences in change processes, intraindividual processes permit to investigate more directly how developmental changes within relationships unfold over time. Particularly, scrutinizing the antecedents, consequences, and functions of intradyadic variability seems to be a promising avenue for future research. The few studies that took this perspective have shown the value of this approach, but further research is warranted. Of particular interest is the question how intradyadic variability is related to changes in content of interactions and relationships. Based on a dynamic systems perspective, we would expect that a temporary period of increased intradyadic variability in interaction behavior would mark a developmental transition from one stable behavioral pattern to another (Fogel, 2000), with the latter pattern reflecting a more egalitarian and reciprocal relationship with parents or friends. This information is also relevant for intervention and treatment: A dynamic systems approach suggests that behavior is most flexible during a transition period, and clinical interventions targeted at these critical transition periods are most likely to be effective and may have a greater influence than interventions during periods of relative stability. Moreover, investigating the role of variability measured over different time intervals and in different contexts will help us understand whether and when variability is beneficial versus detrimental. Further research is needed to examine under which conditions higher levels of variability allow dyadic partners to successfully adapt their interaction patterns to the developmental changes of the dyad members during adolescence and under which conditions they fail to do so.

To conclude, this chapter has discussed a number of issues that are highly relevant when trying to understand the underlying processes of relationship development. We have shown the merits of including both dyadic partners and the larger context in which they are embedded, examining intraindividual processes, including variability as an intrinsic part of relationships, and paying attention to the time intervals over which relationship pathways are examined for understanding the mechanisms underlying relational pathways. We have shown how recent empirical studies have incorporated these themes and advanced our knowledge about processes of relational development. By an increased focus on these issues, future research may provide important insights about interpersonal processes in adolescents' relationships.

∫UGGE∫TED READING∫

Bolger, N., Davis, A., & Rafaeli, E. (2003). Diary methods: Capturing life as it is lived. *Annual Review of Psychology, 54,* 579–616.

Granic, I., & Patterson, G. R. (2006). Toward a comprehensive model of antisocial development: A dynamic systems approach. *Psychological Review, 113,* 101–131.

Lerner, R. M., Schwartz, S. J., & Phelps, E. (2009). Problematics of time and timing in the longitudinal study of human development: Theoretical and methodological issues. *Human Development, 52,* 44–68.

∫ REFERENCE∫

Almeida, D. M., Wethington, E., & McDonald, D. (2001). Daily variation in paternal engagement and negative mood: Implications for emotionally supportive and conflictual interactions. *Journal of Marriage and the Family, 63,* 417–429.

Arriaga, X. B., Reed, J. T., Goodfriend, W., & Agnew, C. R. (2006). Relationship perceptions and persistence: Do fluctuations in perceived partner commitment undermine dating relationships? *Journal of Personality and Social Psychology, 91,* 1045–1065.

Bell, R. Q. (1968). A reinterpretation of the direction of effects in studies of socialization. *Psychological Review, 75,* 81–95.

Boker, S. M., & Laurenceau, J.-P. (2007). Coupled dynamics and mutually adaptive context. In T. D. Little, J. A. Bovaird, & N. A. Card (Eds.), *Modeling ecological and contextual effects in longitudinal studies of human development* (pp. 299–324). Mahwah, NJ: Erlbaum.

Bolger, N., Davis, A., & Rafaeli, E. (2003). Diary methods: Capturing life as it is lived. *Annual Review of Psychology, 54,* 579–616.

Branje, S. (2008). Conflict resolution in mother-daughter interactions in early adolescence. *Behaviour, 145,* 1627–1651.

Bronfenbrenner, U., & Morris, P. A. (1998). The ecology of developmental processes. In W. Damon & R. M. Lerner (Eds), *Handbook of child psychology: Vol 1. Theoretical models of human development* (pp. 993–1028). New York: Wiley.

Charles, S. T., & Pasupathi, M. (2003). Age-related patterns of variability in self-descriptions: Implications for everyday affective experience. *Psychology and Aging, 18,* 524–536.

Chung, G. H., Flook, L., & Fuligni, A. J. (2009). Daily family conflict and emotional distress among adolescents from Latin American, Asian, and European backgrounds. *Developmental Psychology, 45,* 1406–1415.

Collins, L. M. (2006). Analysis of longitudinal data: The integration of theoretical model, temporal design, and statistical model. *Annual Review of Psychology, 57*, 505–528.

Collins, W. A. (1997). Relationships and development during adolescence: Interpersonal adaptation to individual change. *Personal Relationships, 4*, 1–14.

Collins, W. A., Laursen, B. Mortensen, N., Luebker, C., & Ferreira, M. (1997). Conflict processes and transitions in parent and peer relationships: Implications for autonomy and regulation. *Journal of Adolescent Research, 12*, 178–198.

Cook, W. L. (1994). A structural equation model of dyadic relationships within the family system. *Journal of Consulting and Clinical Psychology, 62*, 500–509.

Cook, W. L., & Kenny, D. A. (2005). The actor-partner interdependence model: a model of bi-directional effects in developmental studies. *International Journal of Behavioral Development, 29*, 101–109.

Cox, M. J., & Paley, B. (1997). Families as systems. *Annual Review of Psychology, 48*, 243–267.

De Goede, I. H. A., Branje, S. J. T., Delsing, M. J. M. H., & Meeus, W. H. J. (2009). Linkages over time between adolescents' relationships with parents and friends. *Journal of Youth and Adolescence, 38*, 1304–1315.

De Goede, I. H. A., Branje, S. J. T., & Meeus, W. (2009a). Developmental changes in adolescents' perception of relationships with their parents. *Journal of Youth and Adolescence, 38*, 75–88.

De Goede, I. H. A., Branje, S. J. T., & Meeus, W. (2009b). Developmental changes and gender differences in adolescents' perceptions of friendships. *Journal of Adolescence, 32*, 1105–1123.

Eaton, L. G., & Funder, D. C. (2001). Emotion in daily life: Valence, variability, and rate of change. *Emotion, 1*, 413–421.

Erel, O., & Burman, B. (1995). Interrelatedness of marital relations and parent–child relations: A meta-analytic review. *Psychological Bulletin, 118*, 108–132.

Fogel, A. (2000). Developmental pathways in close relationships. *Child Development, 71*, 1150–1151.

Ford, D. H., & Lerner, R. M. (1992). *Developmental systems theory: An integrative approach*. Newbury Park, CA: Sage.

Furman, W., Simon, V. A., Shaffer, L., & Bouchey, H. A. (2002). Adolescents' working models and styles for relationships with parents, friends, and romantic partners. *Child Development, 73*, 241–255.

Granic, I., Hollenstein, T., Dishion, T., & Patterson, G. R. (2003). Longitudinal analysis of flexibility and reorganization in early adolescence: A dynamic systems study of family interactions. *Developmental Psychology, 39*, 606–617.

Granic, I., O'Hara, A., Pepler, D., & Lewis, M. D. (2007). A dynamic systems analysis of parent-child changes associated with successful "real-world" interventions with aggressive children. *Journal of Abnormal Child Psychology, 35*, 845–857.

Granic, I., & Patterson, G. R. (2006). Toward a comprehensive model of antisocial development: A dynamic systems approach. *Psychological Review, 113*, 101–131.

Grotevant, H. D., & Cooper, C. R. (1986). Individuation in family relationships: A perspective on individual differences in the development of identity and role-taking skill in adolescence. *Human Development, 29*, 82–100.

Hinde, R. A. (1997). *Relationships: A dialectic perspective*. Hove, East Sussex: Psychology Press.

Hollenstein, T., Granic, I., Stoolmiller, M., & Snyder, J. (2004). Rigidity in parent–child interactions and the development of externalizing and internalizing behavior in early childhood. *Journal of Abnormal Child Psychology, 32,* 595–607.

Keijsers, L., Frijns, T., Branje, S. J. T., & Meeus, W. H. I. (2009). Developmental links of adolescent disclosure, parental solicitation, and control with delinquency: Moderation by parental support. *Developmental Psychology, 45,* 1314–1327.

Kelley, H. H., Berscheid, E., Christensen, A., Harvey, J. H., Huston, T. L., Levinger, G., et al. (1983). *Close relationships.* New York: Freeman.

Larson, R., & Almeida, D. M. (1999). Emotional transmission in the daily lives of families: A new paradigm for studying family process. *Journal of Marriage and the Family, 61,* 5–20.

Laursen, B., & Bukowski, W. M. (1997). A developmental guide to the organisation of close relationships. *International Journal of Behavioral Development, 21,* 747–770.

Laursen, B., Coy, K. C., & Collins, W. A. (1998). Reconsidering changes in parent–child conflict across adolescence: A meta-analysis. *Child Development, 69,* 817–832.

Lerner, R. M., & Kauffman, M. B. (1985). The concept of development in contextualism. *Developmental Review, 5,* 309–333.

Lerner, R. M., Schwartz, S. J., & Phelps, E. (2009). Problematics of time and timing in the longitudinal study of human development: Theoretical and methodological issues. *Human Development, 52,* 44–68.

Lewis, M. D. (2000). The promise of dynamic systems for an integrated account of human development. *Child Development, 71,* 36–43.

Lichtwarck-Aschoff, A., Kunnen, S., & van Geert, P. (2009). Here we go again. A Dynamic Systems perspective on emotional rigidity across parent-adolescent conflicts. *Developmental Psychology, 45,* 1364–1375.

Lollis, S., & Kuczynski, L. (1997). Beyond one hand clapping: Seeing bidirectionality in parent–child relations. *Journal of Social and Personal Relationships, 14,* 441–461.

Lyons, K., & Sayer, A. (2005). Longitudinal dyad models in family research. *Journal of Marriage and Family, 67,* 1048–1060.

Moskowitz, D. S., & Zuroff, D. C. (2004). Flux, pulse and spin: Dynamic additions to the personality lexicon. *Journal of Personality and Social Psychology, 86,* 880–893.

Nezlek, J. B. (2001). Multilevel random coefficient analyses of event and interval contingent data in social and personality psychology research. *Personality and Social Psychology Bulletin, 27,* 771–785.

Nezlek, J. B. (2003). Using multilevel random coefficient modeling to analyze social interaction diary data. *Journal of Social and Personal Relationships, 20,* 437–469.

O'Connor, T. G., Hetherington, E. M., & Clingempeel, W. G. (1997). Systems and bidirectional influences in families. *Journal of Social and Personal Relationships, 14,* 491–504.

Papp, L. M. (2004). Capturing the interplay among within- and between-person processes using multilevel modeling techniques. *Applied & Preventive Psychology, 11,* 115–124.

Ram, N., & Grimm, K. (2007). Using simple and complex growth models to articulate developmental change: Matching theory to method. *International Journal of Behavioral Development, 31,* 303–316.

Reis, H. T., Collins, W. A., & Berscheid, E. (2000). The relationship context of human behavior and development. *Psychological Bulletin, 126,* 844–872.

Russell, A., Pettit, G. S., & Mize, J. (1998). Horizontal qualities in parent–child relationships: Parallels with and possible consequences for children's peer relationships. *Developmental Review, 18,* 313–352.

Sameroff, A. J. (1983). Developmental systems: Contexts and evolution. In W. Kessen (Ed.), *Handbook of child psychology: Vol. 1. History, theory, and methods* (4th ed., pp. 237–294). New York: Wiley.

Selfhout, M., Burk, W. J., Branje, S. J. T., Denissen, J. J. A., van Aken, M. A. G., & Meeus, W. H. J. (2010). Emerging late adolescent friendship networks and Big Five personality traits: A social network approach. *Journal of Personality, 78,* 509–538.

Selfhout, M. H. W., Denissen, J. J. A., Branje, S. J. T., & Meeus, W. H. J. (2009). In the eye of the beholder: Perceived, actual, and peer-rated similarity in personality, communication, and friendship intensity during acquaintanceship processes. *Journal of Personality and Social Psychology, 96,* 1152–1165.

Shanahan, L., McHale, S. M., Crouter, A. C., & Osgood, D. W. (2007). Warmth with mothers and fathers from middle childhood to late adolescence: Within- and between-families comparisons. *Developmental Psychology, 43,* 551–563.

Shanahan, L., McHale, S. M., Osgood, D. W., & Crouter, A. C. (2007). Conflict frequency with mothers and fathers from middle childhood to late adolescence: Within- and between-families comparisons. *Developmental Psychology, 43,* 539–550.

Shulman, S., & Knafo, D. (1997). Balancing closeness and individuality in adolescent close relationships. *International Journal of Behavioral Development, 21,* 687–702.

Snijders, T. A. B., Steglich, C. E. G., & van de Bunt, M. (2010). Introduction to actor-based models for network dynamics. *Social Networks, 32,* 44–60.

Thelen, E. (1989). Self-organization in developmental processes: Can systems approach work? In M. Gunnar & E. Thelen (Eds.), *Systems in development: The Minnesota Symposia on Child Psychology, 22* (pp. 77–117). Hillsdale, NJ: Erlbaum.

Thelen, E., & Smith, L. B. (1998). Dynamic systems theories. In W. Damon (Ed.), *Handbook of child psychology: Vol. 1. Theoretical models of human development* (5th ed.). New York: Wiley.

van Doorn, M. D., Branje, S. J. T., Hox, J. J., & Meeus, W. H. J. (2009). Intraindividual variability in adolescents' perceived relationship satisfaction: The role of daily conflict. *Journal of Youth and Adolescence, 38,* 790–803.

van Doorn, M. D., Branje, S. J. T., & Meeus, W. H. J. (2007). Longitudinal transmission of conflict resolution styles from marital relationships to adolescent-parent relationships. *Journal of Family Psychology, 21,* 426–434.

van Doorn, M. D., Branje, S. J. T., Van der Valk, I. E., De Goede, I. H. A., & Meeus, W. H. J. (2011). Longitudinal spillover effects of conflict resolution styles between adolescent-parent relationships and adolescent friendships. *Journal of Family Psychology, 25,* 157–161.

Van Geert, P., & Van Dijk, M. (2002). Focus on variability: New tools to study intra-individual variability in developmental data. *Infant Behavior & Development, 25,* 340–374.

Weigel, D., & Murray, C. (2000). The paradox of stability and change in relationships: What does chaos theory offer for the study of romantic relationships? *Journal of Social and Personal Relationships, 17,* 425–449.

Whiteman, S. D., McHale, S. M., & Crouter, A. C. (in press). Family relationships from adolescence to early adulthood: Changes in the family system following firstborns' leaving home. *Journal of Research on Adolescence.*

Youniss, J., & Smollar, J. (1985). *Adolescent relations with mothers, fathers, and friends.* Chicago: University of Chicago Press.

13

The Role of Gender in Transformations in Adolescent Relationships

Amanda J. Rose

Rhiannon L. Smith

Gary C. Glick

Rebecca A. Schwartz-Mette

C lose relationships are important throughout the life span (Hendrick & Hendrick, 2000; Rubin, Bukowski, & Laursen, 2009). This may be especially true during developmental transitions, including the transition from childhood to adolescence and the transition from adolescence to young adulthood (Collins & van Dulmen, 2006; Laursen & Collins, 2009). Developmental transitions also are important times for gender role development (e.g., Hill & Lynch, 1983; Katz & Ksansnak, 1994). As such,

During the preparation of this chapter, Amanda J. Rose was partially supported by National Institute of Mental Health (NIMH) grant R01 MH 073590, Rhiannon L. Smith was partially supported by a Ridgel Fellowship from the University of Missouri, Rebecca A. Schwartz-Mette was partially supported by NIMH NRSA award F31 MH 0816190 (Amanda J. Rose, Sponsor), and Gary C. Glick was partially supported by a Huggins Fellowship from the University of Missouri.

this chapter focuses on the role of gender in close relationships during these developmental transitions. In particular, we consider girls' and boys' experiences in relationships that are especially central to adolescents: parent–child relationships, same-sex friendships, other-sex friendships, and romantic relationships.

⚜ THEORETICAL OVERVIEW

Significant changes in gender role development take place during adolescence. According to the gender intensification theory (Hill & Lynch, 1983), at the transition to adolescence, youth encounter increased pressure to behave in sex-typed ways and, as a result, gender differences become stronger. The theory also suggests that parents became increasingly invested in rearing same-sex children at this time. This has been proposed to foster closeness between parents and same-sex children. However, given that parent–child closeness tends to decrease at adolescence, Laursen and Collins (2009) suggested that same-sex parent–child relationships may not become closer but may experience less of a decline in closeness. Laursen and Collins (2009) also suggested that increased conflict might arise in same-sex parent–child relationships at this time due to same-sex parents' heightened role as socialization agents.

In regards to peers, gender intensification theory also would suggest that peer influence for sex-typed behavior becomes stronger at the transition to adolescence. However, surprisingly little is known about peer influence on sex-typed behavior beyond the preschool years. As such, in terms of peers, gender intensification theory is typically discussed when considering whether gender differences in peer relationships, including same-sex friendships, increase with age (Rose & Rudolph, 2006). Although there is debate regarding the relative roles of socialization and biology in the development of gender differences, socialization and biological theories converge on the idea that gender differences, including those in same-sex friendships, should increase at the transition to adolescence (see Ruble, Martin, & Berenbaum, 2006).

Then, as youth approach later adolescence and young adulthood, gender differences may become smaller. Gender roles are proposed to be less rigid in later adolescence due to increased cognitive flexibility (Katz & Ksansnak,

1994). As such, girls' and boys' relationships with parents and same-sex friends may become more similar as they move toward young adulthood.

Relationships between the sexes also will be considered in regards to other-sex friendships and romantic relationships. Peer socialization theories, often referred to as "two cultures" theories, have implications for other-sex relationships (Maccoby, 1990, 1998; Underwood & Rosen, 2009). In childhood, sex segregation is strong (Mehta & Strough, 2009), and it has been argued that girls' and boys' groups may even be thought of as different cultures, in which different norms and behaviors are reinforced (Maccoby, 1990; Maltz & Borker, 1982; Thorne, 1986). These sex-linked interpersonal styles are then proposed to create challenges in other-sex interactions later in development (Maccoby, 1990, 1998; Underwood & Rosen, 2009). Moreover, the clash in interpersonal styles has been proposed to be especially challenging for females. Because males are proposed to have more dominant, assertive styles and females are proposed to have more accommodating, interpersonally sensitive styles, it has been suggested that females may have difficulty exerting influence and obtaining support in other-sex relationships (Maccoby, 1990, 1998). We consider these challenges in this chapter but also speculate about the unique challenges that males might face in other-sex relationships.

The two cultures theories do not directly inform predictions regarding developmental differences in other-sex interaction. However, given that other-sex friendships are relatively rare in childhood and become more common throughout adolescence (Mehta & Strough, 2009), challenges of other-sex friendships may be stronger earlier in adolescence when youth have less experience with them. This pattern also may emerge for romantic relationships. Alternatively, because romantic relationships of younger youth may be relatively superficial, challenges related to gender may not be apparent until later in development when these relationships are more central sources of companionship and support (Furman & Buhrmester, 1992).

Finally, although differences between girls' and boys' close relationships are considered, factors that explain within-gender variation are considered too, as the importance of attending to within-gender variation has been increasingly acknowledged (Hyde, 2005; Underwood, 2004). In particular, we consider individual difference factors that may help explain which girls and boys are most likely to have sex-typed experiences in close relationships. We also consider how features of the dyad (e.g., gender composition of parent–child dyads, match between sex-typed interpersonal styles in other-sex relationships) influence adolescents' close relationships.

※ RECENT EMPIRICAL ADVANCES

In this section, we review empirical evidence related to the role of gender in youths' experiences with parents, same-sex friends, other-sex friends, and romantic partners. We focus on the development of these relationships, especially during the transition to adolescence and the transition to young adulthood. In addition, our review focuses on relationship processes that have been central to the study of close relationships, such as social support, disclosure, and conflict.

Parents

Parent–child relationships often are marked by lower levels of support and increased tension at the transition to adolescence as family members negotiate and adjust to new roles. Then, as youth move through adolescence toward young adulthood, parent–child relationships generally become more harmonious (Laursen & Collins, 2009). However, individual differences in these trends are increasingly acknowledged (Laursen, DeLay, & Adams, 2010). We consider this variation by exploring similarities and differences for girls versus boys in relationships with mothers and with fathers.

As noted, positive features tend to decline at adolescence (Laursen & Collins, 2009). These declines are not always found (Bokhorst, Sumter, & Westenberg, 2010; French, Rianasari, Pidada, Nelwan, & Buhrmester, 2001), but when they emerge, they tend to be similar for girls and boys. For example, in one study that tracked youth from sixth to eighth grade (Laursen et al., 2010), youth reported on support from mothers each year (scores based on the admiration, affection, companionship, instrumental aid, intimacy, nurturance, reliable alliance, and satisfaction subscales of the Network of Relationships Inventory [NRI]; Furman & Buhrmester, 1985). Girls' and boys' reports of support declined at similar rates. Likewise, in a cross-sectional study (Furman & Buhrmester, 1992), both girls and boys in the 7th and 10th grades reported less support from mothers and fathers than fourth graders (scores based on the admiration, affection, companionship, instrumental aid, intimacy, nurturance, and reliable alliance subscales of the NRI). In a cross-sectional study in which youth rated the degree to which mothers and fathers helped them with relationship problems (Helsen, Vollebergh, & Meeus, 2000), both girls' and boys' reports of parental support declined between age 12 and mid-adolescence.

Some studies suggest that these declines in positive features may be stronger for girls, but these gender effects do not consistently emerge even across variables within studies. For example, youths' reports on the intimacy subscale of the NRI for fathers were lower in the eighth grade than the second and fifth grades for girls but not boys (Buhrmester & Furman, 1987). However, intimacy with mothers was lower in the eighth grade than the second and fifth grades for girls and boys. In another study (McGue, Elkins, Walden, & Iacono, 2005), twins reported on parent–child involvement, their regard for parents, and parents' regard for them at ages 11 and 14 (using the Parental Environment Questionnaire [PEQ]; Elkins, McGue, & Iacono, 1997). Girls' reports of regard for parents and parents' regard for them declined more than did boys' reports from ages 11 to 14. However, similar declines were found for girls and boys for parent involvement. The data suggest that, when gender differences occur, the transition might be more challenging for girls than boys. However, overall, the data suggest more gender similarities than differences in the drop in positive features in the parent–child relationship at the transition to adolescence.

A different question from whether the developmental trajectories differ for girls and boys is whether there are mean-level gender differences in youths' reports of positive relationship features at these ages. Notably, the mean-level gender differences tend to depend on the parents' gender. In terms of mothers, girls' reports are especially positive. In two of the previously described studies (Furman & Buhrmester, 1992; Laursen et al., 2010), girls reported more support from mothers than did boys. In a third study, girls assessed in the sixth and eighth grades scored higher than boys on the intimacy subscale of the NRI for mothers (French et al., 2001). Finally, 12- to 14-year-old girls reported greater positive relationship quality with mothers than did boys on a scale designed for the study (e.g., assessing time together, admiring, helping; Hair, Moore, Garrett, Ling, & Cleveland, 2008). Although boys do not always report more positive relationship quality with fathers than do girls (e.g., French et al., 2001), when gender differences emerge, they favor boys. For example, boys in Grades 4, 7, and 10 reported marginally more support from fathers than did girls in these grades (Furman & Buhrmester, 1992), and 12- to 14-year-old boys reported more positive relationship quality with fathers than did girls (Hair et al., 2008).

Together, the results suggest that youth may perceive relationships with same-sex parents especially positively. However, the results also suggest that declines in positive qualities in relationships with mothers and fathers are similar for girls and boys. It would be interesting to consider whether declines in relationship quality in relationships that were initially particularly high quality (mothers for girls and fathers for boys) are perceived as especially painful.

The developmental trajectory of negative parent–child interactions, including conflict, at the transition into adolescence also was considered. Some evidence suggests that conflict frequency increases from late childhood to early adolescence. Furman and Buhrmester (1992) found that seventh and ninth graders scored higher than fourth graders on the conflict subscale of the NRI for both mothers and fathers. The effects did not differ by gender. Meta-analytic evidence (Laursen, Coy, & Collins, 1998) indicates that from early adolescence (ages 10–12) to middle adolescence (ages 13–16) conflict frequency then decreases. Although this effect was strongest for conflicts with mothers, the effect did not differ for girls versus boys. Some studies suggest different developmental trajectories in conflict frequency (stability was found from Grades 6 to 8 in French et al., 2001, from Grades 7 to 10 in Furman & Buhrmester, 1992, and from ages 13 to 15 in Smetana, Daddis, & Chuang, 2003; an increase in conflict and criticism was found from Grades 6 to 8 in Laursen et al., 2010). However, none of the studies indicated gender differences in the trajectories. In one longitudinal study (McGue et al., 2005), an increase in youths' reports of parent–child conflict from ages 11 to 14 was found to be strongest for girls (using the PEQ, Elkins et al., 1997). However, this gender difference was the exception rather than the rule. Moreover, gender differences generally were not found in conflict frequency with mothers versus fathers (French et al., 2001; Furman & Buhrmester, 1992; Smetana et al., 2003).

Additionally, the Laursen et al. (1998) meta-analysis highlighted the importance of considering the affective intensity of parent–child conflict as well as frequency. Although the meta-analysis indicated declines in conflict frequency from early to middle adolescence, the intensity of conflicts increased at this time. Interestingly, this increase was significant only for father–son dyads. In a more recent study of conflict with mothers (Smetana et al., 2003), conflict intensity did not increase between ages 13 and 15. However, daughters' conflicts with mothers were perceived as more intense than mother–son conflicts. The studies suggest that same-sex parent–child conflicts may be especially intense during this developmental period.

As stated earlier, as youth move toward later adolescence and young adulthood, parent–child relationships are generally thought to become more harmonious (Laursen & Collins, 2009). For example, in the Helsen et al. (2000) longitudinal study described earlier, the level of support that youth reported from parents stabilized by mid-adolescence and stayed constant until age 24. These results did not differ by gender. In another study (Shanahan, McHale, Crouter, & Osgood, 2007) that tracked youths' reports of parental warmth from about ages 10 to 19, paternal warmth increased starting at about age 16, and maternal warmth increased starting at about age 18. These findings also held across genders. Furman and Buhrmester (1992) also found that college students reported marginally more support from fathers than did 10th graders. Although college men did not report more support from mothers than did 10th-grade boys, college women reported greater support from mothers than 10th-grade girls. This finding highlights the potential significance of the same-sex parental relationship for girls at this transition; however, the bulk of the findings regarding positive qualities suggest gender similarities at this developmental stage.

In terms of conflict, the meta-analytic results (Laursen et al., 1998) indicate a drop in conflict frequency between mid-adolescence (ages 13–16) and later adolescence (ages 17–22). For example, Furman and Buhrmester (1992) found that college students reported less conflict with mothers and fathers did than 10th graders. The results for conflict did not differ by gender.

The findings regarding the transition to later adolescence and young adulthood fit well with the theoretical perspectives described earlier. In particular, gender differences were proposed to be smaller by later adolescence as greater cognitive flexibility increased (Katz & Ksansnak, 1994). In fact, the evidence did indicate gender similarities at the transition to later adolescence and young adulthood with relationships with parents stabilizing or even improving at this time (Furman & Buhrmester, 1992; Helsen et al., 2000; Shanahan et al., 2007).

In contrast, findings related to the transition to adolescence were more mixed in terms of fit with theory. Gender intensification theory suggests that same-sex parent–child dyads might be characterized by increased closeness (or at least buffered from declining closeness) at this transition (Hill & Lynch, 1983; see Laursen & Collins, 2009). Conflict in same-sex parent–child dyads also was suggested to intensify at this time if parents are increasingly active socialization agents for same-sex children (Laursen & Collins, 2009). However, the data provide little support for these ideas. Although youths' perceptions of positive features were found to decline at this transition, the drop was not mitigated for same-sex parent–child dyads. Also, although some data suggested that conflicts were particularly intense in same-sex parent–child dyads, the evidence did not suggest an increase in conflict frequency for same-sex parent–child dyads.

Importantly, though, it is increasingly recognized that sex-typed styles are more apparent in some youth than others (Rose & Rudolph, 2006; Underwood, 2004). This is reflected in the work on families by McHale, Crouter, and colleagues. They propose that sex role socialization will be stronger in homes with children of both sexes as sex roles may be more salient than in homes with only female or male children (McHale, Crouter, & Whiteman, 2003). A prediction that follows from gender intensification theory, then, is that parents will be most intensely invested in rearing same-sex children in homes with children of both sexes.

Research by McHale, Crouter, and colleagues supports this prediction. In one study, in which youth were followed from ages 9 to 11 (Crouter, Manke, & McHale, 1995), girls spent increasingly more time with mothers and boys spent increasingly more time with fathers. Most significantly, these effects were strongest for youth with other-sex younger siblings. As another example, in a cross-sequential study in which parent–child relationships were tracked from about age 7 until age 19 (Shanahan et al., 2007), girls with younger brothers were buffered from a drop in maternal warmth at the transition to adolescence, and boys with younger sisters were buffered from the drop in paternal warmth. These studies highlight the important role of the sex composition of the family in regards to understanding which parent–child dyads are most likely to be characterized by sex-typed interaction styles. Hopefully, this work will stimulate more studies aimed at identifying individual difference and relational factors that help to explain which girls and which boys are most likely to experience sex-typed parent–child interactions.

Same-Sex Friends

Although parents remain important close relationships, friends become increasingly central to youth with age (Collins & van Dulmen, 2006; Furman & Buhrmester, 1992). In childhood, most friends are same-sex peers. For example, one study found that only about 15% of youth in middle childhood had a reciprocal other-sex friend (Kovacs, Parker, & Hoffman, 1996). Although participation in other-sex friendships increases as youth move through adolescence, most close friendships are still same-sex (Mehta & Strough, 2009).

As described, gender intensification theory suggests that differences between girls' and boys' same-sex friendships should increase at adolescence. The strongest support for this idea is reflected in work on intimate disclosure. In our studies (Rose, 2002; Rose, Carlson, & Waller, 2007), third- and fifth-grade children and seventh- and ninth-grade adolescents reported on both self-disclosure about problems in friendships and co-rumination (i.e., extensive problem talk that includes rehashing problems and dwelling on negative affect) in friendships. Girls reported greater self-disclosure and co-rumination than did boys in both childhood and adolescence. However, the gender differences were stronger in adolescence. This was because self-disclosure and co-rumination increased among girls from childhood to adolescence, whereas the disclosure processes either remained stable (self-disclosure) or decreased (co-rumination) for boys. These results are consistent with other work indicating that gender differences in disclosure increase at adolescence (e.g., Buhrmester & Furman, 1987; Zarbatany, McDougal, & Hymel, 2000; also see Buhrmester & Prager, 1995; Rose & Rudolph, 2006). We note that intensification of this gender difference is not found in every study (e.g., French et al., 2001; McNelles & Connolly, 1999). However, gender differences in disclosure generally are found to increase at adolescence.

Less evidence for gender intensification is present for other positive features. For example, in late childhood and adolescence, girls generally report more help and support from same-sex friends than do boys, but the gender differences typically do not increase with age (see Rose & Rudolph, 2006). For example, in a study that tracked youth from 6th to 10th grade (Poulin & Pedersen, 2007), youth reported on the degree to which they received help from same-sex friends when needed. Girls reported more help from same-sex friends than did boys, and the degree of help that girls and boys reported from same-sex friends increased with age. However, this increase was not stronger for girls than boys. Likewise, in a cross-sectional study (Bokhorst et al., 2010), youth ages 9 to 18 reported on perceptions of social support from friends (using the Social Support Scale for Children and Adolescents, Harter, 1985). Although girls reported greater support than boys, the gender difference did not change with age. At least one study in which 12- to 24-year-olds rated the degree to which friends helped them with relationship problems indicated that the gender difference in support intensified at adolescence (Helsen et al., 2000), but this pattern was not found consistently across studies.

Despite gender differences in other domains, girls and boys typically report similar levels of conflict frequency in friendship in late childhood and early adolescence (e.g., Bukowski, Hoza, & Boivin, 1994; Shulman & Laursen, 2002; see Rose & Rudolph, 2006). Developmental trajectories in conflict frequency also may be similar for girls and boys at the transition to adolescence. In one cross-sectional study (Furman & Buhrmester, 1992) fourth- and seventh-grade girls and boys reported similar levels of conflict with same-sex friends (using the conflict subscale of the NRI), and the gender effect did not differ by grade. Likewise, in a study of youth assessed in the sixth and eighth grades, the nonsignificant gender difference in friendship conflict held across grades (using the conflict subscale of the NRI; French et al., 2001).

At the transition to adulthood, some evidence suggests that gender differences in same-sex friendships may become smaller with age. For example, Way and Greene (2006) followed youth from ages 13 and 14 to 17 and 18 and assessed same-sex friendship quality using the NRI (scores based on ratings of affection, companionship, intimacy, reliable alliance, and satisfaction). The strongest gender difference was found at ages 13 and 14, with girls reporting greater positive quality than boys. However, boys experienced greater increases in positive quality over time than girls. As such, by ages 17 and 18, girls and boys reported similar levels of relationship quality. Likewise, a study of college-aged same-sex friends that also used the NRI to assess friendship quality (scores based on ratings of admiration, affection, companionship, intimacy, reliable alliance, and satisfaction; Grabill & Kerns, 2000) also found no gender differences.

Notably, though, other studies suggest that gender differences in same-sex friendships do not disappear entirely by late adolescence and young adulthood. In the study in which 12- to 24-year-olds rated the degree to which friends helped them with relationship problems (Helsen et al., 2000), the gender difference got smaller with age but remained present. Bank and Hansford (2000) found that college women were more likely than college men to report that their same-sex friendships were supportive and intimate (e.g., that they felt concern/affection, that they confided in the friend; using the Close Friendship Scale; Bank, 1994). Williams (1985) also found that college women reported greater frequency and comfort with disclosure and emotional expression with same-sex friends than did men (using a measure created for the study). Last, using observation, Grabill and Kerns (2000) found women to talk more than men with same-sex friends and to report feeling more understood, validated, and cared for in these conversations.

Similar to findings for younger adolescents, gender differences in conflict frequency typically are not found in same-sex friendships in late adolescence and young adulthood. Gender similarities using the conflict subscale of the NRI have been found for 10th graders and college students (Furman & Buhrmester, 1992). In another study of college students (Moilanen & Raffaelli, 2010), in a small sample of Mexican Americans (72 women and 33 men), men scored higher than women on the NRI conflict scale, but gender differences were not found for European Americans, Asian Americans, Cuban Americans, or Latin Americans (with about 400 participants across these groups). Shulman and Laursen (2002) also found that 11th-grade girls and boys reported similar levels of conflict frequency with friends. Interestingly, 11th-grade girls reported more anger than boys when asked about the one friendship conflict in the past week that they thought was most important. Although most research on conflict with same-sex friends focuses on frequency, these results speak to the importance of considering gender differences in conflict intensity in same-sex friendships as well (see Laursen et al., 1998).

Overall, partial support was found for the idea that gender differences in same-sex friendships would intensify at adolescence. Support was strongest for disclosure. For other features, gender differences were not present or robust (e.g., conflict) or typically did not increase at adolescence (e.g., help/support). Consistent with cognitive theories suggesting greater flexibility in sex roles with age (Katz & Ksansnak, 1994), the evidence also suggests that gender differences in same-sex friendship may become smaller as youth approach later adolescence and young adulthood. However, these gender differences did not disappear altogether.

Finally, within-gender variability in same-sex friendships should be considered as well. Considering social cognitions may be useful for determining which youth demonstrate sex-typed styles in same-sex friendships (Rose & Rudolph, 2006). Several of our studies have identified social cognitions that are linked with sex-typed friendship styles, especially disclosure. In one study, youth with social goals such as trying to express caring and to help a friend feel better were likely to adopt strategies of discussing a problem, sympathizing, and giving reassurance (Rose & Asher, 2004). In other research, youth with greater positive expectations for how talking about problems would make them feel (e.g., expecting to feel cared for, understood) and fewer negative expectations (e.g., expecting to feel uncomfortable or weird) were more likely to disclose to friends about problems (Rose et al., in press). In a third study (Smith & Rose, in press), youth who adopted the friend's perspective were most likely to co-ruminate about problems with friends. In one more study (Rose, Swenson, & Robert, 2009), we assessed youths' motivations for *refraining* from prompting friends to talk about problems. Youth who reported more prosocial motivations for not prompting friends to talk (e.g., not wanting to embarrass the friend) and/or more selfish motivations (e.g., feeling like talking about upsetting things was not fun) were most likely to report *not* prompting friends to talk about problems.

In each study, girls were more likely than boys to endorse social cognitions associated with greater disclosure. However, variation within gender in these social cognitions may help to explain which girls and boys are most likely to adopt sex-typed disclosure patterns. Girls with social cognitions more similar to boys may disclose at levels more typical of boys, whereas boys with social cognitions more similar to girls may disclose at levels more typical of girls.

More generally, David Perry's work on gender typicality may be useful for explaining within-gender variability in same-sex friendships. In this work, the degree to which youth feel like typical girls or boys is examined (questions assess, for example, the degree to which youth feel like good examples of girls/boys and the degree to which they feel like their personalities are like other girls/boys; Egan & Perry, 2001). The primary focus has been to examine relations between gender identity and social/psychological adjustment (Carver, Yunger, & Perry, 2003; Egan & Perry, 2001; Yunger, Carver, & Perry, 2004). However, considering gender typicality also might help explain which girls and boys have the most sex-typed same-sex friendships. Perhaps youth who perceive themselves as gender typical are characterized by sex-typed styles in friendships, whereas youth who perceive themselves as atypical are more likely to have other-sex friends and behave in friendships in a way that is similar to other-sex youth.

Other-Sex Friends and Romantic Partners

Although same-sex friendships are primary peer relationships at the transition to adolescence and play an important role throughout adolescence (Mehta & Strough, 2009), other-sex peers become increasingly central as other-sex friends and romantic partners. In regards to other-sex friendships, a study by Poulin and Pedersen (2007) illustrates the increasing role of other-sex friends in the lives of youth. In this study, youth were followed from 6th to 10th grade and listed their 10 best friends each year. The proportion of friends that youth listed who were other-sex friends increased for both girls and boys (from 21% to 33% for girls and from 16% to 19% for boys).

Recall, too, that two cultures theory proposes that other-sex interactions may be challenging because girls and boys approach them with different interpersonal styles (Maccoby, 1990, 1998; Underwood & Rosen, 2009). For other-sex friendships, we hypothesized that these challenges may be strongest earlier in adolescence when other-sex friendships are still relatively novel. Throughout adolescence, same-sex friendships are generally higher quality than other-sex friendships (e.g., Burmester & Furman, 1987; Hand & Furman, 2009). However, the nature of other-sex friendships may improve with age. In one study (Kuttler, La Greca & Prinstein, 1999), 15- and 16-year-olds reported more companionship in same-sex friendships than other-sex friendships (friendship quality was assessed with the Friendship Interview, Berndt & Perry, 1986; modified by Vernberg, Absender, Ewell, & Beery, 1992; Vernberg, Berry, Ewell, & Absender, 1993). However, 17- and 18-year-olds reported similar levels of companionship in same- and other-sex friendships. Also, although 15- and 16-year-old girls reported more prosocial support (i.e., helping) in same-sex friendships than other-sex friendships, 17- and 18-year-old girls reported similar levels of prosocial support in same- and other-sex friendships. No age differences were found in the degree to which same- and other-sex friendships differed in intimacy (i.e., disclosure) or esteem support (i.e., validation). However, the study provided partial support for the idea that other-sex friendships are more challenging earlier in adolescence.

Moreover, as mentioned, the mismatch in interpersonal styles between genders has been proposed to especially disadvantage girls (Maccoby, 1990, 1998). There is some support for this idea. In the study in which youth were tracked from Grades 6 to 10 (Poulin & Pedersen, 2007), boys reported more help from other-sex friends than did girls. In the Kuttler et al. (1999) study, 15- to 18-year-old girls reported less esteem support from other-sex friends than same-sex friends, but boys received as much esteem support from other-sex friends as same-sex friends. Other research that examined 3rd, 6th, 9th, and 12th graders' *expectations* for other-sex friendships (McDougal & Hymel, 2007) suggested that girls may be more accommodating than boys in other-sex friendships. For same-sex friendships, having shared activities was important to boys and intimacy (e.g., disclosure, understanding) was important to girls. Although girls were likely to expect that friendships with boys would include shared activities, boys were not likely to expect that friendships with girls would include intimacy. This suggests that girls may be willing to adapt to boys' expectations more than boys adapt to girls' expectations.

However, girls likely benefit from improvements in other-sex friendships that occur with age. For example, as noted, girls reported less prosocial support from other-sex friends than same-sex friends at ages 15 and 16, but girls reported as much prosocial support from other-sex friends as same-sex friends at ages 17 and 18 (Kuttler et al., 1999). By the 12th grade, girls and boys did not differ in the support that they reported in other-sex friendships (scores based on affection, companionship, enhancement of worth, instrumental help, intimacy, and reliable alliance subscales of the NRI) or in the negative interactions that they reported (based on the conflict and annoyance subscales of the NRI; Hand & Furman, 2009). Similarly, college-aged women and men did not differ in how important they reported their other-sex friendships to be relative to their same-sex friendships (Bank & Hansford, 2000).

Moreover, it is possible that boys face unique challenges in other-sex friendships that have received less attention. For example, boys may find it frustrating if girls expect them to be interested in detailed disclosures and to respond like their female friends do (Underwood & Rosen, 2009). In addition, boys seem to generate considerable fun and excitement in friendship activities (see Rose & Asher, 2011) and may be disappointed or dissatisfied if girls prefer calmer, dyadic, conversation-based interactions. Boys also may find the romantic or sexual potential of other-sex friendships ambiguous and challenging. When interviewed about the rewards of other-sex friendships, boys were more likely than girls to mention physical attraction (Hand & Furman, 2009). Although boys framed this as an advantage of other-sex friendships, the attraction may become a frustration or disappointment if it is not reciprocated given the importance of romantic relationships at this age.

In fact, participation in romantic relationships does increase in adolescence, and romantic partners become central sources of companionship and support for many youth (Furman & Collins, 2009; Laursen & Williams, 1997). Although two cultures theory suggests that challenges in other-sex relationships may be especially salient for girls (Maccoby, 1990, 1998), romantic relationships have been proposed to be less challenging for females than other other-sex relationships if power and influence in romantic relationships are tied more strongly to factors other than gender (e.g., which partner is more attractive or more in love; Maccoby, 1990).

At the transition to adolescence, girls do not seem disadvantaged. In Grades 5 through 8, girls and boys were equally likely to report wanting a romantic relationship (Connolly, Craig, Goldberg, & Pepler, 2004). In Grades 3, 5, 7, and 9, girls were as likely as boys to have the peer they nominated as their boyfriend/girlfriend reciprocate the nomination (Carlson & Rose, 2007). Seventh-grade girls and boys also did not differ in the support (based on admiration, affection, companionship, instrumental aid, intimacy, nurturance, reliable alliance, and satisfaction NRI subscales), conflict, or power they reported in romantic relationships (Furman & Buhrmester, 1992).

At the transition to adolescence, boys even may be more likely to be "in love" (Montgomery, 2005). On average, boys in Grades 7 through 9 reported being in love 1.7 times, and girls reported being in love about 1 time. Interestingly, the number of times youth reported being in love was about the same for older adolescent girls and young adult women as for younger girls, and the number decreased with age for boys. This suggests that youth adjust their perceptions of what it means to be "in love" as they grow older and that this may be particularly true for boys.

Importantly, research generally suggests that girls also are not disadvantaged as the depth and substance of romantic relationships increase later in adolescence and young adulthood. In a study of 5th, 8th, and 11th graders, gender differences were not found on the satisfaction subscale of the NRI for any age group (Carlson & Rose, in press). Similarly, Haugen, Welsh, and McNulty (2008) found no gender differences in relationship satisfaction in their samples of middle adolescents (ages 14–17) and later adolescents (ages 17–21; using the Relationship Satisfaction Scale, Levesque, 1993). Gender differences also did not emerge in 12th graders' reports of support or negative interaction with romantic partners (Hand & Furman, 2009). At least one study suggested that romantic relationships were more challenging for females. Although gender differences in support were not found for seventh graders in the Furman and Buhrmester (1992) study, college women did report less support in romantic relationships than college men. Also, although seventh-grade girls and boys reported similar power in romantic relationships, males' power increased by the tenth grade and college, whereas females' power decreased. However, despite these interesting gender differences, the bulk of the evidence suggests gender similarities. Moreover, as noted in regards to other-sex friendships, there may be unique understudied challenges for males in romantic relationships, such as if males find the level of disclosure and support expected by romantic partners to be extreme.

In regards to within-gender variability, it would be interesting to learn which youth are most likely to have satisfying other-sex relationships. Given that some research suggests that girls perceive same-sex friends to be more helpful and supportive than other-sex friends (Kuttler et al., 1999; Poulin & Pedersen, 2007), girls who are less invested in the helping and support aspects of friendship may have more satisfying other-sex friendships. Likewise, boys who are particularly invested in helping and support may find other-sex friendships an easier fit.

For romantic relationships, most research indicates gender similarities. One study did suggest that older adolescent and young adult females perceived themselves as less powerful than younger girls (Furman & Buhrmester, 1992). In an interesting recent study, adolescent girls perceived themselves as more powerful if they had not yet become sexually active with romantic partners than if they were sexually active (Giordano, Manning, & Longmore, 2010). There may be other individual or relational variables that explain within-gender variability in perceptions of power. However, given that most research indicated gender similarities in romantic relationships, considering across-dyad variability in sex-typed behaviors might be useful, too. For example, some couples may be satisfied if both partners have similar styles (e.g., in terms of disclosure, support, companionship), whereas others may be content with the partners having sex-typed styles if they see these styles as complementary or appropriate for romantic relationships.

Finally, we acknowledge that this section focused on heterosexual attraction, which does not characterize all youth. Although same-sex romantic/sexual attraction in adolescence has received increasing attention (Diamond, 2003; Diamond, Savin-Williams, & Dubé, 1999), it is still understudied. As such, future research is needed that identifies the unique challenges for girls and boys who experience romantic/sexual attraction to same-sex peers.

∭ FUTURE DIRECTIONS

A vast amount of work has examined the role of gender in adolescents' close relationships, but there is still considerable work to do. Although there are many possible future directions, we conclude by highlighting two. First, research aimed at understanding the role of gender in close relationships must continue to move beyond considering mean-level gender differences. It must be recognized that whether there are mean-level gender differences in a relationship variable is a separate question from whether the meaning or impact of the variable differs for girls and boys. For example, in one study (Keijers, Branje, Frijns, Finkenauer, & Meeus, 2010), adolescent boys kept more secrets from parents than adolescent girls. However, only girls' secrecy predicted poorer relationship quality. Future research examining the meaning and impact of relationship variables for girls and boys is important for gaining a nuanced and detailed understanding of girls' and boys' close relationships. Also, as discussed throughout the chapter, work is needed that considers within-gender variability as well as differences between genders. In this chapter, we suggested approaches for examining within-gender variability in regards to parent–child relationships, same-sex friendships, and other-sex relationships.

Second, research is needed that examines the impact of early relationships on later relationships with a focus on gender. Theories regarding the role of gender in close relationships (e.g., Maccoby, 1990; Rose & Rudolph, 2006) have proposed that parents' sex-typed interactions with children socialize them to form sex-typed friendships in childhood and adolescence, which result in their entering romantic relationships in adolescence with sex-typed interaction styles. Despite the intuitive appeal of these ideas, definitive studies of this possible developmental trajectory are lacking. Such research is crucial for increasing our understanding of how gender differences unfold within and across close relationships throughout development.

SUGGESTED READINGS

Laursen, B., & Collins, W. A. (2009). Parent-child relationships during adolescence. In R. M. Lerner & L. Steinberg (Eds.), *Handbook of adolescent psychology: Vol. 2. Contextual influences on adolescent development* (2nd ed., pp. 3–42). Hoboken, NJ: Wiley.

Maccoby, E. E. (1998). *The two sexes: Growing up apart, coming together.* Cambridge, MA: Belknap.

Rose, A. J., & Rudolph, K. D. (2006). A review of sex differences in peer relationship processes: Potential trade-offs for the emotional and behavioral development of girls and boys. *Psychological Bulletin, 132,* 98–131.

Underwood, M. K. (2007). Girlfriends and boyfriends diverging in middle childhood and coming together in romantic relationships. *Merrill-Palmer Quarterly, 53,* 520–526.

〽 REFERENCEſ

Bank, B. J. (1994). Effects of national, school, and gender cultures on friendships among adolescents in Australia and the United States. *Youth & Society, 25,* 435–456.

Bank, B. J., & Hansford, S. L. (2000). Gender and friendship: Why are men's best same-sex friendships less intimate and supportive? *Personal Relationships, 7,* 63–78.

Berndt, T. J., & Perry, T. B. (1986). Children's perceptions of friendships as supportive relationships. *Developmental Psychology, 22,* 640–648.

Bokhorst, C. L., Sumter, S. R., & Westenberg, P. M. (2010). Social support from parents, friends, classmates, and teachers in children and adolescents aged 9 to 18 years: Who is perceived as most supportive? *Social Development, 19,* 417–426.

Buhrmester, D., & Furman, W. (1987). The development of companionship and intimacy. *Child Development, 58,* 1101–1113.

Buhrmester, D., & Prager, K. (1995). Patterns and functions of self-disclosure during childhood and adolescence. In K. J. Rotenberg (Ed.), *Disclosure processes in children and adolescents* (pp. 10–56). New York: Cambridge University Press.

Bukowski, W. M., Hoza, B., & Boivin, M. (1994). Measuring friendship quality during pre- and early adolescence: The development and psychometric properties of the friendship qualities scale. *Journal of Social and Personal Relationships, 11,* 471–484.

Carlson, W., & Rose, A. J. (2007). The role of reciprocity in romantic relationships in middle childhood and early adolescence. *Merrill-Palmer Quarterly, 53,* 262–290.

Carlson, W., & Rose, A. J. (in press). Activities in heterosexual romantic relationships: Grade differences and associations with relationship satisfaction. *Journal of Adolescence.*

Carver, P. R., Yunger, J. L., & Perry, D. G. (2003). Gender identity and adjustment in middle childhood. *Sex Roles, 49,* 95–109.

Collins, A., & van Dulmen, M. (2006). Friendships and romance in emerging adulthood: Assessing distinctiveness in close relationships. In J. J. Arnett & J. L. Tanner (Eds.), *Emerging adults in America: Coming of age in the 21st century* (pp. 219–234). Washington, DC: American Psychological Association.

Connolly, J., Craig, W., Goldberg, A., & Pepler, D. (2004). Mixed-gender groups, dating, and romantic relationships in early adolescence. *Journal of Research on Adolescence, 14,* 185–207.

Crouter, A. C., Manke, B. A., & McHale, S. M. (1995). The family context of gender intensification in early adolescence. *Child Development, 66,* 317–329.

Diamond, L. M. (2003). Love matters: Romantic relationships among sexual-minority youth. In L. Florsheim (Ed.), *Adolescent romantic relations and sexual behavior: Theory, research, and practical implications.* Mahwah, NJ: Lawrence Erlbaum.

Diamond, L. M., Savin-Williams, R. C., & Dubé, E. M. (1999). Sex, dating, passionate friendships, and romance: Intimate peer relations among lesbian, gay, and bisexual adolescents. In W. Furman, C. Feiring, & B. B. Brown (Eds.), *Contemporary perspectives on adolescent romantic relationships* (pp. 175–210). New York: Cambridge University Press.

Egan, S. K., & Perry, D. G. (2001). Gender identity: A multidimensional analysis with implications for psychosocial adjustment. *Developmental Psychology, 37,* 451–463.

Elkins, I. J., McGue, M., & Iacono, W. G. (1997). Genetic and environmental influences on parent–son relationships: Evidence for increasing genetic influence during adolescence. *Developmental Psychology, 33,* 351–363.

French, D. C., Rianasari, M., Pidada, S., Nelwan, P., & Buhrmester, D. (2001). Social support of Indonesian and U.S. children and adolescents by family members and friends. *Merrill-Palmer Quarterly, 47,* 377–394.

Furman, W., & Buhrmester, D. (1985). Children's perceptions of the personal relationships in their social networks. *Developmental Psychology, 21,* 1016–1024.

Furman, W., & Buhrmester, D. (1992). Age and sex differences in perceptions of networks of personal relationships. *Child Development, 63,* 103–115.

Furman, W., & Collins, W. A. (2009). Adolescent romantic relationships and experiences. In K. H. Rubin, W. M. Bukowski, & B. Laursen (Eds.), *Handbook of peer interactions, relationships, and groups* (pp. 341–360). New York: Guilford Press.

Giordano, P. C., Manning, W. D., & Longmore, M. A. (2010). Affairs of the heart: Qualities of adolescent romantic relationships and sexual behavior. *Journal of Research on Adolescence, 20,* 983–1013.

Grabill, C. M., & Kerns, K. A. (2000). Attachment style and intimacy in friendship. *Personal Relationships, 7,* 363–378.

Hair, E. C., Moore, K. A., Garrett, S. B., Ling, T., & Cleveland, K. (2008). The continued importance of quality parent-adolescent relationships during late adolescence. *Journal of Research on Adolescence, 18,* 187–200.

Hand, L. S., & Furman, W. (2009). Rewards and costs in adolescent other-sex friendships: Comparisons to same-sex friendships and romantic relationships. *Social Development, 18,* 270–287.

Harter, S. (1985). *Manual for the Self-Perception Profile for Children.* Denver, CO: University of Denver.

Haugen, P. T., Welsh, D. P., & McNulty, J. K. (2008). Empathic accuracy and adolescent romantic relationships. *Journal of Adolescence, 31,* 709–727.

Helsen, M., Vollebergh, W., & Meeus, W. (2000). Social support from parents and friends and emotional problems in adolescence. *Journal of Youth and Adolescence, 29,* 319–335.

Hendrick, C., & Hendrick, S. S. (Eds.). (2000). *Close relationships: A sourcebook.* Thousand Oaks, CA: Sage.

Hill, J. P., & Lynch, M. E. (1983). The intensification of gender-related role expectations during early adolescence. In J. Brooks-Gunn & A. C. Peterson (Eds.), *Girls at puberty* (pp. 201–228). New York: Plenum.

Hyde, J. S. (2005). The gender similarities hypothesis. *American Psychologist, 60,* 581–592.

Katz, P. A., & Ksansnak, K. R. (1994). Developmental aspects of gender role flexibility and traditionality in middle childhood and adolescence. *Developmental Psychology, 30,* 272–282.

Keijers, L., Branje, S. J. T., Frijns, T., Finkenauer, C., & Meeus, M. (2010). Gender differences in keeping secrets from parents in adolescence. *Developmental Psychology, 46,* 293–298.

Kovacs, D. M., Parker, J. G., & Hoffman, L. W. (1996). Behavioral, affective, and social correlates of involvement in cross-sex friendship in elementary school. *Child Development, 67,* 2269–2286.

Kuttler, A. F., La Greca, A. M., & Prinstein, M. J. (1999). Friendship qualities and social-emotional functioning of adolescents with close cross-sex friendships. *Journal of Research on Adolescence, 9,* 339–366.

Laursen, B., & Collins, W. A. (2009). Parent-child relationships during adolescence. In R. M. Lerner & L. Steinberg (Eds.), *Handbook of adolescent psychology: Vol. 2. Contextual influences on adolescent development* (2nd ed., pp. 3–42). Hoboken, NJ: Wiley.

Laursen, B., Coy, K. C., & Collins, W. A. (1998). Reconsidering changes in parent–child conflict across adolescence: A meta-analysis. *Child Development, 69,* 817–832.

Laursen, B., DeLay, D., & Adams, R. E. (2010). Trajectories of perceived support in mother–adolescent relationships: The poor (quality) get poorer. *Developmental Psychology, 46,* 1792–1798.

Laursen, B., & Williams, V. A. (1997). Perceptions of interdependence and closeness in family and peer relationships among adolescents with and without romantic partners. In S. Shulman & W. A. Collins (Eds.), *Romantic relationships in adolescence: Developmental perspectives* (pp. 3–20). San Francisco: Jossey-Bass.

Levesque, R. J. (1993). The romantic experience of adolescents in satisfying love relationships. *Journal of Youth and Adolescence, 22,* 219–251.

Maccoby, E. E. (1990). Gender and relationships: A developmental account. *American Psychologist, 45,* 513–520.

Maccoby, E. E. (1998). *The two sexes: Growing up apart, coming together.* Cambridge, MA: Belknap.

Maltz, D. N., & Borker, R. A. (1982). A cultural approach to male–female miscommunication. In J. J. Bumpers (Ed.), *Language and social identity* (pp. 196–216). New York: Cambridge University Press.

McDougal, P., & Hymel, S. (2007). Same-gender versus cross-gender friendship conceptions: Similar or different? *Merrill-Palmer Quarterly, 53,* 347–380.

McGue, M., Elkins, I., Walden, B., & Iacano, W. G. (2005). Perceptions of the parent-adolescent relationship: A longitudinal investigation. *Developmental Psychology, 41,* 971–984.

McHale, S. M., Crouter, A. C., & Whiteman, S. D. (2003). The family contexts of gender development in childhood and adolescence. *Social Development, 12,* 125–148.

McNelles, L. R., & Connolly, J. A. (1999). Intimacy between adolescent friends: Age and gender differences in intimate affect and intimate behaviors. *Journal of Research on Adolescence, 9,* 143–159.

Mehta, C. M., & Strough, J. (2009). Sex segregation in friendships and normative contexts across the life span. *Developmental Review, 29,* 201–220.

Moilanen, K. L., & Raffaelli, M. (2010). Support and conflict in ethnically diverse young adults' relationships with parents and friends. *International Journal of Behavioral Development, 34,* 46–52.

Montgomery, M. J. (2005). Psychosocial intimacy and identity: From early adolescent to emerging adulthood. *Journal of Adolescent Research, 20,* 346–374.

Poulin, F., & Pedersen, S. (2007). Developmental changes in gender composition of friendship networks in adolescent girls and boys. *Developmental Psychology, 43,* 1484–1496.

Rose, A. J. (2002). Co-rumination in the friendships of girls and boys. *Child Development, 73,* 1830–1843.

Rose, A. J., & Asher, S. R. (2004). Children's strategies and goals in response to help-giving and help-seeking tasks within a friendship. *Child Development, 75,* 749–763.

Rose, A. J., & Asher, S. R. (2011). *Boys' friendships: What's good about being male?* Manuscript in preparation.

Rose, A. J., Carlson, W., & Waller, E. M. (2007). Prospective associations of co-rumination with friendship and emotional adjustment: Considering the socioemotional trade-offs of co-rumination. *Developmental Psychology, 43,* 1019–1031.

Rose, A. J., & Rudolph, K. D. (2006). A review of sex differences in peer relationship processes: Potential trade-offs for the emotional and behavioral development of girls and boys. *Psychological Bulletin, 132,* 98–131.

Rose, A. J., Schwartz-Mette, R. A., Smith, R. L., Asher, S. R., Swenson, L. P., & Carlson, W. (in press). How girls and boys expect that talking about problems will make them feel: Associations with disclosure to friends in childhood and adolescence. *Child Development.*

Rose, A. J., Swenson, L. P., & Robert, C. (2009). Boys' and girls' motivations for refraining from prompting friends to talk about problems. *International Journal of Behavioral Development, 33,* 178–184.

Rubin, K. H., Bukowski, W. M., & Laursen, B. (Eds.) (2009). *Handbook of peer interactions, relationships, and groups.* New York: Guilford Press.

Ruble, D. N., Martin, C. L., & Berenbaum, S. A. (2006). Gender development. In W. Damon, R. M. Lerner (Series Ed.), & N. Eisenberg (Vol. Ed.), *Handbook of child psychology: Vol 3. Social, emotional, and personality development* (6th ed., pp. 858–932). Hoboken, NJ: Wiley.

Shanahan, L., McHale, S. M., Crouter, A. C., & Osgood, D. W. (2007). Warmth with mothers and father from middle childhood to late adolescence: Within- and between-families comparisons. *Developmental Psychology, 43,* 551–563.

Shulman, S., & Laursen, B. (2002). Adolescent perceptions of conflict in interdependent and disengaged friendships. *Journal of Research on Adolescence, 12,* 353–372.

Smetana, J. G., Daddis, C., & Chuang, S. S. (2003). 'Clean your room!' A longitudinal investigation of adolescent–parent conflict and conflict resolution in middle-class African American families. *Journal of Adolescent Research, 18,* 631–650.

Smith, R. L., & Rose, A. J. (in press). The "cost of caring" in youths' friendships: Examining associations among social perspective-taking, co-rumination, and empathetic distress. *Developmental Psychology.*

Thorne, B. (1986). Girls and boys together . . . but mostly apart: Gender arrangements in elementary schools. In W. W. Hartup & Z. Rubin (Eds.), *Relationships and development* (pp. 167–184). Hillsdale, NJ: Lawrence Erlbaum.

Underwood, M. K. (2004). Gender and peer relations: Are the two gender cultures really all that different? In J. B. Kupersmidt & K. A. Dodge (Eds.) *Children's peer relations: From development to intervention* (pp. 21–36). Washington, DC: American Psychological Association.

Underwood, M. K., & Rosen, L. H. (2009). Gender, peer relations, and challenges for girlfriends and boyfriends coming together in adolescence. *Psychology of Women Quarterly, 33,* 16–20.

Vernberg, E. M., Absender, D. A., Ewell, K. K., & Beery, S. H. (1992). Social anxiety and peer relationships in early adolescence: A prospective analysis. *Journal of Clinical Child Psychology, 21,* 189–196.

Vernberg, E. M., Beery, S. H., Ewell, K. K., & Absender, D. A. (1993). Parents' use of friendship facilitation strategies and the formation of friendships in early adolescence: A prospective study. *Journal of Family Psychology, 7,* 356–369.

Way, N., & Greene, M. L. (2006). Trajectories of perceived friendship quality during adolescence: The patterns and contextual predictors. *Journal of Research on Adolescence, 16,* 293–320.

Williams, D. G. (1985). Gender, masculinity-femininity, and emotional intimacy in same-sex friendship. *Sex Roles, 12,* 587–600.

Yunger, J. L., Carver, P. R., & Perry, D. G. (2004). Does gender identity influence children's psychological well-being? *Developmental Psychology, 40,* 572–582.

Zarbatany, L., McDougal, P., & Hymel, S. (2000). Gender-differentiated experience in the peer culture: Links to intimacy in preadolescence. *Social Development, 9,* 62–79.

Author Index

Subject Index